Arab Intellectuals and American Power

Arab Intellectuals and American Power

Edward Said, Charles Malik, and the US in the Middle East

M. D. Walhout

I.B. TAURIS
LONDON • NEW YORK • OXFORD • NEW DELHI • SYDNEY

I.B. TAURIS
Bloomsbury Publishing Plc
50 Bedford Square, London, WC1B 3DP, UK
1385 Broadway, New York, NY 10018, USA
29 Earlsfort Terrace, Dublin 2, Ireland

BLOOMSBURY, I.B. TAURIS and the I.B. Tauris logo are trademarks of
Bloomsbury Publishing Plc

First published in Great Britain 2021
This paperback edition published in 2022

Copyright © M. D. Walhout, 2021

M. D. Walhout has asserted his right under the Copyright, Designs and
Patents Act, 1988, to be identified as Author of this work.

Cover design: Adriana Brioso
Cover image © [left] Edward Said, 1996 © Ulf Andersen/Getty Images; [right] Charles Malik,
1953 © Lisa Larsen/The LIFE Picture Collection/Getty Images

All rights reserved. No part of this publication may be reproduced or transmitted
in any form or by any means, electronic or mechanical, including photocopying,
recording, or any information storage or retrieval system, without prior
permission in writing from the publishers.

Bloomsbury Publishing Plc does not have any control over, or responsibility for, any
third-party websites referred to or in this book. All internet addresses given in this
book were correct at the time of going to press. The author and publisher regret
any inconvenience caused if addresses have changed or sites have ceased to
exist, but can accept no responsibility for any such changes.

A catalogue record for this book is available from the British Library.

A catalog record for this book is available from the Library of Congress.

ISBN: HB: 978-0-7556-3414-9
PB: 978-0-7556-3922-9
ePDF: 978-0-7556-3415-6
eBook: 978-0-7556-3416-3

Typeset by Deanta Global Publishing Services, Chennai, India

To find out more about our authors and books visit www.bloomsbury.com and
sign up for our newsletters.

Contents

Introduction: Edward Said, Charles Malik, and American Power		1
1	Charles Malik: The Education of a Christian Intellectual, 1906–45	19
2	Charles Malik: The Intellectual as Cold Warrior, 1945–59	37
3	Charles Malik: The Intellectual Out of Power, 1959–75	67
4	Edward Said: The Education of a Secular Intellectual, 1935–67	93
5	Edward Said: The Rebirth of a Palestinian Intellectual, 1967–75	111
6	Charles Malik: The Intellectual as Lebanese Christian Nationalist, 1975–87	133
7	Edward Said: The Intellectual as Palestinian Nationalist, 1975–87	161
8	Edward Said: The Intellectual in Exile, 1987–2003	189
Conclusion: The Intellectual and Power		213
Notes		231
Selected Bibliography		270
Index		284

Introduction

Edward Said, Charles Malik, and American Power

By the time he died in 2003, the Palestinian American scholar Edward Said was quite possibly the most famous literature professor in the world. His academic reputation was established in the late 1970s, starting with *Beginnings* (1975), which helped launch the theory revolution in Anglo-American literary studies. With his knowledge of French, Said was able to draw on the work of such avant-garde Parisian theorists as Roland Barthes and Michel Foucault, many of whom he knew personally. But his most influential scholarly work was *Orientalism* (1978), arguably the founding text of the new field of postcolonial studies. His argument was that Orientalism—the institutionalized study of the Middle East in post-Enlightenment Europe—had produced anything but objective, disinterested knowledge of the Arabs and other "Orientals." On the contrary, it had produced biased scholarship premised on the superiority of European civilization and serving the interests of the European colonial powers.

At roughly the same time, Said was emerging as the leading American spokesman for the Palestinian resistance movement. His first book on the subject, *The Question of Palestine*, was published in 1979, two years after the Camp David peace agreement between Israel and Egypt. As far as Said was concerned, there was only one answer to the Question of Palestine: a single, secular, democratic state in all of Palestine, embracing both Jews and Arabs. The publication of *The Question of Palestine* coincided, more or less, with Said's debut as something of a media star—a handsome, debonair university professor who spoke flawless English with an American accent and who was somehow, at the same time, an elected member of the Palestinian National Council (PNC). From the *New York Times* to the *MacNeil/Lehrer NewsHour* on public television, Said could be counted on to lay the Palestinian case before an American public predisposed to siding with Israel.

A few years before his death, Said published a memoir of his early life entitled *Out of Place* (1999). In it, he recalled his relationship with Dr. Charles Malik, the eminent Lebanese philosopher-statesman, whom he knew as "Uncle Charles." (Malik's wife, Eva Badr, was a first cousin of Said's mother, Hilda Musa.) Nowadays, Malik is a largely forgotten figure outside of Lebanon. Between 1945 and 1960, however, he was the most famous Arab diplomat in America and perhaps the world. As the Lebanese ambassador to the United States and the United Nations, and later as Lebanon's foreign minister, Malik was known as a loyal ally of America, a sharp critic of Israel, and a staunch opponent of Communism. He had friends in high places, from Eleanor Roosevelt, with whom he served on the UN Human Rights Commission, to the Dulles brothers—John

Foster and Allen Welsh—who served as Secretary of State and Director of Central Intelligence, respectively, in the Eisenhower administration.

Malik was not a diplomat by nature, training, or inclination. Like his nephew Edward, he was a Harvard-trained professor long before he stepped onto the world stage. As a student at the American University of Beirut, he had been introduced to the study of philosophy and developed a passion for ideas, logic, and the uncompromising quest for truth. At Harvard, he studied with Alfred North Whitehead, the eminent English mathematician and philosopher. At Freiburg, he studied with Martin Heidegger, the father of existentialism. He then returned to the AUB to teach philosophy the way the Greeks had taught it—peripatetically, dialogically, with a small circle of like-minded pupils, working slowly through classic texts of Western thought. Instead of becoming another Plato or Heidegger, however, he answered the call to public service in the prime of his academic career.

From *Out of Place*, we learn that Malik played an important role in Edward Said's development, both intellectual and political. From Uncle Charles, Edward recalled,

> I learned the attractions of dogma, of the search for unquestioning [sic] truth, of irrefutable authority. From him I also learned about the clash of civilizations, the war between East and West, communism and freedom, Christianity and all the other, lesser religions. . . . During the forties and early fifties Malik's comforting moral certainty and granitic power, his inextinguishable faith in the Eternal, gave us hope.[1]

But Edward's opinion of his uncle began to change as a result of his own political awakening in the late 1960s, until Malik came to represent everything he despised most in religion and politics:

> He began his public career during the late 1940s as an Arab spokesman for Palestine at the U.N., but concluded it as the anti-Palestinian architect of the Christian alliance with Israel during the Lebanese Civil War. Looking back at Malik's intellectual and political trajectory, with all that it involved for me as his youthful admirer and companion, relative, and frequenter of the same circles, I see it as the great negative intellectual lesson of my life, an example which for the last three decades I have found myself grappling with, living through, analyzing, over and over and over with regret, mystification, and bottomless disappointment.[2]

Uncle Charles, one might say, was the father-figure in Edward's intellectual and political life—the conservative teacher who must be slain, symbolically, by the radical student.

The irony was that the two men resembled each other in many respects. Both were Arab Christians, born into minority communities in predominately Muslim lands. Both were educated in American schools, first in the Middle East, then in the States, ultimately earning PhDs at Harvard. Both were fluent in multiple languages—English, French, and Arabic—and passionately devoted to European culture. Both were charismatic teachers who inspired a loyal following among awe-struck students. Both were dedicated to the life of the mind, but neither could resist, when it arrived, the siren call of politics. Both became increasingly devoted to their people, and to their survival as a people—in Malik's case, the Lebanese Christians; in Said's case, the Palestinians. Both denounced terrorism but were willing to countenance violence when they deemed it necessary for national or communal self-defense. Both were proud, averse to criticism, often resorting to verbal intimidation of those who dared question or oppose them. Both were men of principle who hated silence and compromise.

Such similarities suggest that Said might have become a lifelong disciple of Uncle Charles. Instead, they became ideological opposites. Malik remained a devout Greek Orthodox Christian dedicated to reconciliation with Rome who was admired by evangelical Protestants. Said relinquished his family's Protestant faith and renounced all religion while defending Islamic culture against prejudiced Orientalists. Malik held that the discovery of truth was the province of philosophy, of reflection on the nature of things. Said believed that it was the province of philology, of reflection on the nature of words. Malik's library was built on the ancient Greeks, the Church Fathers, and the existentialists—Plato, Aristotle, Chrysostom, Aquinas, Kierkegaard, and Heidegger. Said's library was eclectic, an idiosyncratic collection of eccentric European thinkers—Giambattista Vico, Erich Auerbach, Antonio Gramsci, Michel Foucault. Malik was a conservative anti-Communist who feared Arab nationalism and radical Islam. Said embraced radical politics and the Palestinian resistance movement. Malik loved Lebanon and loved America. Said loved no nation, preferring cosmopolitan cities like Beirut and New York to their provincial hinterlands.

§

Edward Said's earliest memories of Uncle Charles dated from the Second World War, when Charles would stop by the Said apartment on his occasional visits to Cairo, where his mother lived. But it was in the Lebanese mountain village of Dhour el Shweir, the ancestral home of the Badr family, that the bond between Edward and Uncle Charles was forged. The revered patriarch of the Badr family was Eva Malik and Hilda Said's grandfather Rev. Youssef Badr, who had converted to Protestantism, studied with American missionaries, and served as one of the first native Evangelical pastors in Syria and Lebanon. Although Rev. Badr's children and grandchildren had scattered to places like Egypt, the Sudan, and Palestine, they returned to Dhour as often as they could, particularly during the hot summer months. Starting in 1943, the Saids would close their apartment in Cairo each summer and travel to Dhour, whose trees and cool mountain air drew summer residents from Beirut and other Arab cities.

It was in Dhour that Edward's true education began, with Uncle Charles as his tutor. As he recalled in *Out of Place*,

> I was very attracted to [the Maliks'] presence. In the unforgiving sparseness of Dhour, their home, Charles' conversation, and my aunt's evident liking for me further provoked my thirst for ideas, for the great issues of faith, morality, and human destiny, and for a whole gamut of authors. "During the summer of 1930-something," Malik once said to me, "I used to sit by the banks of the Nile and

I read through all of Hardy and Meredith. But I also read Aristotle's *Metaphysics* and Aquinas' *Summa*." No one else I knew then spoke of such things.³

Passages like this suggest that Edward was on his way to becoming a Malik disciple, much like his older cousin George Said, who had studied with Malik at the AUB. Unfortunately, Edward didn't have much to say about George in *Out of Place*, except to note that he moved to Switzerland in the 1950s and, with other Malik disciples, established "a colony of devout men and women who would ready themselves to return to the Muslim world in order to convert people to Christ."⁴

It is very difficult, in retrospect, to imagine Edward following in George's footsteps. For one thing, Edward was originally destined for Oxford or Cambridge, not the AUB. He ended up at Princeton, which Uncle Charles—a true Harvard man—dismissed as "a country club where Harvard sophomores spend their weekends."⁵ Yet it was at Princeton, Edward recalled, that

> I first approached the political currents and issues not only of the period but which in one way or another were to influence my outlook intellectually and politically for the rest of my life. It was then that I heard from Malik about ideology, communism, and the great battle between East and West.... He had an amused contempt for Princeton and me, but he was willing to talk to me at quite some length (conversation, except for an occasional question from me, wasn't really possible).

These talks took place in Washington, in the Lebanese ambassador's residence, where Edward stayed with the Maliks on occasion. "It was in those Washington discussions," Edward wrote,

> that the inherent irreconcilability between intellectual belief and passionate loyalty to tribe, sect, and country first opened up in me, and have remained open. I have never felt the need to close the gap.⁶

Evidently, Uncle Charles' overbearing manner, as well as his devotion to Lebanon's Christian community, was starting to rub Edward the wrong way. Still, they remained on friendly terms for many years.

After graduating from Princeton in 1957, Edward earned his PhD at Harvard and began his academic career at Columbia. His political awakening came in the late 1960s, starting with the humiliating Israeli victory over the Arab armies in June 1967. In December of that year, he paid a visit to the Maliks at their home in Beirut. As he recalled in *Out of Place*,

> I was not too sure of what my errand was, except in some vague way to ask Charles to come out, so to speak, and help guide the Arabs out of their incredible defeat....
> What I was not prepared for was his uncharacteristically passive answer: that this was not his time, that he did not feel he had a role to play anymore, and that a new situation would have to arrive for him to reenter politics. I was stunned by this,

astonished that what I had assumed was a common need to resist and rebuild was not shared by a man whose views and commitments I still had faith in.⁷

By then, Uncle Charles had been out of politics for nearly a decade, having resumed his academic career at the AUB. If he sounded resigned, perhaps it was because he had no confidence in President Nasser of Egypt or the other Arab leaders.

It was the horrific Lebanese Civil War of 1975–90 that finally put an end to Edward's relationship with Uncle Charles. During the war, Edward explained,

> Malik became an intellectual leader of the Christian Right, and long after his death in [December 1987] I still feel profound regret at the ideological gulf that came to separate us, and at the enormous, complicated maelstrom of Arab politics that ultimately divided us, leaving us both with very little positive history and experience to show for it.⁸

In the beginning, the civil war pitted the Maronite Christian militias against the Palestinian *fedayeen* (literally, "those who sacrifice themselves") and their Lebanese allies. To provide political leadership for Lebanon's Christians, the elder statesmen of the Maronite parties—joined by one Greek Orthodox Christian, Charles Malik—organized themselves into the Lebanese Front. At the same time, they agreed to integrate their militias into the Lebanese Forces under the command of young Bashir Gemayel, for whom Charles Malik was an éminence grise. One of their aims was to drive the Palestinians out of Lebanon, with Israeli help if necessary—and that Edward could not forgive.

§

Not only are the lives of Edward Said and Charles Malik fascinating in their own right, but they are also deeply implicated in a larger story—the story of American power and influence in the Middle East. It was in American missionary schools that Charles' lifelong engagement with the United States began. One of those schools was the Evangelical School for Boys in Tripoli, founded by Presbyterians in 1904, which Charles attended in the early 1920s. The other was the American University of Beirut—originally called the Syrian Protestant College—founded by Congregationalists in 1866. The first and second presidents of the AUB—Rev. Daniel Bliss and his son, Rev. Howard Bliss—were both graduates of Amherst College in Massachusetts. Its third president, Rev. Bayard Dodge, was the son-in-law of Howard Bliss and an alumnus of Princeton. It was Bayard's great-grandfather, William E. Dodge, Sr., who, after meeting Daniel Bliss, had given generously to the Syrian Protestant College, arranged for it to be incorporated in the State of New York, and served as the treasurer of its board of trustees.⁹

Charles' years at the Boys' School in Tripoli were decisive ones for the Middle East. After the collapse of the Ottoman Empire, the French occupied Syria and Lebanon while the British remained in Palestine and Transjordan. But President Woodrow Wilson thought that the Arabs ought to determine their own future. So did Howard

Bliss, the president of the AUB, who in January 1919 traveled to Paris to plead the Syrian cause at the peace conference.[10] The idea of inviting an AUB representative to the conference had originated with young Allen W. Dulles—the future Director of Central Intelligence—who, along with his uncle, Secretary of State Robert Lansing, was a member of the American delegation.[11] In Paris, Bliss appealed to President Wilson and addressed the Council of Ten, calling for a commission that would travel to Syria and ask the Syrians what form of government they wanted. It did not hurt that Bliss' son-in-law was Bayard Dodge, whose father, Cleveland H. Dodge, had been a classmate of Wilson's at Princeton and bankrolled his political campaigns.[12]

Bliss got his commission, but the British and the French kept their colonies under the system of mandates instituted by the new League of Nations. By the time Charles Malik matriculated at the AUB in 1923, both Woodrow Wilson and Howard Bliss were dead, as were their hopes for Syrian self-determination under benevolent American tutelage. The AUB, however, remained a hotbed of Arab nationalist sentiment, thanks to a new student society called *al-Urwa al-Wuthqa* ("Tight Bond"). The society took its name from an Arabic newspaper edited in Paris by Jamal al-Din al-Afghani and Mohammad Abdu, two of the leading figures of the Arab *Nahda* ("Renaissance") of the late nineteenth century. Officially, *al-Urwa* was devoted to the cultivation of the Arabic language; unofficially, it promoted Arab self-determination and the end of the British and French mandates. This was especially true after Constantine Zurayk, who led a secret Arab nationalist society known as the Red Book Group, became *al-Urwa*'s faculty advisor in the mid-1930s.[13] President Dodge was hard-pressed to preserve the AUB's long-standing policy of political neutrality—a policy Charles, who feared Arab nationalism, wholeheartedly supported.

The United States played no role in the Levant during the Second World War, other than to broker an armistice after British forces occupied Lebanon and Syria in the summer of 1941 and replaced the Vichy colonial administration with one loyal to General de Gaulle.[14] The war had not yet ended when Charles Malik was asked to serve as Lebanon's ambassador to the United States and the United Nations, whose organizing conference took place in San Francisco in the spring of 1945. Due to French opposition, Lebanon and Syria had not been invited to send delegations to San Francisco until the last minute. Both the United States and the USSR favored their inclusion, however, and so the two Levantine nations received invitations after formally declaring war on the Axis powers. Prominent in both delegations were alumni of the AUB, notably Faris al-Khoury, the Protestant prime minister of Syria. The conference was still in session when de Gaulle ordered his High Commissioner in the Levant to suppress a pro-independence revolt in Damascus. President Harry Truman encouraged Prime Minister Winston Churchill to intervene, and de Gaulle was forced to back down.[15] A year later, the last French troops left Lebanon and Syria.

After the UN organizing conference, Charles embarked upon his new life as a diplomat, shuttling between the State Department in Washington and the United Nations in New York. These years marked the beginning of the Cold War, with the Middle East as a potential battlefield. Oil was a major consideration, with the British dominating production in Iran, Iraq, and Kuwait and the Americans in Saudi Arabia. Lebanon had no oil of its own, but the port of Sidon was the terminus of the new

Trans-Arabian Pipeline, constructed by the Bechtel Corporation for the Arabian-American Oil Company, to which King Ibn Saud of Saudi Arabia had granted an exclusive concession. Ibn Saud was not happy, however, with Truman's support for Zionist aspirations in Palestine. Not only did Truman instruct his ambassador to vote for the 1947 UN resolution calling for the partition of Palestine between the Arabs and the Jews, but he also surprised his own delegation by promptly recognizing Israel when David Ben-Gurion proclaimed its independence on May 14, 1948, angering Charles and the other Arab ambassadors.

With the election of Dwight Eisenhower in 1952, the Cold War began to heat up, thanks in large measure to the appointment of John Foster Dulles as Secretary of State and his brother Allen as Director of Central Intelligence. When it came to International Communism, Foster Dulles condemned the Truman administration's policy of "containment," pushing the architect of the policy, George Kennan, out of the State Department. Dulles wanted to roll back Communism, to liberate nations behind the Iron Curtain and combat Communist influence in the developing world. That meant a more interventionist policy in the Middle East, where nations like Egypt, Syria, Iraq, and Iran were in danger—or so Dulles thought—of falling into the Soviet orbit. It was left to Allen Dulles to oversee the covert operations this policy required, the most infamous of which, Operation Ajax, took place in 1953, when the CIA's Kermit Roosevelt, Jr.—a grandson of former President Theodore Roosevelt, nicknamed "Kim"—traveled to Iran to oust the elected prime minister Mohammed Mossadegh. As for Charles Malik, he remained America's best friend in the Arab world, consulting regularly with both Dulles brothers.

After a decade in the United States, Charles resigned his ambassadorship and returned to the AUB. A year later, however, he was called back into service, this time as foreign minister in the pro-Western government of President Camille Chamoun. Then, in January 1957, President Eisenhower announced what became known as the "Eisenhower Doctrine," promising to protect allies threatened with armed aggression by International Communism. At the time, the Chamoun regime was facing bitter domestic opposition from rival politicians. Worse, the opposition militias were secretly armed, according to the government, by the Egyptians and the Syrians, who in turn were supplied and directed by the Soviets. When Chamoun and Charles asked the United States to intervene under the terms of the Eisenhower Doctrine, however, the Americans demurred. It was not until the violent overthrow of the Iraqi monarchy in July 1958 that Eisenhower finally agreed to send the Marines to Beirut, fearing a wave of anti-Western coups across the region.[16]

However, the American intervention proved a bitter pill for Chamoun and Charles to swallow. After consulting with opposition leaders, Eisenhower's troubleshooter, Robert Murphy, settled on General Fuad Chehab, the neutral commander of the army, as his choice to succeed Chamoun as President of Lebanon. As for Charles, he was exiled to the United States for a few years, after which he returned, once again, to the AUB. By the late 1960s, however, the university's dependence on the US government had become problematic as a wave of anti-Americanism swept the Middle East. The early 1970s saw a series of strikes as students protested everything from faculty dismissals to tuition hikes to Israeli raids on Palestinian camps, earning the AUB the moniker "Guerrilla U." In the spring of 1974, students occupied the campus and started digging through files in College Hall, where President Samuel Kirkwood and other administrators had their offices. Among other documents, they found an evaluation of US military officers enrolled in the AUB's Middle East Area Program, addressed to a military attaché at the US embassy by Professor Joseph Malone. The occupation did not end until Lebanese security forces stormed the campus and restored order.[17]

When Lebanon's brutal fifteen-year civil war erupted in April 1975, Charles aligned himself with the Maronite political parties, led by Camille Chamoun and Pierre Gemayel, as well as the militant monks, headed by Father Charbel Kassis. Together, they formed the Lebanese Front, which initially worked in concert with President Suleiman Frangieh but took an increasingly oppositional stance when the Syrian army, which had entered Lebanon in order to rescue Frangieh and the Christians, overstayed its welcome. That is when the Front and its militia, the Lebanese Forces, turned to the Israelis, who were desperate for allies in the region.[18] Meanwhile, Charles became the Front's senior envoy to Washington. He enjoyed little success with the Carter administration, which sided with Frangieh's successor, Elias Sarkis, a technocrat whom the Front perceived as a creature of the Syrians. With the election of Ronald Reagan in 1980, however, the Front acquired powerful new allies in Washington, notably Secretary of State Alexander Haig and Director of Central Intelligence William Casey.[19]

When Haig gave his supposed "green light" to Israeli defense minister Ariel Sharon, who planned to invade Lebanon in the summer of 1982, the fondest wishes of the Lebanese Front seemed on the verge of fulfillment.[20] Not only did the Israelis force the evacuation of the PLO from Beirut, but Bashir Gemayel, the charismatic young commander of the Lebanese Forces, was elected President of Lebanon with some last-minute assistance from his Israeli patrons.[21] Less than a month after taking office, however, Bashir was assassinated, presumably by a Syrian agent. When some of Bashir's men took out their frustration on defenseless Palestinian refugees as the Israelis looked on, President Reagan agreed to send the Marines to Beirut for the first time since 1958. If Charles was glad to see the return of the Americans, however, he was destined to be disappointed once again. After the devastating suicide bombing of the Marine barracks by Hezbollah militants in October 1983, Reagan ordered the troops to withdraw, leaving Lebanon's fate in the hands of the Israelis and the Syrians.

§

Like Uncle Charles, Edward Said was a product of American schools, beginning with the Cairo School for American Children in Maadi, a garden suburb favored by the British and subsequently by the Americans. Edward attended CSAC for three years in the late 1940s, followed by two years at Victoria College, the most prestigious British public school in the Middle East. These were the last years of the monarchy in Egypt, when King Farouk's throne was tottering. The opposition, including the Muslim Brotherhood, denounced both Farouk and the elected prime minister, Mahmoud al-Nokrashy, for their failure to expel the British and defeat the Zionists in Palestine. In December 1948, in the middle of Edward's final year at CSAC, Nokrashy banned the Brotherhood and was promptly assassinated. Meanwhile, a junta of patriotic army officers, led by General Mohammed Naguib and Colonel Gamal Abdel Nasser, prepared to sweep away both the corrupt monarchy and the ineffective civilian government.

The Free Officers seized power in July 1952, a year after Edward's transfer from Victoria College to the Mount Hermon School in Northfield, Massachusetts. The question of whether or not the Americans conspired with the Free Officers is still open. What is clear is that the Americans welcomed the coup d'état when it arrived. Ambassador Jefferson Caffery and his staff at the US embassy cultivated the Free Officers—who promised to suppress the Communists—and praised them in their reports to Washington. At the same time, the new Central Intelligence Agency, represented by Kim Roosevelt, opened its own channel to the new Egyptian military leaders.[22] Those leaders, in turn, asked Ambassador Caffery, a critic of British imperialism, to help negotiate the withdrawal of British troops from the Suez Canal Zone.[23] Unfortunately, the honeymoon between the Americans and the Free Officers did not survive the transition from the Truman to the Eisenhower administration in 1953, when John Foster Dulles replaced Dean Acheson as Secretary of State.

By 1956, when Edward was an undergraduate at Princeton, Dulles had managed to alienate President Nasser, who had accepted military aid from the Soviet bloc. When Dulles withdrew American funding from Nasser's Aswan Dam project, the Egyptian strongman retaliated by nationalizing the Suez Canal. Determined to put Nasser in his place, the British and the French conspired with David Ben-Gurion and the Israelis to attack Egypt and reassert their control over the canal. They failed to anticipate Eisenhower's reaction, however. When the outraged American president demanded immediate withdrawal from Egyptian territory, the invasion came to a screeching halt. Although Nasser was grateful for Eisenhower's intervention, it did not lead to a second honeymoon. On the contrary, Nasser's embrace of the Non-Aligned Movement, his implementation of "Arab socialism," and the formation of the United Arab Republic—the short-lived political union between Egypt and Syria—only heightened Washington's suspicion.

Relations between the United States and Egypt improved in the early years of the Kennedy administration, when Edward was a graduate student at Harvard. Kennedy's ambassador to Egypt was John Badeau, a former president of the American University in Cairo and a friend of Wadie Said, Edward's father. When Badeau presented his credentials to Nasser in 1961, they had a long talk and agreed to put aside the Question of Palestine, on which the two countries were never going to agree. Badeau's most frequent interlocutor in the Egyptian government was Ali Sabri, one of Nasser's top aides. In the run-up to the summit meeting of the Non-Aligned Movement in Belgrade that September, Badeau advised Sabri that it would be in Egypt's interest to prevent the occasion from turning into an anti-American rally. Afterwards, he congratulated Sabri on bringing off a moderate, constructive conference. When Nasser launched a proxy war against the Saudis in Yemen, however, his relationship with the United States began to sour again, in spite of Badeau's efforts.[24]

By the time Israel launched its preemptive attack against Egypt in June 1967, Edward was a young professor at Columbia. The attack had come in spite of President Lyndon Johnson's warning to Israeli foreign minister Abba Eban—Uncle Charles' old sparring partner at the United Nations—that Israel must not fire the first shot. But the

Israelis knew that Johnson was a friend, having agreed to sell American tanks, missiles, and artillery to the Jewish state. It was these weapons, in addition to those supplied by France and Britain, that enabled the Israel Defense Forces to occupy Gaza, the Sinai, the West Bank, and the Golan Heights before agreeing to a cease-fire at Johnson's behest. The Arab leaders hoped that Johnson would proceed to do what Eisenhower had done after the 1956 Suez War: demand immediate Israeli withdrawal from Arab territory. Johnson, however, was inclined to accept the Israeli principle that land would be returned in exchange for peace, which meant, in practice, that Israel would keep its territorial spoils for the foreseeable future.[25]

One of the consequences of the June War was the takeover of the Palestine Liberation Organization by Yasir Arafat's Fatah movement and new, more radical factions like George Habash's Popular Front for the Liberation of Palestine. In the eyes of the *fedayeen*, both Nasser and the PLO—which Nasser controlled through its first chairman Ahmad Shukairy—had been discredited by the embarrassing Arab defeat. With the Israeli occupation of the West Bank, the *fedayeen* organizations set up shop in the refugee camps on the East Bank of the Jordan River and resumed guerrilla operations against Israeli targets. At the same time, the radicals began to agitate for the overthrow of King Hussein of Jordan, arguing that the defeat of Zionism required nothing less than a social and political revolution in the Arab world. When the behavior of the *fedayeen* became intolerable, Hussein finally decided to crack down, urged on by his advisor Zaid al-Rifai—a former classmate of Edward Said's at Victoria College and a former student of Henry Kissinger's at Harvard—and by Jack O'Connell, the CIA station chief in Amman, who had Kissinger's ear.[26]

After its expulsion from Jordan in 1970-1, the PLO moved its headquarters to Lebanon, which, like Jordan, was a long-standing ally of the United States, thanks in part to Uncle Charles. It was in Lebanon that Edward, who lived in Beirut during a year-long sabbatical in 1972-3, became intimately acquainted with the officials, intellectuals, and poets of the Palestinian resistance movement, including his relative Kamal Nasir. However, it wasn't long before the *fedayeen* began to wear out their welcome, as they had done in Jordan. The difference was that the Lebanese state was weaker than Jordan's, with a government, an army, and a civilian population already divided along sectarian lines. When the PLO was dropped into this volatile mix, it precipitated a civil war, bonding with the Sunni, Druze, and leftist parties and repelling the Maronite Christians. Meanwhile, the Carter administration was committed to solving the Israeli-Palestinian conflict through diplomacy, enlisting Edward as an intermediary between Yasir Arafat and Secretary of State Cyrus Vance.[27]

Following its expulsion from Beirut in 1982, the PLO moved its headquarters to Tunis, where Edward continued to visit Arafat on occasion. Stranded on the other side of the Mediterranean, Arafat had little choice but to explore a diplomatic solution to the Palestinian-Israeli conflict. But it was not until the first *Intifada* in Gaza and the West Bank, which threatened to sideline the PLO, that Arafat decided to accept the conditions laid down by Secretary of State George Shultz for direct talks with the United States, including recognition of Israel's right to exist and renunciation of terrorism. The first step was taken at the Algiers meeting of the PNC in December 1988, when the members—including Edward—voted for a declaration of statehood on the basis of the UN's 1947 partition resolution.[28] One month later, at a special UN session in Geneva, Arafat pronounced the magic words about Israel and terrorism, and Shultz announced the opening of a dialogue with the PLO.

That dialogue led to the 1991 Middle East peace conference in Madrid, cosponsored by the United States and Russia. At the insistence of the Israelis, the Palestinians were represented by non-PLO members from the West Bank and Gaza who formed part of a joint Jordanian-Palestinian delegation. Just before the conference, Edward resigned from the PNC—mostly because he disapproved of the terms of Palestinian representation, but also because he had been diagnosed with leukemia. After the conference, bilateral negotiations between the Israelis and the Palestinians continued for several years in Washington, with little to no progress. The real action took place in Norway, which hosted secret parallel talks between Israel and the PLO. These talks, which even the Americans knew nothing about, resulted in the Oslo Accord, signed by Arafat and Israeli prime minister Yitzhak Rabin on the White House lawn in September 1993. Although Edward was invited by the Clinton administration to attend the signing ceremony, he refused to appear, having concluded that the accord was "an instrument of Palestinian surrender, a Palestinian Versailles."[29]

§

Charles Malik fell into the world of politics in 1945, when American power was perceived as largely benign by intellectuals in the West as well as the so-called "developing" nations. It was US military power that had defeated the Axis powers and would guarantee the freedom of West Germany, Greece, Turkey, and South Korea in the Cold War. It was American economic power that would rebuild Western Europe and Japan and bring the benefits of modern agriculture and industry to the world. And it was the soft power of American culture—its individualism, its egalitarianism, its frankness, its love of liberty—that would inspire young people around the globe. By the time Edward Said entered the world of politics in 1967, however, the attitude of the intellectuals to American power had changed dramatically—not just in Europe and the developing world, but also in the United States itself. American power had been used to overthrow elected governments in Iran and Guatemala, to launch a failed counterrevolution in Cuba, and to fight an immoral and unnecessary war in Vietnam.

This generational difference helps to explain why Edward Said's attitude toward American power differed so dramatically from Charles Malik's. Of course, their contrasting attitudes toward America were also shaped by the cultural bonds and strategic alliances between the United States, Lebanon, and Israel. After the retreat of Britain and France as colonial powers, the United States emerged as the ultimate guarantor not just of Lebanon's independence, but also of the survival of its Christian population. On two occasions—in 1958 and again in 1982—American presidents decided to send the Marines to Beirut in an attempt to restore order in the midst of chaos. Charles Malik played a major role in the first decision and a minor role in the second. To be sure, he was ultimately disappointed on both occasions, frustrated by the limitations Eisenhower and Reagan imposed on the exercise of American power. But there could be no doubt that the United States looked upon Lebanon and its Christians as natural allies in a region rife with anti-American sentiment.

That sentiment, of course, was intimately related to US support for its primary ally in the region—Israel. Granted, Eisenhower's support for Israel was more tepid than that of his Democratic predecessors and successors. It was Eisenhower, after all, who insisted that Britain, France, and Israel bring the Suez War to a halt and withdraw from the Egyptian territory they had overrun—a stance that won the approval of young Edward Said, an admirer of President Nasser. Said's attitude changed, however, after the June War of 1967, when the Israelis launched a preemptive strike against Nasser and his allies with the acquiescence, if not the encouragement, of the United States. He also blamed the United States for failing to use its political and economic influence to force Israel to withdraw from the territories it had occupied during the war. The war had left the Arabs with no part of Jerusalem, the city of his birth, and no part of Palestine, the land he would come to imagine as his lost homeland.

This brings us to another reason why Malik's attitude toward American power differed from Said's. For his part, Malik came to feel at home in America—personally, politically, and spiritually. This is not to say that he tried to assimilate; his difference from Americans was always marked, from his accent to his sense of the weight of existence. Nor is it to say that he did not feel at home in his native Lebanon. His criticism of the "Levantine" character could be severe, but Lebanon was, for better and for worse, his homeland, and he felt it in his bones. He would live and die for Lebanon. If Malik felt at home in two places, however, Said felt at home in no place. He may have been born in Palestine, but he had never really lived there, and after 1967 it was closed to him. He had lived in Egypt, but he had remained a foreigner, a *Shawmi*, a Northerner or Syrian. The same was true of the United States, although he did his best to assimilate in his younger years, eventually becoming a confirmed New Yorker. But America would never be his homeland.

There was a deeper reason for the contrasting attitudes of Malik and Said toward American power, having to do with their understanding of history. Malik believed to the end that America is a benevolent Christian nation, founded on faith in Jesus Christ, appointed by God in the latter days to save the world from Communism. As he put it in a speech in Washington in the early days of the Reagan administration:

> The world promise of America is something providential. Nothing of the order of the American phenomenon can be fortuitous or accidental. America has been schooled and refined precisely for its world promise. It may still have to be chastened further before its authentic word to the world can be uttered. Whatever the trying and the chastening still, doubtless America's word will be articulated and uttered one day.[30]

In short, Malik viewed America much as the Puritan colonists, Abraham Lincoln, and Ronald Reagan did—as the New Israel, the last best hope for earth. And it was Malik's calling, as a prophet sent from the original Holy Land, to school and chasten America until its promise was fulfilled.

Nothing could have been more foreign to Edward Said's understanding of history than his uncle's Theology of America. Said knew, of course, that the United States was a Christian nation in the sociological sense, with a majority of its citizens identifying themselves as Christian. But America was in no sense a providential phenomenon, there being no god working in and through history. Men and women made their own history by purely secular means, although some of them were motivated, to be sure, by religious hopes and fears. Nor was the history of America an especially benign one. The colonization of North America, the decimation of its aboriginal inhabitants, the enslavement of African laborers, the conquest and annexation of Mexican territory—these and other historical crimes were evidence not of a benevolent Christian nation, but of a nation behaving like other nations, driven by greed, racism, and pride. The word of America had been spoken, and it had been a curse as much as a blessing to the world.

Even so, Said did not abandon all hope that the United States might come to play a more constructive role in the Middle East and elsewhere. The true, legitimate power of America, he believed, was to be found not in the state or the corporation, but in civil society. It was the power of dissent, of social movements, of the progressive voices that had always been part of the American tradition, from Anne Hutchinson and Roger Williams to Gloria Steinem and Malcolm X. The truest Americans were not men of power like Dulles and Kissinger, whom Uncle Charles had cultivated and cajoled, but stubborn dissidents like Noam Chomsky and Jesse Jackson, public figures who placed themselves in opposition to power. If the Palestinians could forge alliances with such figures in the United States, he reasoned, they might persuade the American public, and thus Washington, to rethink its unquestioning support for Israel and for repressive regimes in the Middle East and elsewhere. Sadly, they have yet to succeed.

§

At first glance, the pairing of Edward Said and Charles Malik in a biographical study might seem rather idiosyncratic in spite of their family connection and shared history. Yet a dual portrait of these two related Arab intellectuals should prove instructive, as well as entertaining, to a variety of readers. Those interested in Edward Said will acquire greater knowledge of the once-famous uncle Said identified as "the great negative intellectual lesson of my life." Those interested in Charles Malik will acquire greater knowledge of the still-famous nephew who brought Malik's name to the attention of a new generation of scholars. Those interested in politics and international relations will benefit from new perspectives on a century of US involvement in the Middle East as witnessed—and, indeed, shaped—by two Arab intellectuals with sharply contrasting ideas and allegiances. Those interested in the fraught relations between Arab intellectuals and American power will find putative exemplars of two stereotypical positions: on the one hand, that of the "native informant," the friendly indigene who lends his wisdom and expert knowledge to the naïve but well-intentioned Yankee, and on the other hand, the critical intellectual who opposes US imperialism and speaks truth to power.

The book's primary sources include the unpublished papers of Charles Malik and Edward Said as well as their published writings. Malik's papers at the Library of

Congress have been consulted by a variety of scholars over the past three decades, notably Mary Ann Glendon, the author of *A World Made New: Eleanor Roosevelt and the Universal Declaration of Human Rights* (2001).[31] A conservative Catholic, Glendon made no secret of her admiration for Malik as a fellow Christian who built the edifice of human rights on the foundation of natural law, with the freedom and dignity of the individual as its capstone. More recently, Glenn Mitoma researched the Malik Papers for his pioneering article "Charles H. Malik and Human Rights: Notes on a Biography."[32] The Said papers at Columbia University have also begun to attract the attention of scholars, most notably Said's colleague Timothy Brennan, the author of his forthcoming intellectual biography. In addition to the writings and papers of Malik and Said, the book draws on a wide variety of other sources, including pertinent archival records, the published recollections of friends and family members, and US government documents.

The implicit argument of the book—made more explicit in the conclusion—is that power is both an understandable temptation and a grave danger for intellectuals. Until they reached the age of forty or so, neither Charles Malik nor Edward Said took much interest in politics or sought any form of power apart from the power of words and ideas. They were too devoted to reading and writing, to philosophy and literature, to the life of the mind and the spirit. Neither man imagined that he would become anything but a university professor or would one day take an active part in the affairs of nations. Their involvement in politics and diplomacy was wholly fortuitous, the result of circumstance and a strong sense of duty. Both men entered the world of politics with open eyes, knowing full well that they would lose something—perhaps a great deal—of their cherished independence. Both struggled in their role as privy counselors and public apologists for men of power whose actions and principles they could not help but question as men of conscience. Both were asked to do and say things they were not proud of for the sake of the cause. Yet history has judged Said more kindly than Malik, perhaps because he was a critic and not a servant of the imperial power of United States.

Chapter 1 opens with the birth of Charles Malik at the dawn of the twentieth century and ends with his surprise appointment as Lebanon's double ambassador to the United States and the United Nations in 1945. The first half of the chapter emphasizes the influence of American institutions on Malik's intellectual and spiritual formation—the Tripoli Boys' School, the American University of Beirut, the Young Men's Christian Association, the Oxford Movement, Harvard University. During this phase of his life, America was associated not with colonial designs and military might, as were Britain and France, but with the disinterested benevolence embodied in missionary educators like Daniel Bliss and Bayard Dodge. Thanks to the encouragement of these pious educators, Malik developed a passion for Western philosophy—the passion that drove him to Harvard to study with Whitehead and to Freiburg to study with Heidegger. The second half of the chapter underscores Malik's determination to launch his own informal philosophical academy in Beirut and his powerful impact on the young, searching intellectuals of the AUB. The chapter also situates Malik within the small community of interrelated Arab Protestant families that he shared with Edward Said, including the Badrs, the Cortases, and the Makdisis.

Chapter 2 recounts Malik's adventures as the most famous Arab diplomat in the United States and America's best friend in the Arab world. Malik's role in the creation of the Universal Declaration of Human Rights receives considerable attention, as does his participation in the debate over the partition of Palestine and the admission of Israel to the UN. His emergence as a vocal critic of the Soviet Union—which endeared him to anti-Communist liberals as well as conservatives—is documented through his speeches and writings of the period. At the same time, the chapter recounts Malik's interactions with a host of important players on the American scene—Eleanor Roosevelt, her relatives Kim and Archie (both with the CIA), the Dulles brothers, the Rockefeller brothers—all of whom became personal friends as well as political allies. The second half of the chapter narrates Malik's long-expected return to the AUB in 1955, his controversial term as Lebanon's staunchly pro-American foreign minister—which effectively ended his political and diplomatic career—and his brief return to the United Nations as President of the General Assembly in 1958-9.

Chapter 3 covers Malik's resumption of academic life from 1960 until his retirement in 1976. The 1960s were not an auspicious decade for Malik, who found himself out of touch with younger, increasingly radical colleagues and students at the AUB, not to mention the dominant political currents in Lebanon and the United States. The chapter notes Malik's rivalry with various AUB colleagues, notably the philosopher Sadik al-Azm, an atheist and a Marxist who later became a friend of Edward Said's. It also chronicles Malik's private efforts to persuade Washington to oppose the Chehabist regime in Lebanon, which he viewed as dangerously pro-Nasser. But he had few friends in the liberal Kennedy and Johnson administrations. It was only when Richard Nixon was elected president of the United States in 1968, followed by Suleiman Frangieh as president of Lebanon in 1970, that Malik regained some of his earlier influence in Washington and Beirut. With the PLO threatening Lebanese sovereignty, Malik wrote to Nixon and Kissinger and met with them in Washington on occasion, as documented in this chapter.

With Chapter 4, the book shifts its attention to Edward Said, recounting his upbringing in Cairo and his summer vacations in Lebanon, where he enjoyed the company of the Maliks, the Badrs, and the Makdisis, as well as other summer residents. Starting in 1951, the scene shifts to the United States, where Edward completed his education and launched his brilliant academic career at Columbia. Drawing on Said's memoir, the chapter recounts his experiences as a student feeling "out of place" at the Mount Hermon School and Princeton, his loneliness relieved by a number of visits to the Maliks in Washington. It goes on to recount his five years of graduate study at Harvard, his marriage to Maire Jaanus, his introduction to Continental literary theory, and his first four years at Columbia, before his life changed as a result of the devastating 1967 war between Israel and the Arab states. The chapter also introduces some of Edward's Palestinian friends and future political gurus, notably Ibrahim Abu-Lughod and Hanna Mikhail, who were also studying and teaching at American universities.

Chapter 5 begins with Edward's response to the *Naksa*—the setback that was the humiliating defeat of the Arab armies in 1967 and the subsequent loss of Palestine. It documents several attempts on Edward's part to reach out to Uncle Charles for emotional consolation and political wisdom—attempts that brought only disappointing responses. More importantly, the chapter documents Edward's embrace of his identity as a Palestinian in the aftermath of the *Naksa*. Not only did he begin to write and speak on Palestine, but also he took an active role in the new Association of Arab American University Graduates, through which he met important Arab scholars like Hisham Sharabi and Sadik al-Azm—both of whom had studied philosophy with Charles Malik at the AUB—as well as independent radicals like Noam Chomsky and Eqbal Ahmad. The chapter devotes special attention to Said's transformative sabbatical year in Beirut, where he began his intensive study of Arabic and met with various figures in the Palestinian resistance movement—most notably his old friend Hanna Mikhail, now a high-ranking official in Yasir Arafat's Fatah organization.

In Chapter 6, the focus returns to Charles Malik, recounting the final phase of his life as a member of the Lebanese Front following the outbreak of civil war in 1975. The chapter documents Malik's persistent efforts to persuade the Ford, Carter, and Reagan administrations to come to the aid of Lebanon's Christians, threatened first by the PLO and its Druze allies and later by the occupying Syrian army. As a frequent visitor to Washington in the late 1970s and early 1980s, Malik attended prayer breakfasts with presidents, met with State Department officials and legislators, and collaborated with the Lebanese American lobby. Also documented is Malik's role in forging the alliance between the Lebanese Front and Israel, an alliance that culminated in the 1982 Israeli invasion of Lebanon, the expulsion of the PLO from Beirut, and the election of Bashir Gemayel—Malik's young protégé—as President of Lebanon. The chapter ends with the last five years of Malik's life, marked by the bitter disappointment of Gemayel's assassination, the rise of the Shia militias, the near-collapse of the AUB in the midst of assassinations and kidnappings, and the withdrawal of American and Israeli forces from Lebanon.

Chapter 7 turns to Edward Said's growing activism during the same time period (1975–87), when he emerged as the most articulate and photogenic Arab American defender of the rights of the Palestinians. The primary focus is on Said's interventions in the public sphere in the form of books, contributions to newspapers and magazines, lectures, and television appearances. His involvement in such organizations as the Palestine Human Rights Campaign, the Arab American Anti-Discrimination Committee, and the American Middle East Peace Research Institute is noted. Also documented are some of Said's behind-the-scenes meetings with American and Palestinian officials—most notably his friends Hanna Mikhail and Shafiq al-Hout, but also Yasir Arafat himself—as well as his occasional participation in the sessions of the Palestine National Congress. Along the way, the chapter introduces some of Said's new friends, such as Christopher Hitchens and Salman Rushdie, as well as Israeli acquaintances like Yehoshafat Harkabi and Matti Peled.

Finally, Chapter 8 recounts the last fifteen years of Said's life, starting with his and Ibrahim Abu-Lughod's well-publicized meeting with Secretary of State George Shultz in March 1988 and his subsequent encounters with Benjamin Netanyahu, then serving as Israel's ambassador to the United Nations. The chapter goes on to document Said's visits with Arafat in Tunis, his role in the important 1988 Algiers meeting of the PNC, his resignation from the PNC at the time of the 1991 Madrid peace conference, and his public break with Arafat and the PLO over the 1993 Oslo Accord. Drawing on his own published accounts, the chapter also chronicles Said's return to Palestine in 1992 and subsequent visits to Palestine and Lebanon, where he spoke at the AUB on a number of occasions. In addition, the chapter recalls Said's response to the Ayatollah Khomeini's February 1989 *fatwa* against his friend Salman Rushdie, the Gulf War of 1990, the withdrawal of Israeli troops from Lebanon in 2000, al-Qaeda's attack on the World Trade Center on September 11, 2001, and the US invasion of Iraq in March 2003, six months before his death at the age of sixty-seven.

1

Charles Malik: The Education of a Christian Intellectual, 1906–45

The village of Bterram lies in the Kura district of Lebanon, between Beirut and Tripoli. According to tradition, Bterram had been founded by two Syrian brothers, Salem and Malik, after whom the two leading families of the village were named.[1] It was here that Charles Habib Malik was born in 1906. Like most Kura villagers, the Maliks were Greek Orthodox Christians; Charles himself was an incense-carrier for his great-uncle, the village priest.[2] His father Habib was a physician trained at the Syrian Protestant College in the 1890s, when Daniel Bliss was still president. Charles' mother, Zarifa Karam, was the daughter of a Greek Orthodox merchant from Tripoli. Her maternal uncle, Farah Antun, was an intellectual and reformer who had moved to Egypt in order to make a living by his pen.[3] Although Charles never met Antun, who died young, he came to know his sister, Rose Antun Haddad, who edited one of the first women's journals in Egypt.[4]

For some years, Charles attended school in the neighboring village of Bishmizzine, where he met Afif Tannous, a classmate and lifelong friend. Later, both Charles and Afif were sent to the Presbyterian mission school for boys in Tripoli, where they began to develop the faith in America that would guide the rest of their lives. In a memoir, Tannous recalled that both he and Charles were influenced by a young American teacher who proselytized for the Jehovah's Witnesses.[5] Fortunately, they were talked out of joining the Witnesses by the school's new principal, Rev. Leslie Leavitt, whose wife Margaret was the daughter of Rev. Howard Bliss, the second president of the Syrian Protestant College, who had died in 1920.[6] Howard Bliss' other daughter, Mary, was married to Rev. Bayard Dodge, who succeeded his father-in-law as president of the college—which had officially changed its name to the American University of Beirut—in the fall of 1923.

That same fall, Charles matriculated at the AUB, where he studied mathematics and physics. More importantly, he was introduced to the study of philosophy by Rev. Laurens H. Seelye, a graduate of Amherst College and Union Theological Seminary. Seelye's wife Kate was an accomplished scholar in her own right, having studied Arabic at Columbia University with Professor Richard Gottheil, the former president of the Federation of American Zionist Societies of New York, and her fellow graduate student Philip Hitti, an AUB alumnus who went on to a long academic career at Princeton. No doubt the Seelyes introduced Charles to Kate's parents, Rev. William N. Chambers and his wife Cornelia, who had served as missionaries in Adana, Turkey, witnessing the massacre and deportation of the town's Armenian population.[7] They probably knew Charles' father, who had been conscripted into the Ottoman medical corps and sent to Adana, where he, too, witnessed Armenian deportations. As for the Seelye children, Charles would cross paths with several of them later in life, notably future diplomat Talcott W. Seelye.

In addition to teaching philosophy, Laurens Seelye sponsored the West Hall Brotherhood, which had replaced the Young Men's Christian Association chapter on the AUB campus. Just as Howard Bliss had transformed the college into a more liberal institution by exempting non-Christian students from mandatory chapel, so Seelye transformed the YMCA into a theistic "Brotherhood" open to non-Christian students. In an article in the *Journal of Religion*, Seelye noted that the college had enrolled 1,001 students in the year 1920-1, including 490 Christians, 382 Muslims, 66 Jews, 41 Druzes, and 32 Bahais. "In such a situation, with such students," he concluded, "the Christian thing to do is not so much to 'make them Christians' as to provide a way of learning from God by common prayer, song, testimony, and worship."[8] Among those who joined the Brotherhood was Charles Malik.

In the *Students Union Gazette* for 1927, one of Charles' classmates, Edward J. Jurji, offered a humorous sketch of Professor Seelye's eccentricities:

> The Professor has quite a number of paradoxial [sic] characteristics. Out and out he is the faculty champion of free thought and liberty. Not withstanding, he lays so much emphasis on closely sencoring [sic] every single film that comes to West Hall. He abhores [sic] the idea of seeing a lady fashionably dressed.[9]

The same issue of the *Gazette* featured a clever essay by Charles Malik on the evolution of the radio. In it, he prophesied the coming of "Radio-Man":

> A stage might be reached where the apparatus becomes so small that it might be slipped into our ears.... Or, the whole apparatus might change its form and, no longer assuming its present mechanical configuration, become a liquid injected into our system like the anti-typhoid serum. We become virtual radio-men.[10]

In later years, Charles would become a radio-man himself, or at least a frequent guest on American radio and television programs.

In addition to Edward Jurji—who, like Philip Hitti, would enjoy a long academic career at Princeton—Charles' contemporaries at the AUB included two young men who were destined to play important roles in the life of Edward Said: Emile Cortas, a Quaker from the village of Brumanna, and Constantine "Costi" Zurayk, a Greek Orthodox from Damascus. With his brother Michel, Cortas would go on to found the successful Cortas Canning Company. Zurayk would go on to earn an MA from the University of Chicago and a PhD from Princeton—all by the age of twenty-one. He then returned to Beirut, where he taught Arab history at the AUB and married Emile Cortas' sister Najla. Around the same time, Emile married Wadad Makdisi, the daughter of AUB Arabic professor Jirjis Makdisi. Three decades later, their daughter Mariam Cortas would marry Edward Said. And Mariam and Edward would name their daughter after Mariam's aunt Najla.

The future politicians among the AUB student body were drawn to *al-Urwa al-Wuthqa*, the Arabic literary society, which served as an incubator of Arab nationalism. One of Charles' friends from the Brotherhood, Fadhel Jamali—a future Iraqi foreign minister—was also a member of *al-Urwa*. So was Ahmad Shukairy, the son of the *Mufti* of Acre, whose undergraduate career at the AUB lasted less than a year.[11] On May 6, 1927, during the annual Martyrs' Day demonstration in Beirut, the nineteen-year-old Shukairy delivered a passionate oration in which he denounced the French Mandate and called for Arab unity. Afterwards, he was arrested by the authorities, deported to Palestine, and banned from Lebanon for ten years.[12] One month later, Charles Malik graduated from the AUB. Little did he know that, twenty years later, he would be reunited with Ahmad Shukairy at the United Nations, where Shukairy served as a professional diplomat-for-hire.

After graduating from the AUB, Charles stayed on for two years as a "staffite," a young college graduate on a short-term teaching contract. In his second year, Charles was joined by a number of American staffites, most notably Stephen B. L. Penrose, Jr., the son of the president of Whitman College in Walla Walla, Washington. Little did Penrose know that his life was destined to revolve around the Middle East, first as the secretary of the Near East College Association in New York, then as an intelligence officer with the Office of Strategic Services in Cairo, and finally as the fourth president of the AUB. Another new staffite was Lewis G. Leary, Jr., the son of a Presbyterian minister who had taught at the AUB in the early 1900s. During the Second World War, the younger Leary would be tapped by his old friend Penrose to assist him at OSS headquarters in Cairo. In the 1960s, he would be Edward Said's first department chair at Columbia University.

One of Charles' pupils in the late 1920s was Wadad Makdisi—Edward Said's future mother-in-law—who was one of the first women to enroll at the AUB. In March 1928, Wadad sent Charles a conciliatory note after an apparent dispute over a paper she had written for him.[13] Unfortunately, Wadad did not mention Charles in the English version of her memoir. It is obvious, however, that she treasured her experience at the AUB. "While French schools hoisted the colonial flag over their buildings," she recalled,

> the American University hoisted only a white emblem with the cedar tree. We never felt that the Americans pouring onto the campus had any claim over our minds. President Dodge initiated a beautiful tradition on the Prophet Muhammad's birthday intended to foster an appreciation of the spiritual values linking Christianity and Islam. It was in this world of vision and hope that we lived for four years, gaining faith in ourselves, pride in our heritage, and respect for the human ties that bind us to one another.[14]

If Wadad's account reads like a paean to the AUB, it was because her father Jirjis and her uncle Anis had been teaching Arabic there since the early 1900s.

§

In the summer of 1929, after two years of teaching at his alma mater, Charles left Beirut for Cairo, where his family had moved after his father's discharge from the Ottoman medical corps. The following year, Charles took a job as a researcher with the Rockefeller Foundation's bilharzia eradication project, collecting and dissecting some 93,000 snails from the Nile River under the direction of Dr. Claude H. Barlow.[15] Meanwhile, Charles found companionship at the Cairo Central branch of the Young Men's Christian Association, which was run by an American missionary, Rev. James K. Quay, and an Egyptian Protestant educator, Naguib Kelada. In 1930, Charles served with Kelada on the branch's Library Committee.[16] The following year, he joined Quay as a member of the "Principles Committee."[17] More importantly, he joined a Friday discussion circle that Quay convened for the purpose of engaging young, educated Muslims in interfaith dialogue.

After he was introduced to the circle by Quay, Charles declared that he was neither a Muslim nor a Christian but an agnostic. Six months later, however, he confided to Quay, "I want you to know that since I have joined this group the person of Christ is becoming more and more of a necessity in my thinking." In an unpublished memoir, Quay recalled a particularly lively meeting in which Charles had come to his aid in defense of Christianity. "Christianity," Charles reminded his Muslim friends, "has gone through the fires of modernism, criticism and scholarly research and has come through the experience stronger and finer than it otherwise would be. This has not come to Islam as yet." "Personally," he added, "I hope that Islam will stand the test. . . . I am not like Dr. Quay here who is a missionary and who would like to see everybody become Christian." Recalling such exchanges, Quay decided that Charles "had probably the most brilliant mind I have ever encountered."[18]

It is conceivable that Charles also met Wadie Said, Edward's father, at the YMCA's Cairo Central branch during these years, before either man had married into the Badr family. Cairo Central branch reports indicate that William Said (as Wadie called himself in English) made his first small donation in 1931, when Charles was working with James Quay and Naguib Kelada.[19] In *Out of Place*, Edward named Kelada, the general secretary of the branch, as a friend and associate of his father's. He also recalled that one of Kelada's musical daughters used to sing at the American mission church in Ezbekieh, where the Said family worshipped on Sunday evenings, and where Rev. Quay preached on occasion.[20] *Out of Place* offers one other hint of an early acquaintance between Charles Malik and Wadie Said: Wadie, it seems, gave Charles his first typewriter.[21]

In the summer of 1931, Charles was invited to meet with representatives of the "Oxford Group," an evangelistic movement started by an American minister named Frank Buchman, whose intimate "house parties" were popular with students at Ivy League colleges as well as Oxford. Among the representatives were two Princeton men who befriended Charles: H. Alexander Smith, a future US senator from New Jersey, and his son-in-law H. Kenaston "Ken" Twitchell, Jr., who was studying at Oxford.[22] Also traveling to Egypt that summer were a team of students from Wycliffe Hall, the center of Evangelical theological training in Oxford. Leading the team was the principal of

Wycliffe, Rev. George Francis Graham-Brown, who knew Frank Buchman and took a sympathetic interest in the Oxford Group.[23] The following year, Graham-Brown was appointed Bishop of Jerusalem, whose diocese included all of the Levant.[24] Looking back, Charles referred to Graham-Brown as "one of my closest friends."[25]

Meanwhile, Charles was desperate to continue his education in the United States or Britain. He had been reading Bertrand Russell and Alfred North Whitehead, the eminent English philosopher-mathematicians, hoping to follow in their footsteps.[26] So he wrote to both men in January 1932, proposing to study under Russell in London or Whitehead at Harvard. Declaring that "England is moribund," Russell encouraged him to write to Professor Raphael Demos, who taught philosophy at Harvard.[27] Originally from Smyrna, Demos had a background similar to Charles'. Like Charles, he had discovered philosophy as a student at an American missionary school, Anatolia College. He had arrived at Harvard just in time for Russell's lectures there in the spring of 1914. Demos, it is said, was one of the two Harvard students who managed to impress Russell. The other was Thomas Stearns Eliot.[28]

After receiving Russell's letter, Charles wrote to Laurens Seelye at the AUB, insisting that it was "absolutely necessary" that he attend Harvard that fall.[29] In fact, Charles had already been admitted. The problem was money. By August, fortunately, he had managed to scrape together the necessary funds. That was when he notified his friend Stephen Penrose—who, after teaching for three years at the AUB, had been admitted to the graduate program in philosophy at Columbia University—to expect him in New York in early September.[30] A week later, Seelye sent Charles a letter of introduction to Dr. George Sarton, the famous Belgian historian of science, who had an office in Harvard's Widener Library. Providentially, Sarton, who had been learning Arabic in Beirut, had offered to hire Charles as his Arabic tutor upon his return to Cambridge.[31]

§

In Cambridge, Charles learned that a friend from the AUB, Emile Bustani, was coming to study engineering at the Massachusetts Institute of Technology. In the eulogy he delivered at Bustani's memorial service three decades later, Charles recalled some of their adventures in Boston that year—eating Lebanese food with Emile's relatives in the factory towns of Methuen and Lawrence, visiting the grave of the philosopher William James in Mount Auburn Cemetery, interceding between two Iraqi students who had challenged each other to a duel.[32] In the spring of 1933, Charles and Emile attended the twentieth-anniversary celebration of the Syrian American Club of Boston. The *Boston Globe* reported that some 2,000 people turned out to hear the principal speaker—James Roosevelt, the son of the new president of the United States, who promised the crowd, "We have reached the end of a period of depression." According to the *Globe*, both Charles and Emile spoke at the event, along with Faris Malouf of the Syrian American Federation of New England.[33]

Meanwhile, Charles had begun his apprenticeship under Alfred North Whitehead. For three years, he attended every lecture and seminar Whitehead gave.[34] But it was a young Chicagoan, Professor John Wild, who turned out to have the greater impact on Charles. Wild had just returned from a year in Freiburg, Germany, where he had studied with Martin Heidegger. Upon his return to Harvard, Wild set his students, including Charles and Harry Broudy of Brooklyn, to reading Heidegger in German.³⁵ Wild was not the first American to have studied with Heidegger. A few years earlier, in 1928, Julius Seelye Bixler, then a professor of religion at Smith College—and a former AUB staffite—had attended Heidegger's first lecture at the University of Freiburg.³⁶ When Bixler moved to the Harvard Divinity School in the fall of 1933, he was replaced by Laurens Seelye, who happened to be his cousin.

Another of Charles' teachers at Harvard was William Ernest Hocking, a liberal Protestant with a keen interest in Palestine. Originally sympathetic to Zionism, Hocking had changed his mind after a visit to Jerusalem in 1928. As he explained in the *Atlantic Monthly*:

> What I have to say, I say with deep personal regret. For I went to Palestine seized with the idea of Zionism and warmed by the ardor of Jewish friends to whom this vision is the breath of life, prepared to believe all things possible. I came away saddened, seeing that to strive for the perfect body, as things now are, can only mean the loss of body and soul alike. To pursue any campaign for the fulfillment of "the British promise," to force cantonization on Palestine and so to repeat the standing grievance of divided Syria, to press for any further favor of the state, is to work blindly toward another bloody struggle involving first the new settlements, then Great Britain, then no one knows what wider area.³⁷

The degree to which Hocking's anti-Zionism influenced Charles at this stage of his life is difficult to gauge. What is clear is that Charles found himself, a decade later, on the same side of the Palestine Question as Hocking, who continued to oppose Zionism until his death in 1966.

One of Hocking's acquaintances was George Antonius, a Greek Orthodox man of letters from Jerusalem employed by the Institute of Current World Affairs, funded by the American philanthropist Charles R. Crane. In March 1935, Crane sent Antonius on his first lecture tour of the United States, seeking to counteract Zionist propaganda. He gave a number of lectures at Harvard, where he was welcomed by Ernest Hocking and George Sarton. At a dinner in his honor at Adams House, Antonius outlined three Arab grievances against the British administration in Palestine. First, the British had been slow to offer real self-government to the Arabs, a failure he attributed to Zionist pressure. Second, there was growing poverty and unemployment in Palestine, a condition he attributed to the influx of Jewish immigrants. Third, the Zionists had been allowed to purchase Arab land without restriction, creating a "landless proletariat" dependent on charity.³⁸ There is no proof that Charles Malik attended this dinner, but he would have heard about it from Hocking and Sarton.

When he wasn't tutoring Sarton in Arabic, Charles attended worship services at St. Peter's Episcopal Church in Cambridge. The Rector of St. Peter's was Rev. Frederic C. Lawrence, the son of the bishop of Massachusetts and a scion of the wealthy Lawrence family. Fred Lawrence was a leading figure in the Oxford Group, having fallen under Frank Buchman's spell during one of his periodic visits to Harvard.³⁹ In the summer of 1934, Lawrence persuaded Charles to join him on an Oxford Group tour of Canada and the Pacific Northwest, followed by the annual international house party in Oxford.[40] The following spring, Lawrence and Charles spoke at a forum on the Oxford Group at Boston's Ford Hall. What Charles said was not reported, but Lawrence told stories of various captains of industry who, having joined the Oxford Group, had succeeded in bringing a spirit of cooperation to the factory floor—an emphasis of Buchman's in the 1930s, when labor strikes roiled the businesses of his wealthy friends.[41]

§

That same spring, Charles was awarded a coveted Sheldon Traveling Fellowship, which enabled Harvard students to enjoy two years of study in Europe. Inspired by John Wild and Seelye Bixler, Charles was planning to study with Martin Heidegger in Freiburg. What he probably didn't know was the extent to which Heidegger had embraced Hitler's National Socialist revolution. In fact, Heidegger had joined the Nazi Party in 1933, shortly after his election as Rector of the university. Although he had resigned as Rector a year later, he remained a party member until 1945. The sincerity of Heidegger's commitment to Nazism remains a matter of dispute, as does his reputed anti-Semitism. As for popular anti-Semitism in Hitler's Germany, Charles was about to experience it for himself. To the Brown Shirts, he looked like a Jew.

In Freiburg, Charles sat in as many of Heidegger's seminars and lectures as he could. Years later, he recalled the way Der Meister's words had penetrated to the core of his being:

> there is nothing I hate more than fraud and falsehood and sham, and it is this that I loved most in Heidegger's philosophy of *Eigentlichkeit* and *Uneigentlichkeit*.... The fact that I interpreted [his] statements as convicting me personally, while knowing that Heidegger knew nothing about me and could not possibly have been thinking of me as he made them, I kept a close secret to myself; and such guarded secrets whereby one's personal shams are exposed to him without anybody knowing it always produce a genuine catharsis in the human soul.[42]

Apart from Heidegger's cathartic teaching, however, Charles' year in Germany was dark and depressing. As he wrote to Professor Hocking, "I do not know whether you can really appreciate the sting of the terrible feeling of complete existential hopelessness.... It is brought home to me on every side and in diverse subtle ways that I belong to a defeated race ... that Christianity and God are irrecoverably dead."[43]

The following summer, Charles decided to leave Germany two months early. Back at Harvard that fall, he struggled to explain his experience in writing:

> What can I say to impress on you the absolute ubiquity of the Hitler spirit? SA and SS uniforms everywhere. Hitler youth, Hitler girls, Arbeitsdienst, the new army. Swastika flags sticking out of every window on official occasions. Columns of uniformed men—strong, healthy, hopeful, confident—marching; singing, singing. National-socialist papers everywhere; the same controlled news, the same terrible hatred against communists, the French, the Jews and what they call the colored

races. The Professors at the University beginning their classes with the Nazi salute to which the students respond.[44]

Yet Charles emerged from the crucible of Nazi Germany with a renewed sense of vocation. As he wrote to Laurens Seelye, "In God I may have a message that reaches beyond the Near East, at this moment of the world's darkest despair."[45]

Fortunately, Charles was able to secure an assistantship for the 1936-7 academic year. Two of his students that year were Chadbourne Gilpatric and Arthur Szathmary. Gilpatric was a blue blood from New York whose family owned a summer home on Mount Desert Island, Maine, not far from the Eyrie, the ninety-nine-room mansion of the Rockefellers. After graduating from Harvard, Gilpatric went to Oxford as a Rhodes Scholar, served as an intelligence officer in Europe during the Second World War, joined the CIA in Washington for a few years, and spent the rest of his career administering grants for the Rockefeller Foundation. Szathmary, by contrast, was the son of Hungarian Jewish immigrants from Quincy. In his senior year, he won Harvard's Phi Beta Kappa Prize for his essay "The Aesthetic Theory of Bergson." After serving in the navy as an interrogator of Japanese prisoners, he joined the philosophy department at Princeton, where he made quite an impression on Edward Said in the 1950s.

In addition to teaching, Charles hosted weekly Socratic dialogues in his apartment in Cambridge. Among the students who participated was Howard Schomer of Chicago. In a tribute to his mentors, Schomer penned an amusing recollection of these evenings:

> Malik was quite impecunious, always wearing the same outfit—a ridiculous greenish tweed jacket and knickers. . . . Most of us sat on the floor—there were only two real chairs in the room—around a huge pile of oranges. Charles often romanticized about the beautiful mountains of Lebanon and its rich orchards. Before our brainstorming sessions ended toward 2:00 am we usually had consumed quantities of oranges. . . . Charles launched the evening's talkfest by reading a brief provocative passage from some current theologian, philosopher, scientist, or intellectual historian—often a sharp attack on some of the sacred cows of fuzzy American liberalism or pragmatism. Not even Socrates could have been more penetrating in cross-questioning us following our retorts.[46]

Thanks in no small measure to the influence of Charles Malik, Schomer went on to become a pacifist, a Congregationalist minister, a seminary president, and a civil rights activist.

A few months before his graduation from Harvard, Charles received an appeal from the Near East College Association (NECAS).[47] The letter is noteworthy only for its signature—that of Allen W. Dulles, the future director of Central Intelligence. Dulles had a long-standing interest in the Near East, having been posted to Istanbul with the diplomatic corps after the First World War. Following a stint in Washington as chief of the State Department's Near East division, he had joined the Wall Street law firm of Sullivan and Cromwell, where his brother Foster was the managing partner. In the 1930s, Allen Dulles served as a director of NECAS, chairing its Five-Year Stabilization Fund Committee, whose membership included Harold B. Hoskins, vice president of

Cannon Mills, the world's largest manufacturer of sheets and towels. Born in Lebanon to Protestant missionaries, Hoskins had attended Princeton with his cousin, the future diplomat William A. Eddy, another Arabic-speaking missionary son of Lebanon. Hoskins preserved his ties to the land of his birth by serving as a trustee of the AUB.[48]

§

Around the time he received the appeal from Allen Dulles, Charles opened a letter from President Dodge offering him a teaching post at the AUB. He accepted immediately, having decided that the best way to serve Christ in the Near East was to elevate the intellectual, moral, and spiritual character of his alma mater. Thus it was that he found himself back in Beirut in the fall of 1937. One of his colleagues on the faculty was his classmate Costi Zurayk, who had returned from Princeton after completing a doctorate in Islamic history under Philip Hitti. An ardent Arab nationalist, Zurayk was the faculty advisor to *al-Urwa al-Wuthqa*, the student literary club devoted to Arab unity and independence.[49] Another colleague was Albert Hourani, whose father Fadlo had converted to Protestantism, attended the Syrian Protestant College, and immigrated to Manchester. Intrigued by his Lebanese heritage, Albert had decided to teach at his father's alma mater after reading philosophy, politics, and economics at Oxford.[50]

As soon as he got to Beirut, Charles started a weekly philosophy circle. As Albert Hourani recalled, the group "met one evening a week to read texts as they should be read, very slowly, lingering over every word, discussing every problem—Plato's *Republic* in the first year, St. Augustine's *Confessions* in the second."[51] In addition to Hourani, the circle included Costi Zurayk and Najla Cortas, his future wife, who was teaching at the Ahliah School for Girls, headed by Wadad Makdisi. Archie Crawford, the principal of International College—the AUB's preparatory school—sat in on the discussions, as did Fakhri Maalouf, a young AUB physics instructor. Students who joined the circle included Fakhri's brother Rushdi, an aspiring poet, and Angela Jurdak, the daughter of AUB mathematics professor Mansur Jurdak. In addition, the circle included three of Hilda Said's Badr cousins: Albert, an instructor in commerce at the AUB; his wife Lily, who was also his cousin; and Lily's sister Eva—soon to be Charles' wife—who was teaching at the American Junior College for Women.[52]

Two of Charles' favorite students were Edward Said's cousins Evelyn and George Said, who graduated from the AUB in 1940 and 1941, respectively.[53] George became a Malik disciple, as did his friend Fayez Sayegh, the son of a Presbyterian minister from Tiberias. Fayez's older brother Yusif, who was studying economics, also fell under Charles' spell. In a memoir edited by his wife Rosemary, Yusif recalled,

> I audited two courses with Malek [sic]. But it was not in the classroom that Charles Malek was at his most interesting; it was at the house of the Maaloufs. He was a friend of Fakhri's, the eldest Maalouf brother, who was in physics but also had an interest in philosophy, and later took theology and became a Catholic. Charles Malek was interested in bright young students, to win them over to Catholicism— Albert Hourani . . . was influenced by Charles Malek along those lines.[54]

At the time, Yusif and Fayez were living with the Maaloufs in their house on Jeanne d'Arc Street, not far from the AUB campus.

Among the other regulars at the Maalouf salon was one Antun Saadeh, who lived across the street. A native of Shweir, Saadeh had immigrated to the New World after surviving the ravages of the First World War, ending up in South America. Returning to Lebanon in the early 1930s, he built a traditional *arzal* (tree-house) for himself in Dhour el Shweir, where President Bayard Dodge, Professor Anis Makdisi, and other AUB faculty owned or leased summer homes. In an effort to assist the brilliant but impoverished young man, Dodge gave him permission to teach German and other languages to AUB students. In addition to teaching, Saadeh attended lectures and classes, including one in "Semitic Cultures" taught by a young linguist named Anis Frayha, who, some forty years later, would tutor Edward Said in Arabic during a sabbatical in Beirut.[55]

What President Dodge didn't know is that Saadeh had founded a secret political party, the Parti Populaire Syrien (PPS) or Syrian National Party, devoted to the independence of the Syrian Nation, which, in his view, predated the Arabs and extended to Palestine and Transjordan as well as Lebanon. When Dodge learned of the existence of the PPS in late 1934, he seems to have reported it to the authorities.[56] In the fall of 1935 and again in the spring of 1937, Saadeh was imprisoned as a subversive. That did not prevent Fakhri Maalouf from joining the PPS, followed by his brother Rushdi and Yusif Sayigh. As Sayigh recalled:

> [Saadeh] was interested in the Maaloufs, and I was living with them. He wanted us to be his immediate disciples, not to be taught through somebody else. That took months. He always spent five or six months talking to people, testing them intellectually, testing their fiber, before in the end saying, "You are ready to join."[57]

Yusif and his brother Fayez, who joined the PPS a few years later, went on to become high-ranking party officials.

Like its Maronite rival, the Phalange Party of Pierre Gemayel, the PPS was organized along the lines of the European fascist parties of the 1930s, complete with uniforms, military-style exercises, and an oath of obedience to the *Zaim* ("Leader"). Even its emblem, the *zaubaa* ("hurricane"), resembled the Nazi swastika.[58] Charles dismissed these trappings, however, insisting that the similarities between the PPS and the Nazis were merely accidental. The essential purpose of the PPS, he thought, was to give voice to the suffering of the Lebanese diaspora, to express their determination to restore freedom, dignity, and self-respect to their mother country.[59] But he refrained from joining the PPS, which was militantly anti-clerical. If he encouraged his friends and disciples to join any organized body, it was the Roman Catholic Church, not a secular political party.

§

In the spring of 1938, Charles received a visit from his former Harvard student Howard Schomer, who was in the midst of a grand tour of Europe. Charles arranged for Schomer to lecture in West Hall on "Culture and Religion in the New Germany," which he had observed first-hand before coming to Beirut. "Adolf Hitler," Schomer informed his audience, "has accomplished the extraordinary feat of transforming a highly theoretical people and a broad and abstract idea into dynamic action," creating first a political party and then a totalitarian state. As for religion, the Nazi policy was twofold. In the short run, it aims "to constrain the supernational, superracial, supernatural faith of the Christian churches, without losing the support of the many millions of believers." In the long run, it aims to replace Christianity with a religion of "blood and soil and Fatherland and sacrificial devotion to the tribal god." Schomer's talk was not directed at Antun Saadeh—the would-be Führer of Syria—but it might just as well have been so.[60]

Not long after Schomer's visit, Charles gave a speech at the American Junior College for Women on "The Meaning of Philosophy," in which he complained that "we do seem to have a very strong anti-philosophical streak in our very being." He sent a copy to Antun Saadeh, who wrote back immediately, calling the speech "yet another indication of the intellectual awakening of the Syrian nation." Even so, he had a few bones to pick with Charles. One was that he had conflated the Near East with the Arab world, as though it were "one homogeneous coherent group" rather than "a scattering of civilizations, societies and cultures." Another was that Charles had called for a revival of "classical Islamic Arab philosophy," ignoring "our particular [Syrian] classical philosophy which preceded the Islamic Arab philosophy." Saadeh also complained of Charles' tendency to "belittle our people in its own eyes."[61]

In the meantime, Charles continued to enjoy the presence of Eva Badr in his philosophy circle. In May 1938, Eva wrote to apologize for missing one of the meetings. In the same note, she invited him to the Badr home to hear the young poet Said Akl, a Maronite from Zahle. Like Charles, Akl was a regular visitor to the Maalouf house and enjoyed arguing with Antun Saadeh, even though he seems to have been a party member.[62] As Yusif Sayigh recalled, Akl

> was greatly impressed with Saadeh as a person, and with his ideas. But to him, Syria was really Lebanon. In other words, Lebanon wasn't just this little bit of land along the coast, but the whole of Syria. It was an inversion of Saadeh's idea.[63]

In June, however, Saadeh suddenly vanished, having been warned that he was about to be arrested again.[64] No doubt he intended to return to Lebanon as soon as the authorities forgot about him. But when Britain and France declared war on Germany a year later, he was stranded in South America, where he would remain until 1947.

Sometime in 1938, Albert Hourani received a visit from an Oxford friend, Charles Issawi, a Syrian Orthodox economist from Cairo. Hourani introduced him to Charles Malik, who greatly impressed Issawi. As Issawi wrote to Ralph Reed, his former headmaster at Victoria College in Alexandria:

> I spent a few days in Lebanon where I met a prophet who urged me to repent. He's a double Ph.D. (Harvard—where he was Whitehead's favorite pupil and Fribourg where he was with Heidegger), a Syrian Christian, an amazingly fine chap, the only Oriental I've met who will, I think, enrich world thought. . . . He has an interesting scheme concerning the creation of an Everyman's library in Arabic, to consist mainly of translations from Greek, Latin, English, etc.[65]

A few years later, Issawi would quit his job at the Egyptian Central Bank in order to join Charles at the AUB, where he taught politics and economics in the mid-1940s. As for Charles' scheme to translate Western classics into Arabic, it was a venture he would pursue doggedly for years, eventually persuading the United Nations to take it on.

§

In March 1939, Hitler's troops occupied Czechoslovakia following the infamous Munich Agreement. A month later, Charles wrote a letter to C. H. Barlow, his former boss in the Nile bilharzia project. "I myself do not believe that there will be a war," Charles confessed. "Thus I am afraid that Hitler and Mussolini are going to have all they want to have, and nobody is going to do anything about it."[66] Two months later, he went up to Dhour el Shweir for the annual conference of the Bible Lands Union for Christian Education at the invitation of its American general secretary, Rev. George Scherer, who taught at the Near East School of Theology in Beirut.[67] Then, in early September, the Nazis invaded Poland, and Britain and France finally declared war. In Lebanon, the French authorities declared martial law, suspended the Constitution, and banned the PPS, which they suspected of collaborating with the Axis powers. Arrests of party leaders ensued.[68]

That same summer, Albert Hourani left the AUB for the Royal Institute of International Affairs, where he worked with Arnold Toynbee and H. A. R. Gibb.[69] Meanwhile, two of Albert's brothers made their way to Beirut. One of them, George, had just finished his doctorate in Oriental Studies under Philip Hitti at Princeton. He was on his way to Jerusalem to take up a teaching post at the Government Arab College, the most prestigious secondary school in Palestine.[70] The headmaster of the college was Ahmad S. Khalidi, an alumnus of the Syrian Protestant College, whose three sons would all teach at the AUB one day. The other Hourani brother, Cecil, had just finished his studies at Oxford and was invited to join the AUB as a staffite. One of his first assignments was to teach logic as Charles Malik's assistant. Like Albert, Cecil was greatly impressed with Charles, who became a lifelong friend. In his memoir, he paid tribute to Charles as "one of the most brilliant minds of his time."[71]

In the fall of 1939, Charles resumed his philosophy circle. It would appear, however, that some of the participants were put off by Charles' arrogant manner. One of them was Leslie Leavitt, his former principal at the Tripoli Boys' School. In December, Rev. Leavitt reproached Charles in a pastoral letter:

> You say that no one is more open to the truth, more diligent in its search than you, and yet your whole manner contradicts your words. . . . Instead of making people admire the philosopher, you are making us scorn him. . . . But will not a *humble* and *patient* and *loving*—a *Christlike* spirit—in the end triumph?[72]

Another hint of Charles' tendency to pontificate can be seen in the letter he wrote to two other members of his circle, Costi Zurayk and Najla Cortas, upon learning of their engagement. "If you *find everything* in each other and in your several or joint plans," he admonished his friends, "you may become so self-involved as to miss God. And I am very anxious lest you miss God."[73]

Absent from the philosophy circle that fall was Fakhri Maalouf, who had managed to avoid arrest as a member of the banned PPS and was now studying at the University of Michigan, thanks to a scholarship awarded by the AUB. Evidently the scholarship had first been offered to Yusif Sayigh, who turned it down because he needed to work in order to support his family. It was then offered to Eva Badr, whose family, according to Sayigh, refused to allow her to go to America all by herself.[74] So the scholarship was finally offered to Fakhri Maalouf, who traveled to Michigan by way of Europe. In Paris, he was met by Charles Malik's brother Gabriel, who was studying with the Jesuits. Gabriel took him to see the Cathedral of Notre Dame and made him promise to seek out a Catholic priest in Michigan. Fakhri kept his promise and was received into the Roman Catholic Church on November 30, 1940.[75] According Hisham Sharabi, Fakhri's defection left "an unhealed wound" in Antun Saadeh's heart.[76]

§

In the spring of 1941, the war finally came to Lebanon. General Charles de Gaulle, the commander of the Free French forces, was determined to take Syria and Lebanon back from his Vichy foes, but for that he needed British help. In June, British and Free French troops under General Maitland Wilson invaded Syria and Lebanon, where they encountered stiff resistance from the Armée du Levant under General Dentz. In July, Dentz sued for an armistice through the US Consul in Beirut, Cornelius Van Hemert Engert, whose storied diplomatic career had begun in 1914 when he was hired as an interpreter by the US consulate in Istanbul.[77] In the early 1920s, when he was posted in Washington, Engert had befriended Allen Dulles, his boss in the State Department's Near East division. Later, in the early 1950s, Engert would solicit Charles Malik's support for a new pro-Arab organization, American Friends of the Middle East.

The fighting in Lebanon did not prevent Charles from marrying Eva Badr that summer. Among the many friends who wrote to congratulate him was Albert Hourani, who declared, "I owe my understanding of the Arab nation and my belief in Christianity to you, Charles, more perhaps than to any other human being."[78] Albert's brother George wrote from Jerusalem, as did George Said, who had just graduated from the AUB. "I shall always remember you," he promised, "as the first master of my thoughts," adding that he was thinking of returning to the AUB to study for an MA in philosophy.[79] Charles and Eva also received a letter from Elsa Kerr, Eva's colleague at the American Junior College for Women, who was visiting the American School for Girls in Cairo that summer. There she had met Eva's aunt Emelia Badr, who ran the school, as well as Wadie and Hilda Said.[80]

One of Charles' students that fall was future Jordanian diplomat Hazem Zaki Nusseibeh. In his memoir *Jerusalemites*, Nusseibeh remembered Dr. Malik's Eurocentrism:

> At our philosophy classes at the AUB in 1941, Dr. Charles Malik would make invidious comparisons between Western luminaries like Shakespeare, Dante, and Goethe, and Arab poets, claiming the latter were no match for the former.[81]

Although Nusseibeh appreciated Dr. Malik's oratory, his political mentor was Costi Zurayk. As he explained in his memoir:

> The majority of students were too bourgeois to embrace communism; the Greater Syria party, though the best organized, was too confining in its ultimate goal; that left the Arab national movement in the ascendancy. Dr. Constantine Zuraiq was the ideological mentor and I, along with the majority of students, joined the Arab national movement and became its leader in my last year at the AUB.

As Nusseibeh recalled, one of his fellow student leaders in the movement was Yahya Hamoudeh, who would become the chairman of the Palestine Liberation Organization in the late 1960s.[82]

Another future PLO official who took a course from Charles Malik that year was the poet Kamal Nasir, whose mother's cousin was married to Hilda Said's brother.[83] Alas, Kamal failed the course. That summer, he wrote a desperate letter to Dr. Malik from Ramallah, pleading for mercy.[84] Whether Charles bothered to reply is unknown, but in the fall Kamal and fellow poet Tawfiq Sayigh—the younger brother of Yusif and Fayez—moved into St. Justin's House, a new Anglican hostel for AUB students from Palestine. The warden of St. Justin's was Rev. Kenneth Cragg, whose superior, Bishop Graham-Brown of Jerusalem, drove up to Beirut in November in order to dedicate the hostel. Tragically, the bishop was killed on his way back to Jerusalem when his car was struck by a train. As for Cragg, he came to know Charles Malik quite well, eventually succeeding him as head of the philosophy department. "To listen to Charles Malik in full cry," Cragg rhapsodized in a memoir, "was what it must have been like to attend on Demosthenes."[85]

Earlier that fall, Charles had received a letter from George Said, whose father Boulos had recently died of cancer. In his letter, George confessed that he was irritated by the business into which he had been thrust by his father's death. He would much rather be studying philosophy at the AUB with his friend Fayez Sayegh, who was pursuing a Master's degree while working underground to keep the PPS alive in the absence of Antun Saadeh.[86] Together, George and Fayez were reading Kierkegaard's *Fear and Trembling*—one of Charles' favorite texts. George also reported that he had seen Charles' youngest brother, Baheej, in Cairo.[87] Baheej, one gathers, was the black sheep of the Malik family; certainly, he was more worldly than his pious brothers, one of whom, Ramzi, was also studying philosophy at the AUB.

That same fall, Charles received a visit from Harold Hoskins, vice president of the AUB Board of Trustees, who was touring the Near East on a sensitive wartime mission—to lay the groundwork for an Office of Strategic Services operation in the region. On his return, he was to report to President Roosevelt in person.[88] Accompanying Charles to his meeting with Hoskins was Costi Zurayk. According to Hoskins' notes, Charles and Costi complained that the AUB was not graduating enough young men of spirit and character. One reason, they asserted, was that the arts and sciences were regarded as mere appendages; all the resources were going to the professional and technical schools. When Hoskins asked Charles and Costi about the future of Lebanon, they agreed that the country must eventually become independent. In the meantime, they preferred the British to the French, in spite of their fear that Britain would give in to the Zionists' demand for a Jewish state in Palestine.[89]

Hoskins returned to Beirut in February 1943, when he asked President Dodge to help him convince Washington to "subsidize American cultural activities in the Middle East."[90] He also visited old friends from the Syrian Protestant mission, including his cousin Dora Eddy and her husband Harold Close, an AUB chemistry professor who had recently been named Dean of Arts and Sciences. From Beirut, Hoskins made his way back to Cairo, where he met with Brigadier Iltyd Clayton, the spymaster who ran Britain's Middle East Intelligence Centre.[91] It is likely that Hoskins mentioned his earlier meeting with Charles Malik and Costi Zurayk to Clayton, who shared their belief that it was time for the French to leave Lebanon and Syria.[92] When he got back to Washington, Hoskins typed a memo for the State Department regarding a "Cultural Relations Policy for the Near East." Less than a year later, the AUB received its first funds from the US government, laundered through the Near East College Association.[93]

Not long after Hoskins' return to Washington, Stephen Penrose was sent to Cairo as deputy chief of the OSS's Strategic Intelligence branch in the Near East. Penrose had been recruited, no doubt, by Allen Dulles, who knew him through the Near East College Association. To assist him in Cairo, Penrose summoned old friends from his Beirut days, including Archie Crawford, the principal of the International College, and Lewis Leary, a professor of American literature at Duke University.[94] Penrose also recruited Bayard Dodge's son David, a Princeton undergraduate who became one of his field officers.[95] Around the same time, Albert and Cecil Hourani—both British citizens—were assigned to Brigadier Clayton's staff in Cairo, as was Major Aubrey (Abba) Eban, who later became Charles Malik's neighbor at the United Nations. There is no evidence that Charles met Eban in Cairo, although he did travel there on occasion to visit his widowed mother as well as Wadie and Hilda Said.

Albert Hourani's posting to Cairo was due, in large measure, to a report he had written for the Foreign Office, dated March 1943, entitled "Great Britain and Arab Nationalism." According to Hourani, Arab nationalism was possessed of "a double nature: it is itself a symptom of the disease which it attempts to cure." Britain's role, he contended, should be to treat the disease—economic, social, and cultural backwardness—in order to forestall the putative cure—a revolt against the West. Near the end of his report, Hourani suggested that Beirut would replace Cairo as "the centre of living thought" in the Arab world, pointing to lively Arab Christian movements centered around the AUB and the Jesuit Université Saint-Joseph. At the AUB, he noted, "there is a movement for the creation of a Christian philosophy in Arabic, which is associated with Charles Malik, Professor of Philosophy in the University, so far almost unknown but undoubtedly the greatest intellectual figure in the Arab world today."[96] If Brigadier Clayton had not yet heard of Charles Malik, Hourani's report certainly brought the young Lebanese philosopher to his attention.

Clayton paid a visit to Charles in the summer of 1943, a visit that inspired Charles to write a private treatise, *The Problem of Lebanon: An Interpretation*, in which he attempted to explain his beloved homeland and its world-historical significance to the Brigadier. Lebanon, he declared, is defined by five features: its geography and climate, which make it more like Europe than the desert Arab lands; its extensive emigration to the West;

its absence of class and color lines; its Europeanism; and its Christianity. "The roots of [Lebanon's] real life," Charles insisted, "are all European," making it unique in all of Asia and Africa. Even Turkey, to his mind, had no real roots in Europe. "The decisive question," he observed, "is *whether the European tradition is alive in Turkey*, whether the Turks are intellectually and spiritually *oriented* westward, whether they *can* deeply love and understand Plato and Paul and Augustine and Pascal and Leibniz and Shakespeare and Bach and Kant and Dostoevsky."[97] The answer, he implied, was no.

The second part of *The Problem of Lebanon* defended the proposition that Lebanon must be "a Christian-European-Arab state." "When we say Christian," he explained, "we do not mean a theocratic state," but rather a modern secular state that accords equal protection to Christians, Muslims, and members of other faiths. At the same time, however, he left little doubt that he considered Islam to be an inferior religion. "I do not anticipate any primary intellectual-spiritual inspiration coming to us from the Moslem-Arab world," he admitted, "nor do I believe that that world by itself has much real and lasting intellectual-spiritual inspiration *even for itself*." In Baghdad, Damascus, or Cairo, he lamented, "there is in general no freedom of thought at all." What the example of Beirut proves, paradoxically, is that "*only in a Christian country is a Muslim free.* There is freedom only where Christ and Plato reign." And that, he concluded, is why Western powers like Great Britain must ensure that Lebanon remains free to pursue its destiny.[98]

§

In September 1943, Bishara Khoury—who enjoyed the support of General Edward Spears, the head of the British mission in Syria and Lebanon—was elected president of Lebanon. At Spears' insistence, Khoury invited pro-British Sunni politician Riad Solh to serve as prime minister. Together, Khoury and Solh proceeded to amend the Constitution, eliminating all references to the French Mandate. That was too much for the French. On November 11, the French Delegate General had Khoury arrested and replaced him with the Francophile Emile Eddé. Solh was also imprisoned, along with Interior Minister Camille Chamoun—another British ally—and most of the other ministers. The next day, some 200 women, including Chamoun's wife Zelpha and her cousin Klodagh—the sister of PPS chairman Nimah Tabit—led a protest march through the streets of Beirut, stopping at the British and American embassies.[99] The women's march gave birth to a new organization, the League of Lebanese Women, in which Eva Malik played a prominent role. She even translated the women's speeches for Lady Spears.[100]

Confronted with a popular uprising as well as a British military threat, the French authorities relented, releasing the prisoners and recognizing Lebanon's independence on November 22. Meanwhile, Charles continued to correspond with Brigadier Clayton and the Hourani brothers in Cairo. In January 1944, he sent the first part of *The Problem of Lebanon* to Brigadier Clayton at GHQ in Cairo, inviting the spymaster to visit him again in Beirut.[101] In March, he sent the second part.[102] That same month, he received a letter from Cecil Hourani in Cairo. He had seen a good deal of Charles' mother, Cecil reported, as well as his brother Baheej. He had also seen George Said, who appeared restless, unhappy with his inherited position in the family business.[103] A concerned Charles then wrote to George, adding that George's uncle Wadie, "of whom we became quite fond last summer," was planning to come to Dhour again in the summer.[104]

That May, Charles delivered a rousing series of chapel talks at the AUB on the subject of freedom of thought. "In the Near East in general, and in the Arab world in particular," he warned,

> we do not yet know what freedom of thought means. We have not yet tasted the wonderful blessings of real freedom. We have not yet begun the struggle for freedom of thought. Is it possible to think freely and express one's thought in Baghdad, in Aleppo, in Damascus, in Cairo, in Jaffa, in Amman? Here in the University we enjoy much real intellectual freedom.... But outside the University here in Beirut, can you think freely, and publish what you believe? If you think you can, you are out of touch with the real situation.

Unlike material goods, he admonished the assembled students, freedom of thought cannot be imported from the West. "Automobiles may be made in Detroit and brought here; but you cannot buy a freedom that is made elsewhere: you must make it yourself."[105]

Charles was not the only intellectual thinking about freedom of thought in the Arab world. So was Albert Hourani. Indeed, Albert and Charles had been dreaming about an Arab version of Plato's Academy ever since they had read the *Republic* together in Beirut. Charles possessed a copy of a long document entitled "The Idea of an Arab Academy"—probably written by Albert Hourani—along with a list of participants for a proposed meeting in Cairo in August 1944. In addition to Charles, the Hourani brothers, and Brigadier Clayton, the list includes the names of Costi Zurayk and Paul Kraus, an exiled German Jewish Orientalist teaching at King Fuad I University, who had loaned his flat in Cairo to the Hourani brothers.[106] The secretary of the group is identified as Burhan Dajani, a native of Jaffa who had studied economics at the AUB.[107] Unfortunately, I have been unable to verify that the proposed meeting of this illustrious group of intellectuals took place that August.

What we do know is that the Maliks vacationed in Dhour that summer, together with Wadie and Hilda Said and their children.[108] We also know that the Maliks attended a party at the home of President Khoury, along with a hundred other notables, including, probably, Khoury's wealthy brother-in-law, Michel Chiha, the publisher of the influential daily *Le Jour*. It was Chiha who, in 1926, had played a key role in drafting Lebanon's Constitution, which provided for the division of elective offices and public jobs among the country's many sects. More recently, at the request of General Spears, Chiha had launched *The Eastern Times*, an English-language daily edited by Munah Racy, the uncle of Albert and Cecil Hourani.[109] In his diary, Charles described his evening with the Khourys as "terrible, awful, horrible," the guests reeking of "snobbishness, ruthlessness, commercialism, and sensuality." For their part, however, the president and his coterie were impressed by the young Harvard-educated philosopher. By Christmas Eve, Charles was confessing to his diary that he had fallen victim to "political worldly seduction."[110]

In early January 1945, Charles received an invitation from Colonel Bertram Thomas, the famous British explorer, to lecture at the Middle East Centre for Arab Studies in Jerusalem, which he directed. MECAS, housed in the Austrian Hospice, was where British officers and colonial officials went to receive training in Arabic language and culture. Ironically, the principal instructor at the time was none other than Major Aubrey Eban, who had studied Arabic at Cambridge. In his letter, Thomas informed Charles that he had been recommended by two of their mutual friends—Brigadier Clayton and Albert Hourani.[111] In his reply, Charles mentioned that Clayton had visited him in Beirut that very week.[112] Perhaps Clayton wanted to vet him for a possible diplomatic post in the new government of Abdel Hamid Karame, the pro-British prime minister whom he had persuaded President Khoury to nominate.[113]

The United States had accorded full diplomatic recognition to Lebanon and Syria the previous fall.[114] However, the two Levantine nations had not been invited to join the new United Nations, which was due to hold its organizing conference in San Francisco in the spring of 1945. Naturally, the Lebanese and Syrian governments protested their exclusion, as did General Spears, who had returned to London, and a new organization founded by Arab Americans in New York—the Institute of Arab American Affairs (IAAA).[115] The president of the IAAA was Faris Malouf, the Boston lawyer whom Charles had met back in 1933; its executive director was Princeton's Philip Hitti; and its director of Arab Affairs was Ismail R. Khalidi, an AUB graduate who had studied at the University of Michigan and subsequently worked in the Office of War Information.[116] Many decades later, Ismail's son Rashid would become the first holder of the Edward Said Chair at Columbia University.

At the end of March, the Allied powers relented and invited Lebanon and Syria to send delegations to San Francisco. Charles' call to government service came shortly thereafter, evidently on the recommendation of Michel Chiha.[117] "One Friday morning," Charles recalled,

> in the middle of a lecture I was giving, the janitor told me the Foreign Minister had called me. I finished my lecture, called him back, and, at his request, went to see him. I had never met him but knew him to be the owner of one of the greatest stables of Arabian horses in the world. He said to me, "You know I am very fond of horses. Well, I have put them aside to serve the government. I know you are very fond of books. Put them aside. Go to the United States as our Minister and as our delegate to the United Nations Conference in San Francisco." I consulted my wife, and said yes.[118]

In the event, he would serve as Lebanon's ambassador to the United States and the United Nations for the next decade, putting his philosophy books aside for much longer than he expected.

2

Charles Malik: The Intellectual as Cold Warrior, 1945–59

On the eve of his departure for Washington, the AUB threw a bon voyage party for Charles Malik. Among the well-wishers was a young philosophy student named Hisham Sharabi, a native of Jaffa who would become a professor at Georgetown University in Washington, a Palestinian nationalist, and a compatriot of Edward Said's. Sharabi's description of the celebration is worth quoting:

> We gave him a farewell party in West Hall at which a number of students and professors spoke. They all said words to the effect that he was Plato going off to America to realize his philosophy, and that it was our loss and America's gain. It never occurred to us that what Malik would do in the United States was to specialize in attacking communism, praising Christianity, and supporting the Cold War, and that he would return to Lebanon to become the ideologue of the fanatic Christian right.[1]

Sharabi's account was written years later, after his falling out with Charles. But they remained friends well into the 1960s, when Sharabi's politics took a sharp turn to the left.

Before Charles left Beirut, he was contacted by Tuvia Arazi of the Jewish Agency, who told him that the Christians of Lebanon should ally themselves with the Jews of Palestine. Subsequently, Arazi advised the Agency to introduce Charles to "our people in D.C. without delay before people like Hitti hitch him to their wagon."[2] After meeting with Arazi, Charles sailed to Washington, where he signed the United Nations Declaration in the office of Secretary of State Edward Stettinius on the day President Roosevelt died. Then, after presenting his diplomatic credentials to Roosevelt's successor, Harry Truman, at the White House, Charles traveled to San Francisco for the UN organizing conference, accompanied by his AUB colleague Angela Jurdak, the first secretary of the Lebanese legation.

Perhaps the most influential advisor to the US delegation was John Foster Dulles, who until recently had chaired the Commission to Study the Bases of a Just and Durable Peace under the auspices of the Federal Council of Churches. When Dulles was invited to the UN conference, he had turned the Commission over to William Ernest Hocking, Charles' old Harvard professor.[3] Initially, Dulles saw the United

Nations as an opportunity to rebuild international order on a foundation of Christian ideals. Before long, however, Dulles conceded that US national interest required checks on the power of the United Nations in the form of "regional organizations, domestic jurisdiction, and the exclusivity of U.S. security areas."[4] The lone woman in the US delegation was Dr. Virginia Gildersleeve, Dean of Barnard College, who knew Foster Dulles' brother Allen through her work on behalf of the Near East College Association. She took it upon herself to host a luncheon for the twenty-nine Arab delegates who had been educated at American colleges in the Near East, including Charles' classmates Fadhel Jamali and Farid Zeineddine.[5]

More circumspectly, Charles met with the Jewish Agency's observers in San Francisco, notably Eliahu Epstein (Elath), an AUB alumnus to whom he had been introduced in Cairo by Brigadier Clayton. Hoping to enlist Charles' support for a Jewish homeland in Palestine, Epstein invited him to dine with his colleagues Nahum Goldmann and Arthur Lourie at the Sir Francis Drake Hotel. The luncheon, however, proved to be unproductive. As Epstein explained in his diary:

> I was not surprised by Malik's caution in avoiding speaking freely in the company of three members of the Jewish Agency. The mere fact of his meeting us is enough to raise suspicion among his colleagues if the matter becomes known to representatives from the different communities in his own delegation, who do not trust each other and would sabotage each other's positions for communal and personal reasons. A liberal person and a deeply religious Christian, Malik undoubtedly feels himself a stranger to the fanatical Saudi Arabian Wahhabis and must, in addition, guard his behavior and his every word from the suspicion and hostile interpretations of his Arab League colleagues. It was an act of courage on his part to meet us in public at all.[6]

In the event, Charles did not become the ally the Jewish Agency was hoping for. But he maintained cordial relations with Israeli diplomats like Epstein, who found him a worthy opponent.

After the San Francisco conference, Charles returned to Washington to open the Lebanese legation. In early October, he wrote to Ernest Hocking and invited him to meet the young men and women of the new Arab Office in Washington, which represented the League of Arab States.[7] Later that month, Charles met with the new secretary of state James Byrnes, along with the foreign ministers of Egypt, Syria, and Iraq. The ministers, who were concerned about President Truman's recent declaration that 100,000 displaced Jews from Europe should be relocated to Palestine, handed Byrnes an aide-memoire with a sharp warning:

> Regarding the peace of the Near East in general, and of the Arab world in particular, one principle is certain: there obviously can be no peace in that region by sacrificing Arab interests for the sake of the Jews.[8]

Byrnes was hearing the same warning from the Arabists in his own State Department, notably William A. Eddy, the minister to Saudi Arabia, who had served as President

Roosevelt's translator during his famous Red Sea meeting with Ibn Saud in February 1945.

§

In January 1946, Charles received a letter from his friend Fakhri Maalouf, who was teaching at Boston College. After finishing his doctorate in Michigan, Fakhri had moved to Boston for a year of postdoctoral study at Harvard. In Cambridge, he frequented the St. Benedict's Center, a new meeting place for Catholic students. The Center's cofounder was none other than Avery Dulles, the son of John Foster Dulles, who had converted to Catholicism while studying at the Harvard Law School. Following Avery's enlistment in the navy, the direction of the Center had been taken over by a charismatic and controversial priest, Father Leonard Feeney, who took a dim view of the "liberal" Catholics who held sway in Boston. In the late 1940s, Feeney would make the doctrine of *extra ecclesiam nulla salus* ("Outside the Church, there is no salvation") a litmus test of orthodoxy. Under the influence of Father Feeney, Fakhri was becoming more Catholic than the pope.[9]

In his letter to Charles, Fakhri accused his former spiritual mentor of failing to live up to his true calling. "The great tragedy is not that our Christian tradition in Lebanon is threatened," Fakhri wrote, "the real tragedy is that Charles Malik is not on the way of being for us another Athanasius, Ephrem, Gregory, Chrysostom, Damascene." He reminded Charles that "two of your brothers are not only beautiful converts, but converts with a vocation."[10] Fakhri was referring to Charles' brothers Gabriel, whom he had met in Paris, and Ramzi, who had recently experienced a vision while sitting in West Hall at the AUB. In his vision, Ramzi witnessed the future gathering and reconciliation of the children of Abraham—Jews, Christians, and Muslims. Vowing to devote his life to the realization of that vision, he had decided to join the Dominicans.[11] For Charles, Fakhri's rebuke must have hit close to home. But he was not yet ready to abandon politics for sainthood.

Meanwhile, President Truman and Prime Minister Attlee had appointed an "Anglo-American Committee of Inquiry" to study the future of Palestine. In April, the committee issued its recommendations, including the admission of 100,000 new Jewish immigrants. In response, five Arab diplomats in Washington, including Charles Malik and Costi Zurayk—who had joined the Syrian legation—issued a statement warning that further Jewish immigration to Palestine would be resisted by the Arab world "with all the forces at its disposal."[12] Two days later, Cecil Hourani, the new secretary of the Arab Office in Washington, added his voice to the Arab chorus. "All the difficulties which arise from the committee's report," he wrote in a letter to the *New York Times*, "spring from its recommendation that the refugees should go to Palestine, and only Palestine."[13] The following week, Charles and the other Arab ministers met with Under Secretary of State Dean Acheson, exacting a promise that the United States would not act on the committee's recommendations without consulting them first.[14]

That fall, in the UN General Committee, Charles proposed that the United Nations take up the cultural project he had been advocating for years—the translation of "the great classics of human thought" into Arabic and other world languages. When the representative from Ukraine asked sarcastically, "Who is to decide which are the 'great classics of human thought'?" Charles offered his own, decidedly Western, list: "Plato, Aristotle, St. Augustine, St. Thomas Aquinas, Shakespeare, Leibnitz, Pascal, Descartes, Kant, Averroes."[15] In December, the translation project was referred to the UN's Educational, Scientific, and Cultural Organization (UNESCO) and its newly elected Director-General, Julian Huxley.[16] A few years later, an International Committee for the Translation of the Classics into Arabic was authorized by UNESCO, chaired by Charles' old friend Stephen Penrose, who by then had become the fourth president of the AUB.[17]

In January 1947, Charles began what was arguably the most important work of his life: the creation of the Universal Declaration of Human Rights (UDHR). At the first session of the Human Rights Commission (HRC) in New York, Eleanor Roosevelt was elected chair, P. C. Chang of China vice chair, and Charles secretary.[18] As Mary Ann Glendon has noted, Charles initiated the HRC's first argument by posing a philosophical question. When we speak of human rights, he declared, "we are raising the fundamental question, what is man? Is man merely a social being? Is he merely an animal? Is he merely an economic being?" In response, the delegate from Yugoslavia, Vladislav Ribnikar, took issue with the individualistic conception of rights found in capitalist countries. "The psychology of individualism," he observed, "has been used by the ruling class in most countries to preserve its own privileges." In socialist countries, by contrast, "the social principle comes first." This drew a rebuttal from Charles, who insisted that "the deepest danger of the age is the extinction of the human person as such in his own individuality."[19]

§

On March 2, 1947, Antun Saadeh returned to Beirut to reclaim the leadership of the Parti Populaire Syrien. During his long absence, the party had been taken over by younger men, including Fayez Sayegh, who had replaced Charles in the AUB philosophy department in the fall of 1945. The party's rank and file now included another AUB philosophy student, Hisham Sharabi, who had written a paper on the PPS for a class taught by Charles Issawi. After studying Saadeh's writings and interviewing party leaders—including the First Member of the party, George Abdel Masih, and the party's chairman, Nimah Tabit—Sharabi had decided to join. He was among those who greeted Saadeh at the Beirut airport and marched with him to the Tabit home, where the leader delivered a speech denouncing Lebanon's separation from Syria as well as its confessional political system. Within hours, the authorities issued a warrant for Saadeh's arrest.[20]

That same March, Charles traveled to Princeton for a symposium on "Near Eastern Culture and Society" organized by Philip Hitti. From Oxford came the renowned Orientalist H. A. R. Gibb. From Harvard came the professor of Arabic, William Thomson, along with Ernest Hocking and George Sarton. The AUB was represented by many distinguished alumni—Charles, Costi Zurayk, and Edward Jurji among them—as well as by Harold Close, the dean of arts and sciences, and Harold Hoskins, the president of the board of trustees. The US State Department sent a number of representatives, notably William Eddy, now working in the Research and Intelligence bureau of the State Department, and Loy Henderson, the chief of Near Eastern and African Affairs. Aramco was represented by James Terry Duce, and the Rockefeller Foundation by Charles Fahs, a former OSS man. Also present was Donald Wilber, a Princeton-trained expert in Persian architecture, who would soon join the CIA and assist Kim Roosevelt in planning the infamous 1953 coup that overthrew Premier Mossadegh of Iran.[21]

Charles spoke at the conference's concluding plenary session. According to the published summary, he offered an "ontological analysis of Moslem Arab existence," which, he said, "reveals the following phenomena":

> masses, *badu*, discontinuous society and history, weakness of the authority of reason. The literature of this being is of highly imaginative character, with overemphasis on words and rhyme. In the interpretation of events, magic, luck, fatalism and mysticism play a part. The tradition of reformers and rebels is thin. . . . The Arab being is outside the Greco-Roman-Hebrew-Christian European synthesis.

What "Arab man" needed, he continued, was "fearless self-criticism." So far, however, the West had been of little help in this regard. "The historicism of the Orientalist and the self-lost romanticism of Lawrence," Charles complained, merely "confirmed Moslem Arab existence in itself." What America can do to help the Muslim Arabs, he concluded, is to improve the quality of its educational institutions in the Near East, translate the world's classics into Arabic, and uphold Lebanon as a center of freedom of thought.[22]

That June, the committee responsible for drafting the UDHR met for the first time. Mrs. Roosevelt, P. C. Chang, and Charles were members, as were John Humphrey, a law professor at McGill University in Montreal, and René Cassin, the vice president of the Conseil d'État in Paris, a committed Zionist who had lost twenty-nine relatives in concentration camps. Humphrey's draft of an international bill of rights formed the basis of the committee's deliberations. One of Charles' contributions at this stage was to propose that the right to change one's religious beliefs be added to the article guaranteeing freedom of religion. His native Lebanon, he said, was exemplary in this regard, serving as a refuge for those persecuted elsewhere for their beliefs. Although it was opposed by the Saudis, the right to change one's religious beliefs was ultimately included in Article 18 of the UDHR.[23]

Meanwhile, the British had renounced their mandate in Palestine and referred the question to the United Nations. The United Nations, in turn, had created a Special Committee on Palestine, which recommended in September that the land be partitioned between the Arabs and the Jews, much to the dismay of Charles Malik and the other Arab ministers. In October, Charles delivered an alternative Arab League proposal to President Truman's UN ambassador, Warren Austin, calling for a unitary state in Palestine, with a guarantee of cultural and religious freedom for Muslims, Christians, and Jews alike.[24] At the State Department, William Eddy complained to Secretary of State George Marshall that the UN plan authorized the Zionists to build "a theocratic sovereign state characteristic of the Dark Ages."[25] Shortly thereafter, Eddy left the State Department for a job with Aramco; some believe that he joined the CIA at the same time, with Aramco providing non-official cover.[26]

In mid-November, Charles argued the Arab case on ABC's "World Security Workshop," a weekly radio program hosted by Eleanor Roosevelt, who embraced the idea of a Jewish state in Palestine.[27] When Mrs. Roosevelt asked him about the American-Russian accord on partition, Charles played the Communism card:

> I take it that the United States is interested in the security of Greece and Turkey and Iran. I take it also that the Marshall Plan aims at the containment of Communism. But if thousands of Russian and eastern European Jews—and who can tell who is a Jew and who is not a Jew?—have free access to Palestine, is the American government certain Greece and Turkey and Iran will still be secure and Communism will still be contained?[28]

In the end, Charles' efforts to defeat the partition resolution proved futile. With the support of both the United States and the USSR, the resolution was approved by the General Assembly on November 29, 1947.

A few days later, Charles arrived in Geneva to continue his work on the UDHR. Joining Charles as his assistant was his old Harvard friend Howard Schomer, now a missionary living in France. During the war, Schomer, a pacifist, had spent four years working in Civilian Public Service camps in lieu of military service. At Schomer's request, Charles introduced the right of conscientious objection for inclusion in the UDHR, to no avail.[29] His proposal to amend a sentence in Article I, "All men are endowed by nature with reason and conscience," likewise failed. Citing the US Declaration of Independence, Charles proposed that the words "by nature" be replaced with "by their Creator." He was opposed by René Cassin, who protested that references to God would detract from the universality of the document. The representative from India, Hansa Mehta, raised a different concern—namely, that the phrase "all men" would be taken literally in some countries, to the exclusion of women.[30] In the end, "men" was changed to "human beings" and both "nature" and "Creator" were dropped.

§

In January 1948, Harold Hoskins, the chairman of the AUB board of trustees, announced that Stephen Penrose would become the university's fourth president, succeeding Bayard Dodge. As for Charles Malik, the thought of returning to the AUB was never far from his mind. In March, he wrote to Costi Zurayk—Penrose's new vice president—who had pleaded with him to come home, saying that the university needed him. In response to Costi's observation that he was torn between the active life and the contemplative life, Charles retorted,

> I do not believe in politics. I am not interested in diplomacy. I was never tormented between two lures. I am interested only in intellectual and spiritual matters, in the truth, in philosophy.[31]

Why, then, had he not returned to the AUB after a year or two of diplomatic service, as Costi had done? Evidently, he was waiting to be asked in the right way. And then there was the matter of salary: he insisted on being paid more than any other employee of the university, with the possible exception of Penrose himself.[32]

Meanwhile, the Arab lobby and its American friends launched a last-ditch effort to convince the Truman administration to withdraw its support from the UN partition plan. Cecil Hourani persuaded some of his American friends—notably Kim Roosevelt, whom he had met in Cairo during the war—to organize a "Committee for Justice and Peace in the Holy Land."[33] Virginia Gildersleeve was chosen to chair the committee because, as she put it, "I no longer had much to lose from Zionist threats and attacks."[34] In early March, Roosevelt and Gildersleeve met with Secretary of State Marshall in Washington, along with Rev. Daniel Bliss of Greenwich, Connecticut, whose grandfather had been the first president of the AUB; Rev. James Quay, who was now a vice president of the Princeton Theological Seminary; and Dr. Carleton Coon, a professor of anthropology at Harvard, who had served with William Eddy and Kim Roosevelt's cousin Archie in North Africa during the war.[35] Their efforts appeared to bear fruit when the United States reversed course and proposed a trusteeship for Palestine under UN auspices.[36]

When the UN General Assembly met in special session that April, Charles Malik delivered a memorable speech on Palestine. "If this present chance is missed," he warned, "the Near East will be plunged into a terrible period of troubles whose issue . . . is beyond the ken of our present imagination." A good portion of his speech was devoted to convincing Jews that a unitary Palestinian state would enable them not only to develop their own culture but to influence the Arabs as well. As evidence that such cross-cultural influence was possible, he pointed to himself:

> I happen to love the thought of Martin Buber, and his wonderful book, *I and Thou*, exerted a profound influence on me. I doubt whether there is any other instance of cultural influence from the Jewish side to the Arab side. The Jews are culturally non-existent so far as the Arabs are concerned, but let them live in peace together with the Arabs in a unitary Palestine, let the profound existential estrangement vanish which has developed between them, and there is no limit to the cultural boom that is likely then to emerge.[37]

As Charles surely knew, Buber was a member of the small *Ihud* ("Unity") party, which advocated a binational state in Palestine.[38]

Martin Buber aside, the Jews of Palestine were not much interested in what Charles had to say. On May 14, David Ben-Gurion proclaimed the independence of Israel, which was promptly recognized by President Truman. In the UN Security Council, however, Charles insisted that it was too soon to recognize a Jewish state, let alone establish one by force of arms. "The real task of world statesmanship at the present time," he insisted,

> is not to do just that—a very easy thing, indeed—but to help the Jews and the Arabs not to be permanently alienated from each other. The Jews must come to

terms with the Arabs sooner or later. They must do so before they come to terms with the Americans, or the Russians, or the Guatemalans.[39]

Among those who took note of Charles' speech was Hannah Arendt, the exiled German Jewish philosopher, who praised its "calm and open insistence on peace and the realities of the Near East." Charles' remarks, she noted, echoed earlier statements by Martin Buber in favor of Jewish-Arab cooperation.[40]

The day after Charles' speech, Gideon Ruffer (Rafael) of the Israeli delegation met with Francis Kettaneh, a wealthy entrepreneur who claimed to represent Charles and Faris al-Khoury, the AUB-educated Syrian ambassador. Kettaneh was no ordinary businessman. Born in Jerusalem, he had attended the AUB, spied for the British, married a niece of Michel Chiha, and, together with his brothers—two of whom were classmates of Charles' at the AUB—established a lucrative import-export business in Lebanon.[41] Eventually, Kettaneh moved to New York to oversee the United States end of the trade. In July 1942, he met David Ben-Gurion and passed on a disturbing report from Polish exiles in London, namely, that the Nazis were planning to make Poland *judenrein*.[42] After becoming a US citizen in 1946, Kettaneh joined the Council on Foreign Relations and befriended Allen Dulles, who also headed the Near East College Association. Now he proposed to act as an intermediary between Israel and the Arab states. Ruffer told him that the Israelis would participate in direct talks with Arab leaders, without British mediation, if they agreed to respect the 1947 UN boundaries of the State of Israel. Kettaneh promised to convey Ruffer's offer to Azzam Pasha, the head of the Arab League, as well as Lebanese leaders.[43]

That June, the HRC approved the UDHR by a vote of 12-0, with the USSR, Byelorussia, and Yugoslavia abstaining. The final text did not include an article on minorities proposed by the drafting committee:

> In States inhabited by a substantial number of persons of a race, language or religion other than those of the majority of the population, and which want to be accorded differential treatment, persons belonging to such ethnic, linguistic or religious minorities shall have the right, as far as compatible with public order, to establish and maintain schools and cultural or religious institutions, and to use their own language in the Press, in public assembly, and before the courts and other authorities of the State.

In a last-ditch attempt to salvage the article, Charles had suggested a simple alternative: "Cultural groups shall not be denied the right to free self-development." No doubt he was anxious to build some protection for Lebanon's Christians and other minorities into the UDHR. But his motion was defeated. As he noted in his diary, the Americans and Latins were "dead against this idea." As Eleanor Roosevelt explained, the reason states accept immigrants is "to make them part of the nation."[44]

In September, the Maliks traveled to Paris, where the UN General Assembly was meeting that fall. Fortuitously, the Committee on Social, Humanitarian, and Cultural Affairs, which was next to review the UDHR, elected Charles as its chairman. When the discussion turned to Article 2—which specified that everyone is entitled to the rights enumerated in the UDHR without distinction of race, color, sex, religion, or political opinion—the representative from Yugoslavia, Vladimir Dedijer, insisted that the text be amended to include persons in "Trust and Non-Self-Governing Territories," that is, those governed by European colonial powers. His amendment was approved by a narrow margin. Then, in October, the committee heard a report by the acting UN mediator, Dr. Ralph Bunche, on the refugee crisis in Palestine. At the suggestion of the Lebanese delegation, the right to return to one's country was added to Article 13, which guaranteed freedom of movement.[45] Subsequently, the UDHR was approved by the General Assembly by a vote of 48-0, with only the Soviet bloc, Saudi Arabia, and South Africa abstaining.

§

In February 1949, Charles hosted a dinner for Ernest Hocking and the "young Roosevelts"—a reference, no doubt, to Kim and Archie, who had been undergraduates at Harvard when Professor Hocking was nearing retirement.[46] As Charles knew, the Roosevelt cousins shared Hocking's desire to put the Arab case before the American public. To that end, Kim Roosevelt had just written a book about the Near East, *Arabs, Oil and History*, based on his recent travels in the region. Later that year, he would join the Office of Policy Coordination, the State Department's new covert operations arm, soon to be taken over by the CIA. Archie was already with the CIA, finishing up a two-year stint as chief of station in Beirut.[47] The purpose of the dinner may have been to plan a relief effort on behalf of the Palestinian refugees. In any event, both Hocking and Kim Roosevelt became official sponsors of the Holyland Emergency Liaison Program (HELP), which announced its existence later that year.[48]

Meanwhile, Charles was worried about Colonel Husni Zaim, the new Syrian strongman, who ousted the civilian government of President Shukri Quwatli on April 11. Initially, Zaim appeared to be working toward federation with Iraq. Later that month, Charles went to see Tuvia Arazi, who had joined the Israeli delegation at the United Nations, and asked him about Israel's opinion of Zaim. To his relief, Arazi told him that Israel favored an independent Syria—and an independent Lebanon.[49] Whether Charles knew that Arazi had been in contact with Zaim before the coup, which was secretly endorsed by Israel, is unclear.[50] As for US covert assistance to Zaim, it is conceivable that Charles learned of it from one of the Roosevelt cousins or other friends in Washington. Zaim lost no time in announcing that he would ratify an agreement permitting the Tapline—the Aramco pipeline linking the Lebanese port of Sidon to the Saudi oil fields—to transit Syrian territory. He also declared that he was willing to receive 250,000 refugees from Palestine.[51]

Charles' contact with the Israelis was strictly confidential; even his own government may not have known of it. Publicly, he continued to take the Arab League line on Palestine. Thus in May, when the United Nations took up Israel's application for membership, he spoke forcefully against it on the grounds that the new state of Israel was not the Jewish homeland envisioned in the UN partition plan. As he pointed out:

> Israel includes, in the territory now under its control, the whole of the Western Galilee, and the Arab towns of Jaffa, Lydda, and Ramleh, and other Arab areas as

well, that were allotted to the Arab state in the 1947 recommendation; as well as the New City of Jerusalem, for which a separate international regime was planned. . . . There is every indication, moreover, that the Israeli authorities have no intention of giving up anything now in their possession.

To admit Israel under such circumstances, he concluded, would be, "in effect, to condone, by a solemn act of the United Nations, the right of conquest."[52] Once again, however, Charles' argument failed to persuade his fellow representatives, and Abba Eban was seated next to him as Israel's first ambassador to the United Nations.[53]

At the end of May, Charles received a letter from Hisham Sharabi, who was back in Beirut following the completion of his Master's thesis in philosophy at the University of Chicago.[54] Sharabi was writing at the request of President Penrose of the AUB, to whom he had applied for a teaching position. But the question of Sharabi's employment proved to be moot when Antun Saadeh, two years after his return from exile, attempted to stage a premature coup d'etat in early July. Prime Minister Riad Solh and the Lebanese army, it turned out, knew about the plot and quickly crushed the rebellion. Within days of the failed coup, Saadeh was apprehended in Syria and handed over by Husni Zaim to the Lebanese authorities, who hastily tried and executed him. Luckily, Sharabi managed to escape the Syrian dragnet and return to Chicago, where he resumed his studies. But he remained loyal to the Parti Populaire Syrien in spite of—or perhaps because of—the leader's martyrdom.[55]

§

In August 1949, Charles was invited to speak at Princeton by one of Edward Said's future professors, the philosopher Arthur Szathmary. In his letter, Szathmary reminded Charles that he had been Chadbourne Gilpatric's roommate at Harvard, where they had met in the mid-1930s.[56] Conveniently, Gilpatric had recently left the CIA for a job at the Rockefeller Foundation, which had been making grants to the AUB ever since the foundation was established in 1913. Indeed, President Penrose—Gilpatric's former boss in the Central Intelligence Group—had just announced a Rockefeller Foundation grant of $83,000 for the AUB's new Institute of Arabic Studies, the brainchild of Costi Zurayk.[57] Whether the CIA had encouraged Gilpatric to make the move to the Rockefeller Foundation is unknown, but he was certainly the right man for the job, having known the Rockefeller brothers—his summer neighbors on Mount Desert Island—since childhood.

That November, Charles stood before the Political Committee of the United Nations to answer Soviet foreign minister Vyshinsky's call for a peace pact between the five permanent members of the Security Council. Characterizing the Communist doctrine of peace as "war by other means," Charles declared that peace was impossible as long as the Communists had the upper hand. Fortunately, he continued, the Russian spirit was deeper than Communism. And there was no better expression of that spirit, he enthused, than the wonderful Russian literature of the nineteenth century, which

> reflects the mysterious depths of the Russian soul far more authentically than the monotonously true-to-the-party-line dialectical disquisitions of the Soviet

representatives. I honestly believe that the Department of Public Information of the United Nations can do no better service for the cause of peace than to prepare a two-volume compendium of nineteenth-century Russian literature which, by a formal vote of the General Assembly, should be made required reading for every delegate.[58]

World peace through the reading of classic literature—that was vintage Malik.

In late December, Charles joined John Foster Dulles, whom President Truman had appointed to an advisory role in the State Department, and William Yandell Elliott, professor of government at Harvard, at the American Political Science Association's annual convention in New York.[59] Speaking on "The Cultural Aspects of International Cooperation," Charles admonished his listeners that "America means today to the outside world for the most part technology and the atom bomb. I am sure Jonathan Edwards, Thomas Jefferson, Nathaniel Hawthorne and Abraham Lincoln want it to mean much more." He ended by calling on America to return to its spiritual roots. "America was founded under God and developed under the love of Jesus Christ," he proclaimed, "and therefore who can snatch it away from its origins? The ultimate condition of the highest flourishing of American culture is an authentic return to America's creator."[60] So impressed was Elliott that he invited Charles to speak at a conference on "The Near East and the Great Powers" at Harvard the following summer.[61] What Charles may not have known is that Elliott had just signed on as a consultant to the Office of Policy Coordination, Kim Roosevelt's new employer.[62]

Meanwhile, Charles soldiered on in the diplomatic battle over Palestine. On August 1, 1950, he held a frank discussion of Zionist influence in America with George McGhee, assistant secretary of state for Near Eastern Affairs. According to the record of the meeting,

> Dr. Malik said that even he, whose sincerity of friendship for the West could not be disputed, still felt that in any crucial conflict it was a mathematical, foregone conclusion that this Government would be forced by American Zionist pressure to side with the Jews.

Charles went on to suggest that the Truman administration issue

> "a Balfour Declaration in reverse" to the effect not that the Israelis be thrown into the sea but that they will not be permitted to seize further Arab territory—that it would be inconceivable for this country to side with the Jews against the Arabs in any future conflict of interests. Such a declaration would show the Arab world that the US has the "moral guts" to stand against pressure.[63]

Needless to say, no such declaration was forthcoming, however much McGhee, a wealthy Texas oilman, may have favored one.

A week later, Charles and McGhee went to Harvard for Elliott's Near East conference, where they shared the stage with Ralph Bunche and Charles Issawi, who had joined the staff of the UN Secretariat. After praising President Truman's new "Point Four" program of technical assistance to developing nations, Charles insisted that the Near East needed more than technology from the West. "To give one an instrument," he warned,

> without inducing him into communion with the whole spiritual culture which created that instrument in the first place, and without which it would be but a fetish and a fake, is utterly cruel and unjust. As long as there are millions of human beings in the Near East who have never tasted the infinite peace of mind and of reason, as long as the goods of the mind and spirit are deficient in our midst, as long as the great classics of human thought and feeling, which have penetrated and transformed the life and literature and outlook of the West, are totally unheard of by large sections of the Near East, there can be no real prosperity and no genuine human well-being in that part of the world.[64]

That was precisely why UNESCO's new translation program was so important to Charles.

In April 1951, Charles journeyed to Geneva for the annual session of the HRC, where he and Mrs. Roosevelt discussed the political situation in the Near East. After she got back from Geneva, she reported Charles' views to President Truman and the State Department:

> Dr. Charles Malik of Lebanon told me he felt we had missed a great opportunity when the Shah of Persia was here [in late 1949]. We should have had a plan ready to clean up his government and help him to help his people and we should have made him accept it and we should have sent people to help him put it into operation. Dr. Malik openly told me, in confidence of course, that no government in the Near East was anything but rotten, that the King of Egypt was a fool and unless we were going to take hold, the USSR undoubtedly would.[65]

One person who shared Charles' concern was Eleanor's relative Kim Roosevelt, who soon concluded that both King Farouk of Egypt and Premier Mossadegh of Iran had to go—the former because he was lazy and corrupt, the latter because he was, in Kim's eyes, a tool of the Communists.[66]

That June, Charles received a letter from Cornelius Van Hemert Engert, the retired diplomat who had been US counsel in Beirut during the British invasion of 1941. "Van," as his friends called him, was writing to introduce Charles to a new organization, American Friends for the Middle East (AFME), which he served as secretary-treasurer.[67] Along with his letter, Engert enclosed a press release from the president of AFME, the journalist Dorothy Thompson, a former Zionist who had been converted to the Arab cause. What the American public did not know was that AFME was funded almost entirely by the CIA, which used it to cultivate sources and provide cover for its personnel in the Near East. In the months leading up to the first meeting of AFME, Engert had been in touch with his old friend Allen Dulles, the CIA's newly appointed Director of Plans. It was Dulles, it seems, who arranged to channel CIA-controlled funds to AFME through the Dearborn Foundation of Chicago, whose sole purpose was to launder CIA money. Other funds for AFME came from Aramco, courtesy of William Eddy, who sat on AFME's National Council with Philip Hitti, Ernest Hocking, and other old friends of Charles Malik's.[68]

In early September, Charles traveled to San Francisco for the ceremonial signing of the peace treaty with Japan. There he delivered a speech aimed squarely at Secretary of State Dean Acheson, who presided over the conference, and John Foster Dulles, the architect of the treaty. "Mr. John Foster Dulles," Charles observed,

> devoted a whole year to the most painstaking negotiation and elaboration of the draft before us. He has made the entire world his debtor in this great accomplishment for peace. Am I now to be told that the same high quality of statesmanship and reconciliation, so successfully evinced by Mr. Dulles in this instance, cannot somehow be forthcoming with regard to our problems in the Near East? I will not believe it.

He proceeded to list the "fundamental conditions" of peace in the Near East, including "effective promotion of human rights."[69] Years later, Charles told Richard Bayly Winder of Princeton that Dulles kept a copy of this speech in his desk, referring to it often after he became secretary of state in 1953.[70]

§

In January 1952, *Foreign Affairs*, the journal of the Council on Foreign Relations, published a long article by Charles entitled "The Near East: The Search for Truth." He devoted one section to the fate of Islam, naming Toynbee, Gibb, Hourani, Hocking, and Hitti as men who have "brooded" on the matter. His own contribution was no more than an outline consisting of thirty-eight issues. One of them concerned the men he had just named:

> 11. The phenomenon in recent decades of "the Orientalist." How much good and how much harm has Orientalism done? Why a corresponding phenomenon of "the Occidentalist" did not arise?

Another issue was the appearance of research institutes devoted to the Near East:

> 29. The phenomenon of institutes of Islamic and Near Eastern studies in the United States. No greater service can be done the cause of truth than the promotion of these institutes. Distinction, however, between dedication to truth alone and the utilization of historical, sociological, and economic information for political and commercial purposes. Truth is the only savior of the world.[71]

Edward Said, who was a student at the Mount Hermon School when this article came out, never cited it in print. Yet it is striking how closely Uncle Charles' outline anticipated his own future research agenda.

In March, Henry Luce's *Life* magazine published another article by Charles, "From A Friend of The West: He Explains Communism's Appeal In Asia And How To Fight It." The appeal of Communism to "Asiatics," Charles explained, went beyond economics and politics. "Entirely apart from poverty, hunger, Marx, and Lenin," he claimed,

> there are fundamental cultural and racial affinities between the Soviet Union and Asia which place the Western world at a tremendous disadvantage in that continent. Especially is the Western notion of individual freedom and responsibility alien to Asia. It is a Greco-Christian notion. In Asia the effort and initiative of the individual human being are far less important than the weighty tradition of the family, the clan, the class, the caste, the group, the religious community. . . .

With the exception of Islam, Charles asserted, Asian religions tend toward pantheism, lacking the notion of transcendence. "*What then is there to prevent an Asian from worshipping the state?*" he asked. "*He has by his traditions been predisposed to totalitarianism.*"[72]

A week after his *Life* article appeared, Charles was one of the keynote speakers at the National Conference on International Economic and Social Development in Washington, organized by Nelson Rockefeller. I am not sure where Charles and Rockefeller first met, but they were well acquainted with each other by the time of the development conference. In the summer of 1950, Charles had written to thank Rockefeller for his gift of *The Wall* (probably the new John Hersey novel about the Warsaw Ghetto). In exchange, Charles had enclosed a copy of "War and Peace," his reply to Ambassador Vishinsky, which had been published in pamphlet form by the National Committee for a Free Europe, an anti-Communist front organized by Allen Dulles.[73] In his speech at Rockefeller's development conference, Charles called for nothing less than a Marshall Plan for the underdeveloped world, proclaiming that "if only a fraction of the aid extended to Europe and Greece and Turkey were forthcoming for Asia and the Middle East, I believe miracles would be achieved."[74]

Back in Lebanon, meanwhile, opposition to President Khoury and his clique was mounting. In September, Khoury tried to placate his critics by replacing Prime Minister Sami Solh with Saeb Salam, a former classmate of Charles Malik's at the AUB, who asked Charles to join his cabinet. Charles held out for the post of foreign minister, but it was too late.[75] Salam soon joined the opposition and resigned, followed a month later by President Khoury himself. Among the possible successors to Khoury, Charles was the personal favorite of Harold Minor, the US ambassador to Lebanon, and his chargé d'affaires, James Lobenstine. Recognizing that Charles had no Lebanese constituency, however, they recommended that Washington remain neutral.[76] In the end, the candidate favored by the British, Camille Chamoun, was elected president; Alfred Naccache, an old favorite of the French, became foreign minister; and Charles remained in his diplomatic posts in Washington in New York.

That October, Charles met with Rev. Edward L. R. Elson of the National Presbyterian Church in Washington, who was about to embark on a tour of the Middle East on behalf of AFME.[77] Neither man knew it at the time, but Elson was about to become the pastor of both the president of the United States and the secretary of state. After the defeat of Germany in 1945, Elson had served as General Eisenhower's envoy to the ruling Consistory of the German Evangelical Church, which had been controlled by so-called German Christians.[78] When Eisenhower was elected president in November, he decided to attend Elson's church, as did his secretary of state, John Foster Dulles. The director of the FBI, J. Edgar Hoover, had been a member for many years. As for Allen Dulles, he was not much of a churchgoer. But that did not prevent him from being promoted, at long last, to director of Central Intelligence. For the next eight years, American foreign policy would be in the hands of the Dulles brothers. If there was a Malik era in Lebanese diplomacy, it coincided with the Dulles era in American diplomacy.

§

In January 1953, Charles addressed the first annual conference of American Friends of the Middle East at the Delmonico Hotel in Manhattan. In addition to Charles, the featured speakers included Stephen Penrose, Henry Luce, and Ambassador Farid Zeineddine of Syria. At the banquet preceding Charles' talk, he and Eva were seated at the head table with Dorothy Thompson, Van Engert, and Wadia Makdisi, AFME's Beirut representative, who was the sister of Albert and Cecil Hourani and the sister-in-law of Wadad Cortas. In his talk, Charles pointed to the recent revolution in Egypt as a rare instance of "good news" from the Near East. "The emergence of General Naguib," he announced,

> is one of the most significant events in the recent history of the Near East. There is more hope today, not only about Egypt, but about the whole Near Eastern picture, as a result of this event that there has been for decades.

Yet the situation in Palestine, he cautioned, will continue to cause "bitterness and unrest for decades and perhaps generations to come." The only way to restore good will in the region, he said, was for Israel to return territory to the Arabs.[79]

That June, a few days after Edward Said's graduation from Mount Hermon, Charles spoke at Harvard, where he had been invited to receive an honorary law degree. In his talk, entitled "The Historic Moment," he warned that economic development and political freedom alone would never enable the West to defeat Communism. "For the tribal deities of Asia, the Middle East, and Eastern Europe," he explained, "are far more akin to those of Russia than to those of the West. Every radical nationalism of the East is going sooner or later to ally itself with Communism against the West." If such an alliance is to be prevented, he continued, it will require "a fundamental rallying of the Western world around its great humane-spiritual heritage."[80] It was to revive that very heritage that the Harvard Corporation had just elected Nathan Pusey, a classicist and an Episcopalian, to succeed President James Conant. No doubt, Charles, who may have known Pusey when they were graduate students at Harvard in the early 1930s, heartily approved of the Corporation's choice.

In September, Charles delivered the opening address at the American Political Science Association's annual meeting in Washington, emphasizing the limits of democracy in an era of advanced technology, global interdependence, and ideological warfare. In the present age of complexity, he observed, the American people and their elected representatives have no choice but to rely on experts who must operate in secrecy. Future generations, he warned, will not forgive today's leaders if they do not rise to the Communist challenge, blaming their failure to act decisively on "the lethargy of the masses" or "the imperfections of the democratic process." Even political scientists, he insisted, must climb down from their ivory tower and take a stand, for

> there are natural limits to freedom, even to freedom of thought, and even in a free society. These limits are exactly where freedom itself is at stake. When responsible freedom . . . is hated, combated, fundamentally repudiated, then freedom is no longer free to allow that to happen.[81]

Afterwards, Charles sent a copy of his address to John Foster Dulles, who had requested one.[82] Thankfully, the secretary of state also believed in "responsible freedom."

A few months later, Charles addressed a meeting of Congregationalists in Montclair, New Jersey, on the topic of the missionary movement and the Middle East. He began with a reference to Henry Harris Jessup's *Fifty-Three Years in Syria*, which mentions Rev. Youssef Badr and other converts from the Badr family. What struck him in reading Jessup, Charles said, was the contrast between the missionaries of Jessup's day, who were naïve but pure of heart, and those of the present. Nowadays, he lamented, missionaries are quicker to report to the government or the oil companies than their own churches.[83] Perhaps he was thinking of such scions of old missionary families as William Eddy and David Dodge, both of whom worked for Aramco and its subsidiary, Tapline. Or perhaps he was thinking of Arthur and Raymond Close, the sons of Harold and Dora Eddy Close, who had joined the CIA fresh out of Princeton, recruited, no doubt, by their uncle Bill Eddy. At the time, Art was working under diplomatic cover in Damascus; Ray was running a network of informants in the refugee camps in southern Lebanon.[84]

In February 1954, Charles and Eva Malik were invited to dine with Allen and Clover Dulles in Washington.[85] After dinner, one suspects, Charles and Allen retired to the library to chew over two recent, potentially troublesome events. The first was the replacement of General Naguib as prime minister of Egypt by his rival Colonel Nasser, whose case was being handled by Kim Roosevelt, Dulles' chief Middle East operative, with the assistance of his deputy, Miles Copeland.[86] The second event was the ouster of Colonel Adib Shishakli, the military dictator who had ruled Syria since 1951, by a coalition led by the Baath Party and the Communist Party. Shishakli was allied with the Parti Populaire Syrien, which had moved its headquarters to Damascus following the execution of Antun Saadeh. Several of Charles' friends and protégés were still active in the party, notably Ghassan Tueni, a former student who had inherited Beirut's leading newspaper, *an-Nahar*; Said Takieddine, a former classmate who headed the AUB Alumni Association; and Hisham Sharabi, who had just started his academic career at Georgetown. But the PPS was now in serious jeopardy, at least in Syria.

§

In the autumn of 1954, Stephen Penrose finally succeeded in negotiating the terms of Charles' return to the AUB. Thanks to the Ford Foundation, Penrose was able to offer him a threefold appointment as professor of philosophy, dean of graduate studies, and chairman of a special committee for the liberal arts. But then, in early December, Penrose died of a sudden heart attack at the age of forty-six. Fortunately, Costi Zurayk, who took over as acting president, confirmed Penrose's offer to Charles, who planned to resign his ambassadorship and move back to Beirut in the summer of 1955.[87] Meanwhile, a rumor that Harold Hoskins might rush into the breach reached Albert Hourani in Oxford. "I am *horrified*," he wrote to Eva Malik,

> by the prospect that Hoskins should become President. I met him twice only, and disliked him more than almost anybody I have ever known.... I need scarcely add that from the moment I heard of Penrose's death it has been my conviction that Charles and only Charles is suited to fill the position.[88]

In the event, neither man was offered the position, which remained vacant until J. Paul Leonard was appointed in 1957.

In early February 1955, Charles spoke at a joint conference of International Christian Leadership (ICL) and the National Religious Broadcasters at the Mayflower Hotel in Washington.[89] ICL, incorporated as the Fellowship Foundation, had been founded by a Methodist minister from Seattle, Abraham Vereide, who had been inspired by Frank Buchman and the Oxford Group in the 1930s. Its mission was to evangelize men in positions of power and motivate them to apply Christian principles in business and government. The conference, whose theme was "World-Wide Spiritual Offensive," began with the annual Presidential Prayer Breakfast, a tradition inaugurated by President Eisenhower in 1953. Among those who participated in the breakfast were Senator Frank Carlson of Kansas, who chaired the ICL's International Council; Conrad Hilton, who hosted the breakfast; Vice President Nixon, who read from Scripture; Senator A. Willis Robertson of Virginia, who prayed; and Rev. Billy Graham, who preached.[90] It was the first of many prayer breakfasts for Charles, who would come to know several generations of American politicians through ICL.

Later that month, Charles was recalled to Beirut for consultation following the signing of the Baghdad Pact. The Pact, which brought Turkey and Iraq into an alliance with Britain, Iran, and Pakistan, had been denounced by President Nasser and King Saud, both of whom regarded Iraq as a traitor to the cause of Arab unity. Before leaving Washington, Charles hurried to the State Department with an invitation for Secretary Dulles from President Chamoun, who was under strong pressure to follow Syria's lead in opposing the Baghdad Pact.[91] Then, on March 3, Allen Dulles brought a communication from Charles to a meeting of the National Security Council. In it, Charles proclaimed that the Baghdad Pact marked the end of the Arab League's power and the rise of Western influence in the region. After summarizing Charles' report, Dulles reported that Syria "was ripe for a military coup d'etat."[92] He may have heard the same thing from his spies in Damascus, including Art Close.[93]

In April, Charles flew to Bandung, Indonesia, for the landmark Asian-African Conference that gave birth to the Non-Aligned Movement. It was John Foster Dulles who had talked him into going.[94] In Bandung, Charles did his best to prevent the anti-Western, anti-white outcome Dulles feared. For example, he convinced Premier Zhou Enlai of China to accept a watered-down acknowledgment of the UDHR in the conference's final communiqué.[95] Charles also joined Fadhel Jamali and Ahmad Shukairy—all of whom had attended the AUB together in the mid-1920s—on a subcommittee that met in President Nasser's quarters to draft a statement on Palestine. The statement, which called for a peaceful end to the conflict contingent on Israel's acceptance of the relevant UN resolutions, was adopted by the conference.[96] In spite of such rhetorical victories, however, Charles came away from Bandung with an abiding suspicion of Nasser and his fellow neutralists. In a world menaced by International Communism, he believed, there could be no neutrality.

After a stop in Australia, Charles returned to Washington and reported to Foster Dulles. He was pleased that the twenty-eight nations represented at Bandung had decided to continue working through the United Nations, although he regretted their failure to condemn International Communism in their final communiqué. As for the prospect of the "colored" races uniting against the white race, Charles thought the conference was inconclusive. On balance, he thought, the Bandung conference "did more harm than good" to relations with the West, although it could have been worse.[97] Charles then warned Dulles about an imminent Communist takeover in Syria, to which he had been alerted by Faris al-Khoury, the recently ousted pro-Western prime minister. On Khoury's behalf, Charles recommended "clandestine operations . . . to support conservative elements in Syria," notably the PPS, which was "absolutely and irrevocably anti-Communist."[98]

Two days after meeting with Foster Dulles, Charles met with Allen Dulles and Kim Roosevelt, probably to discuss Syria.[99] Around the same time, one of his acquaintances, Major Wilbur "Bill" Eveland, attended a reception given by the Maliks. Eveland had recently joined the staff of the Operations Coordinating Board (OCB), which supervised the activities of the various agencies involved in national security, including the CIA. At the reception, Eveland invited Charles to relate his impressions of the Bandung conference at an OCB meeting. The next morning, Eveland mentioned the idea to Elmer Staats, the executive secretary of the OCB, who had some surprising news for Eveland: Allen Dulles wanted to borrow him for a special assignment in Syria, namely, to assist Ambassador James Moose in rallying pro-Western politicians behind a strong candidate for the presidency. That afternoon, Kim Roosevelt confirmed that "Allen and Foster" wanted the CIA and the State Department to step up their efforts in Syria. Evidently, the Dulles brothers were taking Charles' warning of a Communist takeover seriously.[100]

That June, Charles went to San Francisco to celebrate the tenth anniversary of the founding of the United Nations—a fitting finale to his ten-year diplomatic career. Meanwhile, some seventy persons accused of plotting to assassinate Colonel Adnan Malki, the deputy chief of staff of the Syrian army, were put on trial in Damascus. The Malki assassination, prosecutors charged, was part of a larger conspiracy involving the PPS, the Iraqis, and the Americans. Their evidence included a letter from Hisham

Sharabi to George Abdul Masih, Antun Saadeh's successor as the chairman of the PPS, found in the home of Saadeh's widow in Damascus. The letter revealed that Sharabi had been talking to a representative of the American government, who had suggested that the PPS send its secretary general, Issam Mahayri, to Washington for talks. And who was this representative of the American government? According to the prosecutor, it was none other than Charles Malik, who could easily have met with Sharabi in Washington.[101]

On August 26, shortly before the Maliks left for Beirut, Foster Dulles gave a speech at the Council for Foreign Relations in New York in which he laid out his solution to the Arab-Israeli conflict.[102] Afterwards, he hosted a dinner for Charles and Harold Hoskins at his home on East 91st Street, where they discussed, no doubt, the future of the AUB.[103] Hoskins had recently resigned as chairman of the AUB board of trustees in order to direct the State Department's Foreign Service Institute. His replacement turned out to be John Case of Socony Mobil, one of the Aramco partners. A few days later, Van Engert hosted a bon voyage party for the Maliks in Washington, presenting them with a silver tray on behalf of American Friends of the Middle East.[104] Then it was off to Beirut, where Charles received a belated farewell letter from Nelson Rockefeller, who was serving as a special assistant to President Eisenhower, representing the White House on the OCB.[105] Regretting that he had not seen more of Charles over the years, Rockefeller urged him to continue his work in international relations.[106]

§

The AUB to which Charles returned in the fall of 1955 was a different institution from the one he had left a decade earlier. Thanks to the efforts of Harold Hoskins and Stephen Penrose, it was in the midst of a costly expansion, with a new school of engineering, a new department of agriculture, and new programs in public administration and public health. The money for this expansion came from a variety of private and public sources, including the Rockefeller and Ford Foundations and the Bechtel Corporation, which had built much of Aramco's infrastructure in the Middle East, including the Tapline. That spring, President Chamoun had joined Stephen D. Bechtel, Sr.—an AUB trustee—at the dedication of the new Bechtel Engineering Building.[107] More controversially, the university was receiving aid from the US government through the International Cooperation Administration.[108] The head of the ICA, Harold Stassen, was also a member of the Operations Coordinating Board—an illustration of the close link between foreign aid and national security in the Eisenhower era.[109]

Not surprisingly, Charles found himself in demand as a public speaker. In November, he addressed the annual meeting of Pierre Gemayel's Phalange Party in Beirut, stressing compromise as a fundamental principle of the Lebanese polity.[110] In December, he eulogized his old friend Stephen Penrose at a memorial service, declaring that "the cause of peace with justice never had a better champion than Steve Penrose."[111] That same month, he addressed the AUB Alumni Association on the theme of "What One Learns." Among the many things one learns at the United Nations, he declared, is that

> internationalism is a fiction, whereas the reality is interculturalism. The ultimate unit is not the nation, but the group of nations which partake of more or less

the same culture. Thus you are not really dealing at the United Nations with the 60 or 80 nations of the world, but with the 6 or 8 cultural groupings throughout the world. It is not an accident that there is a clearly definable Latin-American world, Anglo-Saxon world, West-European world, Arab world, South-Asian world, Asian-African world, and Slavic world, and that each one of these worlds acts internationally more or less as a unit. . . . The law of nations is in reality the law of cultures.[112]

Note that Charles' analysis of world cultures anticipated Samuel Huntington's controversial "Clash of Civilizations" thesis—roundly condemned by Edward Said—by some forty years.[113]

More surprisingly, Charles was welcomed into Beirut society. In March 1956, he attended a party hosted by William Eddy, who had moved to Beirut from Dhahran. In addition to Charles, Eddy's guests included Donald Heath, the American ambassador; Abdulhamid Ghaleb, the Egyptian ambassador; Farid Chehab, the director of the Lebanese Sûreté Générale; St. John Philby, the former confidant of Ibn Saud; Elmo Hutchinson, the Middle East representative of AFME; Sam Pope Brewer of the *New York Times*; and Harry Kern, formerly of *Newsweek*, who was starting a newsletter for the oil companies called *Foreign Reports*.[114] Like other reporters of the time, Kern had friends in high places. As he later admitted to journalist Carl Bernstein, "When I went to Washington, I would talk to Foster or Allen Dulles about what was going on."[115] His partner was his former *Newsweek* colleague Sam Souki—the son of one of Wadie Said's old friends from Cairo—who, according to Bill Eveland, was also a paid informant for the CIA's station chief in Beirut.[116]

A few weeks later, Charles attended another Beirut party, hosted by John Fistere of *Fortune*, one of the magazines owned by his friend Henry Luce. The guest of honor was the American novelist Philip Wylie, whose father had been John Foster Dulles' pastor at Park Avenue Presbyterian Church in the 1930s. Wylie described his encounter with Charles in the book he wrote about his travels, *The Innocent Ambassadors*. To Wylie, Charles embodied man "in man's best shape":

> Charles Malik is a husky man, a gray man. . . . He has a large, shagged, gray head; he smiles often and speaks softly. In repose, and only then, deep seams in his countenance tell how his character was made: of uncountable disappointments transcended each in turn by his hope.

Arriving late, Charles cornered Wylie and asked him to explain the basic policy of the West, which, he said, he had never been able to fathom. Irritated, Wylie declared that Americans have no notion of "the West" and care nothing for policy—they act on their own, and they do so impulsively. Later, Fistere informed him that Charles had been telling all his friends that, thanks to Wylie, he had finally understood America.[117]

Meanwhile, the trustees of the AUB were having a hard time agreeing on a replacement for the late Stephen Penrose. For that reason, perhaps, the possibility of appointing the first non-American to the office was discussed in Washington. Costi Zurayk, the acting president, was an obvious candidate, but Charles' name was also mentioned. According to a June 1956 memo addressed to the OCB, Charles' selection would serve "to forestall neutralist and nationalistic trends in the area which might endanger the University." But since Charles was "not a good administrator," the memo continued, he would need an American vice president to run the university while he "acted as a front man in Lebanon and in the US."[118] That the OCB monitored the presidential search illustrates the AUB's importance to high-ranking officials in Washington—particularly Allen Dulles, who represented the CIA on the OCB. At least one interested party, Francis Kettaneh, had written directly to Dulles to recommend someone for the office.[119]

That July, *Foreign Affairs* published another article by Charles entitled "A Call to Action in the Near East." "The consummation of [Communist] penetration" in the Near East, he warned,

> has occurred in the last 12 months, but the studied preparation for it has been going on for perhaps 30 years. Agents have been trained or primed or enlisted or placed in key positions—in trade unions, in the press, in government, in the community at large and perhaps even in Western capitals.[120]

The Western response to this penetration, he argued, must include "vast schemes of economic and social development."

> If America, for instance, in the characteristically generous American spirit, comes to Egypt with the offer *to present Egypt with the Aswan Dam without any conditions*, ... this act would make the strongest possible positive impression upon both the government and the people of Egypt.[121]

Alas, it was not to be. Just one week after Charles' article appeared, John Foster Dulles, angered by Nasser's acceptance of Soviet aid and facing a recalcitrant Congress, yanked American funding for the dam.[122]

Nasser's response was to nationalize the Suez Canal Company, which was owned by French shareholders and the British government, in order to pay for his dam. Less than two weeks later, Nasser asked Charles—through the Egyptian ambassador in Beirut, Abdulhamid Ghaleb—to convey a personal message to Secretary Dulles. The message was that Nasser would not accept international control of the canal, but would guarantee free transit pending a new international convention. Ambassador Ghaleb added that any resort to force on the part of the Western powers would result in the destruction of oil facilities in other Arab nations. Charles carried both messages to Donald Heath, the American ambassador in Beirut, adding a confidential message of his own for transmission to Dulles. While he personally liked Nasser, Charles informed Dulles, it was not in the West's best interest that he remain in control of Egypt.[123]

What neither Charles nor Dulles knew was that the British, the French, and the Israelis were secretly plotting a military response to Nasser's seizure of the canal. In late October, Israeli troops marched into Gaza and the Sinai as British and French planes bombed Nasser's airfields. President Eisenhower was furious, demanding an immediate halt to the invasion. In Lebanon, the Suez War provoked a cabinet crisis when Prime Minister Abdallah Yafi and Oil Minister Saeb Salam resigned over President Chamoun's refusal to break off diplomatic relations with Britain and France. In November, Chamoun asked veteran Sunni politician Sami Solh to form a new government. Although he had just returned to academic life, Charles—a favorite of Ambassador Heath—agreed to join the Solh cabinet as foreign minister.[124] After a decade of defending his government's foreign policy in Washington, he was finally in a position to make policy himself.

§

Among those who wrote to congratulate Charles on his new appointment was John Fistere, who offered his services as a public relations expert, proposing to arrange press interviews and television appearances for him in the United States.[125] Perhaps Fistere was merely drumming up business. But it is equally possible that he was acting on behalf of his friends in and around the Eisenhower administration. After all, his boss at *Fortune*, C. D. Jackson, had been Eisenhower's special advisor on psychological warfare. And Jackson's boss, Henry Luce, was an admirer of Charles Malik's as well as an unofficial publicist for President Eisenhower and Secretary Dulles. Fistere himself was a former OSS man who, like Stephen Penrose and Kim Roosevelt, had been stationed in Cairo, where he directed Morale Operations.[126] It was in Cairo, no doubt, that he had acquired his fascination with the Middle East and his taste for adventure. Those motives would soon lead him to return to Beirut, where he lectured at the AUB while working for the Kingdom of Jordan at the behest of the CIA.[127]

In early January 1957, Charles flew to Cairo to meet with President Nasser, whom he had last seen at Bandung. Because Lebanon had not severed diplomatic relations with France and Britain over the Suez invasion, Charles was in a position to serve as a messenger. Nasser's message was that the only way to resolve the crisis was to return to the status quo ante, with complete Israeli withdrawal from the Sinai and Gaza.[128] From Cairo, Charles flew to Paris and London to deliver Nasser's message before going on to New York, where he met with Bill Eveland.[129] Then, in early February, Charles met with Foster Dulles in Washington, warning him that Egypt and Syria were conspiring with the Communists to bring down the Chamoun regime in Lebanon. For that reason, he said, the coming elections to the Chamber of Deputies, which would choose the next president in 1958, were critical. He then turned to his meeting with Nasser, which had convinced him that the Egyptian leader was a tool of Moscow. The United States, he declared, must "drive a wedge" between the Arab nationalists and the Communists.[130]

Meanwhile, Bill Eveland and the Damascus CIA station, including Art Close, had been plotting regime change in Syria. According to Eveland, a planned coup, which involved the British, the Iraqis, and the PPS as well as the Americans, had been called off when the British suddenly attacked Egypt in October, leading him to wonder whether the Syrian plot had been a mere diversion.[131] The following month, the Syrians, who had known of the plot all along, charged forty-seven persons with treason, including Adib Shishakli, the former Syrian dictator, and Mikhail Ilyan, the secretary general of the National Party (Eveland's primary asset). In the course of the trial, the name of Charles Malik came up again, as it had during the Malki assassination trial in 1955. On February 2, 1957, Sam Brewer reported from Damascus that the prosecutor had accused the United States of using Charles to influence Syrian dissidents. When Brewer asked Ambassador Moose about the Syrian charges, he declined to comment.[132]

In January 1957, President Eisenhower had proclaimed the so-called Eisenhower Doctrine, which promised US protection for countries threatened by "overt armed aggression from any nation controlled by international Communism."[133] A few weeks later, Charles returned to New York, where he addressed a closed meeting of the Council on Foreign Relations on US policy in the Middle East. The moderator was Frank Altschul, formerly of Lazard Frères, one of the founders of the CFR and an old friend of Allen Dulles. Charles began by comparing President Nasser of Egypt to the hero of a Greek tragedy—a simple, noble man who is inadequate to the situation in which he finds himself. It is Moscow, he warned, that ultimately determines policy in both Egypt and Syria. He then urged the United States not to banish Britain and France from the Middle East, inasmuch as Europeans understand the region far better than Americans do. As for the proposition that Islam is a bulwark against Communism, Malik called it "a fallacy," pointing to the collaboration between the Muslim Brotherhood and the Communists in Egypt. It is the "intellectuals," not the "reactionaries," who will determine the future, he claimed.[134]

Charles' calendar indicates that he met with Kim Roosevelt in Beirut in early April.[135] No doubt they discussed the coming Lebanese elections, which Charles had mentioned to Foster Dulles in February. Like Charles, Ambassador Heath had been urging Washington to counteract Egyptian and Syrian subsidies to anti-Western candidates. The OCB agreed, and Bill Eveland was assigned to work personally with President Chamoun. Once he got to Beirut, Eveland turned to Ray Close for advice on Lebanese politics. Close explained that, because of Charles Malik's promise that Lebanon's adherence to the Eisenhower Doctrine would bring unlimited US aid, something dramatic had to be done before the elections. Otherwise, considerable funds would have to be expended to reduce Nasser's appeal to the Lebanese electorate. In the event, Eveland became the CIA's bag man, delivering briefcases full of cash to the presidential palace.[136]

Ironically, Charles turned out to be one of the direct beneficiaries of the CIA's largesse. According to Eveland, Ambassador Heath was keen to procure Charles a seat in the Chamber of Deputies, where he could defend the Eisenhower Doctrine and help choose the next president of Lebanon. The Lebanese Constitution limited presidents to a single six-year term, but there were rumors that Chamoun planned to push through an amendment permitting him to run for a second term. The problem was that Charles had no political base in his native region of Kura. So the incumbent—who happened to be a relative of his—would have to be paid off. According to Eveland, who sat up with the Maliks in their Beirut apartment as they debated what to do, they concluded that Charles should not be a candidate. But then Ambassador Heath turned up in his Cadillac and talked Charles into running.[137]

In the midst of the elections, which took place in May and June, syndicated columnist Joseph Alsop—who happened to be Kim Roosevelt's cousin—appeared in

Beirut, where he spent an evening with the Maliks. His admiration for his hosts was evident in his column that week:

> Greetings have hardly been exchanged when there is a screech of automobile tires somewhere down the street, followed by a loud, dull boom. Charming Mrs. Malik, bringing drinks, stops short with her tray for an instant, then says with careful casualness,
> "That would be another bomb."
> "Of course," replied Malik, and launches unconcernedly into a discussion of the recent events in Lebanon.

Alsop's ulterior motive was to cast an air of legitimacy over the elections. The opposition parties, he claimed,

> wished to avoid at all costs the proof that any Arab country could decisively reject in a fair vote the peculiar brand of Arab nationalism peddled by their real leader and director, Egypt's President Gamal Abdel Nasser. Therefore, with the active help of the Egyptian, Syrian, and Communist agents who swarm in Lebanon, the opposition parties have sought to make the coming vote seem unfair, by the simple expedient of staining it with blood.[138]

In reality, the elections had already been bought by President Chamoun with the help of the CIA.

Meanwhile, the opposition press was busy trying to smear Charles Malik. That June, an alleged correspondence between Charles and Israeli ambassador Abba Eban was published in Egyptian and Lebanese newspapers. The authenticity of the correspondence, in which the two ambassadors proposed to establish diplomatic relations between their nations, was immediately disputed by the Chamoun government. The editor of one Beirut paper, an AUB graduate named Hanna Ghosn, was arrested and charged with publishing forged documents. He was later released after convincing the authorities that he did not know they were forgeries.[139] But were they? We know from Eban's autobiographies that he was on cordial terms with Charles, with whom he exchanged notes on occasion. In this case, however, the documents may well have been a dirty trick on the part of the Soviet KGB.[140]

After the elections, Said Takieddine—whose own political party, the PPS, had thrown its weight behind Charles—penned a satirical pamphlet entitled *Bridge under the Water: This Is How We Chased Eisenhower out of La Republique Libanaise*. After reviewing some of the theories as to why Charles had decided to run for political office, Takieddine offered his own: "Personally I believe that the man has a weakness for anything official. If left to his own counsel he would run for the vice-mayor of Zarooria (pop. 562)." He went on to explain how Charles' opponent was paid off by Chamoun. "Malik's case," he concluded, "is tragic in two ways":

> From a national point of view he was another promising leader who . . . stooped to practice the ways of the common politician when that procedure became a

necessity for him to attain his ends. And for the same reason he became a very poor advertisement for democracy in action.[141]

If Charles saw this pamphlet, it surely ended his friendship with Takieddine, whose daughter Diana, a concert pianist, would later play in recitals with Edward Said.[142]

§

In September 1957, Charles flew to New York for the opening of the UN General Assembly. One morning, he went to the Waldorf Astoria for a long talk with Secretary Dulles, reminding him that Communist agents were sowing subversion all over the Middle East. As soon as the Communists felt secure in Syria, Charles predicted, Jordan would be the next domino to fall, followed by Lebanon, Iraq, and Saudi Arabia. He told Dulles that Soviet ambassador Andrei Gromyko, whom he had called on recently, was obviously preoccupied with Syria. Dulles replied that the United States, while it would keep its promise to defend Lebanon under the Eisenhower Doctrine, would not launch an attack on Syria. The initiative, he said, must come from Syria's neighbors.[143] Later that month, syndicated columnist Drew Pearson had breakfast with Charles at the Harvard Club. He recorded Charles' table talk in his diary, calling it both "illuminating" and "frightening." "We have three months to head off Russia in the Near East," Charles warned. "After that, we are gone."[144]

Returning to Beirut in November, Charles stood before the Chamber of Deputies to clarify the terms of Lebanon's adherence to the Eisenhower Doctrine. As Sam Brewer reported in the *Times*, Charles announced that the United States had promised "unlimited military and economic aid within the bounds of Lebanon's capacity to absorb them with benefit." He also read a letter from Secretary of State Dulles, who confirmed that Lebanon would not be required to fight on behalf of the United States or participate in American diplomatic initiatives (such as peace talks with Israel). As for those who think "that the West is going to withdraw into itself or accept defeat in this cold war," Charles warned, they are "committing a very great error. . . . The determination of the West to prevent any domination of the Middle East has never been stronger."[145]

Two months later, Egypt and Syria announced the formation of the United Arab Republic. Immediately, Lebanese opposition leaders Rashid Karame and Saeb Salam made pilgrimages to Damascus and Cairo to pay homage to President Nasser.[146] Around the same time, a new US ambassador, Robert McClintock, arrived in Beirut, replacing Donald Heath. As deputy chief of mission in Egypt during the Free Officers' Revolt of 1952, McClintock had come to know Nasser personally. Camille Chamoun, who had enjoyed Heath's confidence, evidently considered McClintock to be something of a Nasserite. As for Charles Malik, McClintock regarded the outspoken foreign minister as a political liability. Within a few weeks of his arrival, McClintock was asking Foster Dulles to arrange a graceful exit for Charles. "Something must be done for Malik, the apostle of Americanism," McClintock cabled Dulles. "In my judgment, he should go fairly soon as he is focusing anti-American opinion on himself."[147]

On May 8, 1958, the editor of a leading opposition newspaper, Nassib Metni, was gunned down in Beirut. That same day, President Chamoun sent Charles to offer his condolences to Metni's widow. The following day, an estimated 15,000 people joined the funeral procession from St. George's Greek Orthodox Cathedral to the cemetery.[148] The assassination of Metni proved to be the spark that ignited the Lebanese Civil War of 1958, which pitted militias backing the opposition United National Front, headed by Saeb Salam, against those loyal to Chamoun, with the small Lebanese army, under the command of General Fuad Chehab, doing its best to remain neutral in the political struggle. Among the militias fighting on behalf of Chamoun was that of the Parti Populaire Syrien, which was supplied with arms by Chamoun, by the Iraqis, and—as Ray Close admitted fifty years later—by the CIA.[149]

The Chamoun government asked the United States how it would respond to a request for American military assistance in putting down the rebellion, which was aided and abetted, it charged, by the United Arab Republic. In response, the United States insisted that Lebanon first bring a formal complaint against the UAR to the UN Security Council, which was scheduled to meet in June.[150] At the end of May, therefore, Charles boarded a plane for New York in order to present evidence of armed aggression by the UAR. To ensure his security as he made his way to the airport, the Foreign Ministry had resorted to a ruse, announcing that he would hold a press conference in Beirut that same day.[151] A few days later, on June 6, Charles stood before the Security Council to accuse the UAR of attempting to overthrow the elected government of Lebanon. "The only sin of Lebanon in the eyes of the United Arab Republic," he declared, is that "it is independent and follows a policy of cooperation and friendship with the Western world. We plead guilty on both counts."[152]

A month later, on the evening of July 14, Charles met with Foster Dulles in Washington to beg that American troops be sent to Lebanon.[153] By then, news of a bloody military coup in Baghdad had arrived in Washington. King Faisal II and Crown Prince Abdul Illah had been summarily executed; Fadhel Jamali was missing and presumed dead.[154] Ironically, the army brigades that led the coup, under the command of General Kassem, had been on their way to Jordan to defend King Hussein, who had agreed to confederate with Iraq after the formation of the UAR. The next day, President Eisenhower authorized Operation Blue Bat, and the Marines, who had been waiting offshore with the Sixth Fleet, waded ashore in Beirut. Once they had secured the airport, William Eddy flew in from Aleppo. For months, Eddy had been warning Ambassador McClintock—and anyone else who would listen—that sending American troops to Lebanon would be "a catastrophe to American interests."[155] As a proud ex-Marine, however, he put on his Colonel's uniform and saluted the troops.[156]

On July 16, Eisenhower named Deputy Under Secretary of State Robert Murphy his personal envoy to Lebanon. Before leaving for Beirut, Murphy conferred with Charles.[157] A few days later, Charles met with Foster Dulles and read him a message from President Chamoun, who urged a "general cleaning up" in the Middle East, not a mere "holding action" in Lebanon and Jordan. Chamoun was concerned that Eisenhower would turn responsibility for Lebanon's security over to UN peacekeepers, whose capabilities he doubted. When Dulles asked what Chamoun wanted the Americans to do, Charles offered a few ideas of his own, namely, that the United States should land

20,000 troops in Lebanon and another 20,000 in Jordan to protect King Hussein. He also suggested that the United States invite the Turks to deal with both Syria and Iraq. Finally, President Eisenhower should issue a "strong warning" to Nasser.[158]

On July 21, John Fistere wrote to Charles urging that President Chamoun step down immediately, rather than waiting until the bitter end of his term.[159] Presumably, Fistere's advice reflected the opinion of his friends in Washington. But Chamoun was not ready to give up the fight. Meanwhile, Robert Murphy was talking to Saeb Salam, Rashid Karame, and other opposition leaders. His intermediary and translator was William Eddy, with whom he had served in North Africa during the Second World War.[160] Influenced by Eddy and Ambassador McClintock, Murphy quickly settled on the neutral General Chehab as the best replacement for Camille Chamoun. A parliamentary vote was scheduled for July 31, and Charles Malik returned to Beirut to cast his ballot. Observed by Sam Brewer, Charles received "a warm handshake" from opposition leader Rashid Karame as they entered the chamber together. To no one's surprise, the American-approved Chehab was elected by a vote of 48 to 7.[161]

§

It would be nearly two months, however, before General Chehab took office, and the fighting continued in desultory fashion. Meanwhile, controversy arose over who should represent Lebanon at the upcoming special meeting of the UN General Assembly, called by the United States and the USSR to discuss the crisis in the Middle East. President Chamoun asked Charles to head the delegation, and Chehab concurred. Once again, Charles' departure was kept secret in order to guarantee his safety. He landed in New York on August 14, a few days ahead of Nassim Majdalany, a member of Kamal Jumblatt's Progressive Socialist Party, who had been sent by the opposition as an observer. In New York, Majdalany admitted that Charles had a good chance of being elected president of the General Assembly. But he would certainly not remain as Foreign Minister in the new Chehab government. "He will remain nothing," Majdalany told the *New York Times*. "He will become a professor at Harvard or somewhere else."[162]

Although he did not become a professor at Harvard, Charles did accept President Pusey's invitation to speak at a September conference celebrating the fiftieth anniversary of the Harvard Business School, where he shared the dais with Vice President Nixon. Nixon, looking ahead to the 1960 presidential campaign, used the occasion to deliver a major speech on the economy. First, however, he addressed the latest crisis involving the islands of Quemoy and Matsu in the Taiwan Strait, which the Chinese Communists were threatening to attack. "Our aim here as it was in Lebanon," Nixon insisted, "is solely the maintaining of peace but we have learned that in dealing with dictatorships you do not maintain peace by appearing to be weak but only by maintaining strength militarily and diplomatically."[163] Charles, who had met Zhou Enlai at Bandung, could not have agreed more. His own speech, entitled "The Businessman and the Challenge of Communism," soon appeared in *Fortune*, courtesy, no doubt, of John Fistere.[164]

After the Harvard conference, Charles returned to New York as a candidate for the presidency of the UN General Assembly. His opponent was the Sudanese foreign minister, Mohammed Mahgoub, who charged that Charles represented neither the

Arabs nor Lebanon. "He represents Charles Malik," Mahgoub quipped. According to Bill Eveland, however, President Eisenhower instructed his UN ambassador, Henry Cabot Lodge, Jr., to do whatever was necessary to ensure that Charles was chosen over Mahgoub. Eveland himself was sent to New York to reassure Charles, who, on September 16, was elected by a vote of 45-21. After a reception at the Waldorf, the Maliks invited Eveland to ride with them in their new UN limousine to the Harvard Club for a private dinner.[165] What Eveland didn't mention was that, shortly before leaving the Waldorf, he introduced Charles to one of his CIA colleagues, Jack O'Connell, who was on his way to Amman as King Hussein's new case officer.[166]

A few weeks after taking office, Charles angered the government of new French president Charles de Gaulle by meeting with Mohammed Yazid of the Front de Libération Nationale (FLN), which was fighting to liberate Algeria from French colonial rule. The Algerians hoped to plead their case on the floor of the United Nations; the French regarded the conflict as a purely domestic affair over which the UN had no jurisdiction.[167] Charles may have decided to intercede at the urging of his friend Cecil Hourani, who had left the AUB to serve as an advisor to President Habib Bourguiba of Tunisia, the leader of that nation's successful independence movement. According to Hourani, an alliance between the FLN, which had established a provisional government in Cairo, and President Nasser would spell the end of Bourguiba's moderating influence; hence the urgent need of an accord between the FLN and President de Gaulle.[168]

When the holidays arrived, Charles decided to remain in New York rather than returning to Beirut. Although he was no longer a member of the cabinet—now led by Prime Minister Rashid Karame—his friends and family were concerned about his safety. So, on New Year's Eve, he celebrated by drinking German beer with his old friend Charles Issawi, who had left his job at the UN for a faculty position at Columbia University.[169] Two weeks later, Charles received a blunt missive from his brother Baheej, who advised him to forget about his security and return to Beirut as "a naked citizen." Camille Chamoun, he noted, goes about the city without fear and even drives into the mountains to hunt, and Sami Solh—who, like Charles, had prudently left the country when his term expired—was expected to return soon. If he was not going to come back, Baheej added, Charles should resign his seat in the Chamber of Deputies, as he was doing his constituents no good in New York.[170]

In February 1959, McGeorge Bundy, Dean of Arts and Sciences at Harvard, offered Charles a one-year appointment in Harvard's new Center for Middle Eastern Studies. Bundy may have been prompted by Charles' friend William Elliott, who had played a role in the founding of CMES. The Center's director was the famous Orientalist H. A. R. Gibb, who had left Oxford for Harvard in 1957. Gibb's two assistants were Derwood Lockard, an anthropologist who had served as Kim Roosevelt's assistant in the CIA, and A. J. Meyer, an economist who had come to Harvard from the AUB.[171] Among the students enrolled in CMES at the time were Edward Said's friend Hanna Mikhail and future US diplomat Hume Horan. Charles, however, objected to being attached to CMES and turned down Bundy's offer.[172] Evidently, the presence of his nephew Edward, then a first-year graduate student at Harvard, was not enough to lure him back to his alma mater.

That May, Charles accompanied New York mayor Robert Wagner to the Coliseum for the opening of the city's World Trade Fair. After the ceremony, he and the mayor visited a number of the exhibits, including one sponsored by the government of Israel. As it happened, one of the Israeli trade officials, Nathan Raviv, was a former student of Charles' at the AUB. An alert *New York Times* photographer snapped a picture of Charles enjoying a glass of Israeli champagne with his hosts. When the photograph appeared on the front page of the *Times* under the title "Mideast Amity Marks Opening of Trade Fair Here," there was outrage back in Beirut.[173] Charles was forced to issue an immediate disclaimer. "I do not represent Lebanon," he stated. "Nor can this incident have any significance with regard to the unaltered position either of me or of the Arab world toward Israel."[174]

When the UN General Assembly opened on September 15, Charles was not there to pass the gavel to his successor, Victor Belaunde of Peru. In a final act of political retribution, Prime Minister Karame flew in from Beirut to take Charles' place in the ceremony.[175] And with that, Charles' official diplomatic career came to an end. He had served his country for nearly fifteen years, years that could have been his prime years as a teacher and a scholar. It was not too late to resume his academic career, but it was too late to achieve academic distinction as a philosopher. He had studied with Alfred North Whitehead, but Whitehead's philosophical stock had fallen since the 1930s. Martin Heidegger's stock was on the rise, but Charles had not devoted his life to existentialism and phenomenology as his teacher John Wild had done. Meanwhile, Charles' contemporaries at Harvard—W. V. O. Quine, C. L. Stevenson, William Frankena—had made names for themselves as analytical philosophers. If Charles' academic star had set, however, a new star was about to rise from Harvard—that of his nephew Edward Said.

3

Charles Malik: The Intellectual Out of Power, 1959–75

In January 1960, Charles returned to the United States to take up a visiting professorship at Dartmouth College, leaving Eva and Habib in Beirut. In February, Eva wrote to say that Hilda Said had come from Cairo to see her daughter Rosemarie, who was studying for a Master's in history at the AUB. She also mentioned that Mrs. Eddy (presumably Mary Eddy, the wife of William A. Eddy) had invited her to tea. On the way up to the Eddy apartment, she had shared the elevator with Wadad Cortas—Edward Said's future mother-in-law—whom she called "the same old crazy woman." Finally, she told Charles that her cousins Albert and Lily Badre had invited her to dinner at the Bristol Hotel, along with Wadad Cortas' cousins Nadim and Samir Makdisi, who was all but engaged to Edward Said's sister Jean.[1] Nadim had just submitted his doctoral dissertation on the Parti Populaire Syrien to American University in Washington; Samir was starting his dissertation at Columbia under the direction of Charles Issawi.

That April, Charles traveled to Hartford, Connecticut, to participate in Trinity College's annual convocation. Among the other invited speakers were McGeorge Bundy of Harvard and Walt Whitman Rostow of MIT, both of whom would soon be serving in the administration of President John F. Kennedy.[2] Some weeks later, Charles met Rostow again, this time at the Asilomar retreat center on the Monterey Peninsula, where the World Affairs Council of Northern California was hosting a conference on "Competitive Coexistence." Also invited to speak were Dean Rusk of the Rockefeller Foundation—soon to be Kennedy's secretary of state—and Lyman Kirkpatrick of the CIA. Charles had known Rusk since the late 1940s, when Rusk was under secretary for United Nations Affairs in the Truman State Department. As for Kirkpatrick, he was hounded by reporters inquiring about the secret U-2 spy plane that had been shot down by the Soviets on May 1.[3]

Then, on June 11, Charles Malik delivered an oration in Colonial Williamsburg—the living-history museum financed by the Rockefellers—on the anniversary of the historic Virginia Declaration of Rights. Speaking of the growing Soviet threat to West Berlin, he challenged the doctrine of containment, calling for "an active policy of liberation." "When the late John Foster Dulles spoke of liberation shortly after he became Secretary of State," Charles asked,

> was there a Communist or fellow-traveling or Olympian or soft-headed pacifist or appeasing voice in the world that did not attack him? . . . But only a believing,

active, sustained, and bold looking forward to a free Eastern Europe, a free Russia, and a free China is worthy of the magnitude of the gigantic world struggle.

The struggle, as Charles saw it, was primarily an intellectual and spiritual one—a struggle in which the West enjoyed superior firepower:

> The civilization at whose heart pulsate Aristotle and Augustine and Aquinas and Dante and Newton and Shakespeare and Pascal and Kant and Lincoln, the civilization which has been blessed and transformed by Christ, needs only a mighty hand to shake it out of its slumber.[4]

Just whose "mighty hand" was needed he did not say.

In spite of the fact that it received very little coverage in the national press, Charles' Williamsburg speech became an instant classic of conservative anti-Communism, with some 130,000 copies distributed by the Colonial Williamsburg Foundation that year alone.[5] It was also excerpted in conservative mass-circulation periodicals like *US News and World Report* and *Reader's Digest* and reprinted in the *Congressional Record*. Among the Washington politicians who read and admired the speech was Vice President Nixon, the front-runner for the Republican presidential nomination. After the Republican convention formally nominated him in July, Nixon wrote to Charles at Dartmouth, thanking him for his remarks at Williamsburg and confessing to having "borrowed" a few of his ideas for his acceptance speech.[6] It is fair to say that it was his Williamsburg speech, as much as anything, that made Charles the darling of American conservatives.

Two days after his Williamsburg oration, Charles traveled to Boston College, where he delivered the commencement address and received an honorary degree. "In a world gripped by revolution on every side," he declared, the West needed a revolutionary idea and a charismatic leader of its own. Possibly he was thinking of Richard Nixon. But a more attractive leader for a revolutionary West would be Senator John F. Kennedy of Massachusetts, whose brother Robert was on the platform at Boston College that day, listening to Charles' speech.[7] In fact, Bobby Kennedy had resigned his post as counsel to the Senate Permanent Committee on Investigations in order to run his brother's presidential campaign. Charles' diplomatic career may have come to an end, but he knew a promising Washington contact when he met one.

That summer, Charles returned to Cambridge to teach, once again, at the Harvard Summer School. In early August, he shared the stage with his friend William Elliott at a conference on "Cultural Aid to Underdeveloped Areas."[8] At the time, Elliott was advising Vice President Nixon as he geared up for the fall presidential campaign against Senator Kennedy—a former student of Elliott's at Harvard. In his speech, Charles admonished his listeners:

> You inherit the Graeco-Roman, Hebrew-Christian, Mediterranean, Western European, scientific, democratic, humane, American tradition. You are that. You should be proud of it. . . . In its positive, humane, universal elements, there is nothing to be reticent about or to be ashamed of. And it is these humane and

universal elements alone that will enable you to establish creative international cultural relations with others today.⁹

Edward Said did not hear Uncle Charles' speech, having returned to Cairo to work for his father that summer. But his reading of Joseph Conrad—the subject of his doctoral dissertation—taught him that cultural aid to underdeveloped areas might reveal a heart of darkness.

On November 8, Kennedy narrowly defeated Nixon, whose political career, like Charles Malik's, appeared to be over. Meanwhile, President Leonard of the AUB—who, it seems, had been under the influence of Charles' rivals—announced that he would retire after only three years in office. With Leonard now a lame duck, Charles wrote to John Case, the chairman of the board of trustees, and agreed to return to the AUB.¹⁰ Around the same time, however, he received a letter from Hisham Sharabi, who had been lobbying the Georgetown administration to bring Charles to Washington. Sharabi told him to expect an offer of a joint appointment at Georgetown and American University.¹¹ When American University subsequently offered him an eighteen-month appointment in the School of International Service and the Department of Philosophy and Religion, Charles accepted, further delaying his return to Beirut. Shortly thereafter, veteran State Department official Norman Burns, who had worked with Charles' friend John Fistere at UNRWA, took over from Leonard as president of the AUB.¹²

The following May, Charles delivered the keynote address at the second Corning Conference in Corning, New York, before a select gathering of 100 notables from around the world, including his friend David Rockefeller, whom he had known since 1953, if not longer.¹³ The opening line of Charles' keynote address, "The Individual in Modern Society," made quite an impression: "The derivation of man from and the reduction of man to material, economic, and social conditions is the great heresy of this age." In fact, the concept of the "individual in modern society" was itself a product of this reductionism. "When you speak of the individual in the modern society of Japan, or China, or India, or the Middle East, or Russia, or Africa, or the United States, or Latin America," he explained,

> you are ignoring the specific cultures, religions, moralities, forms of government, and fundamental outlooks on life and existence of these various countries, and are concentrating wholly on the degree, rate, manner, and possibilities of their economic development and socialization.

He went on to distinguish "seven types of society and seven corresponding types of individual," concluding that "the differences are far more important than the similarities."¹⁴

Meanwhile, the Parti Populaire Syrien was plotting to overthrow the government of President Fuad Chehab of Lebanon on December 31, 1960. According to Adel Beshara, the party sent an emissary to Washington that fall to inform Charles of the plot. The new Chairman of the PPS was Dr. Abdullah Saadeh, a distant relative of the party's martyred founder who had studied at the AUB in the late 1930s. Dr. Saadeh, it appears, had already consulted with former president Camille Chamoun and other opposition leaders, including Patriarch Meouchi of the Maronite Church. Charles' role would be to secure American recognition of the new government once Chehab had been ousted.[15] In the event, the coup failed, Dr. Saadeh was arrested, and the PPS was suppressed yet again. Afterwards, the Lebanese ambassador to the United States, Nadim Dimechkie, asked for a meeting with President Kennedy. Kennedy assured Dimechkie that the United States had nothing to do with the attempted coup, adding that he had no evidence of British or Jordanian involvement either.[16]

Coincidentally, Hisham Sharabi wrote the preface to his first major scholarly book, *Governments and Politics in the Middle East in the Twentieth Century*, in the weeks immediately following the failed coup in Lebanon. If his dedication of the book to Issam Mahayri is any indication, Sharabi was still sympathetic to the PPS. Mahayri had been the secretary general of the party until his imprisonment following the Malki assassination in April 1955. At the time Sharabi dedicated his book to him, Mahayri was still rotting in prison in Damascus. As for Charles Malik, Sharabi identified him in the book as a Christian who considered Arab nationalism a threat to Lebanon's unique character as a meeting place between the Christian West and the Muslim East. In addition to Charles, Sharabi named the politician Pierre Gemayel, the poet Said Akl, and the historian Fuad Bustani as representatives of this school of thought.[17]

§

In the fall of 1962, Charles returned to the AUB as distinguished professor of philosophy. Among those who had joined the AUB faculty during his six-year absence were Walid, Usama, and Tarif Khalidi, the sons of Ahmad S. Khalidi, the former principal of the Government Arab College in Jerusalem. Ahmad Khalidi's second wife—the mother of Usama and Tarif—was Anbara Salam, the sister of Saeb Salam, the leader of Beirut's Sunni community, who had led the opposition to the Chamoun-Malik regime in 1958. Walid Khalidi's wife was Rasha Salam, his stepmother's much younger sister. Like Albert Hourani, Walid Khalidi had settled into the peaceful life of an Oxford don after the Second World War. Following the British attack on Suez in 1956, however, he had resigned in protest, choosing to teach instead in Beirut, where his connection to the Salam family gave him entrée to society and the corridors of power.

In November, Charles wrote the introduction to his book *Man in the Struggle for Peace*, a copy of which was owned by Edward Said.[18] "Man struggles for peace," Charles began, "because he is *essentially* a struggling being." He ended with a call for a Western revolution, led by a spiritual vanguard of committed intellectuals:

> If there are a hundred men, *well placed* in government, in the press, in industry, in labor, in the universities, and in the churches, one hundred men *who really work as a team*, who really see through the sham and vacuity of Communist existence, who really understand that it is a matter of life and death for the highest and deepest they believe in, and who really believe that there is nothing like the values of the mind and spirit and man and God which have come down to Mediterranean-Western civilization from the last four thousand years . . . , then we can rest . . .

because the revolution has started, because everyone will be called to do his part in it, and because the Communists are already on the run.[19]

Just who these 100 disciplined anti-Communist cadres might be, Charles did not say. But surely he himself was among them.

In May 1963, Charles flew to Chicago for a conference on Lebanese democracy organized by Leonard Binder, the founder of the University of Chicago's new Committee on Middle Eastern Studies, who had studied under H. A. R. Gibb at Harvard. The conference was sponsored by the university's Committee on the Comparative Study of New Nations, which included, in addition to Binder, the sociologists Edward Shils and Clifford Geertz. Although Shils, who gave the conference's opening address, was active in the CIA-funded Congress for Cultural Freedom, the Lebanon conference was not a CCF event. It did receive funding, however, from another CIA front, American Friends of the Middle East, which was represented at the conference by its vice president for research, Erich Bethmann.[20] Just how much Bethmann knew about the CIA's funding of AFME is uncertain, although he certainly knew that Kim Roosevelt was a member of AFME's board of directors, having retired from the CIA a few years earlier.

The Chicago conference turned out to be another unofficial AUB reunion. Philip Hitti was there, along with Albert Hourani and Charles Issawi. Also present was UCLA political science professor Malcolm Kerr—the son of Charles' longtime colleagues Stanley and Elsa Kerr—who had studied with Hourani at Oxford. Other participants included Harvey Hall of the Ford Foundation, a former AUB staffite; the historian Kamal Salibi, an AUB graduate who had studied under Bernard Lewis in London before returning to the AUB; and the political scientist George Grassmuck, a former AUB professor and campaign consultant to Richard Nixon. In addition, the conference reunited Charles with two of his students from the 1940s, Hisham Sharabi and Muhsin Mahdi, who had been roommates at the University of Chicago. Mahdi, who had joined the Chicago faculty, was close to his mentor Leo Strauss, under whose influence he had switched from economics to medieval philosophy.[21]

A number of those who presented papers at the conference, including Malcolm Kerr, discussed the Lebanese Civil War of 1958. According to Kerr, President Chamoun's mistake had been to attempt to turn his pro-Western foreign policy to his own domestic political advantage:

> In any case, having made his choice against a diplomatic break with Britain and France and having put Dr. Charles Malik in charge at the Foreign Ministry, Chamoun then felt it necessary to reinforce these decisions by bolstering his own parliamentary and public positions. As for Parliament, he could use the familiar powers of machine politics associated with his office to obligate deputies to himself, and in mid-1957, to secure the election of a new Chamber overwhelmingly favorable to himself and morally committed to amend the Constitution and reelect him to a second term in 1958. As for the public, . . . whose preferences were diverging on increasingly sectarian lines, Chamoun found it expedient to encourage rather than bridge this divide, preferring to pose as the indispensable (hence reelectable) champion of Christian Lebanon.[22]

Charles could not have been happy with Kerr's criticism of Chamoun and, by implication, himself. After all, he had known Malcolm since he was a little boy climbing trees on the AUB campus.

A number of prominent Jewish scholars also participated in the Chicago conference, including, in addition to Leonard Binder, J. C. Hurewitz of Columbia, Manfred Halpern of Princeton, and Nadav Safran of Harvard. Binder, a native Bostonian, and Safran, who was born and raised in Cairo, had both fought with the Jewish army in 1948. Binder had been captured during the siege of Jerusalem and imprisoned in Transjordan, where he began to learn Arabic.[23] Hurewitz and Halpern, who had been born in Germany but immigrated to the United States in the 1930s, had both served with the OSS during the war. From 1948 to 1958, Halpern had worked with Wendell Cleland, Charles' former American University colleague, at the State Department. Coincidentally, the Council on Religion and Foreign Policy had just published a pamphlet by Halpern entitled *The Morality and Politics of Intervention*, in which he analyzed the US military intervention in Lebanon in 1958.

Halpern, who presumably had access to the State Department's intelligence on Lebanon, pulled no punches in his analysis of the "real story" behind the landing of the Marines, which he regarded as unwarranted and counterproductive. "In order to perpetuate the status quo," he wrote,

> Chamoun rigged the 1957 election enough to give himself that two-thirds parliamentary majority required to amend the constitution so that parliament could re-elect him for a second six-year term. Then, in order to make up in foreign backing for what he had lost in domestic support, he agreed to the Eisenhower Doctrine.

To these allegations Halpern added one other, namely, that "most politically active Lebanese believe that there is conclusive evidence that the Lebanese president and foreign minister, though they failed to consult other members of their government, had from the start acted in concert with the CIA."[24] That foreign minister, of course, was Charles Malik, who had quite a few friends in the Agency.

§

In the fall of 1963, Charles' former student Sadik al-Azm, having earned his PhD from Yale with a dissertation on the moral philosophy of Henri Bergson, returned to the AUB as a member of the philosophy department. The scion of an aristocratic Sunni family from Damascus, Azm had attended the Protestant Boys' School in Sidon before enrolling at the AUB. At Sidon, Azm had become interested in the ideas of Antun Saadeh, notably his commitment to science and his insistence on the separation of church (or mosque) and state. After graduating from the AUB, he had married Fawz Tuqan, the daughter of Ahmad Tuqan of Nablus, who had been a contemporary of Charles' at the AUB in the mid-1920s. A former member of Jordan's UN delegation, Tuqan had worked for many years as an education advisor to UNRWA and the World Bank. On her mother's side, Fawz was related to the Khalidi family of Jerusalem, which was well represented on the AUB faculty.[25]

That September, just as Edward Said was starting his teaching career at Columbia, Charles traveled to New York at the invitation of David Rockefeller to address the International Management Congress. Charles was by no means the only participant from Lebanon. His brother Baheej, a self-employed businessman, came with him to New York, as did Fuad el-Khazen, one of the directors of the Contracting and Trading Company, co-founded by Charles' old friends Emile Bustani and Shukri Shammas. Lebanese bankers in attendance included Pierre Eddé of the Riyad Bank—an opponent of the Chehab regime who had gone into voluntary exile in Paris—and George K. Hakim of Intra Bank, founded by Yusef Beidas, an old friend of the Said family. Representing the Middle East Business Services and Research Corporation was Sam Souki, whose partner was Charles' former student Ghassan Tueni, the publisher of *an-Nahar*. The sole participant from Jordan was businessman Raja Farradj, the brother of George Said's wife Huda.[26]

In one of the plenary sessions, Charles shared the platform with Dr. Courtney Brown, Dean of the Columbia Business School, and Lee Iacocca, Vice President of the Ford Motor Company. In his paper, later published in the *Harvard Business Review*, Charles addressed the problem of leadership in the newly independent nations of Africa and Asia. "It will take decades or even generations," he admitted, "before some of these new nations ... are able ... to generate their own stable leadership independently of the rest of the world." But it is not enough, he warned, to train the future leaders of Africa and Asia in the techniques of scientific management. What is most necessary, he insisted, is to share the ideas and ideals of Western civilization with these leaders, lest human beings in the new nations be treated as means and not as ends. "Socrates, Plato and Aristotle, Christ and Paul, Augustine and Aquinas, Pascal and Kant," he admonished his audience, "are not going to be impressed by the perfection and efficiency of your techniques alone."[27]

While he was in New York, Charles met with Attorney General Robert Kennedy about the 1964 elections in Lebanon.[28] In the memo he handed to Kennedy at their meeting, Charles wrote:

> Just as last time [1958] the United States played a decisive role, so this time the United States is certain to play a decisive role.... The present regime, with total United States blessing and encouragement, is Nasserite-dominated. I beg you that the coming regime be completely free of Nasserism.[29]

Although Charles did not mention the AUB, he knew that the Kennedy administration took an interest in the university, which Bobby Kennedy had visited most recently in February 1962.[30] On the same day that Charles met with Bobby Kennedy in New York, in fact, Hugh D. Auchincloss, Jr., the assistant to AUB board chairman John Case, wrote a letter to Bobby's brother John thanking him for his administration's support of the AUB.[31] It didn't hurt that Auchincloss, known to his family as "Yusha," happened to be the step-brother of Jackie Kennedy.

§

In early January 1964, Charles Malik accompanied Athenagoras I, the Ecumenical Patriarch of Constantinople, to Jerusalem for his historic meeting with Pope Paul VI.[32]

Landing in Amman, they drove to Jerusalem, which had been a divided city since the war of 1948. The papal entourage did the same. It was the first time in history that a pope had visited Jerusalem—or traveled by air—and the first meeting between a pope and a patriarch since the Council of Florence in the mid-fifteenth century. Charles himself was a Roman Catholic in all but name, having been asked by the pope to refrain from formal conversion in order to persuade his Orthodox brethren to reconcile with Rome.[33] The meeting in Jerusalem was the first fruit of this effort. Still photographs and film footage of the meeting—which took place in the residence of Benediktos I, the patriarch of Jerusalem, on the Mount of Olives—show Charles standing behind the pope as he receives the gift of an encolpion (a chest medallion) from Athenagoras.[34]

That March, Charles received a visit from Richard Nixon in his office on the AUB campus. According to the notes Nixon took during their meeting, Charles criticized the Republicans for their defeatist attitude regarding the 1964 presidential election, which Lyndon Johnson was destined to win in a landslide over Barry Goldwater. Johnson, however, was evidently not Charles' idea of the leader of the Free World. What America needed, he declared, was a proud patriot and pillar of strength, like Charles de Gaulle of France. If the United States refused to stand up for itself in the world, he warned, the new nations would lose their respect for America and turn instead to the Soviets.[35] While nothing in Nixon's notes indicates that Charles urged him to run for president in 1964, the possibility was not far from either man's mind. Four years later, following Nixon's comeback victory in 1968, Charles would be among the first to offer his congratulations.

That same March saw the publication of *The Conservative Papers*, a collection of statements by leading conservative intellectuals solicited by Representative Melvin Laird of Wisconsin on behalf of a group of Republican congressmen that included Gerald Ford of Michigan. In addition to Charles Malik, Laird solicited papers from, among others, Henry Kissinger, Milton Friedman, Edward Teller, and Harry Jaffa, who argued that the rights of free speech, freedom of association, and so forth do not extend to Communists and Nazis (although he added that it was preferable, for pragmatic reasons, to tolerate them). The papers were then edited by Ralph de Toledano and Karl Hess with the help of Laird's legislative assistant, William J. Baroody, Jr.[36] Charles' contribution, entitled "The Challenge to Western Civilization," was a compilation of his recent speeches, including the famous one he had delivered at Colonial Williamsburg in 1960.

A few months later, Charles' nemesis in the AUB philosophy department, a Chicago native named Roland Puccetti, was notified that the AUB board of trustees would not renew his contract. The reasons for his dismissal had already emerged in Puccetti's conversations and correspondence with various trustees, notably Dr. John Wilson of the University of Chicago's Oriental Institute. First and foremost, Wilson told Puccetti, board members were troubled by his public profession of atheism, which, some feared, he was inculcating in his students. He had also been accused of excessive drinking. In response, Puccetti reminded the trustees that he had identified himself as a "humanist" in his original job application and denied that he taught atheism to his students. As for the drinking charge, he said that it was based on a single incident at a faculty party.[37] But the trustees had made up their minds. Charles Malik, for one, shed no tears over Puccetti's demise.

That fall, Charles took a leave of absence from the AUB and returned to the United States for a series of speaking engagements. At the end of November, he spoke at the Healy Conference on Freedom and Man at Georgetown, which concluded with a special convocation featuring President Lyndon Johnson, who had defeated Barry Goldwater in a landslide a few weeks earlier.[38] In his talk, entitled "The Metaphysics of Freedom," Charles offered a theological account of personal freedom. "This is an age of group freedom," he warned his audience. "The individual person is assimilated to his group.... He is not 'a free man,' he is 'a group man,'" in thrall to what Heidegger named *das Man* ("the They"). As Charles noted:

> Modern existentialism, from Kierkegaard to Heidegger and Sartre, is a revolt against group freedom. Not . . . the group but the individual human is the real thing. Freedom resides in the decision of each existing individual.[39]

What Heidegger and Sartre failed to realize, he added, is that true freedom comes only from God.

A year later, in October 1965, Charles returned to the United States for a conference sponsored by the Council for Religion in Independent Schools. Although the theme of the conference was "Youth's Crisis in a Changing World," Charles devoted most of his opening address to a deeply felt confession of his own Christian faith. Among those who found Charles' address disappointing was Rev. William Sloane Coffin, Jr., the increasingly radical chaplain of Yale University, who spoke the following morning. Mr. Malik, he told his audience, "represents the kind of 'back-to-God' American legionnaire, poster kind of religion that is not going to solve the crisis one bit as far as our youth are concerned." He added, apologetically, that he had "complete admiration for Mr. Malik, whom I trailed around as a kid at the United Nations, thinking this was one of God's finest gifts to the world, and I still think so." Although Charles did not attend Coffin's talk, the two men sparred at a later discussion session, with Coffin challenging Charles' "abjectly conventional approach to religion."[40]

The following March, Charles flew to New York for a conference sponsored by the Harvard Business School, where he offered his "Reflections on the Great Society." In Charles' view, the "Great Society" envisioned by President Johnson was far from a reality. In America, he lamented,

> atheism is not only tolerated; it has become fashionable and militant. Perversion has become respectable. Materialism is thoroughly rationalized. The crassest hedonism has made its way into life. Rebellion is not only an adolescent phase: it is now a total spirit. When the soul of youth . . . is hungering for some fare of satisfying truth, departments of philosophy are engaged literally in splitting words. There is no correlation between the place and power of America in the world today and what is being spun by the philosophers.[41]

As this diatribe suggests, Charles was no admirer of student radicalism or of Anglo-American philosophy, with its logic-chopping style of argument—a style he associated with the Roland Puccettis of the world.

After his speech, Charles went out to lunch with a pair Columbia University deans, Courtney Brown of the Business School and Andrew Cordier of the School of International Affairs, whom Charles knew from their many years together at the UN.[42] Among the topics they discussed, it seems, was the possibility of bringing Charles to Columbia, where he would have been reunited with Edward Said, Charles Issawi, and other old friends on the faculty. It is hard to imagine that Charles would have agreed to teach at a business school, even one as prestigious as Columbia's. But he must have given Brown some hope, because Brown went ahead and proposed the idea to his colleagues. Not surprisingly, they rejected it as too unconventional.[43]

Meanwhile, the Puccetti Affair continued to dog Charles. In June, an article appeared in the *New York Times* bearing the title "Problems Plaguing American University of Beirut." Reporting from Beirut, correspondent Thomas Brady offered the following account of Puccetti's firing:

> Professor Pucetti [*sic*] has charged that he was dismissed because he was an atheist and that Prof. Charles Malik, now chairman of the philosophy department in which Professor Pucetti taught the Philosophy of Religion, was a major opponent of his tenure appointment.
>
> Professor Malik . . . is a Lebanese Christian. He was not chairman of the department when the university decided not to keep Professor Pucetti, and he said recently that he had not been formally consulted by university authorities on the matter.[44]

If Edward Said read the *Times* that day, he must have been thankful to be teaching at Columbia, where even atheists enjoyed academic freedom.

Not long after the *Times* story appeared, Charles flew to Washington, where he arranged to meet with Walt Rostow, McGeorge Bundy's successor as Johnson's national security advisor. Unfortunately, Rostow had to miss the meeting, so he sent two Near East experts from his staff, Harold Saunders and Howard Wriggins, in his place. I am not sure why Charles wanted to see Rostow, but the letter he wrote in response to Rostow's note of apology reveals that he feared for the freedom of Lebanon. One sign that freedom was in danger, he told Rostow, was the recent assassination of the editor of "the freest and finest newspaper in the Arab world."[45] He was referring to Kamel Mroueh, the pro-Western editor of *al-Hayat* and *The Daily Star*, who had been gunned down in his Beirut office that May. His assassins, it appeared, were militant Nasserites.[46]

While he was in Washington that summer, Charles visited his friend Hisham Sharabi, who handed him an article he had published in the *Middle East Journal*, "The Transformation of Ideology in the Arab World." In effect, Sharabi was throwing down the gauntlet to his old teacher, announcing his conversion to the revolutionary socialism of Nasser and the Algerian FLN. "For the Western-oriented intellectuals," he noted,

> the cause of Europe's failure lay in the sickness which has gripped the entire West in the twentieth century. Thus, for Charles Malik . . . it is only "when [Western] culture mends its own spiritual fences, [that] all will be well with the Near East."

For these intellectuals, reconciliation still seems possible, but not on the transient plane of nationalist or revolutionary action: "East and West can come together in peace only if they repent together under transcendent judgment."

Sharabi then summarized the Marxist position:

To the revolutionary elite this position is reactionary, the remnant of bourgeois moralistic intellectualism. The Graeco-Christian tradition no longer has meaning or relevance. In the midst of the starved and illiterate millions, the only true values are those of bread, dignity, and power. Truth is a human not a transcendent value.[47]

In August, Charles responded to Sharabi's article in a letter, complaining that his views of truth and being were unclear. What Sharabi needed, he said, was "ultimate conviction with respect to ultimate things."[48]

§

By the fall of 1966, Charles was busy preparing for the AUB's centennial festivities. His primary task was to organize a symposium on the theme of "God and Man in Contemporary Religious Thought"—or, more accurately, *two* symposia, since the Muslim participants were to convene in February 1967 and the Christians in April. This segregation disappointed at least one of the participants, the liberal Catholic theologian Hans Küng, whom Charles had met at the Georgetown "Man and Freedom" conference. When Küng asked Charles why the Muslims and the Christians could not meet together, Charles replied, "*Cher Professeur, c'est trop tôt!*"[49] But the real explanation, one suspects, is that President Samuel Kirkwood did not want to risk further sectarian conflict in the wake of the Spagnolo Affair, in which an AUB history professor—John Spagnolo, a former student of Albert Hourani's at Oxford—had been forced to leave Lebanon over an excerpt from the *Summa Theologica* in which Thomas Aquinas abused the Prophet Muhammad.[50]

On December 3, 1966, the AUB celebrated its Centennial Day, starting with a breakfast featuring Van Engert, whose memories of the AUB dated back to the year 1919. At the age of seventy-nine, Engert was still active in American Friends of the Middle East. After Engert's talk came a chapel service featuring trustee Daniel Bliss and two senior professors—Anis Makdisi, who read a poem he had written for the occasion, and Charles Malik, who delivered an address entitled "Faith, Truth, Freedom." "In the faithlessness of this age," Charles vowed,

the University can and will remain faithful; in the lostness of this age, the University can and will remain truthful; and amidst the slavery which has afflicted the men of this age, both their body and their soul, the University can and will remain free— and the free dispenser of freedom.[51]

The day's festivities concluded with a banquet at the Bristol Hotel, where Bliss offered his recollections of his grandfather and history professor Joseph Malone ventured a lighthearted account of how the AUB had changed over the years.

As the director of the Middle East Area Program at the AUB—funded by the US Army's Advanced Research Projects Agency—Malone mentored the young officers who were sent to Beirut for training.[52] He had started teaching at the AUB in 1959, having completed his studies at the University of London and the Middle East Centre for Arab Studies in Shemlan—the so-called spy school run by the British government. Inevitably, there were rumors that Malone was CIA—rumors he enjoyed feeding.[53] Dean of Arts and Sciences Terry Prothro joked that "[Malone] is the only CIA man I know whose cover is being a CIA man."[54] Malone's sense of humor was on display at his talk at the Bristol Hotel banquet, in which he proposed that the AUB, which had benefited from the munificence of the Rockefeller family for decades, should invite David Rockefeller to be the university's comptroller.[55]

The AUB's Centennial Day festivities were important enough to be covered by Thomas Brady, the Beirut correspondent of the *New York Times*, who could not resist inserting a reminder of the Puccetti Affair:

[Malik] reaffirmed the religious aspect of [the] university, a subject of controversy since the board of trustees declined to renew the contract two years ago of Roland P. Pucetti [sic], an assistant professor and self-proclaimed atheist.

"Without God and faith in God," he reminded his audience, "this university would never have come into being, nor would it have endured. And I believe without God and faith in God, it will not last and shine."[56]

For his part, Charles asked Doug Coe—Abraham Vereide's right-hand man at International Christian Leadership—to get one of his congressional friends to read his Centennial Day speech into the *Congressional Record*.[57] A few months later, the speech was duly printed in the *Record*, courtesy of Senator Mark Hatfield of Oregon, Coe's former professor at Willamette University.[58]

In February 1967, the Islamic half of Charles' centennial symposium on "God and Man" convened at the AUB. Among the local participants were Sheikh Nadim al-Jisr, the *Mufti* of Tripoli, and Imam Musa al-Sadr of Tyre, the Iranian-born leader of Lebanon's Shia community. At the time, Sadr was organizing the Supreme Islamic Shia Council, a representative body intended to unite Lebanon's Shia and give them a voice in national affairs.[59] Sadr's paper, entitled "Islam and the Dignity of Man," traced the Islamic concept of the dignity of man to the Koranic teaching that man is God's *khalifah* (vice-regent) on earth. According to the Koran, he noted, even the angels fell down before Adam—all but Iblis, who was too proud. To the angels' complaint that man will do evil and spill blood, God had replied, "I know what ye know not," which Sadr interpreted to mean that freedom—even the freedom to do evil—is essential to man's dignity. That freedom, he added, includes freedom of thought or *ijtihad*—the free use of reason to interpret the Koran and tradition—which Islam therefore protects.[60]

Ironically, the "God and Man" symposium drew its sharpest criticism from one of Charles' own colleagues, Sadik al-Azm, who had previously criticized both Sheikh al-Jisr and Imam al-Sadr for their futile efforts to reconcile Islam and modern science.[61] Soon after the symposium, Azm delivered a scathing review of the proceedings at the Arab Cultural Club in Beirut, portions of which were subsequently published in

Ghassan Tueni's *an-Nahar* newspaper. The whole symposium, Azm charged, served the interests of the conservative Islamic movement, which was hostile to Arab nationalism in general and to President Nasser in particular.[62] As Azm recalled many years later, his critique of the symposium resulted in "une rancoeur dévastatrice de la part de Charles Malek, qui a joué un rôle déterminant dans mon éviction de l'Université américaine."[63] Indeed, Azm soon learned that his contract with the AUB would not be renewed beyond the 1967–8 academic year.[64]

The following month, Charles flew to Washington to address an open session of the Near East subcommittee of the House Committee on Foreign Affairs. His remarks were reported by Si Kenen, the founder of the American Israel Public Affairs Committee (AIPAC) and the editor of *Near East Report*. It was Kenen who, a few years earlier, had exposed the CIA's covert funding of American Friends of the Middle East.[65] Not knowing that Israel was about to go to war, Charles told the subcommittee that the most crucial issue facing the Arab countries was no longer Israel, but, rather, the growing influence of Communism and the absence of freedom of thought. The Communists, he charged, had "massively infiltrated" every aspect of life in the Near East, including the trade unions, the press, and the universities. The assassination of Kamel Mroueh, he lamented, had terrorized other editors in Lebanon. Even the AUB, he complained, was losing its regional influence by "taking more and more students from Asia and Africa."[66]

Charles returned to Beirut in time for the Christian half of his "God and Man" symposium, which brought together a number of prominent Orthodox, Catholic, and Protestant theologians. W. A. Visser 't Hooft of the Netherlands, who had recently stepped down as general secretary of the World Council of Churches, addressed the question of the church's relevance in the wake of Comte, Marx, and Nietzsche.[67] Hans Küng read a paper entitled "The Church and Sincerity." Contrasting the modern passion for sincerity with the church's history of dishonesty, Küng issued a call for renewed truthfulness on the part of the church.[68] Harvard philosopher John Wild—who had introduced Charles to the work of Martin Heidegger some three decades earlier—spoke on Christian faith in an age of science. The true ground of faith, he suggested, is to be found not in nature, but in human experience, including the mystical experiences studied by William James.[69]

A few weeks later, Sadik al-Azm burned his last bridge to Charles Malik, critiquing the symposium in a talk at the University Christian Center, subsequently published in *an-Nahar*. Listening to the speakers, Azm said,

> I could not resist the feeling that although the Christian theologians have blessed this uneasy peace with the forces of secularization and have come to regard the loss of the Church's old domains and bastillions as a liberation which permits it now to manifest its true character and mission, still deep in their hearts they seem to regret that this should have happened at all.

Turning first to Visser 't Hooft, Azm mocked the Dutchman's assertion that the God who was declared dead by Nietzsche was not the living Christian God, but merely the abstract God of the philosophers. "Surely Nietzsche did not write down a vacuous tautology," Azm protested, "to the effect that the dead God is dead." As for Hans Küng's dedication to sincerity, Azm asked why sincerity requires the church to do away with Mariology, Papal infallibility, and scholastic theology, but not with the Incarnation, the Resurrection, or the miracles of Jesus. "As long as one is inside the Church," he concluded, "the kind of sincerity that Father Küng is supposedly talking about can be pressed only to certain limits while sincerity in fact requires us always to go all the way, no matter what."[70]

§

After the final "God and Man" symposium, Charles returned to the United States for his usual round of university commencement speeches. He was in the Midwest on June 5 when Israel launched a preemptive war against its Arab neighbors, which had been massing forces along its borders. A few days later, Charles visited Metropolitan Philip Saliba of the Antiochene Orthodox Church at his home in Brooklyn. As Saliba recalled that visit a few years later:

> It was hard to believe that the June War was decided in favor of Israel in a few hours, and it was heart breaking to see the defeated Egyptian army wandering in Sinai aimlessly. But the most tragic and disgusting thing was to see how the Arab diplomats were begging the United Nations for a cease-fire. I will never forget how Dr. Charles Malek [sic], who was visiting me that day, and I wept while watching the proceedings of the United Nations General Assembly. After a few tearful moments, Dr. Malek turned to me and said, "The Middle East will never be the same."[71]

Nor, for that matter, would the relationship between Charles Malik and Edward Said ever be the same. For it was the *Naksa* ("Setback") of June 1967 that turned Edward Said into a Palestinian, and it was the consequences of the *Naksa* that turned Uncle Charles into an enemy of the Palestinians.

The following month, Charles traveled to Istanbul for the historic visit of Pope Paul VI to the Ecumenical Patriarchate in Phanar.[72] After their previous meeting in Jerusalem in 1964, Pope Paul and Patriarch Athenagoras had issued a joint statement repealing the mutual excommunications of 1054, known as the "Great Schism." Now Paul became the first Roman pontiff to visit the Phanar since the time of Constantine. Joining Charles in the patriarch's entourage was the Greek American business tycoon Thomas A. Pappas, who had been a leading backer of Richard Nixon's 1960 presidential campaign and would be again in 1968, funneling cash from Greece's brutal military rulers into Nixon's coffers.[73] Then, in November 1967, Charles accompanied Athenagoras on his return visit to Rome, where he and the pope conducted a service together in St. Peter's Basilica. Afterwards, Charles asked the patriarch, "Were you satisfied with your meeting with the Pope?" "My son," Athenagoras replied, "more than satisfied. In fact, we agreed on everything."[74]

On January 31, 1968—the day the North Vietnamese Army launched its famous Tet Offensive—Charles spoke at an International Christian Leadership seminar in Washington. The next day, he attended the Presidential Prayer Breakfast at the Shoreham Hotel, which featured some sober remarks from President Johnson. "We weary of the winter," Johnson confessed, "and despair of the coming of the spring. We are tempted to turn from the tasks of duty and to lay down the works that are ours to do."[75] Johnson was thinking, obviously, of the war in Vietnam. What no one in the room knew, however, is that he had already decided not to seek reelection. Certainly Vice President Hubert Humphrey, who spoke at an ICL luncheon later that day, gave no indication that he would run for president that year. Charles, however, was preoccupied with the Middle East, which he discussed with a number of senators and representatives, including Ross Adair of Indiana, the senior Republican member of the House Committee on Foreign Affairs, who was active in ICL.[76]

Charles then returned to the AUB, which, like many other universities, was experiencing a student uprising that spring. In March, students formed a Committee on Academic Freedom to protest the administration's refusal to renew Sadik al-Azm's contract and called for a one-day strike. At the time, Azm was gathering some of his speeches and articles into a book about the causes of the Arab defeat in the June War. As usual, he spared no one, not even President Nasser, whom he accused of "middle-roadism." What the June defeat showed, he declared, is that Nasser's Arab socialist revolution "is not sufficiently revolutionary and not sufficiently socialist."[77] The AUB student strike, however, had no effect, other than to elicit a statement from President Kirkwood confirming the cover story that Azm was being let go for purely academic reasons.[78] But Azm blamed Charles Malik.

§

In November 1968, Richard Nixon returned from the political wilderness, defeating Hubert Humphrey in the US presidential election. Shortly thereafter, the *New York Times* published a story, datelined Beirut, under the title "Arabs Hope Nixon Will Bring Change." The first Arab quoted was Charles Malik, who praised the president-elect as "a man of great moral values" who will bring "peace based on justice" to the Middle East.[79] With Nixon back in the White House, Charles obviously hoped to stage a political comeback of his own, regaining some of the access and influence he had enjoyed in Washington during the Eisenhower years. After all, Nixon had praised his Williamsburg speech during his first presidential run and visited him in Beirut during his "wilderness years." Surely he would be more responsive to Arab concerns than Lyndon Johnson, the most pro-Israel president since Truman. More importantly, Nixon would understand the urgency of saving Lebanon from the Nasserites and the Communists.

By early December, Charles was back in New York, staying as usual at the Harvard Club. There he composed a long letter to Nixon, warning him about Soviet inroads in the Middle East. "The Communist presence," he observed,

> has been making itself more and more felt in the Eastern Mediterranean and in certain parts of the Middle East, and the presence of the West has correspondingly retreated. Teachers, students, poets, intellectuals, governments, the press, the

elements forming and guiding opinion and attitude, are for the most part now fundamentally oriented along Communist and anti-Western lines.

And yet, Charles continued, he was more optimistic now than ever before. As he told Nixon:

> A wholly new vision for the Middle East is called for. I have more confidence now that in you such a vision can come to full articulation than I ever had with respect to any other person.[80]

The next step was to get the letter to Nixon. Evidently, Charles entrusted it to his old friend Lowell Thomas, who handed it to veteran Nixon advisor William Casey, who passed it on to Nixon.[81]

Charles had come to New York to address a special meeting of the UN General Assembly on December 9, the twentieth anniversary of the Universal Declaration of Human Rights. Although the influence of the UDHR over the past twenty years had been "incalculable," he admitted that the year 1968, which the United Nations had designated "The International Year for Human Rights," had been "a sad one for human rights." In the Middle East, for example, the Arab refugees had been deprived of their rights—"their homes, property, liberties and land." But the deepest challenge, he continued, was "not to excite people further about their rights," but to stress their duties to one another—"to instill solidarity, obligation, the sense of belonging together and of a common human destiny." "Human rights," he proclaimed, "flowered naturally in the soil of love."[82] Until the stony ground of the Middle East was nourished by love between Arab and Jew, he implied, human rights were destined to wither on the vine.

In February 1969, Charles returned to the United States as a fellow of the new Institute for Advanced Religious Studies at the University of Notre Dame. Meanwhile, President Nixon had started a program of Sunday morning sermons in the White House. In late September, Charles preached one of these sermons on the theme of peace and war. His congregation included not only Nixon, who introduced him "as a personal friend" and "a friend of anyone who has a great desire for this world to have peace," but also the sixty country directors of the Peace Corps, along with many of the ambassadors from those countries. "Peace," Charles proclaimed, is not the absence of conflict, but, rather,

> the perpetual struggle for the preservation and enhancement of the deepest values. Therefore it is always a matter of faith in these values, for where there are no values which man is not prepared to part with, there is no difference between peace and war: man then is like a jellyfish adjusting to and fro to every wind and wave.[83]

These values, he continued, are five in number: objective truth, reason, the original freedom of man, man as an end in himself, and the unchanging essence of things.

The problem facing America, Charles implied, was not that the nation was at war in Vietnam, but that it was losing faith in the values it was fighting for—a problem he blamed on the intellectuals. "Entirely apart from any external menace," he warned, within the Western world itself philosophies have been fermenting for two hundred years or more which preach ... false doctrines. It is the maturing of these philosophies in the highest intellectual circles that has, more than anything else, been at the base of the tribulations which have so tragically afflicted the university in recent years.[84]

These false philosophies included, no doubt, Freudianism, Marxism, and other godless ideologies that had begun to attract many of Charles' former students—not to mention his nephew Edward, whose interest in Marxist thinkers like Lukacs and Gramsci as well as avant-garde French theorists like Barthes and Foucault was bound to disturb him.

Back in Beirut, meanwhile, Sadik al-Azm had published a collection of his articles on religion, including his critique of Charles Malik's Christian symposium, under the title *Naqd al-Fikr al-Dini* ("Critique of Religious Thought"). In early December, the Sunni *Mufti* of Beirut, Hassan Khaled, asked the Lebanese government to ban the book. The authorities complied, citing a law against publications intended to incite religious strife, and issued a warrant for Azm's arrest. Azm then placed himself under the protection of the Democratic Front for the Liberation of Palestine (DFLP), the most intellectual of the leftist *fedayeen* organizations. After some negotiation with the Lebanese authorities, he surrendered himself for interrogation in early January.[85] Interestingly, both Nadim al-Jisr and Musa al-Sadr, whom Azm had criticized by name in his book, took the position that he should be allowed to publish his heresies—a fact that Azm recalled with gratitude when he revisited the affair some three decades later.[86]

Around the time that Sadik al-Azm turned himself in, Charles Malik wrote a letter of recommendation for a young Iraqi mathematician who was applying for a faculty position at the AUB.[87] The letter was addressed to the chairwoman of the mathematics department, Mary Hanania Regier, a cousin of George Said's wife Huda.[88] As for the subject of the letter, he was none other than Dr. Ahmad Chalabi, the future head of the Iraqi National Congress. It is not clear from his letter that Charles knew Chalabi personally, but he knew other members of the Chalabi family, which had relocated to Beirut after the overthrow of the Iraqi monarchy in 1958. What he may not have known is that the Chalabis, including Ahmad, were conspiring to bring down the Baathist government in Iraq. In the summer of 1969, Ahmad and his brother Hassan had traveled to Iran to meet with Nematollah Nassiri, the head of the shah's secret police, and Mulla Mustafa Barzani, the rebellious Kurdish leader, regarding a possible coup in Baghdad.[89] The coup never materialized, but Chalabi got the job at the AUB.

§

On April 16, 1970, Charles met with President Nixon in the White House for half an hour. According to James R. Stocker, he recommended that the US work with other Arab states to cut off funding for the *fedayeen* and supply arms to the Christian parties in Lebanon. At one point during the meeting, Nixon picked up the phone and called CIA director Richard Helms, perhaps to inquire what the Agency was already doing in Lebanon.[90] Charles also handed Nixon an Arabic letter from Cardinal Meouchi, the Maronite patriarch, along with his own English translation. In the letter, Meouchi requested US aid for "conservative" and "free" elements in Lebanon, meaning, presumably, the "Tripartite Alliance" consisting of Camille Chamoun, Raymond Eddé, and Pierre Gemayel.[91] Charles did not always see eye to eye with Meouchi, who had backed Fuad Chehab over Chamoun in 1958. By 1970, however, Meouchi had withdrawn his support for Chehab, who was about to announce his candidacy for a second term as president of Lebanon.[92]

The US ambassador to Lebanon, Dwight Porter, thought that Charles coveted the presidency for himself. As he recalled many years later:

> Camille Chamoun, who had been the president and evicted in 1958 when the country almost went through a catastrophe and the Marines landed to preserve law and order, was very anxious to be reelected. Of course, it was a) an impossibility and b) it would have sent the country into another tailspin. Among others was Charles Malik, who was of course well-known at this stage and who always was at prayer breakfasts at the White House. I am told that Charles Malik went around later saying that he was responsible for getting me kicked out of Lebanon, simply because I had not endorsed his candidacy for the presidency.[93]

Porter was neither the first nor the last American ambassador who did not care for Charles' high-handedness. But his story about Charles' interest in the presidency sounds rather implausible.

That July, Charles typed a fifty-page memorandum on the upcoming Lebanese elections, which he sent to the White House via Ambassador Porter. His concern was to secure American assistance for a candidate capable of defeating Fuad Chehab, whom he accused of presiding over a corrupt military dictatorship for the past twelve years (the last six via his protégé Charles Helou). Not surprisingly, Charles' preferred candidate was Camille Chamoun, who, he thought, could win the election if Chehab could be persuaded not to run, or if a certain number of deputies could be persuaded to vote for Chamoun. The White House, Charles believed, could easily bring about this result if it wanted to. He took care not to ask for money, although he noted that Chehab had greater financial resources at his disposal than Chamoun did. Henry Kissinger's executive secretary, Theodore Eliot, took the hint, noting in his cover letter to his boss that, as far as Charles was concerned, "U.S. funds might play a role."[94]

In the end, a dark horse candidate for the presidency, Suleiman Frangieh, won the necessary majority by a single vote, defeating Elias Sarkis, the Chehabist candidate. It was Charles' former protégé Ghassan Tueni, the publisher of *an-Nahar*, who persuaded the other Christian leaders to back Frangieh, the Maronite *Zaim* of northern Lebanon.[95] Frangieh was an unlikely statesman, a provincial man of the mountains with a well-armed private militia, the Marada Brigade. In an effort to shore up his support among Sunni Muslims, Frangieh asked Saeb Salam—who had led the opposition to the Chamoun-Malik regime in the late 1950s—to form a new government. Charles himself was too unpopular to hold office again, but he became an unofficial advisor to President Frangieh on relations with the United States, making several trips to Washington on Frangieh's behalf over the next six years. It must have seemed almost like old times, with a pro-American president in Baabda Palace and a pro-Lebanese president in the White House.

Soon after the election, Charles' old friend Hisham Sharabi arrived in Beirut, where he would spend the next year working at the PLO's Planning Center and teaching at the AUB. By now, Sharabi had left the PPS and embraced the Palestinian resistance movement, which he had been researching on-site during his summer vacations. In November, he was invited by a group of local expatriates, Americans for Justice in the Middle East, to address the question of a political settlement of the Israeli-Palestinian conflict. Sharabi explained that, "from the Palestinian point of view, Israel is a colonial enclave established, like all colonial settlements, by force of arms. It cannot be dealt with except by force." Curiously, he made no mention of the devastating defeat of the PLO at the hands of King Hussein's army that September. He did concede that "so long as Arab regimes are more interested in their own political survival than in fighting Zionist colonialism, the full impact of Palestinian resistance will not be felt." But the Palestinians, he noted, "take the long view. They see the world as changing, the *status quo* as subject to sudden radical transformation."[96]

Sharabi's turn to the Left all but ended his long-standing friendship with Charles Malik. In his memoir, Sharabi recalled a day in the fall of 1970 when Charles called him into his office in Bliss Hall and closed the door. "I've heard," Charles announced,

"that *Al-Sayyad* magazine says you're a Marxist. Is that true?" He then continued, "I'm concerned about you. We have to speak frankly on this subject. Marxism is something unreasonable. I don't believe it is possible you have taken this road."

"Strangely," Sharabi confessed,

it never occurred to me to ask why his thought tended to be metaphysical, or to say to him, "Your ideology is reactionary, and it is better for you to abandon it." From that time on, however, the old bond which held me to Charles Malik was broken, and it was no longer possible for me to justify much of a relationship with him.[97]

The following spring, Sharabi received a letter from President Kirkwood informing him that his teaching contract would not be renewed. One suspects that Charles Malik had a hand in this personnel decision, too.[98]

§

In mid-January 1971, Charles flew to California for a conference on the twenty-fifth anniversary of the founding of the United Nations. The conference, sponsored by the Hoover Institution at Stanford University, was opened by Ambassador Henry Cabot Lodge, Jr., President Nixon's new envoy to the Vatican. Charles knew Lodge quite well from their days at the United Nations, where Lodge had served for seven years following his defeat by John F. Kennedy in the 1952 Massachusetts senatorial race. After he and his running mate, Richard Nixon, were defeated in the 1960 presidential election, Lodge had served as Kennedy's ambassador to Vietnam, green-lighting the military coup that overthrew Ngo Dinh Diem in 1963. Reappointed to a second term by Lyndon Johnson, Lodge had presided over the escalation of the war in 1965 and 1966. That is why his Stanford speech was interrupted by anti-war protesters chanting "Fascist pig!" and "What did you do in Vietnam?"[99]

Charles' speech, entitled "The United Nations as an Ideological Battleground," seems not to have been disrupted. But he had some strong words about student radicals, warning,

> The greatest thing that America and the West must face up to now is the terrible moral rot that has crept into Western existence: radical hedonism in living, the worship of instruments and things, the terrible decline of reason, the quest of the moment, the rebellion against truth and value—especially in the universities—moral irresponsibility, the destruction of order and respect, the disappearance of shame and honor, the voluptuous flirtation with death itself.[100]

Even as Charles was issuing his dire warning at Stanford, however, students at his own university in Beirut were rebelling against the traditional curriculum, announcing the creation of a "Free University." As student leader Namir Cortas explained, the Free University was

> a kind of challenge to the regular university, for in effect we are saying that our interests and priorities are vastly different from the university's as decided by administrators and department heads, and therefore we will study what we deem important in spite of the program that they set for us.[101]

Namir happened to be the son of Michel and Mona Malik Cortas and the cousin of Edward Said's wife Mariam.

Namir Cortas was hardly the only AUB student to protest the administration's policies that spring. In March, the Student Council condemned David Rockefeller's upcoming visit to Beirut, where the banker hoped to see his friend Charles Malik.[102] In May, the Council called a strike to protest a tuition increase and demand student representation on faculty committees, occupying Bliss Hall (where Charles Malik had his office) and other campus buildings. As usual, Charles was one of the primary targets of the radicals, who denounced him as an American lackey. On May 18, when the Faculty Senate was meeting in Marquand House—the historic residence of the AUB presidents—students surrounded the building, refusing to let Charles and the other senators leave. At one point, as Charles' colleague David Gordon recalled, someone passed around a copy of Cavafy's "Waiting for the Barbarians" (one of Edward Said's favorite poems). The senators ended up spending the night in Marquand House, with Charles sleeping under a grand piano.[103]

In late November, the *Daily Star* carried an interview with Charles about student unrest at the AUB, subsequently reprinted in the *Congressional Record* at the request of Senator Hatfield. In response to the question of how to avert future uprisings, Charles replied, "By patience and love; by long-suffering and foresight; by understanding and forgiveness. . . ." More generally, he said, the AUB must be depoliticized. "I wish to assure the students and everybody categorically," he declared, "that the University has nothing to do with United States policy in the Middle East or elsewhere." When the friendly interviewer suggested that Charles himself was as qualified to be president of the AUB as any American, Charles agreed that presidents should be chosen on the basis of their qualifications, not their nationality. But he disavowed any personal interest in the position, admitting that "administrative jobs do not fit my temperament, principally because I covet my freedom above everything else."[104]

Having denied that the AUB had anything to do with US policy, Charles sat down and typed a four-page memo for Richard Nixon in which he described the AUB as "the most important single American interest in the Middle East." President Kirkwood, he averred, was "a splendid leader." But the AUB, he warned, was beset by a host of enemies, including current faculty and even trustees. These he declined to name, although he did report a rumor that the chairman of the board of trustees coveted the presidency for himself.[105] The man in question was Dr. Calvin Plimpton, who had just stepped down as president of Amherst College. Charles' suspicion of Plimpton was probably related to Plimpton's support for Dean Terry Prothro, who, like other liberals on the faculty, resented Kirkwood's intolerance of dissent.[106] There is no proof, however, that Charles' memo ever got to Nixon, who had more important things to worry about than campus politics at the AUB.

The following spring, Charles wrote again to Richard Nixon, warning that Lebanon could not absorb the Palestinian *fedayeen* and refugees and asking, once again, for US involvement in Lebanese elections. He had no way of knowing it, but the general election of April 1972 would be the last one in Lebanon during his lifetime, thanks to the civil war of 1975–90. He also complained that the United States wasn't doing enough to stop the spread of Communism in the region. The letter was supposed to arrive before Nixon's summit meeting with Leonid Brezhnev in Moscow at the end of May, but its delivery seems to have been delayed. Eventually, it found its way onto the desk of Henry Kissinger, who sent Nixon a summary that summer, telling his boss, "You know his thinking."[107] By that time, Nixon was looking forward to winning a second term in office at the expense of his Democratic challenger, Senator George McGovern, whose accusation of a whitewash in the Watergate investigation failed to sway Nixon's silent majority.

§

In September 1972, Palestinian terrorists calling themselves "Black September" massacred eleven members of the Israeli Olympic team in Munich. Two months later, Charles read a remarkable paper to the Westinghouse Developing Nations Advisory Committee in Pittsburgh. "The problem of the Fidayeen [sic]," he told the committee, "is the most important single problem with which Lebanon has to contend."

> You can bomb them as much as you like, as Israel keeps bombing their camps in Lebanon and Syria, or you can kill them as much as you like, as the German police did last September, or you can condemn them as much as you like, as everyone has done during the last few days, but you cannot extirpate them or suppress their

movement, until the root cause of the whole thing is identified, dealt with and remedied.

He went on to compare the Palestinian movement to Zionism itself. "Just as the Jewish diaspora of the last 19 centuries produced over the years a mystique and an urge that finally materialized itself in the state of Israel," he observed, "so the contemporary diaspora of the two or three million Palestinian Arabs is inducing a counter mystique and urge whose ultimate materialization cannot now be foreseen."[108]

Meanwhile, the Israelis were systematically assassinating PLO officials they blamed for the massacre in Munich. On the night of April 9–10, 1973, an Israeli hit team landed in Beirut and brazenly assassinated three PLO leaders, including AUB alumnus Kamal Nasir. That same April, Charles gave an interview to *an-Nahar* in which he drew a sharp contrast between Israeli progress and Arab backwardness. Calling Israel "a first-rate modern state," he noted that she had won the respect of hundreds of millions of non-Jews. But it was not Israel that he feared. "What I fear most," he explained,

> is ourselves rather than anything else. I fear the primitiveness of Arab thinking and Arab planning. I fear the Arabs' grudges against each other. . . . I fear the ornamental phrases which captivate the Arabs so much that they become their prisoners. I fear their impatience with everything that is not Arab, as though it were contaminated. I fear their mixing of religion with politics. I fear, too, the lack of conscious and responsible relationship between word and reality; the blind adherence to demagogy. . . .

Among those who took note of this remarkable interview was the Israeli journalist Nissim Rejwan, who immediately translated it into English for the Israeli monthly *New Outlook*, devoted to Israeli-Arab coexistence.[109]

For much of May, the AUB was closed because of fighting between the PLO and the Lebanese army. When classes were finally resumed at the end of the month, members of the League of Lebanese Students, known as *Rabita*, armed themselves with slingshots and attacked Palestinian students, who defended themselves with trays from the cafeteria. According to *Outlook*, the pro-Palestinian student weekly, the "Day of the Slingshots" marked a turning-point in *Rabita*'s history:

> The Lebanese League has always assumed a defensive posture deliberately, never [entering] a fight unless provoked. . . . It appears that a far more extreme right-wing element of a different mentality and leadership was the source [of the aggression], for *Outlook* does not recall that the Lebanese League ever prodded for violence, or that [Charles] Malik ever had a central role in student disturbances, or the administration has ever invited the police to beat up progressive students.

It's hard to imagine Charles Malik condoning student violence of any kind. But even *an-Nahar* reported that he had taken *Rabita*'s side in the confrontation.[110]

That summer, Charles escaped to Boulder, Colorado, where he taught at the Institute for the Study of Comparative Politics and Ideologies, an anti-Communist summer school directed by Dr. Edward Rozek.[111] But Charles had a more important reason for visiting the United States that summer, namely, to carry a secret message from President Frangieh to Washington. In late June, he met with Secretary of State William Rogers, warning him that the Palestinian *fedayeen*

> constitute the greatest and most permanent danger Lebanon faces. The fedayeen are better armed than the Lebanese army and are receiving arms from Syria and Iraq which are ultimately provided from Soviet and Chinese Communist sources.

Colonel Khadafi of Libya, he added, was funneling millions of petrodollars to various parties in Lebanon in an attempt to turn Lebanon into a Muslim state. When Charles asked how far the United States was prepared to go in order to guarantee Lebanon's security, Rogers was noncommittal. He noted, however, that the United States' improved relations with the Soviet Union and Communist China promised to make things safer for countries like Lebanon.[112]

Two weeks later, Charles met with National Security Advisor Henry Kissinger. According to a memo prepared by Kissinger's Middle East experts, Harold Saunders and William Quandt, Charles was likely to convey a request from President Frangieh to arm villagers who supported the government against the *fedayeen* and their Syrian allies.[113] Perhaps Saunders remembered Charles from the day of his graduation from Princeton in June 1952, when Charles had received an honorary doctorate.[114] Since then, Saunders had earned a PhD in American Studies from Yale, worked for the CIA as an analyst, and joined the staff of the National Security Council, eventually becoming the senior Middle East expert. As noted earlier, Saunders had met with Charles at least once before, when he was working for Walt Rostow in the Johnson administration. As for Quandt, he had written a doctoral dissertation on the Algerian revolution and was working for the RAND Corporation when he met Saunders, who asked him to come to Washington as his deputy.[115] No doubt Kissinger gave Charles the usual assurances about US support.

The month of December found Charles back in New York.[116] On December 5, he attended the annual dinner of the International League of the Rights of Man, at which Soviet dissident Andrei Sakharov was awarded a Human Rights Prize in absentia.[117] The following evening, he attended another dinner, this one sponsored by the National Institute of Social Sciences, which presented a Gold Medal to Elliot Richardson, who had resigned in October rather than obeying Nixon's order to fire Watergate Special Prosecutor Archibald Cox.[118] A few days later, Charles returned to the United Nations to celebrate the twenty-fifth anniversary of the Universal Declaration of Human Rights. There he was reunited with John Humphrey, who had served for twenty years as the director of the United Nations Human Rights Division. While Charles praised the international character of the Declaration, Humphrey pulled no punches:

> Men and women who are being denied their most basic rights can hardly be blamed if they do not share our enthusiasm for an event, which to them can only seem a colossal joke. It might have been more appropriate if the United Nations had dedicated this 25th anniversary of the adoption of the Universal Declaration

of Human Rights to the countless people whose rights it has not been able to protect.[119]

In private, Charles must have shared Humphrey's gloomy assessment of the UN's record on human rights.

In March and April 1974, a thousand striking students occupied the AUB campus and held it for over a month.[120] Afterwards, Charles tried to explain the situation to his friend Nelson Rockefeller, who had asked him to recommend names for his latest project, the Commission on Critical Choices for Americans.[121] The work of the Commission was scheduled to be completed in time for the US Bicentennial in 1976—and, more importantly, the presidential race, which Rockefeller hoped to enter. When Charles offered to serve on the Commission, Rockefeller invited him to submit a paper for the "Quality of Life" panel, scheduled to meet that June in Rockefeller's New York office. Not surprisingly, Charles defined quality of life in moral and spiritual terms. If America's quality of life has decayed, he said,

> it is because the Bible has been neglected; and if you seriously want quality of life at its truest and deepest, restore by 1985 or by the year 2000 love and reverence for the Bible into the heart of America; for without the Bible America would never have come into being, neither would it have flourished and endured.[122]

Some of the other panelists objected to Charles' analysis, however, arguing that it was improper for the Commission to concern itself with moral and spiritual issues.[123]

On September 1, *an-Nahar* carried an article by Charles on American policy in the Middle East. On the subject of the Palestinians, Charles opined that "as long as Saudi Arabia, Israel, and America do not agree to the elimination of Jordan, the Palestinians will have to come to an agreement with King Hussein on their fate." But the Palestinian problem will never be solved, he continued, until its existential dimension is admitted:

> Faced with their distress, their bitterness and their revolution, I feel that I myself am the cause. If this bitterness, distress, and revolution continues, there can be no peace in the Middle East, and quite possibly no peace in the world. Regardless of any cheap threat to peace, the mere fact of their homelessness is a challenge to my humanity and the humanity of every human being. . . . As long as the Americans, Arabs, and Israelis are not profoundly ashamed as human beings to see the Palestinians tormented, homeless, wretched and desperate, we are all liars and hypocrites.[124]

No doubt Charles' feeling of shame was genuine. Even so, he was not about to sit by and watch his own home overrun by the homeless Palestinians.

A week later, Charles wrote a letter of congratulations to Nelson Rockefeller, who had been nominated as vice president by President Gerald Ford, Richard Nixon's successor. Among other things, Charles mentioned his recent article in *an-Nahar*, denounced the dominant philosophies in American universities, and complained about the sorry state of America's military after Vietnam. But he ended on a prophetic note, telling

Rockefeller that the world was waiting for the fundamental "Word of America" to be spoken.[125] The following week, he wrote another letter of congratulations, this time to William J. Baroody, Jr., whom Ford had decided to retain as director of the Office of Public Liaison.[126] With Lebanon on the brink of civil war, Charles needed his friends in the Ford administration to facilitate his continued access to the White House.

§

In November 1974, Charles hosted a symposium at the Goethe Institute in Beirut to commemorate the eighty-fifth birthday of Martin Heidegger. Testifying to Heidegger's profound influence on his own life and thought, he recalled how Der Meister would dwell on a single proposition in a text for hours, bringing his knowledge of the entire history of Western philosophy to bear upon it. Those moments of "dwelling," Charles explained, "constituted the most valuable experience I had under Heidegger. They were moments of sheer joy. In them time simply stopped. . . ." But his primary purpose that evening was to define the limits of Heidegger's philosophy. Heidegger, he explained, had set out to "detheologize theology," which left him unable to answer three of humanity's perennial questions: *why* we exist, *which* possibilities of existence to choose, and *how* to become what we want to be. Charles held out hope, however, that Heidegger would return to the Christian faith before his death. "If in God's providence this should happen," he concluded, "then we would have one of the greatest events of the twentieth century, perhaps even more important than the event of Solzhenitsyn!"[127]

The following January, Charles hosted a meeting at his home on the subject of Lebanese émigrés.[128] Among those present at the meeting was Bashir Gemayel, the younger son of Phalange leader Pierre Gemayel, who had trained as a lawyer (including a brief period of study in the United States in the early 1970s) but was also a leading figure in the party's militia. There was bad blood between Bashir and the Palestinian *fedayeen*, who had kidnapped him back in 1970 following a Phalangist attack on a *fedayeen* convoy as it drove through the village of Kahhala.[129] According to Shafiq al-Hout, the PLO's Beirut representative, a Lebanese newsman had photographic evidence that Bashir was one of the gunmen in Kahhala. When Bashir was subsequently kidnapped by the *fedayeen*, Interior Minister Kamal Jumblatt asked Hout, who knew the Gemayel family, to negotiate his release.[130] It was a humiliation Bashir would never forget.

That same January, Charles received a visit from a New York rabbi, Israel Mowshowitz, who was touring the Middle East, talking to Arabs as well as Jews. As Mowshowitz wrote in a published account of his trip, Charles

> welcomed me into his beautiful home, situated on top of one of the hills overlooking Beirut, with true Arab hospitality. He was not impressed with the PLO and the manner in which it was conducting the affairs of the Palestinians. "They are now in a state of euphoria," he said. "Everyone is courting Arafat since his appearance at the United Nations. Everyone is running after him." This, he was convinced, would not last for long because of the very nature of the PLO program, which had nothing positive to offer by way of a solution of the Middle East problem.

Arafat sent out feelers to meet him a number of times, but he had declined. It was too early, he maintained, to accept Arafat as the ultimate spokesman to the Palestinians.[131]

One wishes that Charles had consented to meet with Arafat. It would not have averted the terrible civil war that was about to erupt, but his nephew Edward, for one, would have appreciated the gesture.

A week or two later, Charles received another Jewish visitor from New York—Norman Cousins, the veteran editor of the *Saturday Review*, who was also touring the Middle East, asking Arab and Israeli leaders about the prospects for peace. When Cousins asked Charles what he saw as the essentials of a durable peace, Charles replied that "the main essential for peace—indeed, the quintessential—is the need for the Arab world to accept Israel's existence." But a second essential, he added, is that "Israel must be prepared to pay a steep price," starting with the return of the entire Sinai to Egypt. In the case of the Golan Heights, Charles believed that internationalization offered the best chance for peace between Israel and Syria. But the hardest problem of all, he confessed, was the Palestinians. Echoing the PLO's new line, he opined that Israel must be prepared for "a separate Palestinian state carved out of the fertile area contiguous to Jordan." Cousins came away impressed by Charles' intelligence and sense of justice. "Charles Malik," he decided, "would be an ideal peace-maker."[132]

That February, Charles wrote a remarkable piece for *Monday Morning*, Beirut's English-language weekly. Suppressing the private reservations he had voiced to Rabbi Mowshowitz, he called on the US government to "deal directly and openly" with the PLO:

> The Arab states and most of the countries of the world have recognized the Palestine Liberation Organization as representing the Palestinians. The next indicated step appears to me to be for the United States to recognize openly and formally the Palestine Liberation Organization and to enter into active formal discussion with it on all aspects of the Arab-Israeli conflict.

The United States, he added, should not impose conditions on the PLO before taking this next step:

> To ask [the Palestinians] now to change their declared will before America can recognize and deal with their representatives seems to me to be unnecessary. Such change can come, if it comes at all, only after and as a result of recognition and negotiation.[133]

A few weeks later, Charles sent a copy of this statement to Vice President Rockefeller, explaining that the moderates were now in charge of the PLO.[134] The following month, Rockefeller thanked Charles, adding that he had shared Charles' article with Henry Kissinger.[135] By that time, alas, the PLO and the Christian militias had turned Beirut into a battle zone.

4

Edward Said: The Education of a Secular Intellectual, 1935–67

In the autumn of 1935, as Charles Malik was beginning his studies with Martin Heidegger in Freiburg, Edward Wadie Said was born in his uncle Boulos' house in Jerusalem. His father, Wadie Ibrahim Said, was a native of the Holy City who, on the eve of the First World War, had immigrated to the United States in order to escape the Ottoman draft and seek his fortune. There he had remained for the better part of a decade, anglicizing his name to "William," fighting with the American Expeditionary Force in France, and earning US citizenship. It was his widowed mother who persuaded him to return to Jerusalem after the war and enter into a business partnership with his cousin Boulos Said—the founder of the Palestine Educational Company, a bookshop located at Jaffa Gate—who had married Wadie's sister Nabiha. After a few years in Jerusalem, Wadie had gone off to Cairo to open an Egyptian branch of the family business, the Standard Stationery Company, which soon prospered under his American-style management.[1]

Edward's mother, Hilda Musa Said, was the daughter of Rev. Shukri Musa, a Texas-educated Baptist minister from Safad, and Munira Badr, the daughter of Rev. Youssef Badr of Shweir. In 1928, Hilda had accompanied her cousins Eva—the future wife of Charles Malik—and Lily Badr to Beirut, where they studied together at the American School for Girls and, a few years later, at the new American Junior College for Women. Following the sudden death of her father, however, the family's finances did not permit Hilda to continue her education in Beirut. Instead, she returned to Palestine and married Wadie Said in a match arranged by Nabiha Said and her friend Mrs. Marmura, the wife of Rev. Elias Marmura, Canon of St. Paul's Church in Jerusalem.[2] After a honeymoon in Europe, Hilda moved to Cairo with Wadie.

Following Edward's birth, the Saids relocated to Zamalek, a leafy, cosmopolitan neighborhood where many of Cairo's wealthy Jewish and European residents lived. In the early 1940s, they took an apartment in the New Grotto House at 1 Aziz Osman Street, across the street from the Nile Aquarium Grotto, where Edward and his sisters played. Another resident of the New Grotto House was the Francophone poet Edmond Jabès, whom Edward would surely have mentioned in *Out of Place* had he remembered him.[3] Perhaps Edward's sisters played with the Jabès girls, who were the same age. Just down the street from the New Grotto House stood the Villa Goodman, the home of Aaron ("Alec") and Victoria Alexander. The Alexanders were ardent Zionists, hosting receptions for Chaim Weizmann and other visiting dignitaries. Their daughter Eileen was a close friend of future Israeli ambassador Aubrey Eban, whom she had met at Cambridge. Eban's future wife, Suzy Ambache, lived in the Villa Mosseri, on the same street as the Villa Goodman.[4]

In the fall of 1941, Edward was enrolled in the Gezira Preparatory School, a British Council school on Aziz Osman Street, where his classmates included various Mosseris and other Cairene Jews. The following spring, his first year at GPS ended abruptly when, with Rommel's Afrika Korps threatening Cairo, the Saids piled into Wadie's black Plymouth and escaped to Palestine. They rented a summer house in Ramallah, the home town of the Nasir family. As previously noted, the two families were related by marriage: Hilda Said's oldest brother, Dr. Munir Musa, had married Latifeh Nasir, the daughter of Rev. Butros Nasir. Kamal Nasir was also in Ramallah that summer, writing to Charles Malik about the failing grade he had received in his course that spring. The Saids remained in Palestine until November, when Montgomery's victory over Rommel at the second battle of El Alamein made it safe to return to Cairo.[5]

It was in Cairo during the war years, Edward recalled, that he first became aware of Charles Malik, who had married Aunt Eva in the summer of 1941. Starting in the summer of 1943, he also saw the Maliks in Dhour el Shweir, along with various other Badr relatives and Beirut friends. In *Out of Place*, Edward painted a rather bleak picture of Shweir, claiming that he had always felt out of place in the Christian hamlet. What he neglected to mention is that Shweir was the home of Antun Saadeh and the Partie Populaire Syrien. Admittedly, the PPS had been forced underground during the war years, with the party banned and its founder in exile. In any case, Edward was too young to know the politics of his neighbors in Shweir, such as the family of Anis Makdisi, whose eldest son, Nadim, was a fellow traveler, if not a member, of the PPS.[6] Another Makdisi— Anis' nephew Bahij, a well-known structural engineer—had reportedly designed the party's swastika-like emblem, the *zaubaa*, at the request of Saadeh himself.[7]

Although Wadie Said must have known about the PPS, he was devoted to a very different organization: the Young Men's Christian Association. In 1944, he served on the Management Committee of the Cairo Central YMCA, along with Uncle Charles' old friends James Quay and Naguib Kelada. Another member of the committee was W. Wendell Cleland, a veteran administrator at the American University in Cairo, who later taught with Uncle Charles at American University in Washington.[8] Edward did not mention Quay or Cleland in *Out of Place*, but he did name two of Cleland's AUC colleagues—John Badeau, Dean of Arts and Sciences, and Worth Howard, Chairman of the English Department—as friends of his father's. Both Quay and Badeau preached on occasion at the American Mission Church in Ezbekiah, where the Saids worshipped on Sunday evenings.[9] As for Naguib Kelada, Edward recalled the "phenomenal" voice of his daughter Isis, who sang at the services of the American Church.[10]

The Saids returned to Dhour in the summer of 1944, as did the Maliks. Afterwards, Wadie Said wrote to Charles regarding a matter they had discussed in Dhour, namely, a scholarship to the AUB he had offered to endow in his father's name.[11] Wadie wanted the scholarship to go to a Protestant or Greek Orthodox student from Palestine, but Charles, it turned out, had already nominated one of his own philosophy students, Raymond Karam, a Maronite from Lebanon. When Charles wrote back to apologize, Wadie graciously agreed to the selection of Karam, who, inspired by Charles' example, was eager to pursue graduate study at Harvard with his classmate Ghassan Tueni, another Malik protégé.[12] Once enrolled at Harvard, however, Karam met Fakhri Maalouf, fell under the influence of Father Feeney, and abandoned his studies, becoming one of the brothers of the St. Benedict Center in Still River, Massachusetts.[13]

Meanwhile, Wadie Said's business continued to prosper thanks to his connection with a number of American firms, most notably the Royal Typewriter Company, for whom he was designing an Arabic typewriter. When Charles Malik was chosen to represent Lebanon at the United Nations in the spring of 1945, Wadie saw an opportunity to put his wife's relative to work. In June, he asked Charles to meet with the Royal people in New York regarding any corrections the typewriter might need prior to production. He also let Charles know that the Saids would be in Dhour in August, staying at the Hotel Kassouf, a watering hole for wealthy Arab and European tourists.[14] The hotel made quite an impression on young Edward, who, fifty years later, wrote a piece about Lebanon's grand hotels entitled "Paradise Lost" for *Travel & Leisure*.[15] By that time, alas, the Kassouf lay in ruins, having been bombarded repeatedly during Lebanon's endless civil war.

In the fall of 1946, Edward was enrolled in the sixth grade at the new Cairo School for American Children (CSAC), which had opened its doors in 1945 thanks to the initiative of the American consul in Cairo, Ralph Miller, who procured the necessary funds from American oil companies. As Edward recalled in *Out of Place*, it was the first time he had seen so many Americans, and he did his best to fit in, going so far as to conceal his perfect command of Cairene Arabic. In addition to Miller's own children, Edward's schoolmates at CSAC included a number of faculty kids from the AUC, notably the children of John Badeau, who had recently become president of the university, and Worth Howard, who had replaced Badeau as dean of arts and sciences. The sixth-grade class was taught by a Miss Clark, whom Edward remembered fondly as "the first great martinet and sadist of my life."[16]

The following summer, the Saids relocated to Dhour as usual. Did Edward know that the Parti Populaire Syrien maintained a camp in Dhour, or that Antun Saadeh spent the summer of 1947 there, dodging the authorities? One young man who did know was Hisham Sharabi, who, after graduating from the AUB that June, went up to Dhour to join Saadeh's entourage. Sharabi had been accepted for graduate work in philosophy at the University of Chicago, but he decided to delay his departure so that he could sit at the leader's feet for the rest of the year.[17] Also in Dhour that summer was Fayez Sayegh, who spent the month of August writing an essay entitled "A Call from the Depths: Reflections on Man and Existence." Like Sharabi, Sayegh had been accepted—thanks to a recommendation from Uncle Charles—for graduate study at an American university (Georgetown). Unlike the worshipful Sharabi, however, Sayegh was troubled by Saadeh's autocratic manner and did not hesitate to criticize the leader to his face. Before the year was out, Sayegh had quit—or been expelled by—the party.[18]

§

Rather than returning to Cairo that fall, the Saids went to Jerusalem, where Edward joined his cousins Albert and Robert—Nabiha Said's twin boys—at St. George's School.

One of his teachers there was Michael Marmura, whose father, Rev. Elias Marmura, had married Wadie and Hilda in 1932 and baptized Edward in 1937. Another teacher was H. P. Boyadjian, a survivor of the Armenian massacres of 1915, whose son Haig was Edward's age. Both Michael Marmura and Haig Boyadjian would later vouch for Edward when Justus Reid Weiner questioned whether he had ever been a student at St. George's.[19] The senior Arabic teacher at St. George's was Khalil Beidas, a Russian-educated man of letters and early Palestinian nationalist, whose son Yusef had worked at the Palestine Educational Company and stood as best man in Wadie and Hilda's wedding. All Edward knew of Khalil Beidas at the time, however, was that he was his father's second cousin—and that they played backgammon together for hours at a stretch.[20]

That November, rioting broke out in Jerusalem in the wake of the United Nations resolution calling for the partition of Palestine, which Uncle Charles had adamantly opposed. The Jewish Agency decided to accept the resolution, knowing that the Arab Higher Committee, backed by the Arab League, would reject it out of hand. Meanwhile, the British government had announced that it would withdraw from Palestine by May 15, 1948. Just before Christmas, with both sides preparing for war, Wadie and Hilda Said decided that it was time to return to Cairo. In the months to come, they would be joined by refugees from both sides of the family, including Nabiha Said and her children. The last to leave the family home in Talbiyya was Nabiha's oldest son Yousif, who moved with his pregnant wife to a rented house in Baqa, bringing his hunting rifle with him. In April, after the Deir Yassin massacre, they escaped to Lebanon, leaving a relative in charge of the house. When the Haganah broke in a few weeks later, they found Yousif's rifle, threw the relative into prison, and claimed the house. That, at least, is what Yousif told Edward many years later.[21]

In July, with the battle for Palestine still raging between cease-fires, the Said family sailed to New York—Edward's first visit to the city he would later call home. Also sailing to New York that month were Wadie's widowed sister-in-law Emily Said and her children, who were starting a new life in America following the death of Wadie's older brother Assaad. As for Wadie Said, he was scheduled for kidney surgery at Columbia-Presbyterian Hospital, where a recent graduate of the AUB medical school, Dr. Fouad Sabra, was in residency. Sabra was all but engaged to Hilda Said's cousin Ellen Badr, the youngest sister of Eva Malik, whom he would marry the following summer. In *Out of Place*, Edward recalled having lunch with Dr. Sabra at the Cedars of Lebanon on 29th Street before his father's surgery.[22] He made no mention of seeing Uncle Charles and Aunt Eva, although Wadie had written to Charles prior to their departure for New York.[23]

The following summer, Edward was confirmed as a member of the Church of England and took his First Communion in All Saints' Cathedral in Cairo. In *Out of Place*, he recalled his disappointment after the ceremony:

> My hope that I might gain insight into the nature of things or a better apprehension of the Anglican God proved fanciful. The hot and cloudless Cairo sky, my aunt Nabiha's disproportionately large hat perched on her small head and body, the placidly flowing Nile immediately in front of us in its undisturbed immensity as we stood on the cathedral esplanade: all these were as I was, exactly the same.[24]

Shortly thereafter, the Saids left for Dhour, where Edward was tutored in geometry prior to matriculating at the new Cairo branch of Victoria College. The famous parent branch of VC, located in Alexandria, drew students from across the Arab world, including the future King Hussein of Jordan and the future billionaire Adnan Khashoggi. But the Cairo campus also boasted its share of achievers, such as Zaid al-Rifai, a future prime minister of Jordan, and Gilbert de Botton, the future London financier, whose mother was the Jewish Agency's top spy in Egypt until her arrest and deportation.[25]

In the fall of 1950, the Cairo branch of Victoria College moved to a new, larger campus. That was when the trouble started for Edward. The older Arabic-speaking boys began to bully him, demanding that he write their English exams for them. Then, after he and his classmates defied their English teacher one day, Edward was sent home by the headmaster, Mr. Griffiths, whom he described in *Out of Place* as his bête noire. After a whipping from his father and a two-week suspension, he was allowed to return to school. But Griffiths made it clear that Edward could not expect a recommendation to Oxford or Cambridge. Under the circumstances, Wadie Said thought an American boarding school would be the best option for his delinquent son, as it would allow Edward to establish residency in the United States. For advice, he turned to John Badeau, who recommended the Mount Hermon School, a private Christian academy in Northfield, Massachusetts, whose new headmaster, Howard Rubendall, was a former AUC instructor.[26]

§

In the summer of 1951, Edward and his parents made the long journey to Northfield, sailing from Southampton to New York. As Edward recalled in *Out of Place*, his mother protested the whole way. "I hate America and Americans," she declared. "Must we take the boy there? You know he'll never come back." For his part, Wadie was delighted to be returning to his beloved America; he was even thinking of buying a house there. From New York, the family traveled to Princeton to visit acquaintances and to Washington to see the Maliks. Uncle Charles had gone to San Francisco to sign the peace treaty with Japan, but Aunt Eva invited the Saids to stay with her in the Lebanese minister's residence near Embassy Row, offering to serve as Edward's guardian while he was at Mount Hermon.[27]

By his own account, Edward's first year at Mount Hermon was a lonely one, although Howard Rubendall did his best to make him feel welcome. He did manage to make a few friends among his peers, notably Tony Glockler, who had grown up in Beirut and spoke French and Arabic as well as English. Tony's English father Henry was the treasurer of the Presbyterian mission in Lebanon and the business manager of the mission's printing press; his American mother Annie was a teacher at the American School for Girls, where Hilda Said and Eva Malik had studied in the late 1920s.[28] Whether Edward knew that Tony's great-grandfather, Rev. Samuel Jessup, had ordained his own great-grandfather, Rev. Youssef Badr, is doubtful.[29] Edward also formed a friendship of sorts with Neil Sheehan—the future Vietnam War correspondent—who, as the son of an Irish Catholic farmer, was another ambitious outsider at Mount Hermon.[30]

During the holidays, Edward did not go to Washington to visit Aunt Eva and Uncle Charles, who were away in Paris for the UN General Assembly. Instead, he stayed with Aunt Emily, his father's sister-in-law, in Queens. Emily Said and her family attended the Syrian Protestant Church in Bay Ridge, whose Princeton-trained pastor, Rev. K. A. Bishara, had lobbied Congress to admit refugees from Palestine after the *Nakba*.[31] Bishara's associate and successor at the church was Rev. Dr. Edward Jurji of Princeton, Uncle Charles' old classmate from the AUB, who had also spoken out on Palestine, charging that US support for Israel was undermining Muslim trust in America—trust that had been built up, he said, by generations of Christian missionaries.[32]

Back in Cairo, meanwhile, revolution was in the air. On January 26, 1952—a day remembered as "Black Saturday"—hundreds of foreign-owned businesses in Cairo, including Wadie Said's Standard Stationery Company, were torched during an anti-British riot in which both the Communists and the Muslim Brothers played a role. Edward learned of the riot two days later from Howard Rubendall, who had spoken with Wadie Said by phone. The next day, Edward picked up a copy of the *Boston Globe* and was startled to see the name "William A. Said" in a story about American properties burned by the mob.[33] In Washington, Kim Roosevelt was already meeting with Allen Dulles, the deputy director of the CIA, about a plan to save King Farouk, whom he had befriended during the war. According to his deputy Miles Copeland, however, Roosevelt's trip to Cairo that February persuaded him that Egypt could not be saved as long as Farouk was on the throne. Roosevelt subsequently turned to Colonel Gamal Abdel Nasser and his cadre of "Free Officers" as the best hope for Egypt.[34]

That summer, the Free Officers overthrew the Egyptian government, deposed King Farouk, and installed General Muhammad Naguib as president and prime minister of Egypt. The evidence suggests that the Americans had known that a military coup was in the works and welcomed it, but did not plan it or participate in it.[35] Uncle Charles, too, welcomed the coup, having long since dismissed King Farouk as a fool, as he had confided to Mrs. Roosevelt. As for the Saids, they had already left Cairo for Dhour by the time of the coup. As Jean Said Makdisi recalled, her parents followed the news from Egypt that summer with mixed feelings, fearing another Black Saturday but anticipating a new era of clean government.[36] King or no king, Edward longed to return to Cairo with his family instead of going back to Mount Hermon for his senior year. He spent his last night in Dhour in his parents' bedroom, begging them not to send him back to Northfield.[37]

In the spring of 1953, Edward made the curious decision to attend Princeton rather than Harvard. In *Out of Place*, he attributed his choice to a pleasant visit he and his parents had made in 1951 to the Princeton home of the relatives of some Dhour el Shweir neighbors.[38] He did not identify their hosts, but Princeton was full of people, both American and Arab, who had lived in Cairo or Beirut. James Quay, Wadie Said's old associate at the Cairo YMCA, was now vice president of the Princeton Theological Seminary. Edward Jurji, whom Edward could have met at his aunt's church in Bay Ridge, taught comparative religion at the seminary. Philip Hitti was still teaching in the Near Eastern Studies Program, along with his son-in-law, Bayly Winder, who had met Uncle Charles at the AUB during the Second World War.[39] Bayard Dodge, the former president of the AUB, had retired to Princeton, where he lectured in Near Eastern

Studies. And William Eddy's son, Rev. William Eddy, Jr., was Princeton's Episcopalian chaplain.

After his graduation from Mount Hermon, Edward and his father returned to Cairo. Also traveling to Cairo that summer were three former colleagues in the Counter Intelligence Corps, sent by the CIA's Kim Roosevelt to liaise with the Free Officers who now ran Egypt. They were James Eichelberger, a former ad man with the J. Walter Thompson agency, operating under diplomatic cover; Miles Copeland, who had taken a position with the management consulting firm Booz, Allen & Hamilton; and Frank Kearns, a reporter for CBS News. The Copeland family rented a villa in Maadi, where the older children attended the CSAC, as Edward had done some years earlier.[40] Meanwhile, Frank Kearns and his wife leased a luxurious apartment in Zamalek, where the three couples gathered regularly to socialize and, in the eyes of the Egyptians, conspire.[41] The apartment happened to be in the new Badrawi Buildings on Saleh Ayoub Street, just two blocks from the New Grotto House, where the Saids lived.[42]

§

In August 1953, Edward arrived in Princeton for Freshman Week. Also moving to Princeton that summer was Michael Marmura, Edward's former mathematics teacher at St. George's School in Jerusalem. Marmura had recently graduated from the University of Wisconsin in Madison, where the Saids had visited him in the summer of 1951, prior to enrolling Edward at Mount Hermon.[43] Now Marmura was planning to study philosophy at Princeton. No doubt Edward's parents were delighted that Marmura, the son of their old Jerusalem friends, would be in town to keep an eye on their formerly wayward son. However, Marmura left Princeton after just one year and transferred to the University of Michigan, where he earned a PhD in Near Eastern Studies under George Hourani, the brother of Albert and Cecil. He would go on to enjoy a long academic career at the University of Toronto, specializing in medieval Islamic philosophy.[44]

Edward's arrival in Princeton coincided with a Colloquium on Islamic Culture organized by Bayard Dodge and cosponsored by the US State Department, which was attempting to cultivate anti-Communist Muslims. To that end, Dodge and his colleagues brought a number of prominent Islamists to Princeton and Washington—notably Said Ramadan, the son-in-law of Hassan al-Banna, the founder of the Muslim Brotherhood, which may well have been responsible for the burning of Wadie Said's stores the previous year. Among the American scholars attending the colloquium was John Badeau, who had recommended Mount Hermon to the Saids. Since then, Badeau had left Cairo and moved to New York to head the Near East Foundation, one of the charities founded by the Dodge family. As for Uncle Charles, he was listed in the program as a "visiting scholar," although he seems not to have attended the Princeton portion of the colloquium.[45]

On New Year's Eve, Edward arrived at the Malik residence in Washington for a brief stay. According to Eva Malik's calendar, two of her Badr relatives arrived from New York a few days later, probably to attend to her during the birth of her first and only child, Habib Charles Malik. Meanwhile, Uncle Charles was busy writing letters on behalf of Samir Makdisi, the younger son of his colleague Anis Makdisi, whose summer home in Dhour was not far from the Said house. At the time, Edward's sister Jean—Samir's future wife—was just thirteen years old. Samir, who had just graduated from the AUB, was hoping to do graduate work at Harvard or another American university and needed a scholarship. One organization to which Charles wrote on Samir's behalf was American Friends of the Middle East, which was represented in Washington by Dorothea Seelye Franck, the daughter of Laurens Seelye, his old AUB professor.[46]

Returning to Princeton for his second semester, Edward enrolled in a course on the philosophy of art taught by Arthur Szathmary, who had hosted Uncle Charles at a Princeton philosophy forum back in 1950. The *Daily Princetonian* for February 17, 1954, published a front-page photograph of Szathmary seated with his students—including one who must be Edward—on the steps of a campus building, enjoying a rare February heat wave. Did Edward enroll in Szathmary's course on the recommendation of Uncle Charles? Did Szathmary know that Edward was Charles Malik's nephew? Whatever the case, the provocative Szathmary quickly became one of Edward's favorite teachers. As he wrote in *Out of Place*, "For a number of disaffected outsiders, Szathmary came to represent, and even embody, the intellectual life." The other Princeton professor who made a lasting impression on Edward was R. P. Blackmur, with his "sheer genius in uncovering layer after layer of meaning in modern poetry and fiction (despite his gnarled and frequently incomprehensible language)."[47]

In the summer of 1954, Edward joined his family for their usual vacation in Dhour. At a new tennis club near the Hotel Kassouf, he met the Emad sisters, Eva and Nelly, the daughters of a wealthy soap manufacturer from Tanta, north of Cairo. Like the Saids, the Emads were *Shawam*—Northerners or Syrians—having moved to Egypt from their native village near Shweir.[48] Back in Egypt, meanwhile, US Information Service libraries in Alexandria and Cairo were set on fire, along with the Rivoli Cinema, where Edward had heard the Berlin Philharmonic in 1951. Once the saboteurs were apprehended, President Nasser announced that they were Zionist terrorists whose purpose was to disrupt negotiations over the Suez Canal and sow dissension between Egypt and the United States. In the same speech, Nasser denounced all those who opposed the Suez agreement he had concluded with the British in late July, naming the Muslim Brothers and the Communists as well as the Zionists.[49]

In September, Edward returned to Princeton for his sophomore year. By chance, he met a new graduate student who would become his political "guru"—Ibrahim Abu-Lughod. In a tribute published after Ibrahim's death, Edward recalled their first encounter at the campus ticket office where he was working:

> One especially hot, slow afternoon in September a young man with a brisk manner, piercing blue-green eyes and a heavy accent came in, asked for tickets, showed me his identity card quickly ... and then, as he was leaving, turned and asked me what I had said my name was. When I told him again he came all the way back into the office and asked me where I was from. I said something like I'm *from* Egypt now, but formerly I was from Palestine. His face lit up: I'm from Palestine too, he said, from Jaffa.[50]

Like many of Jaffa's residents, Ibrahim had fled in 1948 and found himself unable to return home. He ended up in Chicago, where he married a University of Chicago graduate named Janet Lippman and attended the University of Illinois before moving to Princeton.

Eva Malik's calendar indicates that Edward and his sister Rosemarie, a freshman at Bryn Mawr College in Philadelphia, came to Washington for a visit in early January 1955.[51] It must have been during this visit that Edward discussed Egyptian politics with Uncle Charles. As he recalled in *Out of Place*:

> [Malik] had an amused contempt for Princeton and me, but he was willing to talk to me at quite some length (conversation, except for an occasional question from me, wasn't really possible). Later I understood that Nasser's approach to the Soviet Union coupled with his Islamic faith were the real problem for Malik; hidden beneath the discourse of statistics and demographic trends were Communism and Islam. I was unable finally to sustain any kind of counterargument: Malik's manner kept reminding me that I was only a sophomore, whereas he lived in the real world, dealt with great people, was so much more elevated in vision, etc.[52]

In fact, Nasser's approach to the Soviets would not become known until later in the year; in early 1955, he was still negotiating with Kim Roosevelt and the Americans. But it is likely that Uncle Charles was beginning to cool on Nasser, who had recently removed President Naguib from office and placed him under house arrest.[53]

At the beginning of June, Edward returned to Cairo for the summer. Thus he missed the annual commencement exercises of the Princeton Theological Seminary, which featured a sermon by Uncle Charles on "The Peace of Man and the Peace of God." "Peace," Uncle Charles opined at one point, "is not worth the ticket unless the civilization which germinated in the Mediterranean and developed and matured in the West is able at least to hold fast to its fundamental persuasions." For that reason, he continued, "the peoples of this civilization, which comprises the Christian and Moslem worlds, must rediscover and realize the natural bonds of unity among them."[54] To say that "the natural bonds of unity" between the Christian and the Muslim worlds must be "rediscovered" implied that they had been lost. It would be up to the beneficiaries of Mediterranean-Western civilization, such as Edward Said, to reforge those bonds.

The following April, one of Edward's future *bêtes noires*, Professor Bernard Lewis of the School of Oriental and African Studies in London, came to Princeton at the invitation of the Program in Near Eastern Studies. Lewis was spending the year in Los Angeles as a visiting professor at UCLA. In December, he had contributed a series to the *Los Angeles Times* in the wake of the Soviet-Egyptian arms deal of 1955, charging the Arab lobby with inconsistency in condemning Western colonialism while ignoring the Soviet conquest of Muslim lands in Central Asia.[55] The theme of Lewis' talk at Princeton, "The Muslim Discovery of Europe," was of considerable interest to Edward's friend Ibrahim Abu-Lughod, whose dissertation was entitled *The Arab Rediscovery of Europe*. It is tempting to think that Edward, too, heard Lewis for the first time that evening. Alas, Lewis' lecture conflicted with a poetry reading by Robert Frost, which probably held more interest for Edward and his literary friends.[56]

Later that month, Edward's classmate Ralph Schoenman—a radical thorn in the side of conservative Princeton—arranged for the accused spy and convicted perjurer Alger Hiss to address the Whig-Clio Society. The announcement of Hiss' lecture launched a wave of protest that rippled all the way to Washington. Senator H. Alexander Smith of New Jersey—Uncle Charles' old friend from the Oxford Group—accused Whig-Clio of bringing "discredit and negative publicity on Princeton's good name."[57] On campus, Princeton's contentious Roman Catholic chaplain, Father Hugh Halton, organized a counter-lecture by veteran red-baiter Willard Edwards, the Washington correspondent of the *Chicago Tribune*. Halton's intervention, in turn, drew criticism from his fellow chaplains, including Rev. William Eddy, Jr., who regretted "that the lively debate about issues should degenerate into the judgment of persons."[58] It was not the last time Edward would see Alger Hiss. Many years later, he would welcome Hiss to Columbia for an all-day teach-in on "The New Cold War."[59]

§

In the summer of 1956, as Edward and Eva Emad were declaring their love in Dhour, President Nassar nationalized the Suez Canal Company and closed the canal to Israeli shipping. Once Edward got back to Princeton, he tried to interest his fellow students in the Suez crisis. His classmate Thomas Kean—the future governor of New Jersey and chairman of the 9-11 Commission—remembered following the crisis at Princeton's Campus Club, of which Edward was president.[60] In early October, Edward contributed a column entitled "Nasser and his Canal" to the *Daily Princetonian*, defending the Egyptian leader as "a sincere, dedicated (if inexperienced) man." He also attempted to explain the Arab view of the United States to his fellow students. "The U. S.," he pointed out, "is viewed as Israel's chief abettor in that state's struggle against the Arabs."[61] Two weeks after Edward's column appeared, the Israeli army marched into Gaza and the Sinai as British and French planes bombed Egyptian airfields.

At the time of the Suez War, Edward's sister Jean was in her final year at the English School in Cairo. "Though the attacks were mostly on the Canal area," she recalled,

> air-raid sirens wailed even in Cairo. At night, we had blackouts. As in those earlier times in my childhood—the Second World War and the Palestine War—we sat in the corridors during air raids, and Joyce, who specialized in this reaction, vomited regularly.

After the war, the English School was nationalized, along with Victoria College and other English and French interests in Egypt. As Jean recalled:

> Our old teachers were ordered out of the country: my friends and I went on a round of farewell visits. . . . Those we visited did not express the slightest regret that Britain, among others, had invaded Egypt, the country in which they had lived and worked all those many years.

Eventually, the school reopened as the *Madrassat al-Nasr* ("Victory School"), with Egyptian teachers in place of the departed British.[62]

That same autumn, a Protestant minister from Jerusalem, Rev. Fuad J. Bahnan, arrived in Princeton to study for a Master's degree at the seminary. Like many of Edward's relatives, Bahnan had been scarred by the Israeli conquest of Palestine. In 1948, his father had been shot by the Haganah and died in his arms.[63] The following year, he had moved to Beirut to attend the Near East School of Theology, still headed by Uncle Charles' friend George Scherer. It is unlikely that Edward encountered Bahnan at Princeton, although he would make his acquaintance decades later, after he had become Hilda Said's pastor in Beirut. When Hilda moved to Washington in the mid-1980s to live with her daughter Grace, she was reunited with Bahnan, who had immigrated to the United States a few years earlier. In her memoir, Jean Said Makdisi recalls that Bahnan visited her mother on her deathbed and prayed with her in Arabic.[64] Later, Bahnan would preach the sermon at Edward's own memorial service in Manhattan's Riverside Church.

Meanwhile, Edward was applying for postgraduate scholarships, including a Rhodes Scholarship. Naturally, he asked Uncle Charles to write letters of recommendation for him. Uncle Charles was happy to oblige. "In these days of crisis," he wrote to the Rhodes Committee of New Jersey, "a young man like Edward Said, with his background and experience, holds out real promise for the service of the United States in its critical relations with the Near East."[65] Evidently, Uncle Charles had come to regard his nephew as something of a protégé—one who could carry on his own work as an intellectual ambassador, bringing the best of Western philosophy and literature to the Arab world. Serving the United States, however, was not what Edward had in mind, nor was he particularly interested in the Near East. What he wanted was simply to escape a life of drudgery at the Standard Stationery Company in order to pursue the life of the mind.

In February 1957, Uncle Charles' former student Fayez Sayegh, the acting director of the Arab States Delegation Office in New York, came to Princeton to talk about President Eisenhower's recent declaration that any Near Eastern ally threatened by the forces of International Communism could expect American aid.[66] Sayegh's speech revealed the extent to which his political views had started to diverge from those of Uncle Charles. After warning against the use of American aid as a political tool, Sayegh went on to call the Eisenhower Doctrine "doubly defective." On the one hand, the doctrine ignored the threat to the Arab nations from the old colonial powers as well as Israel. By its silence on the matter, it made further aggression on the part of Britain, France, or Israel more likely. On the other hand, the doctrine exaggerated the threat to the Arab nations from the Soviet Union. A better way to reduce the appeal of Communism, Sayegh opined, would be to distribute aid unconditionally and take a bolder stand against European colonialism and Zionist expansionism.[67]

That spring, Edward's main task was to complete his senior thesis, entitled *The Moral Vision: André Gide and Graham Greene*, which he dedicated to "E. E." (Eva Emad) and his parents.[68] In his preface, he thanked his advisor, Richard Ludwig, a young specialist in American literature with a PhD from Harvard, where Edward would soon begin his own graduate studies. André Gide, he explained, had always been one of his favorite authors—a confession that would have disappointed Uncle Charles, who undoubtedly regarded Gide as a prime instance of decadent French literature. As for Graham Greene, Uncle Charles would likely have been repulsed by his joyless, masochistic Roman Catholicism. What drew Edward to both Gide and Greene, however, was precisely their religious eccentricity, their refusal to follow the conventional road to salvation.

In June 1957, Edward graduated from Princeton with honors. Wadie and Hilda came from Cairo for the ceremonies, which included the usual awarding of honorary degrees. Edward didn't mention it in his memoir, but one of the honorees that year was none other than the Director of Central Intelligence, Allen W. Dulles, a proud member of the Princeton class of 1914.[69] If Uncle Charles had mentioned to his friend Dulles that his nephew Edward was a Princeton undergraduate, America's top spy might have been tempted to recruit him. After all, the CIA was a veritable Princeton alumni club, from Dulles himself to the various Eddys and Closes who were his field officers in the Arab world. Like these sons of Protestant missionaries, Edward was a Princeton-educated Arabic speaker who had grown up in the Middle East. Better yet, he was an Arab. In his heart, however, Edward was not a Princeton man, let alone a future foot soldier of the American empire.

§

Following in the footsteps of Uncle Charles, Edward was determined to pursue graduate study at Harvard, which had offered him "a fat fellowship."[70] His father, however, was still grooming him to take over Standard Stationery one day. So he deferred his studies for a year in order to learn the business and, more importantly, to court Eva Emad, who lived in nearby Alexandria. With no specific responsibilities at the office, he spent much of his time playing the piano and writing poetry, some of which appeared in *The Middle East Forum*, a magazine published by the AUB Alumni Association, under the title "Desert Flowers." A brief excerpt from an unrhymed sonnet will suffice to reveal his mood at the time:

> There is no future here,
> Time's tether completed, eaten away
> By the ridiculous vermin of hope—
> A sterile vision fraught with rhythmic cant,
> Decisive, but frighteningly restrained.[71]

Perhaps Edward was influenced by the poetry of Keith Douglas, the soldier-poet who had died in North Africa and written a poem called "Desert Flowers."

In the summer of 1958, the Saids avoided Dhour because of the civil war in Lebanon, which ended with the removal of Uncle Charles as foreign minister. Instead, Edward spent the summer touring Europe in a car bought for him by his father. In Switzerland, he was hospitalized after a head-on collision with a motorcyclist, who was killed. Fortunately, he recovered in time to begin the fall term at Harvard, where he was reunited with his American girlfriend—a former classmate of his sister Rosemarie's—

as well as Princeton friends like Tom Farer, who was studying law.[72] Coincidentally, an exiled family friend from Jerusalem—a gifted tenor named Afif Alvarez Bulos—was beginning a doctoral program in music at Harvard that fall.[73] Another Palestinian friend was Hanna Mikhail, a student in Harvard's new Center for Middle Eastern Studies, headed by the renowned Orientalist H. A. R. Gibb. As Edward recalled, Hanna's switch from chemistry to Middle Eastern Studies was "a necessary one for someone like himself who needed to know more about the historical traditions and culture of his people."[74] Eventually, Edward would experience the same need.

Returning to Cairo in the summer of 1959, Edward was anxious because of Nasser's program of "Arab socialism," which targeted foreign-owned companies like Standard Stationery. "Entering the city from the airport," he remembered, "I felt a direct sense of being threatened, an insecurity so profound that it could only come, I thought, from the sense of our being torn up by the roots, such roots as we had in Egypt. Where would our family go?"[75] He had reason to be anxious for family friends as well. That year, Nasser's secret police had been rounding up suspected Communists, including Dr. Farid Haddad, who assisted Edward's aunt Nabiha in caring for poor refugees in Cairo. Originally from Jerusalem, Dr. Haddad had gone to school in Cairo with Elie Raffoul, a fellow man of the Left, who had been arrested in 1948 and gone into exile in France.[76] There he had changed his name to Eric Rouleau and been hired by *Le Monde*, where his reporting on the Middle East would later draw high praise from Edward Said. As for Dr. Haddad, he would die in prison in November 1959, tortured to death by his interrogators.

In his second year at Harvard, Edward became a "section man," the leader of a small discussion section in a large general education course. In Edward's case, the course was "The Interpretation of Literature," popularly known as "Hum 6," which had been transplanted from Amherst to Harvard by Professor Reuben Brower. One of the young instructors who taught Hum 6 at the time, Richard Poirier, became one of Edward's closest friends. Another Hum 6 instructor was an older doctoral candidate from Belgium, Paul de Man, who was writing a dissertation on Mallarmé and Yeats under Harry Levin and Renato Poggioli.[77] Although Edward must have crossed paths with de Man during the two years they were together at Harvard, he didn't befriend him until the late 1960s, by which time de Man had established himself as one of the world's foremost literary theorists. He knew nothing of de Man's shady past, which included an abandoned family and association with Nazi collaborators in his native Belgium.

On May 5, 1960, Uncle Charles came to Harvard to deliver the first annual Douglas L. Rights Peace Lecture in Memorial Church. If Edward was in the audience that night, he would have heard, in addition to a call for peaceful international relations, an emotional *apologia* on the part of Uncle Charles:

> Babylon is not over against us, way across the desert, as though we could choose to have nothing to do with it: we are at one and the same time citizens of both Jerusalem and Babylon; we are both Babylonian and heavenly. And sometimes I think that, because they have plunged into the dirt of the world and taken its corruption upon themselves, and because while the world is still on our hands they had to do the job or else the dogs would do it, the politicians, the diplomats, and

the statesmen, by reason of the immensity of their self-sacrifice, are more entitled to intercede for us in heaven than even the saints.[78]

To abandon a life of contemplation for one of action, to dirty one's hands with politics and intrigue and CIA money and coup plots—that is the ultimate self-sacrifice, one a Christian statesman must make, lest the world go to the dogs.

That summer, Edward returned to Cairo, where he pretended, once again, to work for his father. It turned out to be his last visit to Cairo—the only home he had ever known—for fifteen years. In his memoir, he blamed his long exile on a questionable business contract his father asked him to sign that summer. Evidently, the contract violated Egyptian law, because the police came looking for him some months later, only to learn that he had returned to the United States.[79] In the meantime, the Saids went to Dhour el Shweir as usual, along with the Badrs, the Makdisis, and their other summer friends. Not long after their arrival, Edward's sister Jean, who was about to begin her senior year at Vassar College, announced her engagement to Samir Makdisi, who was finishing his doctoral dissertation on the Syrian economy at Columbia. The wedding was planned for the following summer.[80]

§

In September 1960, Edward and Jean returned to the States. It must have been that fall, or perhaps the following spring, that Jean introduced her brother to one of her Vassar classmates, Maire Jaanus, a brilliant, beautiful German-Estonian student of comparative literature, to whom he would soon become engaged. Here we come to a missing chapter in Edward's autobiography. He told interviewers that his memoir stopped in 1962 because he did not want to write about his first marriage, which ended badly. Indeed, Maire's name appears nowhere in *Out of Place*. Similarly, Jean makes no mention of Maire in her family memoir, which was published after Edward's death in 2003. Perhaps Edward and Jean had agreed to bury what must have been a painful memory for both of them. Back in 1960-1, however, Edward was quite in love with Maire. Whatever lingering thoughts he had about marrying Eva Emad or his American girlfriend were soon forgotten.

In the summer of 1961, the Saids gathered in Lebanon for Jean and Samir's wedding. Unfortunately, the marriage had to be postponed when Wadie was diagnosed with malignant melanoma and underwent several operations at the AUB Medical Center.[81] Meanwhile, President Kennedy had ordered a dramatic expansion of the Selective Service draft as Nikita Khrushchev threatened to start World War III over West Berlin. In his memoir, Edward stated that Ralph Nader—who had been two years ahead of him at Princeton—helped him "resist" the draft.[82] A few months later, Aunt Eva invited him to spend the holidays in Washington, where Uncle Charles was teaching at American University. Edward politely declined, noting that he would be in England with Maire, who had received a Fulbright Fellowship for a year of postgraduate study at Cambridge. He said that he looked forward to seeing the Maliks in Washington, however, when Jean and Samir—who had accepted a job with the International Monetary Fund—

arrived from Beirut. He proposed "a long walk and talk with Uncle Charles, something I cherish very highly."[83]

On February 2, 1962, Jean Said and Samir Makdisi were finally married in Beirut's National Evangelical Church, where Edward's great-grandfather had once been the pastor. At the time of Jean's wedding, both pastors were refugees from Palestine and graduates of the Princeton Theological Seminary. The senior pastor was Rev. Farid Audeh, who had been ordained by Bishop Graham-Brown—Uncle Charles' old friend—in Jerusalem in 1934.[84] The junior pastor was the aforementioned Rev. Fuad Bahnan, who had completed his studies at Princeton in 1957, the year Edward graduated.[85] Meanwhile, Edward's parents had decided to relocate to Beirut.[86] Wadie's cancer aside, the timing of the move seems to have been dictated by Nasser's Egyptianization decrees of January 1957, which gave foreign-owned import firms like Standard Stationery five years to turn their management over to Egyptian nationals.[87] Beirut seemed the obvious choice for the Saids: Wadie still owned the Beirut branch of Standard Stationery, and Hilda would enjoy the company of her Lebanese relatives.

That June, Edward and Maire were also married. In *Out of Place*, he mentioned the wedding only in passing.[88] Maire, too, remained silent about the marriage—apart, that is, from her 1984 novel *She*, in which the narrator's first husband, a Greek named "Robert," is a thinly disguised Edward. At one point, the novel's first-person narrator—a college professor who finds herself falling for a student—is reminded of

a scene in Athens, before my marriage to Robert, when his mother had said, "We don't know you, but we know our son," and I had gone and packed my suitcase to leave, but Robert persuaded me to stay.[89]

That Robert's mother is based on Hilda Said is confirmed by Edward's description of her determination to dissuade Eva Emad from marrying him:

"I know my own son," she would say sanctimoniously, pinning me down with her disapproval and insistence that she knew what I would always be—a disappointment in the long run.[90]

Like Edward, the Robert character in *She* had an oedipal relationship with his mother, who, unable to prevent her son's marriage, proceeded to ruin it.

In the fall of 1962, the newlyweds returned to Harvard, where Maire started the doctoral program in comparative literature and Edward resumed his work on Joseph Conrad. One of his directors was Monroe Engel, who had published a novel and written a dissertation on Charles Dickens at Princeton before coming to Harvard in 1955. His other director was Harry Levin, who had been a Junior Fellow at Harvard when Uncle Charles was in graduate school. In *Out of Place*, Edward recalled that his reading of Conrad was informed by such continental thinkers as Heidegger and Sartre, whom he had discussed with Uncle Charles, no doubt, during their rambles. He also read Georg Lukacs' *History and Class Consciousness*, which had been translated into French but not yet into English. He may have been put onto Lukacs by Fredric Jameson, who had come to Harvard from Yale, where he had studied with Erich Auerbach, the eminent

German Jewish scholar. Not only did Jameson become a lifelong friend of Edward's, but Auerbach—who had written his magnum opus, *Mimesis*, in exile in Istanbul—would also become an important intellectual figure for Edward.

§

In the fall of 1963, Edward joined the Department of English and Comparative Literature at Columbia University in New York. The chairman of the department was none other than Lewis Leary, the former AUB staffite who had invited Uncle Charles to participate in Columbia's bicentennial conference back in 1954.[91] It is conceivable that Uncle Charles—who came to New York that September at the invitation of his friend David Rockefeller—told Edward of his acquaintance with Leary and that Edward, in turn, told Leary that he was Charles Malik's nephew. In any case, Uncle Charles was well known to other members of the Columbia faculty, notably Charles Issawi, a member of Columbia's Middle East Institute. The MEI was part of the School of International Affairs, where Andrew Cordier, Uncle Charles' longtime colleague at the UN, had recently become the dean. Also teaching in the SIA was Doak Barnett, a China expert who had married Jeanne Badeau, Edward's former classmate at the CSAC.[92] Jeanne's father John—who had recommended the Mount Hermon School to Wadie Said—was Kennedy's ambassador to Egypt, where he may well have seen the Saids again before their move to Beirut.

As for the Columbia English department, its faculty included a number of senior scholars who had made names for themselves in the radical 1930s, notably Lionel Trilling and F. W. Dupee, both of whom befriended Edward. Diana Trilling—Lionel's wife and a literary force in her own right—would become a lifelong confidante, living into her nineties. Another member of this generation was Robert Gorham Davis, who had taught writing at Harvard in the 1930s and been a member of Harvard's Communist cell. Among the junior faculty was one of Edward's friends from Harvard, Robert B. Alter, who would later make a name for himself as a critic and translator of the Hebrew Bible. As an undergraduate at Columbia in the 1950s, Alter had studied with Trilling and Dupee and composed a senior essay comparing two Jewish writers, Franz Kafka and S. Y. Agnon, whom he read in German and Hebrew, respectively.[93] Like Edward, he had written his dissertation under the direction of Harry Levin.

In his first year at Columbia, Edward witnessed the birth of campus protest over the Vietnam War. On February 28, 1964, the University Committee to Protest the War in Vietnam, a coalition of New York City faculty, published an open letter to President Johnson in the *New York Times*. "We are waging an immoral and inhumane war," the committee charged, "that has brought untold suffering to the people of South Vietnam." The signers of the letter included some eighty faculty from Columbia alone, including retired English professor Mark Van Doren and a young religion instructor named Susan Sontag.[94] Edward did not sign the letter, although he undoubtedly shared its sentiment. Another professor who did not sign was Zbigniew Brzezinski, the director of Columbia's Russian Institute, who had defended Johnson's recent decision to bomb North Vietnam.[95] On March 3, Brzezinski again defended the American bombing at a "Forum on Vietnam" on the Columbia campus. He was opposed by the octogenarian socialist Norman Thomas, who denounced the war as "a chess game played with people."⁹⁶

Meanwhile, Edward was revising his dissertation on Conrad, which was under contract to Harvard University Press. In June 1965, Hilda Said wrote to congratulate him on its publication, adding that his sister Joyce had just taken her exams for her Master's degree in philosophy at the AUB.⁹⁷ She wrote again in December, explaining that she and Wadie were having second thoughts about the house being designed for them by Raymond Ghosn, the dean of engineering and architecture at the AUB. The house was to be built in the new hilltop development in Rabieh where the Maliks lived. The problem, Hilda complained, was that "we don't know anybody up there, beside the Maliks, and they're not much company, as you know."⁹⁸ Rabieh was in the foothills above East Beirut, far from the Ras Beirut community where the Saids lived near the Makdisis, the Cortases, and other friends attached to the AUB. In the end, the Saids decided not to make the move. Had they done so, Edward would undoubtedly have seen more of the Maliks over the years.

In June 1966, a statement opposing the war in Vietnam appeared in the *New York Times*, along with three pages of signatures by academics and professionals from across the nation, including Edward Said.⁹⁹ It was the first public indication of his incipient political radicalism. Shortly thereafter, he traveled to East Jerusalem with his father and his sister Jean for the wedding of his cousin Robert, the youngest son of Boulos and Nabiha Said. As Jean recalled in her memoir:

> This was the first time my father had been to Jerusalem since 1948, and I shall never forget his face as we surveyed the whole city, now so changed, from the top of the YMCA building near the Mandelbaum Gate, separating the two parts of the divided city.¹⁰⁰

The long-serving general secretary of the East Jerusalem YMCA was Labib Nasir, the brother of Latifeh Nasir Musa, Hilda Said's sister-in-law. Little did anyone know that a year later, Labib and his family would be forced to take refuge in the basement during the June War, in which the building was badly damaged by artillery shells.¹⁰¹ Robert Said would be more fortunate, having opened a branch of the family business, the Jordan Educational Company, in Amman.

In October, Edward traveled to Johns Hopkins University in Baltimore for the epoch-making Franco-American conference that simultaneously introduced structuralism to America and gave birth to the school of criticism known as "post-structuralism" or "deconstruction." Edward, who had studied French at Princeton, was already immersed in the work of phenomenological critics like Georges Poulet as well as Marxist critics like Lucien Goldmann.¹⁰² Both Poulet and Goldmann came to Baltimore for the conference, along with such avant-garde Parisian intellectuals as Roland Barthes, Jacques Lacan, and Jacques Derrida. Another participant was Paul de Man, who had been dividing his time between Cornell University and the University of Zurich. Over the course of the next decade, Edward would establish his own reputation as a leading American interpreter of French theory, most notably in his second book, *Beginnings*.

That same fall, Edward's sister Joyce enrolled in a Master's program in English literature at Columbia, having completed her thesis at the AUB on *The Finitude of Man in the Philosophy of Maurice Merleau-Ponty*. Unfortunately, she broke her leg in early 1967 and had to spend a few days in a New York hospital. It was at her bedside that Edward—still married to Maire Jaanus—first met Mariam Cortas, his future second wife. As Mariam told her daughter Najla:

> Your aunt Joyce broke her leg. She had been my friend at university. I went to visit her in the hospital. When I walked into the room, your father was sitting in a chair, eating popcorn. He looked at me and said, "All right, Joyce, your friend is here. That means I can go," and he left.

When Najla pointed out that her mother's story was not very romantic, Mariam replied, "I thought he was rude. It is true."[103]

5

Edward Said: The Rebirth of a Palestinian Intellectual, 1967–75

On June 6, 1967—the second day of the Six-Day War—*The New York Times* published an editorial calling on the Arab states to recognize Israel. "No matter how the present war turns out," the *Times* declared, "there will be the explosive material of war unless or until the fundamental fact of history is accepted that there is an Israeli nation and that it has a right to exist in peace."[1] The following day, the *Times* published a full-page appeal, paid for by Americans for Democracy in the Middle East, calling upon President Johnson to open the Straits of Tiran, which Egypt had closed to Israeli shipping in late May. Although the appeal had been written before war broke out, the authors noted, "it is even more urgent now." It was signed by some fifty intellectuals and writers, including Hannah Arendt, Irving Howe, Alfred Kazin, Dwight MacDonald, and even Lionel Trilling, whom Edward Said considered a friend.[2] On June 8, the *Times* ran the same ad with two full pages of academic signatories, listed by university affiliation. Columbia alone was represented by some sixty professors, including one of Edward's closest friends on the faculty, the philosopher Sidney Morgenbesser.[3]

It is not difficult to imagine the frustration Edward must have felt during those six days in June as he followed the war on a transistor radio. He happened to be on jury duty, the only Arab in a room full of jurors who referred to the Israelis as "we," asking him, "How are we doing?" As he recalled many years later, "I found I was unable to say anything—I felt embarrassed."[4] And so he sat down and wrote a letter to the *Times*, protesting that the Arabs, too, are a fundamental fact of history, that their suffering must be measured on the same moral scale as that of the Jews. He went on to accuse Israel of Western-style imperialism, comparing Israel's war against the Arabs to America's war in Vietnam—a war the *Times* itself had called into question.[5] Unfortunately, the editor declined to publish Edward's letter, which would have marked his public debut as an intellectual champion of the Palestinian people.

On June 19, Edward sent a copy of his unpublished *Times* letter to Uncle Charles, who, as he had learned from a mutual friend, was in New York. "Dear Uncle Charles," he pleaded,

> We are very anxious to see you now, as we are aghast at [what] is going on around us—so much so that one can scarcely know whether the entire world has lost its senses or not. My chief difficulty—I will be frank—is in trying to fathom what it is

that the Arabs are up to; I very much fear that confusion and anger will bottle up either thought or vision, whichever is needed most, and take them to the wrong position or strategy.[6]

Unfortunately, Uncle Charles did not receive Edward's letter until he was about to return to Beirut. His belated reply, dated July 12, counseled patience:

> This part of the world has gone through a great convulsion and we do not yet see our way out of the mess. I know how the Arab case is not properly heard in the United States and the reasons why. We must suffer the situation until God shows us His will and His light.[7]

It's hard to imagine that Uncle Charles' pious words offered much consolation to Edward, who expected more from the statesman who had once been the Arabs' most effective voice in the United Nations.

In September, Edward left for the University of Illinois, which had offered him a year-long fellowship to write a book on one of his favorite authors, Jonathan Swift. Once in Illinois, however, he found it difficult to concentrate. Not only was his marriage in trouble, but he was also haunted by the Arab defeat, which had prompted much soul-searching on the part of Arab intellectuals.[8] One of those intellectuals was Cecil Hourani, whose manifesto "The Moment of Truth" appeared that November in the *Sunday Times* as well as *Encounter*. The lesson of the Arab defeat, Hourani wrote, is that victory cannot be won on the battlefield. In order to come to terms with the fact of Israel, he opined, the Arabs must win a victory over themselves, over their tendency to pretend that unpleasant realities do not exist. As for the PLO, Hourani had nothing good to say about its grandiloquent chairman, who had sabotaged President Bourguiba's 1965 peace initiative, which Hourani himself had secretly cleared with Washington.[9] "What greater proof of our capacities for self-delusion and moral cowardice," he asked, "than that Ahmed Shouqairi stills sits with our responsible leaders?"[10]

We know that Edward admired Hourani's essay from a letter he wrote to his friend Robert Alter, who had moved to Berkeley that fall after five years at Columbia. Edward's letter was prompted by an essay Alter had contributed to a special report on the June War published by *Commentary*, the magazine of the American Jewish Committee, edited by Norman Podhoretz. "Israel's stunning victory," Alter exulted, "has knocked askew a whole row of stereotypes of the Jew," including the assumption that Jews are unworldly and must be held to a higher moral standard than other people. It was only American Jewish intellectuals, Alter complained, who continued to be "enslaved" by such stereotypes, condemning Israel for behaving as other nations do.[11] One of his prime examples was Noam Chomsky of MIT, whose offense had been to sign a petition calling for compassion for Arab refugees and respect for Islamic holy sites. Other signers had included Arnold Toynbee of Chatham House, George Makdisi of Harvard, and Charles Issawi of Columbia.[12] In his letter, Edward recommended that Alter read Hourani's essay for an enlightened Arab perspective on the war.[13]

§

In January 1968, Edward flew to Beirut, where his parents had been living for the past five years, enjoying the company of the Maliks and Hilda's other Lebanese relatives (and some of Wadie's exiled Palestinian relatives as well). As for Edward's sisters, Rosemarie was completing a doctorate on the Gulf states at the School of Oriental and African Studies in London, where Bernard Lewis—the future bête noire of her brother Edward—was a member of the faculty. Jean and Samir Makdisi were still living in Washington, where Jean had earned a Master's in English literature from George Washington University.[14] Joyce, having returned from her year of graduate study at Columbia, was teaching English at the AUB, along with Fawz al-Azm, whose husband Sadik was in his final year at the university. Like the Azms, Joyce was drawn to the emerging Palestinian resistance movement in Beirut.[15] Grace was in the middle of her senior year at Duke University, soliciting the usual letters of recommendation from Uncle Charles.[16]

One day Edward drove up to Rabieh to visit Uncle Charles and Aunt Eva at their hilltop villa. As he recalled in *Out of Place*:

> I was not too sure what my errand was, except in some vague way to ask Charles to come out, so to speak, and help guide the Arabs out of their incredible defeat. A stupid idea perhaps, but at the time it seemed plausibly worth pursuing. What I was not prepared for was his uncharacteristically passive answer: that this was not his time, that he did not feel he had any role to play anymore, and that a new situation would have to arrive for him to reenter politics. I was stunned by this, astonished that what I had assumed was a common need to resist and rebuild was not shared by a man whose views and commitments I still had faith in.[17]

Edward may not have understood the extent to which Uncle Charles, the former Chamounist, was still reviled in Egypt, Syria, and Lebanon itself. In any case, it was not a militant Israel that Uncle Charles feared the most; it was the militant Arab regimes that remained in power even after their defeat.

While he was in Beirut that January, Edward gave a lecture at the AUB on "Recent Trends in Literary Criticism."[18] His audience probably included his sister Joyce, if not Uncle Charles. If Sadik and Fawz al-Azm were in attendance, Joyce may well have introduced them to her brother, who was becoming something of an authority on contemporary European criticism, having attended the structuralism conference at Johns Hopkins in 1966 as well as Paul de Man's Princeton seminar in 1967. After his vacation in Beirut, Edward traveled to Zurich for a seminar on literary interpretation hosted by de Man, which featured many of the original Johns Hopkins conferees, including Jacques Derrida and J. Hillis Miller (who heard Derrida typing his famous lecture "La différance" in his hotel room).[19] Also in Zurich was Edward's contemporary Tony Tanner, a fellow of King's College, Cambridge, with whom he quickly became "fast friends." As Edward recalled many years later, "Tony and I sat there as decidedly second-rank soldiers . . . both dazzled and repelled by the overwhelming displays of learning, profundity, and polyglot disputatiousness of these redoubtable figures in European thought and interpretation."[20]

After the Zurich seminar, Edward returned to Illinois, where he was being courted by university officials. In early February, he informed Lewis Leary, his department chair at Columbia, that both he and Maire, who was finishing her doctoral dissertation at Harvard, had received tempting offers from the University of Illinois. After consulting with Barry Ulanov of the Barnard College English department, Leary countered with an offer of an associate professorship for Edward and a faculty appointment at Barnard for Maire, which they quickly accepted.[21] Edward was still in Illinois, however, when student radicals, led by Mark Rudd of Students for a Democratic Society, took over the Columbia campus that April, occupying buildings and issuing demands. When President Grayson Kirk called an emergency faculty meeting, someone sent Edward a telegram urging him to attend. So he flew to New York, only to find himself barred from campus by the police for lack of proper identification.[22]

The following month, Edward read a paper at a "Conference on Norms" at New York University. He had been invited by an old friend from Princeton and Harvard, Tom Farer, then a research fellow at the Carnegie Endowment for International Peace. It was at this conference, probably, that Edward met Richard Falk, the Milbank Professor of International Law and Practice at Princeton, who was active in the antiwar movement. Other speakers included Conor Cruise O'Brien, the Albert Schweitzer Professor of Humanities at NYU, then in his radical phase, and the literary critic Leslie Fiedler, who had been the Gauss Lecturer at Princeton during Edward's senior year. In his paper, Edward deconstructed norms as "signs of difference"—the difference between the general and the particular and between the act and its result. He even used the term "logocentricity," citing Jacques Derrida, whose *De la grammatologie* had been published the previous year.[23] Edward, of course, had read the book in French; Gayatri Chakravorty Spivak's English translation would not appear until 1976.

That summer, President Kirk was forced to resign over his mishandling of the Columbia student rebellion. He was replaced by Andrew Cordier, Uncle Charles' former UN colleague.[24] Meanwhile, Ibrahim Abu-Lughod had asked Edward to contribute an article on the representation of the Arab in the Western media to a special issue of *Arab World*, a glossy magazine published in New York by the Arab League.[25] In his article, entitled "The Arab Portrayed," Edward chose to examine Western responses to the June War, which he had been clipping from newspapers and magazines. He began, however, with the reunion of the Princeton class of 1957, which had taken place in early June, while the war was still in progress. The prescribed costume for the reunion (announced before the war) included thobe, sandals, and *keffiyah*. Unfortunately, some of Edward's former classmates decided to carry signs reading "How d'ya expect to win if ya gotta wear skirts?' and "See the pyramids—visit Israel" while others paraded with their hands up in mock-surrender.[26] But it was not so much the war, Edward complained, as "the American consciousness of the Arab" that "permitted this tasteless demotion of a people into a stupid and offensive caricature."[27]

After criticizing his Princeton classmates, Edward turned to pundits who were just as guilty, in his eyes, of caricaturing the Arabs. Among them were Harvard professors Michael Walzer and Martin Peretz, who had published an essay entitled "Israel Is Not Vietnam" in the New Left magazine *Ramparts*. Both Walzer and Peretz had been graduate students at Harvard at the same time as Edward, although it is uncertain whether they had crossed paths there. More recently, Peretz had married a wealthy heiress, Anne Labouisse Farnsworth, who happened to be the daughter of Henry Richardson Labouisse, the former director of UNRWA and the current director of UNICEF, both of which provided aid to Palestinian refugees. Unlike his new father-in-law, however, Peretz was a staunch partisan of Israel, which, he argued, was not a product of European colonialism, like South Vietnam, but a nation whose independence had been opposed by the colonial powers.[28]

Returning to Columbia in the fall of 1968, Edward was invited to speak at a meeting of Students for a Democratic Society. According to Harold Veeser, who was a Columbia freshman that fall, Edward was introduced by the radical heiress Josie Duke:

Tonight we are getting some ... support, we are getting some solidarity, man, and it's coming tonight from a faculty member, a professor in the English Department. . . . This is Professor Edward Said. . . . Professor Said is going to make a statement. Professor Said!

By the time he came to the subject of Palestine, Veeser recalls, "the dandy-like and introspective professor had morphed into a swingeing Palestinian Billy Sunday":

And have you in SDS ever said so much as a word on the Palestinians' behalf? . . . No, you haven't! . . . You call for "many Vietnams." Well, Palestine today IS another Vietnam![29]

Edward's equation of Palestine and Vietnam was, no doubt, a conscious retort to Walzer and Peretz's *Ramparts* essay.

In May 1969, Edward was invited by a group of Harvard graduate students to speak at a forum on the Arab-Israeli conflict at the Harvard Divinity School. One of them was Ismail Serageldin of Egypt, a PhD candidate in economics and an officer of the Organization of Arab Students, who went on to a long career at the World Bank. Another was Stephen P. Cohen, who, along with Harvard psychology professor Herbert Kelman, would go on to host a number of problem-solving seminars involving various Arab and Israeli participants, including Edward.[30] Among the Jewish speakers at the forum were Shimon Shamir, a future Israeli ambassador to Egypt and Jordan; J. C. Hurewitz, Edward's colleague at Columbia; and Rabbi Arthur Hertzberg, who taught religion courses at Columbia.[31] As Hertzberg recalled, Edward called for a secular, democratic state in Palestine embracing Jews as well as Arabs—a formula the PLO had just adopted under its new chairman, Yasir Arafat. Hertzberg demurred, opining that, given the historic antagonism between the two peoples, separate states were the only realistic alternative.[32]

§

In the summer of 1969, Edward flew to Beirut to visit his family and, perhaps, to escape his marital trouble. From there he traveled to Jordan to observe the Palestinian revolution for himself. Many of his relatives from the West Bank were living in Amman, including Kamal Nasir, who had recently been elected to the executive committee of the PLO.[33] Among others, Edward spoke with "a clergyman who had been active in West Bank resistance . . . imprisoned by the Israelis, abused, then deported."[34] The clergyman was undoubtedly Rev. Elia Khoury, an Anglican priest from Ramallah, who happened to be Kamal Nasir's brother-in-law.[35] In February of that year, a bomb had exploded in a crowded supermarket in Jerusalem, killing two and wounding eight. Khoury had been among those arrested by the Israelis, who accused him of carrying instructions and smuggling explosives.[36] Four years later, when Kamal Nasir was assassinated by the Israelis, Khoury would replace his brother-in-law as the Christian representative on the PLO executive committee.

After his return to New York, Edward penned a semi-autobiographical essay on the emergence of "Palestinianism," inspired by his recent visit to Amman. The essay, which appeared in the *Columbia University Forum*, was Edward's contribution to the literature of Arab self-criticism. The Arab defeat of 1967, he announced, had awakened the Palestinian to the limitations of his self-proclaimed allies, including Arab nationalists as well as the international Left. The Palestinian, he lamented,

> has no benefits to gain from Western good-thinkers who sympathize so effortlessly with the Vietnamese peasant, the American black, or the Latin American laborer, but not with him. And this is only because he is an "Arab" who is opposed by "Jews." To live in America, for example, and to know this truth as a Palestinian Arab is especially painful.[37]

No doubt Edward was thinking of intellectuals who were identified with the New Left but were also defenders of Israel, like Michael Walzer and Martin Peretz, as well as Students for a Democratic Society.

At the same time, the essay offered up a strong dose of self-criticism on Edward's part—a painful examination of his own suppression of his identity as a Palestinian. At one point, he recalled his response (or lack thereof) to the first Arab-Israeli war:

> In 1948 I was twelve, a student at an English school in Cairo. . . . My closest friend at the time was a Jewish boy who had a Spanish passport. I remember his telling me that autumn how shameful it was that six countries were pitted against one; the appeal, I believed, was to my sporting instinct developed at cricket and soccer games. I said nothing, but I felt bad.[38]

He continued to say nothing, he confessed, right up until 1967, telling people he was from Lebanon, because that is where his family lived. But the June War had put an end to his self-alienation. "The present stage of the Palestinian experience," he declared, "is a problematic early transition from *being* in exile to *becoming* Palestinian once again."[39]

In February 1970, Edward had the issue of the *Forum* containing his essay mailed to Uncle Charles, along with an invitation to respond.[40] Charles, who did not write a response, would have been particularly pained by his nephew's remarks on the religious dimension of the conflict over Palestine. Having placed his hope in an eventual political settlement, Edward issued a caveat to his readers:

> Nevertheless, many imponderable forces also intersect at the essential node of the conflict. They range from great power competition to, equally irrational

and perhaps even more compelling, the subliminal forces of primitive religious emotion and mythic racism. For it must never be forgotten—and this may be the clue to the entire imbroglio—that Palestine carries the heaviest weight of competing monotheistic absolutisms (Jewish, Christian, and Islamic) of any spot on earth.[41]

This was a theme dear to Uncle Charles' heart—the Middle East as the cradle of the three Abrahamic faiths. But what Uncle Charles regarded as a mark of divine blessing, Edward regarded as an unmitigated curse for the people of Palestine.

The following month saw another protest rally and march at Columbia, this one sponsored by a group calling itself the "December 4th Movement" in honor of Black Panthers Fred Hampton and Mark Clark, killed in a police raid in Chicago on December 4, 1969. The purpose of the rally was to demand that Columbia aid the defense in the conspiracy trial of twenty-one Panthers from New York. Among the speakers were Afeni Shakur, one of the Panther 21; Jean Genet, the celebrated French author; and Abbie Hoffman, the leader of the so-called Yippies. Before Hoffman spoke, D4M leader Jay Facciola asked for a moment of silence for Ted Gold, the former vice-chairman of the Columbia chapter of SDS, who had died in an explosion in a Greenwich Village townhouse the previous week. Gold was a member of the Weathermen, the underground offshoot of SDS responsible for several bombings in the past six months. Hoffman was obviously in the know, asking the crowd:

> Have you heard the weather report? Well, Mark Rudd gave the weather report on the Today Show and I'll tell you about the weather map. Seattle—boom! San Francisco—boom! New York—boom! boom! boom!

Following the rally, D4M led a crowd of 400 in a march around the campus, smashing some forty windows.[42]

Edward attended the rally because he wanted to hear Jean Genet, whose books he had taught in his courses. Genet spoke with the help of a translator—a former student of Edward's—but Edward understood his French well enough to note

> the stark contrast between the declarative simplicity of Genet's French remarks in support of the Panthers, and the immensely baroque embellishment of them by my erstwhile student. Genet would say, for example, "The blacks are the most oppressed class in the United States." This would emerge in the translator's colorful ornamentation as something like "In this motherfucking son-of-a-bitch country, in which reactionary capitalism oppresses and fucks over all the people, not just some of them, etc. etc." Genet stood through this appalling tirade unruffled.[43]

And who was this former student who had agreed to translate for Genet? Edward did not name him, but he seems to have been Paul Auster, the future novelist, who had polished his French in Paris during his junior year abroad.[44]

Later that spring, Edward participated in a symposium on the Palestinians moderated by Richard Hudson, the editor of *War/Peace Report*, a monthly funded by the New York

Friends Society. The other participants were Marver Bernstein of Princeton, whom Edward may have remembered from his undergraduate years; Joseph E. Johnson, the president of the Carnegie Endowment for International Peace; and Don Peretz of the State University of New York at Binghamton, who had worked with the American Friends Service Committee on its recent report *The Search for Peace in the Middle East*. Peretz noted that only one Palestinian leader, Nayef Hawatmeh of the DFLP, had made "a practical political proposal," namely, "a bi-national State in which both groups would co-exist equally." But only Edward thought Hawatmeh's proposal was workable. The others agreed with Bernstein that a Palestinian state in the West Bank and Gaza, perhaps federated with Jordan, was the most the Israelis would concede. Hudson asked, "Professor Said, would you find it acceptable to live in a separate, sovereign Palestinian state of the kind Professor Bernstein has outlined?" Edward's reply was unequivocal: "No. It would be a kind of vassal state. I would be excluded from other parts of Palestine."[45]

§

In an effort to conciliate the PLO, King Hussein of Jordan appointed a new prime minister at the end of June 1970. He was Abdul Munim al-Rifai, an AUB alumnus who, as Jordan's pro-Western ambassador to the United States and the United Nations in the 1950s, had spent many hours in the company of Uncle Charles. In his letter to Rifai—which was released to the press—the king instructed his new prime minister to prepare for battle with Israel.[46] However, Rifai's nephew Zaid al-Rifai—Edward's classmate at Victoria College—was among those urging the king to confront the *fedayeen* before it was too late. Another hard-liner was the CIA's station chief in Amman, Jack O'Connell, who had been introduced to Uncle Charles by Bill Eveland back in 1958. In preparation for the showdown with the PLO, O'Connell moved to a safe house just before his own house was firebombed. Throughout the crisis that summer, Zaid al-Rifai was O'Connell's primary intermediary with the king, who was holed up at his palace at Hummar, several miles outside of town.[47]

As civil war loomed in Jordan, Edward Said arrived in Beirut to visit his family and, more importantly, to ask Mariam Cortas to marry him, now that his divorce from Maire was official. The Saids didn't know it, but it would be their last family reunion in Dhour el Shweir.[48] As for her engagement to Edward, Mariam recalled:

> In the summer of 1970, I decided to marry Edward Said. Mother was delighted because he was a professor. They held similar political views and got along very well. What she did not like was that we would be living in the United States, far away.[49]

Mariam did not mention her father's reaction to the news, but he must have shared his wife's enthusiasm, as, one assumes, did Uncle Charles and Aunt Eva. Admittedly, the Maliks did not particularly care for Wadad Cortas or her political views, which were decidedly pro-Palestinian. But, as fellow Christians and AUB alumni, they belonged to the same social circles. Besides, the two families were already joined by marriage through Charles' relative Mona, the wife of Emile Cortas' brother Michel.[50]

Later that summer, Edward visited Amman for the second year in a row. His relative Kamal Nasir introduced him to various comrades in the resistance movement, including Hanna Mikhail, who had recently quit his faculty position at the University of Washington. "I was unprepared," Edward recalled, "for the transformation in my gentle, even pacifist old friend." What particularly struck Edward was "the grandeur and generosity of his gesture in coming to Amman in the first place," in trading "a secure academic job in the United States" for the uncertainty and danger of "a volatile and hostile Arab environment." Edward did not say that he was tempted to make a similar sacrifice, but the thought surely entered his mind. One day, he accompanied Hanna to a mass demonstration at which Yasir Arafat crowed over the PLO's rejection of Secretary of State William Rogers' plan for a cease-fire and UN mediation of the conflict with Israel—a plan recently accepted by President Nasser as well as King Hussein. After the speech, Hanna introduced Edward to the PLO leader. "But I distinctly remember Hanna's discomfort around Arafat," Edward wrote—a discomfort he shared.[51]

At the end of August, Edward returned to Amman to observe an emergency two-day session of the PNC, where he was reunited with a number of old friends. Helping to organize the session was Sadik al-Azm.[52] Also in attendance was Ibrahim Abu-Lughod, who had just flown in from Cairo. At the time, Ibrahim still considered himself an Arab Nationalist of the Nasserite variety. In Cairo, however, Nasser's confidant Mohammed Heikal had invited him to lunch with Yasir Arafat, Abu Iyad, Farouk Kaddoumi, and other PLO members. The only one he knew was Kaddoumi, a former classmate from Jaffa. After lunch, Arafat said, "Doctor, you must come to the Palestine National Council meeting." So he flew to Amman and made his way through the lines of soldiers and commandos guarding the building where the meeting was to take place. As he was waiting in the hall, he saw Hanna Mikhail. Then Arafat came over and embraced him. Looking back on the PNC meeting near the end of his life, Ibrahim commented, "It was a decisive moment for me. . . . I became a Palestinian."[53]

In the end, the Council declared Palestine-Jordan "a single arena of struggle."[54] PFLP commandos soon took matters into their own hands, ambushing the king's motorcade. Then, on September 6, PFLP hijackers commandeered three airplanes, landing two of them at Dawson Field, east of Amman. Some of the passengers were still in captivity on September 16 when King Hussein imposed a new military government under General Muhammad Daoud, who declared martial law and ordered the *fedayeen* to surrender their weapons. In the bloody street-fighting that ensued—known to Palestinians as "Black September"—the army seized control of Amman and forced the *fedayeen* to retreat to northern Jordan. On September 26, Hussein agreed to a cease-fire and asked Ahmad Tuqan—Sadik al-Azm's father-in-law—to form a new civilian government. The next day, the king flew to Cairo, where he and Yasir Arafat, who had been smuggled out of Amman, signed an agreement in the presence of President Nasser. A few hours later, Nasser died of a sudden heart attack, and Anwar Sadat became president of Egypt.

§

Back at Columbia, Edward Said continued to veer to the Left, aligning himself, according to his student Paul Berman, with the DFLP.[55] On October 7, 1970, an Israeli academic and advisor on Arab affairs, David Farhi, spoke at the Men's Faculty Club at the invitation of Columbia's Center for Israel and Jewish Studies. Outside the club, members of the Jewish Defense League clashed with SDS activists, who were picketing the event. Edward immediately fired off a letter to the *Daily Spectator*, comparing Farhi's visit to that of a white South African official in charge of "black affairs." The aims of Farhi's work, he noted, were to wean the inhabitants of the West Bank from the Palestinian resistance organizations and to choose leaders subservient to Israel. If SDS and others were beginning to connect Israel with Western imperialism, he added, it's because there is such a connection. As evidence, he pointed to a recent article in the *New York Times* revealing a secret agreement between Israel and the United States to intervene, if necessary, on King Hussein's side in his recent showdown with the Palestinian commandos.[56]

Edward's letter was read with indignation by his father's old friend John Badeau, the director of Columbia's Middle East Institute, who chastised his younger colleague in a letter to the *Spectator*. According to Badeau, David Farhi had resigned from his government position and was now a full-time university professor. Moreover, the original invitation to Farhi had come from Badeau himself, not the Center for Israel and Jewish Studies. What really troubled Badeau, however, was Edward's apparent disregard for academic freedom. "I find it nothing short of incredible," he exclaimed, "that a senior member of the faculty of a great university should propose the muzzling of free and controversial discussion on the campus." As for Edward's comparison of Farhi to a white South African in charge of black affairs, Badeau said he would welcome an opportunity to hear such a man's views. He concluded by linking Edward to the extremists of SDS and the JDL, who would deny free speech to those who disagreed with them.[57]

Edward replied to Badeau in a second letter marked by the *ad hominem* tone that would come to characterize his polemical writing. "Dr. Badeau's letter," he began, "is outrageous. Not only does he say things about my letter that are totally untrue, but he has the breath also to preach to me an unsolicited sermon on free discussion in the university." (Edward knew, of course, that Badeau was an ordained minister.) Proclaiming that he, too, believed in free discussion, Edward insisted that he was not attempting to prevent Farhi from speaking, merely putting his speech in its political context. He added that regional studies institutes—including, presumably, Columbia's Middle East Institute—also operate in a political context, serving the interests of the United States. "[Badeau's] dark hints about my views on free discussion," he concluded, "ought properly to be directed to the Israeli government, at present holding over 200 Arab writers and intellectuals under house arrest and without trial."[58]

At the end of October, Edward flew to Chicago for the third annual convention of the Association of Arab-American University Graduates at Northwestern University, Ibrahim Abu-Lughod's home institution. There he joined Maxime Rodinson of the École Pratique des Hautes Études and Noam Chomsky of MIT in a session on "The Future of Palestine." Rodinson regarded Israel as a colonial-settler state, although he doubted that revolution was the answer to the Palestinian Question. Edward, too, endorsed the "radical" view of Israel as a settler state, a product of Western colonialism and racism, as opposed to the "liberal" view of Zionism as a movement of national liberation. He even quoted a passage from Frantz Fanon, the theorist of the Algerian revolution, whose writings had reportedly inspired Arafat and other PLO leaders. As he had done before, Edward rejected the idea of partition, which, he said, "would perpetuate the extreme nationalist Zionist principle of an exclusively Jewish state, with the Arabs of Palestine confined in a Bantustan to the east," in favor of "one common state, or perhaps two or four loosely federated structures."[59]

The respondent was the Pakistani scholar Eqbal Ahmad, who had worked for Cecil Hourani in Tunisia while researching his Princeton doctoral dissertation.[60] Later, Ahmad had befriended the radical priest Daniel Berrigan, later convicted of destroying draft records in the army recruiting office in Catonsville, Maryland. By the time of the Evanston convention, Ahmad, along with Daniel Berrigan, his brother Philip Berrigan, and five of their Catholic friends, was being investigated by the FBI for conspiring to kidnap National Security Advisor Henry Kissinger—a harebrained scheme that had been quickly dismissed. The FBI had been alerted to the alleged conspiracy when it received a copy of a letter to Philip Berrigan from his wife. On Thanksgiving, FBI Director J. Edgar Hoover would appear on television to announce the discovery of the kidnapping plot. In January 1971, Ahmad would be arrested, along with the rest of the "Harrisburg Eight" (named after the city of Harrisburg, Pennsylvania, where their trial took place).[61]

As fate would have it, the Israeli ambassador to the United States, Yitzhak Rabin, happened to visit the Northwestern campus during the November AAUG convention. When he learned of the visit, Ibrahim Abu-Lughod quickly organized a "Free Palestine" demonstration outside the lecture hall where Rabin was speaking. Meanwhile, a group of American Jews staged a demonstration of their own outside the banquet hall where the AAUG was meeting. According to Abu-Lughod, one of the AAUG's organizers, Hatem Husseini, got into an altercation with the Jewish demonstrators, who left the scene after Abu-Lughod called the police.[62] According to former AAUG president Cherif Bassiouni, however, it was Edward Said who got into the altercation with the Jewish intruders, who were merely seeking to open a dialogue with their Arab counterparts. In Bassiouni's version, the Jewish delegation was led by Yehoshafat Harkabi, the famous general-turned-Arabist from Hebrew University.[63]

Whatever really happened in Evanston, the record of these years indicates that Edward Said welcomed dialogue and debate with Jewish supporters of Israel. In late November, he traveled to Boston for a Ford Hall Forum on the Arab-Israeli conflict hosted by Roger Fisher of the Harvard Law School. Edward's opponent at the forum was the veteran Labor Zionist Marie Syrkin, an old friend and biographer of Israeli prime minister Golda Meir. Until her retirement in 1966, Syrkin had taught English literature at Brandeis University; her former students included Michael Walzer and Martin Peretz. Years later, Peretz claimed that Syrkin had "kick[ed] the shit out of [Said]" at Ford Hall.[64] In fact, Syrkin's defense of Israel turned on a number of controversial claims: that Palestinian nationalism had not existed before the creation of Israel; that there had been no displaced Arabs in Palestine prior to 1948; that the refugee problem was comparatively easy to solve because of the vast scope of the Arab lands.[65]

Two weeks later, Edward and Mariam Cortas were married in New York. As their daughter Najla remembers the story:

> On December 15, 1970, my father woke up in his apartment in New York, assessed the weather (an enormous blizzard was descending on the city), and said to my mother, who was living with him, I suppose: "Mariam! Let's go to City Hall and get married."

When they arrived at City Hall, however, Mariam, who was wearing pants, was informed by a clerk that a dress was required. As Edward's anger threatened to boil over, Mariam

> disappeared into the bathroom only to emerge five minutes later with her pants removed. Her turtleneck sweater was long enough to cover the upper part of her thighs, and so was the crocheted vest she wore, which her favorite aunt, Najla, had made for her.[66]

Mariam's aunt Najla, it will be recalled, was the wife of Costi Zurayk of the AUB, to whom Edward was now related by marriage.

§

Meanwhile, Wadie Said, a lifelong smoker, was dying of lung cancer in a Beirut hospital. Toward the end of January 1971, he fell into a coma. Edward and his sister Jean, who was still living in Washington, caught the first flight to Beirut. By the time their plane landed, however, Wadie was already dead. The funeral was held the next day at All Saints, the church of the Palestinian Anglican community in Beirut, whose parish priest was Rev. Samir Kafity, a native of Haifa who had studied at the AUB and the Near East School of Theology.[67] Uncle Charles stopped by the Said residence that morning to offer his condolences, explaining that an important luncheon with the papal nuncio would prevent him from attending the funeral. Judging from his account in *Out of Place*, Edward was deeply offended—at least in retrospect—by Uncle Charles' decision to keep his lunch date.[68]

While he was in Beirut that January, Edward had a conversation with his mother-in-law Wadad, who, missing her only daughter, persuaded him to accept a job with the Institute for Palestine Studies, founded by Walid Khalidi of the AUB. Wadad herself served on the board of the IPS, which was chaired by Costi Zurayk, her brother-in-law. If Edward had taken the position, his life would have followed a very different trajectory. In all likelihood, he would have joined the staff of the IPS's new journal, *The Journal of Palestine Studies*. (In the event, Hisham Sharabi became the journal's first editor.) Eventually, he would have been invited to join the faculty of the AUB, becoming a colleague of Uncle Charles, Walid Khalidi, and other friends and relatives. According to Mariam, Edward came home excited at the prospect of moving to Beirut. She surprised him, however, by saying that she preferred to live in New York.[69]

On May 1, Edward returned to Cambridge to speak at the Harvard-MIT Arab Club. Among those present, it seems, was a young Iraqi architecture student named Kanan Makiya.[70] Years later, Edward and Makiya would quarrel over the first Gulf War, which Edward opposed and Makiya supported. In 1971, however, Makiya was a student radical, an opponent of the Vietnam War and a partisan of the Palestinian resistance movement. In his talk, entitled "The Palestinian Situation Today," Edward sounded every bit as radical as Sadik al-Azm in his diagnosis of the PLO's recent defeat at the hands of King Hussein's army. "Does my people's movement accept its revolutionary character or not?" he asked. "In failing to say yes outright, we were defeated." "Revolution is a serious business," he admonished the students, "and it must begin concurrently in the mass and the individual." True revolutionaries must fight for the oppressed everywhere, Jews as well as Arabs. As for the Palestinians, they must not settle for a piece of land, nor should they tolerate the corruption that caused other Arab nationalist movements to rot from within.[71]

That summer, Edward and Mariam—already pregnant with their first child—returned to Beirut, where they stayed with Mariam's parents. Edward spent much of his time talking to his friends in the Palestinian resistance movement, becoming increasingly disillusioned in the process. As he complained in a letter to his friend Sami al-Banna, a doctoral candidate in Columbia's School of Engineering, the Palestinians were "in a mess." Nabil Shaath, the director of the PLO Planning Center, told him that the Palestinians should become urban guerrillas, like the Tupamaros in Uruguay. When Edward inquired, "How? Why? Where?" no answer was forthcoming. Edward also spoke with his friend Hanna Mikhail and urged him to overthrow Arafat or leave Fatah. As for the PLO Research Center, he noted, "There is a lot of dirty shit going on between Anis Sayegh [the director of the Research Center] and [Walid] Khalidi's Institute [for Palestine Studies]." "I've volunteered a great deal of my time and effort," he concluded, "only to find it wasted on a bunch of children."[72]

When he got back to New York, Edward sat down and wrote a postmortem on Black September for *Le Monde Diplomatique*. The mood on the streets of Beirut, he observed, had changed dramatically since his last visit in the summer of 1970:

> In July and August 1970 the organized Palestinians outside Israel and those inside the occupied West Bank seemed the brightest popular hope in the Middle East. A year later nothing to me so humbly and yet significantly demonstrates the Palestinian fall from favor, their almost total paralysis, as the sight of some young men in a car trying unsuccessfully in Beirut to *give* away a copy of the Fatah newspaper.

He left no doubt as to who was ultimately responsible for the defeat of the *fedayeen*:

> No conspiratorial view of history is needed to remark how, both since 1967 and since Hussein's war on the Palestinians, American investments in the Middle East have not only remained unharmed but have been enhanced.[73]

In other words, American investments require stability; anything that threatens the status quo, such as the Palestinian resistance movement, must therefore be contained.

In October, Edward, who was serving a one-year term as vice president of Arab-American University Graduates, attended the organization's annual convention in Boston. Among the participants were Hisham Sharabi, back at Georgetown after his nonrenewal by the AUB, and Tony Zahlan—Edward's future brother-in-law—who had returned to the AUB after a brief stint with the new Royal Scientific Society in Amman. Also participating was Sami al-Banna, who, like Edward, had embraced the Palestinian cause after the 1967 war. A Chaldean Christian from Baghdad, al-Banna had attended Jesuit schools there—Baghdad College and al-Hikma University—before they were nationalized by the Baathists, who expelled the Jesuits from Iraq in the late 1960s.[74] In his AAUG paper, al-Banna chastised Iraq's Baathist regime for failing to come to the aid of the Palestinians in Jordan in September 1970. He blamed Western intelligence agencies for conspiring with "indigenous reactionaries" to liquidate any truly revolutionary movement in Iraq.[75]

Another participant in the Boston conference was Sadik al-Azm, who delivered a devastating postmortem on Black September, accusing the leaders of the Palestinian resistance—Arafat's Fatah in particular—of having learned nothing from the Arab defeat in 1967. He even coined a new term, "Fathawism," to describe the "reformist" theory and practice of Fatah, comparing it to the "petit bourgeois" ideologies of Nasserism and Baathism. As for the PFLP and the DFLP, Azm credited them with a correct understanding of the need to revolutionize the Arab masses in Jordan and throughout the Arab world. But these same organizations, he concluded, "remained unable to live up to what they mentally saw and preached."[76] Instead, they relied on spectacular feats like hijackings that stimulated the masses temporarily but did not require sacrifice on their part. The implication of Azm's critique was that the *fedayeen* were unprepared to wage a revolutionary war in Jordan or anywhere else.

§

In July 1972, Edward, who had been granted a year-long sabbatical, moved to Beirut with Mariam and their young son Wadie, taking an apartment in the building owned by the Cortas family on Jeanne d'Arc Street. One of his goals for the year was to "re-educate" himself in Arabic philology and grammar. To that end, he arranged for Anis Frayha, a retired professor of Arabic at the AUB and an old friend of his father's, to tutor him for three hours each morning.[77] (This was the same Professor Frayha who, some forty years earlier, had taught Semitic culture to the young Antun Saadeh.) The main purpose of his sabbatical, however, was to complete his second book *Beginnings*, in which he grappled with the avant-garde French theorists he had been reading. Evidently, he discussed his work with Sadik al-Azm, whom he thanked on the "Acknowledgments" page when *Beginnings* was published in 1975. Conveniently, the Azms lived within walking distance of the Cortas' building.[78]

In early September, Edward flew from Beirut to Poland for a week-long conference on his favorite author, Joseph Conrad, sponsored by the Polish Academy of Sciences. On September 5—the first day of the conference—members of the Palestinian terrorist organization Black September struck the Munich Olympics, capturing and eventually murdering eleven members of the Israeli team. Edward learned of the attack from Gustav Morf, a Jungian analyst and amateur Conrad scholar who had left his native Switzerland for Montreal. "They are killing people in Munich!" Morf announced, pointing to Edward, who quickly found a television set.[79] What Edward didn't know was that Morf had taken a professional interest in terrorism through his work with imprisoned members of the Front de Libération du Québec (FLQ), two of whom had trained with the PLO in Jordan.[80]

After the Conrad conference, Edward traveled to Linz, Austria, to read a paper at a conference on "Spheres of Influence in the Age of Imperialism," hosted by Vladimir Dedijer on behalf of the Bertrand Russell Peace Foundation. A former partisan fighter and companion of Field Marshal Tito, Dedijer had represented Yugoslavia in the United Nations Third Committee, chaired by Uncle Charles, in the fall of 1948. It was Dedijer who had proposed the article specifying that the Universal Declaration of Human Rights applies to people in "Trust and Non-Self-Governing Territories."[81] More recently, Dedijer had assisted Jean-Paul Sartre at the Bertrand Russell War Crimes Tribunal, which had been organized by Russell's secretary, Ralph Schoenman—Edward's former Princeton classmate—in order to try American officials for their alleged war crimes in Vietnam.[82] Both Sartre and Noam Chomsky had lent their names to the Linz conference, although neither appeared in person.

Edward's paper, entitled "United States Policy and the Conflict of Powers in the Middle East," was written in the bureaucratic style of the government reports he had been reading. His aim was to expose the tactics by which the United States pursues its strategic interests in the Middle East. "One consistent tactic," he observed,

> is to confuse ties among the Arabs, thus making states with sharply different constitutions, populations, economies, and avowed foreign policies (Israel, right-wing Arab states) unwittingly similar in the positions they adopt. Any force challenging these regimes, either externally or internally, is labeled radical, and an unspoken alliance develops, for economies and class balances are deeply threatened by change.

His example was the case of Jordan in September 1970, when the threat of US and Israeli intervention dissuaded the PLO's allies from coming to its rescue. "The U.S. response to the Jordanian crisis was impressive," Edward conceded, "for it set in train a remarkable series of events that almost literally destroyed every progressive movement in the Arab world, and of course strengthened the U.S.-Israel position accordingly."[83]

Curiously, one of Edward's fellow panelists at the Linz conference was "Lyn Marcus," a.k.a. Lyndon LaRouche, the guru of the cult-like and increasingly violent National Caucus of Labor Committees. Edward may have heard about LaRouche from his students at Columbia, where LaRouche's young disciples, led by Tony Papert, had played a leading role in the campus occupation of 1968.[84] Or perhaps he had been warned about LaRouche by Noam Chomsky, who knew several of LaRouche's followers.[85] Just how LaRouche got himself invited to Linz is something of a mystery. Perhaps he responded to the call for papers published in the *New York Review of Books* the previous December, issued under the names of Chomsky, Dedijer, and Sartre. After the conference, LaRouche (writing under the pseudonym "Hermyle Golthier, Jr.") praised Edward's paper in his magazine, *The Campaigner*.[86]

At the end of September, one of Edward's future PLO friends, Shafiq al-Hout, spoke in a movie theater in West Beirut, where a crowd of several hundred had gathered to commemorate the second anniversary of the death of President Nasser. "We will continue what we began at Munich," he vowed, referring to Black September's massacre of the Israeli Olympic athletes. He rejected the charge that the *fedayeen* had perpetrated "terror against innocents." "No eleven Israelis," he declared, "are worth more than the lives of one of the women and children that the Israeli bombers have killed in our camps."[87] It was not just the camps that the Israelis had been bombing. That July, Mossad had sent letter bombs to a number of PLO officials in Beirut, including Hout himself. Fortunately, the bomb mailed to his office was detected before it could do any damage. Anis Sayegh, the director of the PLO Research Center, was not so lucky. The bomb sent to his office had exploded in his hands, taking several of his fingers and leaving him partially blind.[88]

That fall, Edward saw Hanna Mikhail on a number of occasions, including, it would seem, Hanna's wedding, presided over by Edward's Quaker father-in-law, Emile Cortas. Hanna's bride was Jihan Helou, a former AUB classmate of his cousin Hanan Mikhail and a fellow member of Fatah, who was assisting Hisham Sharabi in the task of editing the *Journal of Palestine Studies*. One evening in early October, Hanna brought a visitor from France to meet Edward at his apartment. It was none other than Jean Genet, whom Edward had seen in 1970 at the Black Panthers rally on the Columbia campus.[89] As he wrote to Monroe Engel, his old professor at Harvard, Edward found Genet "a strange bird" who talked a great deal about his childhood and religion.[90] When Genet's posthumous memoir of his travels among the Palestinians, *Un captif amoureux*, was translated into English in 1989, Edward praised it as "one of the strangest and most extraordinary books of the decade."[91]

Another of Edward's new Beirut acquaintances was a young American student of Lebanese descent named Charles Glass. Glass, who had just graduated from the University of Southern California with a degree in philosophy, had come to Beirut to continue his studies with Uncle Charles and the AUB philosophy faculty. In a tribute published on the occasion of Edward's death in 2003, Glass recalled their first meeting on the AUB campus in the fall of 1972, after a lecture by Edward on Michel Foucault. "It was not always easy to follow," Glass admitted, "especially for an American like me who got lost when his lectures bounced from English to Arabic to French and back again."[92] If Uncle Charles was also in the audience that evening, he would have had no difficulty with Edward's Arabic and French. But he would have been dismayed by his nephew's interest in Foucault, for whom concepts like Man, Freedom, and Truth were products of a historically conditioned system of thought—one whose time was coming to an end, according to Foucault.

Just before Christmas, the US embassy in Beirut was hit by several American-made anti-tank rockets. Whoever did it left a note reading, "With the compliments of the friends of Vietnam, who will hit you wherever you go." The attack came just days after President Nixon's decision to resume the bombing of Hanoi in response to an impasse in the Paris peace talks.[93] A few days later, Edward and Mariam gathered with the other members of the Cortas family for their annual Christmas celebration. Wadad Cortas' memoir includes a family photograph taken at that time. Edward sits between Wadad and Mariam with his young son Wadie on his lap. On the other side of Wadad sit two of her sisters-in-law, Mona Malik Cortas and Najla Cortas Zurayk. Behind them stand their husbands, Emile and Michel Cortas and Costi Zurayk. Around them are gathered Mariam's brothers and cousins, all of whom had attended the AUB, and some of whom had joined the faculty (including Ilham Zurayk, Costi's eldest daughter, who had studied physics at Columbia in the mid-1960s).

Although Edward, too, had hoped to teach at the AUB during his sabbatical, he was unable to work out a satisfactory arrangement. As he explained in a letter to one of his graduate students, Ferial Ghazoul, what the AUB wanted him to teach did not interest him. "Anyway," he added,

> I think it's an absolutely hopeless and even pernicious place, and . . . I won't have anything to do with it. . . . Anybody good—although poor old Halim B. is a mild enough man compared to Sadek al-Azm—is just shelved, castrated, or thrown out, whichever can be done most cheaply.[94]

"Halim B." was Halim Barakat, a Syrian sociologist and novelist who was denied tenure because of his leftist, pro-Palestinian views—or so his students believed. As in the case of Azm, a student strike was organized, only to be called off at Barakat's request.[95] Although Uncle Charles was probably not involved in the Barakat decision, Edward surely knew of his alleged role in the ouster of Azm and other leftists.

As for Azm, he was about to publish a new book (in Arabic) entitled *A Critical Study of the Thought of the Palestinian Resistance*—an expanded version of the paper he had read at the AAUG conference in Boston, in which he blamed Fatah for the PLO's defeat in Jordan. Having been threatened over one of his previous books, he knew the personal risk he was taking. As Edward observed in a letter to Sami al-Banna in early February, Azm expected to go into hiding in the next few weeks.[96] Unfortunately, his fear turned out to be justified. When Fatah leader Kamal Adwan threatened him, he fled to Damascus. He also lost his job when Anis Sayegh, the director of the PLO Research Center, relieved him of his duties and banned him from the pages of *Shu'un Filastiniyah*, the Center's monthly publication, which forced him to write under a pseudonym. Many years later, Sayegh apologized to Azm, admitting that the order to fire him had come from Yasir Arafat himself.[97]

Meanwhile, Edward spoke on at least two occasions that spring at the Beirut College for Women, where his mother had been a student in the early 1930s and where his sister Jean now taught English, having returned to Beirut after a decade in Washington.[98] Coincidentally, the College had hired his mother's cousin, Dr. Albert Badre, to oversee its transition to a coeducational institution under a new name, Beirut University College. On March 30, Edward joined two AUB English professors, John Munro and Richard M. Murphy, for a panel discussion of Lawrence Durrell's *Alexandria Quartet*.[99] As Charles Glass, who was in the audience, recalled:

> Many of the Westerners in the room imagined themselves Durrellian heroes in a latter-day Alexandria of intrigue and romance. Said attacked the book's triviality, incomprehensible metaphors and meaningless plot.[100]

Edward's dislike of Durrell had been confirmed, no doubt, by a friend's report that he had seen a copy of the *Alexandria Quartet* on the secretary of defense's desk in the Pentagon.[101]

One evening in early April, Edward recalled, he was dining with his cousin Albert Said, Albert's wife Sylvia, and Kamal Nasir, the PLO spokesman. The evening was cut short, however, by a telephone call informing them that Albert's mother Nabiha had died in Amman. Albert and Edward decided to drive to Amman that very night. Unfortunately, Edward was turned away at the Syrian border because he had accidentally brought his son Wadie's passport instead of his own. Returning to Beirut the next morning, he found the city in an uproar. Kamal Nasir, he was told, had been shot dead in his bed.[102] The assassins, it was reported, were Israeli commandos who had landed on the beach under cover of darkness, led by a blond woman. Two other high-ranking PLO leaders, Yussif Najjar and Kamal Adwan—the official who had threatened Sadik al-Azm—had been killed the same night, along with Najjar's wife and five other *fedayeen*.

Within hours of the raid, Prime Minister Saeb Salam resigned, accusing the Christian army commander of ignoring his order to engage the Israeli commandos. Meanwhile, the PLO charged that the Israelis had received assistance from American undercover officers operating out of the US embassy. That same day, a thousand students marched on the embassy, only to be turned away by heavily armed police.[103] On the following day, April 12, an estimated 100,000 mourners joined the funeral procession leading from the al-Omari Mosque to the PLO Martyrs Cemetery near the Sabra and Shatila refugee camps. A number of foreign correspondents covering the funeral, including Juan de Onis of the *New York Times* and Georgie Anne Geyer of the *Chicago Daily News*, were detained at the Fatah office in the camps. The guerrillas, it seems, were fearful of Israeli spies masquerading as journalists.[104] In Geyer's case, they even suspected that she was the blond woman who had led the Israeli raid.[105]

Not long after the Israeli raid on Beirut, Edward, Mariam, and Wadie left for Paris, where Edward was scheduled to lecture at Reid Hall, home of Columbia University's Paris program. There he ran into Jacques Derrida one day. When he mentioned that he had seen Jean Genet in Beirut, he was surprised to learn that Derrida and Genet were friends and fellow football fanatics. At the time, Derrida was writing *Glas*, his most experimental book, with its parallel columns of commentary on Hegel and Genet. When *Glas* was published the following year, Edward was peeved that Derrida had not used his name, referring to him only as "un ami" who had seen Genet in Beirut.[106] It is conceivable that Edward also met up with his former student Paul Auster, who was living in Paris with another former Columbia student, Lydia Davis, the daughter of his colleague Robert Gorham Davis. Among the poets Auster was starting to translate was Edmond Jabès, who had once lived in the same Cairo apartment building as the Said family.[107]

§

His sabbatical over, Edward returned to New York in August 1973. One of his first tasks was to write a paper for the annual conference of the AAUG, scheduled for mid-October in Washington. Just two weeks before the conference, during the Jewish festival of *Yom Kippur*, Egypt and Syria launched their dramatic surprise attack on Israel, which managed to turn the tide of the war with the help of an emergency airlift authorized by President Nixon. A week later, Edward sent the opening paragraphs of his AAUG paper to the *New York Times*, which published them under the title "Arab and Jew: 'Each Is the Other.'" Recalling his own childhood in Cairo, he described his "felt correspondence" with his Jewish classmates. Since then, he lamented, a "corporate Arab-Jewish identity" has emerged, resulting in a "diminished human reality." What was needed, he implied, was some way of returning to the colorful social mosaic that existed before 1948, when Arab and Jewish identities were "mixed."[108]

The following week, Edward read his "Arab and Jew" paper in Washington, where he shared the platform with Daniel Berrigan—Eqbal Ahmad's fellow "conspirator" in the Kissinger kidnapping case—and Dr. Israel Shahak of Hebrew University, a Holocaust survivor and the president of the Israeli League for Human and Civil Rights. Speaking to his fellow Arabs, Edward sounded a surprisingly cautionary note. "Although in many ways, the war from the Arab viewpoint went better than one had expected," he warned, "there are strong reasons for thinking of this war in particular as having been a very dangerous business indeed." One danger was that "many former doves in Israel and perhaps in America have now seen that they were wrong and 'unrealistic'" in their hopes for peace. Another danger was "that, in parallel with the Israelis, we [Arabs] will start to believe that our Middle East can be restored to us either by war or by negotiation as a pristine, unspotted land, free of its past enemies, ours for the taking."[109]

Unfortunately, Edward's timely warning was destined to be overshadowed, as far as the New York press was concerned, by Daniel Berrigan's passionate "I am a Jew" speech. "I am a Catholic priest," Berrigan began, "in resistance to Rome. I am an American, in resistance against Nixon. And I am a Jew, in resistance against Israel." The Jews, he declared, were called by their own prophetic books to be "the arbiter and the advocate of the downtrodden of the earth." Tragically, however, Israel had closed its sacred books, replacing their prophetic wisdom with "an Orwellian nightmare of double talk, racism, fifth-rate sociological jargon, aimed at proving its racial superiority to the people it has crushed." Only in his conclusion did Berrigan address the Arabs, chastising them for "betray[ing] their resistance for rhetorical violence and blind terrorism." He ended with a nod to his friend Eqbal Ahmad, calling on the Palestinians to engage in a massive campaign of nonviolent resistance, following the example of Gandhi, Martin Luther King, and Cesar Chavez.[110]

After the conference, Daniel Berrigan's speech appeared in *American Report*, the newsletter of Clergy and Laymen Concerned, the organization he had co-founded in 1965 to oppose the war in Vietnam. Among the first to respond was Edward's colleague Arthur Hertzberg, who accused Berrigan of concealing "old-fashioned, theological anti-Semitism" underneath "the language of the New Left."[111] Taken aback, the editors of *American Report* decided to devote a whole issue to the Arab-Israeli conflict. Among those who agreed to contribute was Edward Said, who declared that the fundamental conflict in the Middle East was not between Arabs and Jews, or Jews and anti-Semites, or communists and capitalists, or Americans and Russians. Rather, the fundamental conflict was between the modern state and the rights of the individual—the right to live where one pleases, to participate in the political process, to enjoy the economic benefits of one's society regardless of nationality, religion, or ethnicity. As for peace between Israel and the PLO, Edward proposed a Palestinian national authority in the West Bank and Gaza—a proposal he had previously rejected.[112]

In January 1974, Edward returned to Harvard as a visiting professor. One of Uncle Charles' AUB colleagues, the sociologist Samir Khalaf, happened to be a research fellow at Harvard's Center for Middle Eastern Studies that year. Ironically, it was Khalaf whom Halim Barakat blamed for his failure to receive tenure the previous year.[113] That did not stop Edward from befriending Khalaf, who persuaded him—in spite of what he had written to Ferial Ghazoul from Beirut—to think seriously about a permanent position at the AUB. At Mariam's suggestion, Edward wrote to Costi Zurayk about it in February, adding that he had already received offers from Harvard and Johns Hopkins.[114] Zurayk's reply is unknown, but it would seem that the AUB did not show enough interest for Edward to pursue the matter. It was just as well, considering the tsunami of violence that was about to break over Beirut.

That same February, Harvard professors Michael Walzer and Martin Peretz—whom Edward had criticized in his 1968 "Arab Portrayed" essay—returned from a state-sponsored trip to Israel, where they had interviewed Prime Minister Golda Meir, Defense Minister Moshe Dayan, and Foreign Minister Abba Eban, among others. Edward could have read about it in the *Harvard Crimson*, which interviewed Walzer and Peretz after their return to campus. According to Walzer, Golda Meir had reported that the so-called Allon Plan of 1967, which proposed the return of most of the West Bank to Jordan, was now official Israeli policy. Peretz added that American liberals and radicals were wrong to think of Israel as "a Sparta, a garrison state. If there is anywhere that is less like that it is Israel."[115] The *Crimson* did not invite an Arab response, but one can imagine Edward's disgust at the thought of Harvard professors lending their names to an Israeli public relations campaign.

That summer, after finishing the semester at Harvard, Edward attended an international conference on Joseph Conrad in Canterbury, where he read a paper on Conrad and Nietzsche. One of the featured speakers was the Trinidad-born writer V. S. Naipaul, who was beginning to be recognized as a major postcolonial author, having won the Booker Prize a few years earlier for his book *In a Free State*. In his lecture at the conference, "Conrad's Darkness and Mine," later included in *The Return of Eva Peron* (1980), Naipaul recounted his long struggle to come to terms with Conrad as his literary predecessor in the exploration of the "half-made societies" of Africa, Asia, and South America.[116] It was in Canterbury, perhaps, that Edward's dislike for Naipaul and his Olympian perspective on the postcolonial world was born. After the conference, or perhaps before, Edward flew to Beirut with his family, including newborn daughter Najla.[117] It would be their last peaceful summer in Lebanon before the horrible civil war.

In November, Edward was invited to the Waldorf Astoria to meet with Yasir Arafat, who had come to New York to address the UN General Assembly. Arafat's entourage—which included Shafiq al-Hout and the poet Mahmoud Darwish, who became good friends of Edward's—took up two whole floors of the hotel. According to Hout, he and Darwish, along with Walid Khalidi, had written the Arabic text of Arafat's speech, based on an initial draft by Nabil Shaath. This was the famous "gun and olive branch" speech, in which Arafat declared that he had come to the United Nations bearing a gun in one hand and an olive branch in the other. Edward was invited to translate the speech into English with the help of Randa Khalidi el-Fattal—Walid Khalidi's sister—who had published his "Arab Portrayed" essay back in 1968.[118] What Edward didn't know was that Arafat's chief of security, Ali Hassan Salameh, was meeting with the CIA's new Beirut station chief in another room—one of the secret back-channels between Arafat and the US government.[119] Before long, Edward would agree to serve as something of a back-channel himself.

6

Charles Malik: The Intellectual as Lebanese Christian Nationalist, 1975–87

In the spring of 1975, as Charles was teaching what turned out to be his last courses at the AUB, his old friend Bill Eveland returned to Beirut with the Fluor Corporation. In an after-dinner conversation with Eveland, Charles complained that Henry Kissinger had sacrificed his leverage over Israel by agreeing to resupply its military without getting anything in exchange. The best hope for peace, he said, would be a return to the negotiating table in Geneva, where the Soviets could manage the Syrians and the Palestinians could be represented. As for the PLO, he noted that it would not have been recognized as the sole representative of the Palestinian people had Kissinger persuaded the Israelis to return the Golan Heights to Syria and the West Bank to Jordan. It was Lebanon, Charles lamented, that bore the brunt of Kissinger's failure, forced to host a Palestinian state-within-a-state whose sovereignty had now been recognized by most of the world.[1]

As fate would have it, Eveland's return to Beirut coincided with the beginning of the Lebanese Civil War. On Sunday, April 13, 1975, Pierre Gemayel, the founder of the Phalange, attended mass in the East Beirut neighborhood of Ain al-Rumanneh. As he left the church, it was reported, Palestinian gunmen fired at him, killing his bodyguard. In retaliation, Phalangists attacked a bus carrying Palestinian workers through the Christian district, killing twenty-two. Immediately, the fighting spread to other quarters of the city.[2] That evening, Eveland received a phone call from his old friend Abu Said, *Time* magazine's veteran Beirut stringer, warning him not to leave his hotel (the Phoenicia). Unable to sleep, Eveland stood on his balcony, listening to the gunfire in the streets below and watching the rockets launched by the Druzes—allies of the Palestinians—from their mountain stronghold in the Shouf. The Maliks begged him to join them in Rabieh for his own safety, but he chose instead to move to the Holiday Inn.[3]

Later that month, Charles managed to fly out of Beirut on his way to Washington, where on April 29—the eve of the fall of Saigon—he dined with Vice President Nelson Rockefeller at his mansion on Foxhall Road. By chance, a reporter from UPI, Clay Richards, was following Rockefeller around town that day. Richards described the scene:

> He dines alone at Foxhall with Dr. Charles Malik, former president of the UN General Assembly. "It's mostly social. I've known him for years . . . an extremely

well-informed man." At the great mahogany table, which seats 24, they enjoy a simple meal tailored to Rockefeller's diet—veal chops and kidneys, stuffed tomatoes, spinach, stewed pears and a rose wine, which Rockefeller substitutes for his favorite. Dubonnet. Rockefeller, who usually relaxes in the evening by watching detective shows on television, chats with Malik until 10:30 p.m., when his guest leaves and Rockefeller retires an hour early.[4]

Richards didn't reveal what Rockefeller and Charles talked about, but one can be sure that the fighting in Beirut came up.

That fall, Charles returned to Washington to lobby on behalf of Lebanon's Christians. On the evening of November 12, he attended a dinner hosted by Senator Jesse Helms of North Carolina, a supporter of presidential hopeful Ronald Reagan. The following morning, he attended a prayer breakfast hosted by Mayor Walter Washington of the District of Columbia.[5] Later, he met with Senator George McGovern, who chaired the Senate Foreign Relations Subcommittee on the Near East.[6] On December 10, he met with Nelson Rockefeller again, hoping to enlist the vice president in his effort to increase the State Department's budget for the AUB. Prior to the meeting, Robert Oakley of the National Security Council staff sent a "talking paper" to his boss, National Security Advisor Brent Scowcroft, for delivery to Rockefeller. Oakley did not conceal his impatience with Charles, whom he described as "an aging former Lebanese statesman . . . whose fondest memories of US-Lebanese relations are of the 1958 landing of the Marines."[7] Oakley did not mention that Charles had been a visiting dignitary when he received his diploma from Princeton back in 1952.

Charles' frequent trips to Washington were frowned upon by the US ambassador to Lebanon, G. McMurtrie "Mac" Godley, who was casting about for a moderate Maronite to succeed Suleiman Frangieh in 1976. He found one in Elias Sarkis, the banker who had lost the 1970 election to Frangieh by a single vote. Shortly before Christmas, Godley had a long talk with Sarkis, who told him that Frangieh now believed that the best hope for Lebanon lay in the partition of the country. When Godley asked Sarkis whether he planned to visit Washington, Sarkis said that he was willing to go if invited. On Christmas Eve, Godley cabled Henry Kissinger for instructions. "It has . . . occurred to me," he told the secretary of state,

> that we have been receiving a series of relative idiots such as Raymond Edde and Charles Malik, etc., and there might be something to be gained in meeting with one of the few still stable and rational Lebanese. As Department is aware, Sarkis is definitely still among the 4 or 5 leading candidates for the presidency.[8]

Godley may have been the first American ambassador to call Charles Malik an "idiot," but he was neither the first nor the last to complain about Charles' meddling.

Meanwhile, Charles had joined a group of Maronite monks and intellectuals who met regularly at the Université Saint-Esprit de Kaslik to explore the idea of a Christian "mini-state." In late December, Karim Pakradouni, a Phalange official who belonged to the Arabist wing of the party, warned Godley about the Kaslik group, which, he said, had a militia of its own, the *Tanzim* ("Organization"). When Godley asked whether the group had made contact with the Israelis, Pakradouni didn't have an answer. But he did say that Pierre Gemayel, the founder of the Phalange, would be meeting with Father Charbel Kassis, Camille Chamoun, and Charles Malik on December 31 in an effort to enlist their support for a Syrian-sponsored peace initiative. In exchange for modest political reform, according to Pakradouni, the Syrians would guarantee the good behavior of the Palestinian *fedayeen* and their allies in the Lebanese National Movement, the alliance of leftist parties headed by Druze leader Kamal Jumblatt.[9]

§

After a lull, the civil war reignited in January 1976 when Maronite forces butchered hundreds of Muslim men, women, and children in the slums of Karantina, the old quarantine area of Beirut. Within days, the PLO and its allies took their revenge on the Christian town of Damour. Then a rebel lieutenant named Ahmed Khatib announced the formation of a "Lebanese Arab Army."[10] At the end of the month, Lebanon's Christian power brokers met in Kaslik to lay the groundwork for cooperation among the Maronite parties. Those present at the meeting included Pierre Gemayel of the Phalange; Camille Chamoun of the National Liberal Party; Father Charbel Kassis of the Maronite Order; Shaker Abu Suleiman of the Maronite League; Fuad Shemali of the *Tanzim*; Said Akl of the Lebanese Renewal Party; and Charles Malik, the only non-Maronite in the group. Calling themselves "The Front for Freedom and Man in Lebanon"—a Malik-inspired name if ever there was one—they signed a statement demanding the expulsion of foreigners from Lebanon, specifically the Palestinians.[11] The following day, however, the group received an emissary from President Frangieh, who persuaded them to go along with the Syrian peace initiative he had brokered.[12]

Charles and the other leaders of the FFML may have been resigned to the necessity of Syrian intervention, but they hedged their bets by forging a secret alliance with Syria's most powerful enemy—Israel. On March 12, an emissary of the Phalange, Joseph Abou Khalil, boarded an Israeli naval vessel and was taken to Haifa, where he met with Prime Minister Yitzhak Rabin and Foreign Minister Yigal Allon, proposing an alliance between the Maronites and Israel. According to Israeli journalists Zeev Schiff and Ehud Yaari, Rabin was more skeptical than Allon, agreeing only to investigate the situation. A few days later, an Israeli team headed by Colonel Benyamin Ben-Eliezer left for Junieh, the Maronite-controlled port north of Beirut. There they met Bashir Gemayel and his older brother Amin, neither of whom made a good impression. When Ben-Eliezer and his team returned to Israel, they recommended further investigation. In the meantime, the Israelis continued to supply the Maronite militias, as they had been doing for some time.[13]

When the FFML met again in Kaslik in early April, Charles drafted a document officially welcoming "the gracious Syrian initiative."[14] What he really wanted, however, was for the West to take responsibility for Lebanon. As reported by Jack Foisie of the *Los Angeles Times*, who was present at the Kaslik meeting, several participants hoped that the arrival of Dean Brown, Kissinger's special envoy to Lebanon, signaled a more serious peacemaking effort on the part of Washington. Eventually, someone invited Charles to speak his mind. The Americans, he exploded, "don't give a damn about

Lebanon." Then, having vented several decades' worth of frustration, he calmed down. "I understand there can be no direct intervention," he admitted. "I appreciate the isolationist feeling that stems from Vietnam." But some external force had to intervene, he insisted, in order to guarantee an effective cease-fire. When asked what force he had in mind, he could offer only negative answers—not the Arabs (because of their internal divisions), not the United Nations (because of the Soviet veto), not the Syrians (because of their unpopularity).[15]

On May 8, 1976, Elias Sarkis, the Syrian-backed presidential candidate, defeated Raymond Eddé in a near-unanimous vote. After the election, *Monday Morning* published reflections on the election by a number of leading political figures, including Charles. In his contribution, entitled "The Impossible and the Possible," Charles called on all parties to rally around Sarkis. He then named three "impossibles" in the present situation. The "thoughtless bourgeois existence" of the past, he warned, was no longer possible. But it was also impossible, he lamented, "to tell all the truth you know" in "this atmosphere of terror." As for the "possibles," Charles listed ten. "It should be possible," he ventured, "for acts of violence and war to stop completely and for good." It should also be possible "for the Lebanese and the Palestinians to love and respect one another," realizing that "their inalienable destiny is to live as neighbors and brothers, each in the full dignity of their independence and integrity as a people."[16] Whether it was possible for them to live as independent peoples within the borders of Lebanon, Charles did not say.

By mid-May, a Lebanese National Movement offensive, supported by the PLO, was threatening the Maronite heartland in Mount Lebanon. For the first time, the PLO publicly asked the Syrians to leave Lebanon, accusing them of shelling the Palestinian suburb of Burj al-Barajneh and imposing a blockade on arms intended for the PLO. In an effort to prevent a complete break between the PLO and Syria, Shia leader Musa al-Sadr went to Damascus to plead with President Assad.[17] Evidently, he was unsuccessful. At the beginning of June, Assad ordered regular Syrian army units into Lebanon, where they faced formidable resistance from the LNM militias and the PLO. The Maronites took advantage of the Syrian invasion to redouble their siege of Tal al-Zaatar, the last Palestinian stronghold in Maronite territory, which ended with another massacre of innocent civilians. Among those who observed the siege was Colonel Ben-Eliezer, who was meeting with the leaders of the rival Maronite militias—Bashir Gemayel, Camille Chamoun's son Dany, and President Frangieh's son Tony.[18]

§

By July 1976, Beirut had become so dangerous that the PLO was asked to provide security for the evacuation of over 300 Americans and other foreigners. The evacuation was overseen by Deputy Assistant Secretary of State for African Affairs Talcott Seelye, who had been sent to Beirut to run the embassy after the assassination of Ambassador Francis Meloy that June. Before the evacuation, Seelye telephoned his father's old friend Charles Malik to ask for a guarantee that the Maronite militias would not open fire on the Palestinian security forces. Charles took the opportunity to invite Seelye to visit the Maronite zone, which he described as perfectly safe. Seelye cabled Henry

Kissinger that he was inclined to go, even though such a visit would be seen as proof that the Americans were collaborating with the Maronites and the Syrians. He hoped to persuade the Maronite leaders to "come off their high horse," as he put it.[19] But Kissinger seems to have denied his request.

On August 29, Charles delivered a speech entitled "Why You are Fighting" at a rally of new recruits to the Phalange militia.[20] The next day, the Phalange and the other Maronite militias announced the formation of a "Joint Command Council" to be headed by Bashir Gemayel. In theory, the JCC would transform the separate militias into a single, integrated Christian army known as the "Lebanese Forces." Then, on August 31, Charles and Fuad Bustani, the former president of the Lebanese University, met with Camille Chamoun to discuss their upcoming trip to the United States, where they planned to meet with Lebanese expatriates.[21] All three men were members of the new "Lebanese Front," whose membership differed somewhat from the original Front for Freedom and Man in Lebanon. In addition to Chamoun, Charles, and Bustani, the new Front included Pierre Gemayel, Suleiman Frangieh, Charbel Kassis, Edward Honein (an MP allied with Raymond Eddé, who wanted nothing to do with the Front), and the historian Jawad Boulos.[22]

Having resigned from the AUB, Charles returned to the United States that fall as a representative of the new Lebanese Front. In early October, he sent a telegram to Pierre Gemayel and the "Three Presidents" (Chamoun, Frangieh, and Sarkis) from Washington, reporting that he had met with Nelson Rockefeller and that Henry Kissinger had asked to meet with him.[23] That same month, Charles received a copy of a "Prospectus for a Public Affairs Program for Free Lebanon" from Martin Ryan Haley and Associates, a well-known Washington consulting firm.[24] Then, at the end of October, Charles met again with Henry Kissinger, who promised him a "bold plan" for Lebanon after the American presidential election.[25] Accompanying Kissinger to the meeting was Under Secretary of State for Political Affairs Philip C. Habib. Afterwards, Kissinger told Israeli ambassador Simcha Dinitz, "We have had some Lebanese people here and they say you have slowed down supporting them." Dinitz replied, "Not that I know of. You mean Charles?" Kissinger replied, "Yeah. I said I don't want to know what is going on but just as long as it was not done at our urging."[26] The fact that Dinitz referred to Charles by his first name indicates just how close the alliance between the Lebanese Front and the Israelis had become.

There was just one problem: if President Ford should lose the election to Jimmy Carter, Henry Kissinger would be out of a job. So Charles wisely decided to hedge his bets. A few days after meeting with Kissinger, he met with David Rockefeller and Cyrus Vance, a member of the executive committee of the Rockefeller Foundation and Carter's future secretary of state.[27] If Nelson Rockefeller had offered Charles access to the Ford administration, it was his brother David who introduced him to the Carter administration-in-waiting. A few years earlier, David Rockefeller had founded the Trilateral Commission, an elite forum for public officials, academics, and corporate executives interested in greater cooperation between the United States, Western Europe, and Japan. The man Rockefeller had asked to take charge of the Commission was Zbigniew Brzezinski, Edward Said's colleague at Columbia and Carter's future national security advisor. After dining with Carter in London, Rockefeller had decided to invite the Georgia governor to join the Commission.[28] That is how Carter had met Brzezinski and Cyrus Vance, another Trilateralist.

On November 2, Jimmy Carter won the presidential election, ending Henry Kissinger's eight-year monopoly on US foreign policy. A week later, Charles attended a meeting of the Lebanese Front in the village of Kfur, in the mountains northeast of Junieh. As reported by the US embassy in Beirut, the Front decided to send him back to Washington to obtain stronger assurances of American support.[29] In December, he sought an audience with the president-elect. Among those who tried to help was the televangelist Pat Robertson, who had backed Carter's presidential campaign and interviewed him on his cable television show, *The 700 Club*. Robertson's father, Senator A. Willis Robertson of Virginia, who had been active in Congressional prayer groups and International Christian Leadership since the late 1940s, was an admirer of Charles.[30] In a letter to Carter, which began "Dear Jimmy," Pat Robertson referred to Charles Malik as a friend and "a warm-hearted evangelical Christian." If Carter would agree to see Charles, Robertson said, he would offer Charles the use of his own private jet.[31] Evidently, Carter declined Robertson's invitation.

On December 8, Charles met for an hour with Philip Habib, whom Cyrus Vance had decided to retain in his State Department post.[32] As the son of Lebanese Christian immigrants, Habib could be expected to follow through on Kissinger's pledge of a bold plan for Lebanon. Two weeks later, Charles met with Vance again and handed him a document entitled "Free Lebanon" with the request that he pass it on to Jimmy Carter. Then, over the holidays, Charles produced a revised version of "Free Lebanon," which he sent to Vance in early January. In it, he blamed a "Palestinian-communist-international terrorist alliance" for the civil war in Lebanon. He also warned Vance and Carter that "to allow what has already been gained between Israel and Lebanon to turn out to be totally in vain is a mistake."[33] The alliance between Israel and the Lebanese Front was hardly a secret. That September, *Time* had reported that Shimon Peres, the Israeli defense minister, had made no fewer than four trips to Lebanon during the summer months, accompanied on one occasion by Prime Minister Yitzhak Rabin.[34]

§

On January 23, 1977, the leaders of the Lebanese Front met at the convent of the Sisters of the Cross at Saydet el-Bir, east of Beirut. According to Karim Pakradouni, they adopted three fundamental resolutions. First, they endorsed a federal system for Lebanon in which each community would control its own affairs, including education, finance, and security. Second, they called for the distribution of the Palestinians among the various Arab countries. Third, they voiced concern over the penetration of Syrian troops into Christian areas in the wake of the agreement brokered by the Arab League in October 1976, which authorized a Syrian-dominated Arab Deterrent Force to keep the peace in Lebanon. The Front also decided to prepare a memorandum for Cyrus Vance, the new US secretary of state, who was due to visit Lebanon in February.[35] As usual, the task of composing the memorandum fell on Charles Malik, who produced a fifteen-page document that was duly signed by Camille Chamoun, Suleiman Frangieh, Pierre Gemayel, and Charbel Kassis.

The memorandum began with an epigraph from the Book of Isaiah: "Is it not yet a very little while, and Lebanon shall be turned into a fruitful field." After laying out the Front's vision for a federal Lebanon and asking the Arab Deterrent Forces to respect Lebanon's unique identity, Charles turned to the Palestinians. "Had it not been for the Palestinians," he declaimed,

> and their hollow ambitions in Lebanon, and their conceit, and this war which this conceit prompted them to unleash on Lebanon, and the fact they allowed themselves to be swept by international communism and allied themselves with it, had it not been for all these facts there would have been no need for any intervention, Arab or non-Arab.

He went on to recommend that the responsibility for the Palestinians be turned over to the Joint Arab Command, that the Palestinians in Lebanon be distributed among the other Arab League states, and that those states adopt a uniform law regarding the status of their Palestinian residents.[36]

The memo was delivered to the new US ambassador to Lebanon, Richard Parker, who presented it to Cyrus Vance when he visited Beirut on February 18. Vance then handed it to William Quandt of the National Security Council, who was accompanying him on his tour of the Middle East.[37] That same day, the new Lebanese foreign minister, Fouad Boutros, shared a vehicle with Vance and Parker. According to Karim Pakradouni, Boutros accused Vance of working parallel diplomatic channels—an open, official channel with the Sarkis government and a secret, unofficial channel with the Lebanese Front, represented by Charles Malik. He demanded that Vance say whether or not the United States wanted a Christian state in the Middle East—"a second Israel"—as envisioned by the Lebanese Front. Vance replied that United States continued to support the unity of Lebanon as well as the policies of President Sarkis. As for Charles Malik, Vance defended his decision to give him a hearing, noting that he was an old friend of the United States.[38]

In April, Ambassador Parker had a long talk with Karim Pakradouni, which he immediately reported to Secretary Vance in Washington. According to Pakradouni, whom Parker considered the most reasonable and moderate of the Phalangists, Christian hard-liners were claiming that the United States had a "double echelon" policy in Lebanon, secretly endorsing the separatist agenda of the Lebanese Front while publicly supporting a unified Lebanon. The hard-liner most responsible for this lie, he said, was Charles Malik, who had met with both Kissinger and Vance in Washington. "Unfortunately," Pakradouni complained, "the myth of Charles Malik's influence in Washington was born in 1958, when, it is said, he sought US intervention in Lebanon despite the opposition of the US ambassador in Beirut." Underlying this myth, he continued, was another myth, namely, that the "other echelon" of US policy was conducted by the CIA.[39]

A few weeks after Pakradouni complained about him to Ambassador Parker, Charles published another long piece in *an-Nahar*, entitled "Between Hope and

Despair." He began with the Palestinians, whose cause, he claimed, he had "defended ... at the United Nations and in diplomatic conversations and notes perhaps more than any other human being." The Lebanese, he noted,

> attribute the devastation of considerable parts of Beirut and other cities, towns, and villages, the destruction or desecration of 50 or more churches and monasteries, the slaughtering of nuns and monks and innocent women and children, the importing into Lebanon of thousands of mercenaries motivated by fanatical hatred, wholly ungrounded in truth and in fact, for the most part to the Palestinians.

"I am at a loss as to where we were to blame," he continued, "and I would be the first to apologize publicly to the Palestinians for any offense we may have committed against them." Next, he apologized to Lebanon's Muslims. "If I knew where we erred towards our Muslim brothers," he declared, "except in not loving them enough, in not being sensitive enough to their needs, I would be the first to apologize to them; and for our insensitivity and lack of love I do apologize."[40]

A week later, Menachem Begin's Likud Party won a majority of the seats in the Israeli Knesset. After Begin took office in June, Charles attended a meeting of the Lebanese Front.[41] Either before or after the gathering, he typed up thirty-three talking points for "a most fateful meeting" with the new Israeli leaders. Point 14 revealed the Front's growing resentment of the Syrian occupation: "Is Israel prepared to cooperate with us to the full with a view to liberating ourselves from Syrian domination?" Point 21 voiced the Front's frustration with the Carter administration:

> Everything emanating from Washington these days aims at discouraging us from having anything to do with Israel, and urging us to support Sarkis and the Syrians, and cooperate with the Arabs. . . . Is Israel prepared to cooperate with us in bringing about a change of attitude in Washington?

To top it off, Point 32 appeared to contemplate a coup d'état against the Sarkis government:

> There is no substitute for the youthful leadership who fought the 2-year war coming to political power in Lebanon. Total coordination between us and Israel towards that end is essential.[42]

Eventually, the youthful leader of the Lebanese Forces, Bashir Gemayel, would come to power with the help of the Israelis—but not until 1982, when Sarkis' six-year term ended.

The meeting between the Lebanese Front and the Israelis took place later that summer. There is no evidence that Charles attended the meeting, although the Malik Papers contain unsigned copies of three notes, dated August 8, 1977, addressed to Prime Minister Menachem Begin, Defense Minister Ezer Weizman, and Mossad director Yitzhak Hofi, thanking each of them for the previous week's "first contact."[43] Hofi was the most skeptical of the three, but his deputy and rival David Kimche believed that the

Christians of Lebanon deserved Israeli assistance. Kimche had traveled to Lebanon on several occasions during the previous year, forming a close bond with Bashir Gemayel. On one trip to Beirut, Kimche recalled,

> our car was stopped by a Syrian patrol; the Syrian soldiers stared at me for a long minute before accepting the driver's explanation that his companion was a European journalist. When we reached a second Syrian post, the driver, Bashir Gemayel, crashed through the barrier. The Syrians were too surprised to shoot.[44]

Kimche made no mention of Charles Malik, but it is possible that the two men had been introduced on one of Kimche's visits to Beirut. Charles, after all, had become Bashir's trusted mentor.

In December, Bashir Gemayel called on Ambassador Parker at his residence in Yarze, southeast of downtown Beirut. As Parker recalled:

> [Gemayel] was bent on becoming president of Lebanon. He came to see me at my residence in December of '77 and told me he was about to move on the presidential palace which was about two-hundred yards down the road from us. And he was going to take over. I told him not to be a damn fool. We weren't going to support that, and neither would anybody else. . . . He was very disappointed, and he went away.

"He thought that you would give support to him?" asked the incredulous interviewer. Parker replied:

> Yes, he had because he had been misled I think by Charles Malik, who had kept coming back here [to Washington] and seeing Vance and other people and going back to Lebanon and saying, "Parker doesn't know what he is talking about. Parker is pro-Syrian—Vance is with us."

Parker went on to describe Charles as "a man of great intellect and even greater ego who was, I found, a very destructive influence in Lebanon in the time I was there."[45]

§

In late January 1978, Charles traveled to Washington for the Presidential Prayer Breakfast, the annual gathering sponsored by International Christian Leadership, now headed by Doug Coe, who referred to it simply as "The Family." In his talk at the breakfast, President Carter mentioned his recent meetings with Menachem Begin and Anwar Sadat. He liked and admired Prime Minister Begin, Carter said, because Begin has the "fervor of a deeply committed, religious man who . . . worships the same God you and I do." And he had "felt an instant friendship with President Sadat," who "never fails to point out that the Egyptians and the Jews are sons of Abraham, worship the same God, share a common heritage and a common faith."[46] This was the sort of theological language that Charles himself used when communicating his own vision of peace in the Middle East. But he never became a confidant of Jimmy Carter's, even though Carter was on friendly terms with Doug Coe and The Family.[47]

Charles' schedule indicates that he met with a number of individuals after the prayer breakfast, notably Doug Coe and Mark Hatfield, the evangelical Christian senator from Oregon, who had been Coe's political science professor at Willamette University.[48] Coe has been criticized for cultivating such brutal dictators as Haiti's Duvalier and Indonesia's Suharto, but Hatfield was one of the most liberal Republicans in the Senate, an opponent of the Vietnam War and an early advocate of the Palestinian cause.[49] He had made several trips to the Middle East over the years, visiting refugee camps and calling on the United States to increase its support for UNRWA. He was also a friend of the AUB, which he had visited on at least one occasion and whose US government funding he had defended in Congress.[50] One suspects that Charles' meeting with Hatfield was not devoted to spiritual matters alone; no doubt he took the opportunity to remind the senator of the threat Syria posed to Lebanon's Christians.

Sadly, Lebanon's Christians also posed a threat to each other. In northern Lebanon, an intra-Maronite turf war broke out between the Frangieh family and the Phalangists. Some of Bashir Gemayel's men, it seems, were trying to muscle their way into the local rackets, and the Frangiehs didn't like it. The bad blood between the two Maronite camps reached its nadir on June 13, when Phalangists led by Samir Geagea launched a surprise attack on the Frangieh summer home in the village of Ehden, murdering Tony Frangieh, his wife, his three-year-old daughter, and some thirty others.[51] In July, the Syrians—longtime allies of the Frangiehs—took their revenge by shelling Christian East Beirut, killing hundreds of civilians and forcing tens of thousands to flee to the mountains. In response, Israeli jets flew low over Beirut as a warning to the Syrians to stay out of the city.[52] In Washington, the American Lebanese League sent 150 demonstrators to the Syrian embassy and took out a full-page ad in the *Post* calling on President Carter to halt the "genocide" of Lebanon's Christians.[53]

Soon after the July crisis began, the Lebanese Front prepared for an emergency meeting with the Israelis. The Malik Papers contain a "note" and "points for discussion" dated July 14, 1978, evidently composed by Charles but reflecting the opinions of Camille Chamoun and other Front leaders. The note, which begins by blaming the three-year civil war on the Palestinians, the Syrians, and their Muslim and Leftist allies, announces that the Christians of Lebanon have "reached an historic turning point." "The immediate and urgent objective today," the note continues, "is to change the 'nominal' government which oppresses the Christians by the use of foreign occupying forces." It goes on to propose a new state incorporating "the greatest possible number of Christians on the largest possible tract of land." One of the points for discussion accuses President Sarkis of being a Syrian agent covering up "the genocide of the Christians." Another insists that, in order to change the attitude of the United States, "we need the active support of the Israeli world information services." A third point recommends pressuring the Druzes to change sides.[54]

In August, Charles returned to Washington to rally American support for Lebanon's besieged Christians. On August 16, he appeared before the Senate Subcommittee on

Near Eastern Affairs, chaired by Senator Richard Stone, a friend of Israel. "The other day," he testified,

> I watched Beirut at night burning and getting destroyed. In a reverie . . . I imagined Nero fiddling and chuckling as he saw Beirut burning and reduced to ashes. And who was Nero, to me, at that moment? He was the whole of the civilized world.

Lebanon, he said, was a sick man in need of a doctor. But the partition of the country, he insisted, was not a cure that anybody wanted. In fact, he said, Lebanon had already been partitioned—not just physically, politically, and militarily, but also psychologically. "The question then," he concluded, "is not partition but the exact opposite: How to reassemble the already splintered parts, how to reconstitute the whole."[55]

A week or so after the Stone hearing, Lucien Kinsolving, a veteran Arabist assigned to the American embassy in Beirut, sent a sharply worded telegram to the State Department in Washington. The department, he advised, must take a

> firm line with the American Lebanese lobby and its supporters. While Charles Malik should of course be received for old times' sake, we believe [Morris] Draper should talk to him very toughly indeed and ask him if he does not think it a disgrace that a former eminent professor of philosophy should now be stooping to the inciting role he is playing in a civil war fueled to large degree by religious intolerance.[56]

The following day, Deputy Secretary of State Warren Christopher reported back to Beirut on Charles' meetings with Draper and other officials. In one meeting, Charles had warned that the Syrians intended to "annihilate" the Christian community in Lebanon, charging the United States with complicity in the "Islamization" and "Arabization" of the country. Over dinner with Draper, he had insisted that the Christians be allowed to maintain their predominance, lest they become a persecuted minority like the Copts in Egypt.[57]

At the same time, Charles was giving interviews arranged by the Lebanese Information and Research Center, the new Washington office of the Lebanese Front, directed by a Lebanese American engineer named Alfred Mady.[58] In early September, Charles sat down with a reporter from the *Washington Star*, who asked him about the role of Syrian peacekeeping forces in Lebanon. They had done a good job in the beginning, he admitted. But "something happened about eight or nine months ago which appears to have changed the policy of Syria." Just last month, he lamented, the Syrians had destroyed several Christian suburbs of Beirut, forcing some 300,000 civilians to flee to the mountains. When the reporter asked about Israel's role in Lebanon, Charles defended it, claiming that Israeli reprisal raids were aimed exclusively at the PLO. To the accusation that the Israelis had turned South Lebanon over to Christian forces who were refusing entrance to UN peacekeepers, Charles retorted that the United Nations had been unable to prevent thousands of armed Palestinians from returning to the area. That same day, the interview was read into the *Congressional Record* by Representative

Edward Derwinski, Republican of Illinois, who had recently introduced a measure to suspend all US aid to Syria.[59]

In October, Charles was joined in his Washington lobbying effort by Dory Chamoun, the younger son of Camille Chamoun. On October 20, Edward Cody of the *Washington Post* reported that Senator Daniel Patrick Moynihan, Democrat of New York, had hosted a luncheon for congressmen and reporters to hear from Charles and Chamoun. In the same story, Cody documented the cordial relationship between the American Lebanese League and the American Israel Public Affairs Committee (AIPAC). A State Department official told him, "It's common knowledge that they're working together." Even Robert Basil, the president of the ALL, admitted, "We contact one another every three or four weeks, you know, but we're very careful about it. There are times when our interests merge and there are times when they don't." Not all Lebanese Americans in Washington were happy with the ALL, however. Senator James Abourezk, Democrat of South Dakota, complained, "What they represent is a small right-wing minority with a lot of money who are determined to use the money and their alliance with Israel to restore themselves to power."[60]

The ALL was forging ties with other American Jewish organizations as well. At the end of October, Charles accompanied Monsignor Elias Hayek, the founder of the ALL and the director of its Washington office, to Cambridge, Massachusetts, for a dinner hosted by the American Jewish Committee. At the dinner, Charles told his hosts that they found themselves "at one of the most mysterious and significant moments in the history of the world." He was referring to the recent signing of the Camp David Accords by Presidents Begin and Sadat. The question now, he continued, is whether the United States would

> let slip away the opportunity for making peace between all the children of Abraham, and not only between the Moslems and the Jews. Only when Jews, Christians, and Moslems are secure, and the whole region is Abrahamic, can there be peace in the world.

After his speech, Charles received a standing ovation. His host, Rabbi Marc Tannenbaum, declared that "American Jews would not sit by while the innocent men, women, and children of Lebanon were being annihilated."[61]

§

The beginning of 1979 found Charles back in Washington, where he attended the Presidential Prayer Breakfast on January 18, just two days after the shah of Iran had fled the country. In his remarks at the breakfast, President Carter alluded to the Islamic revolution:

> I would guess that one of the great news stories of 1979 will be the impact around the Persian Gulf, in the Middle East, of religious fervor and the searching for some compatibility between a modern, rapidly changing, technological world on the one hand, and an inclination on the part of devout religious leaders to cling to

stability and security predicated on past social and personal habits. So, as you can well see, in various ways, even in a modern world when we consider it to be highly secular, the great events that move the people here and in other nations are intimately related to religion.[62]

A year earlier, the Carters had celebrated New Year's Eve with the shah and Empress Farah in Niavaran Palace in Tehran. In words that had already come back to haunt him, he had toasted the shah in front of the assembled guests, saying, "Iran, because of the great leadership of the Shah, is an island of stability in one of the most troubled areas of the world."[63]

After the Ayatollah Khomeini's triumphant return to Iran on February 1, the shah's government collapsed. Charles happened to be staying at Arrowhead Springs near San Bernardino, California, a former desert spa that served as the headquarters of Bill Bright's Campus Crusade for Christ. At the time, Bright was in the midst of a global campaign called "Here's Life, World!" which sent teams of evangelists into the developing world. Charles served on the executive board of Here's Life International— the nonprofit that ran the campaign—along with such wealthy entrepreneurs as Wallace E. Johnson, the founder of the Holiday Inn chain; W. Clement Stone, the Chicago insurance magnate who had donated millions to Richard Nixon's presidential campaigns; and Nelson Bunker Hunt, the Dallas oilman who backed the John Birch Society and other conservative causes.[64] As for the revolution in Iran, Charles feared that the United States was in retreat after Vietnam. "I see you doing *nothing*," he told a reporter from San Bernardino.[65]

A week later, Charles published an op-ed in the *New York Times* entitled "Ultimate Questions of the Middle East." In Cold War fashion, he attributed Lebanon's problems, and those of the Middle East at large, to a Communist plot, much as he had done in the Eisenhower era. "What is happening in Lebanon," he asserted,

> is an organic part of a grand strategic encircling movement that has been unfolding for years. The encircling subject is the Soviet Union and the encircled object is the entire Middle East, with its unique strategic position and its immense natural resources. The events in Iran, Afghanistan, Ethiopia, the Horn of Africa, Yemen, Lebanon, Turkey, as well as the Arab opposition to the Camp David accords, all belong to the same encircling phenomenon.[66]

Unfortunately, there was no Eisenhower or Dulles to break the Communist circle. Instead, the West was stuck with mild-mannered peacemakers like Jimmy Carter and Cyrus Vance.

A month later, on March 26, Prime Minister Sadat and President Begin came to the White House for the signing of the peace treaty between Egypt and Israel. That evening, Charles delivered a major speech at the Cosmos Club, where he often stayed when he was in Washington. "These signings," he admonished his audience,

> solemnize and formalize and publicly declare to the whole world that the effective extension of the domain of the West to include the Eastern Mediterranean is now

guaranteed by the economic and military might of the United States. You have no idea of the depth and extent of your inextricable involvement in the Near East now.

Not surprisingly, he saw the hand of God in the signing of the treaty. "There is a mystery," he observed,

> in Carter the Christian reconciling Sadat the Moslem and Begin the Jew. Let a Communist atheist try to bring them together! He could not. Let an Indian pantheist try to bring them together! He could not. Let a Western cynic try to bring them together! He could not. Only Carter the Christian could—at least so far.[67]

In fact, Sadat and Begin had forced Carter to abandon his dream of a comprehensive Middle East peace, settling, instead, for a bilateral agreement of the sort preferred by Henry Kissinger.

Turning to the revolution in Iran, Charles called it "the Pearl Harbor of our day." But he interpreted the event through the lens of the Cold War. Admitting that "all analogies are more or less misleading," he ventured,

> I believe Khomeini is the Kerensky of the Iranian revolution. I believe he is going to be superseded by a Marxist-communist regime closely linked to the Soviet Union. His historical function is precisely not to last, but only to get rid of the shah in order to pave the way for this supersession of himself. Soviet communism has the power of dominating Iran even under cover of Islamic Shi'ism. The West has no such power.[68]

Khomeini may not last long, Charles continued, but in the meantime he has a vital message for the West—namely, that the West is in desperate need of its own spiritual revival, a return to its own roots in the Judeo-Christian tradition. Among those inspired by Charles' speech was Senator Jesse Helms, who later read it into the *Congressional Record*, introducing it as "a remarkable address, by a man who has the insight to penetrate to the heart of our problems."[69]

That June, Charles attended a dinner at the Hyatt Regency in Washington hosted by the Coalition for a Democratic Majority, founded by Democratic Cold Warriors in the wake of Nixon's landslide victory over George McGovern in the 1972 presidential election. Two of its leading figures were Senators Henry Jackson of Washington and Daniel Patrick Moynihan of New York, who cochaired the dinner at the Hyatt. Charles was there to receive a "Friends of Freedom" award, along with nine other individuals and organizations. Among those receiving awards in absentia were Ida Nudel, a Russian Jewish "refusenik" who had been exiled to Siberia; Huber Matos, a Cuban revolutionary who had been sentenced to twenty years in prison after breaking with Fidel Castro; and Jonathan Netanyahu, who had died during the 1976 Israeli rescue operation that had freed the passengers of a hijacked jet in Uganda. Netanyahu was represented by his brother Benjamin, the head of a new anti-terrorism institute in Jerusalem named after the martyred Jonathan.[70]

In November, Charles returned to Arrowhead Springs to address a Protestant pastors' conference. One of the pastors in attendance was Rev. John F. MacArthur, Jr., a radio preacher who found Charles' talk to be a sign of the End Times. According to MacArthur, Charles warned that Christianity was retreating in the face of three successive revivals: the revival of atheism, the revival of Judaism, and the revival of Islam, the last of which threatened to "sweep the world," starting with Iran. The only hope for the West, Charles proclaimed, was an alliance between the Roman Catholic Church and the Eastern Orthodox Church. According to MacArthur, Charles even prophesied the reunification of all of Christendom—Protestants included—under the authority of the pope. "Folks," MacArthur told his congregation, "when I heard that, knowing what I know about the book of Daniel, I started hopping on my seat. I knew that was coming. I just didn't think I'd hear it from somebody who claimed to be a Christian."[71]

In Lebanon, meanwhile, Bashir Gemayel was reunifying Christendom by force of arms. On July 7, 1980—the "Day of the Long Knives"—he sent his Lebanese Forces to crush the Tiger militia of his last remaining rival in the Maronite camp, Dany Chamoun. The following month, Charles wrote an open letter to the Maronites. Rather than dwelling on the fratricidal wars between the Gemayels, the Chamouns, and the Frangiehs, he chose to remind the Maronites of how much they had been given, starting with Mount Lebanon itself, "among the strongest fortresses in the Near East." In addition, the Maronites had been given an Aramaic-Syrian heritage, including the Aramaic language—the language of the Maronite rites, the language of Jesus himself. Because of this heritage, the Maronites had been given "the opportunity to be the closest people, morally, and culturally, to both the Arabs and the Jews." Moreover, the Maronites have been given "great vigor" in all spheres of life. In the sphere of poetry, this vigor was exemplified by the incomparable verse of Said Akl. In the sphere of politics, it was exemplified by the longevity of the Phalange Party, which, Charles noted, "is forty-five years old today."[72]

§

On September 13, 1980, Charles spoke at the dedication of the Billy Graham Center at Wheaton College in suburban Chicago. "What could be more wonderful," he asked, "than for a Center named after the greatest evangelist of our age to aim at achieving . . . the twofold miracle of evangelizing the great universities and intellectualizing the great evangelical movement?"[73] Then he rushed back to Lebanon for an important meeting with Bashir Gemayel and his counselors at Saydet el-Bir. According to Alain Ménargues, the purpose of the meeting was to determine strategy following the defeat of Dany Chamoun's militia and the unification of the Lebanese Forces. To that end, Bashir had asked two of his counselors, Antoine Najm and Colonel Michel Aoun, to prepare a report, entitled "Étude de la prise du pouvoir par Bashir," which presented two options for seizing power in Lebanon—one by force, the other by constitutional means, with or without the support of President Sarkis. After much discussion, Bashir and his counselors decided to keep both options on the table. In the meantime, they would "prepare the environment" for a seizure of power no later than 1982, the final year of Sarkis' term in office.[74]

That December, Cecil Hourani asked Charles to deliver a copy of a letter from Major Haddad, the renegade commander of the Israeli-backed South Lebanon Army, to President-Elect Ronald Reagan. In his letter, Haddad urged Reagan to get the Syrians and the Palestinians out of Lebanon. He also requested that Reagan send an emissary directly to "Free Lebanon," as he called the area controlled by his forces.[75] Reagan may not have known who Haddad was, but he was well acquainted with a California evangelist named George Otis, who had built a "Voice of Hope" radio station in southern Lebanon on land donated by Haddad. In addition to playing gospel music, the station was used for Arabic broadcasts by Haddad and his spokesmen.[76] It was Otis who, in 1970, had prayed with Governor Reagan, prophesying that God would put him in the White House one day.[77] In 1976, during Reagan's first presidential campaign, Otis had interviewed the former governor, eliciting Reagan's affirmation that he had, indeed, been "born again."[78] In 1980, he had served as honorary chairman of "Christians for Reagan."[79]

Just before Christmas, Charles attended a meeting of the Lebanese Front at the monastery in Aoukar, between Beirut and Junieh. At the conclusion of the meeting, the senior leaders of the Front, including Camille Chamoun and Pierre Gemayel, endorsed a Malik-drafted document entitled "The Lebanon We Want To Build." In it, they called for a reconsideration of the 1943 National Pact, one that might result in "some kind of decentralization or federation or confederation" designed to prevent future sectarian conflict. They also called for "total liberation from the two occupations," namely, the Syrian and the Palestinian. In order to prevent Palestinians from settling in Lebanon, the Front proposed to abrogate "all the sales or transfers of real estate which occurred here and there with a view to enabling Palestinians ... to own Lebanese property." The document's penultimate section was addressed to the Western democracies. "We are persuaded," the leaders insisted, "that part of the responsibility for the havoc that has afflicted Lebanon falls on your shoulders."[80]

In January 1981, Charles attended the Inauguration of Ronald Reagan as president of the United States. Before he left Beirut, he paid a visit to Bashir Gemayel, who authorized him to make as many contacts with the new administration as possible. When he arrived in Washington, he learned that Richard Allen, the new national security advisor, was willing to meet with him. As they started to talk, Charles was surprised by Allen's knowledge of Lebanon's problems and, more particularly, of the aspirations of Lebanon's Christians, which Charles attributed to Israeli tutelage. When Allen asked, "What do you want from the United States?" Charles replied, "To get rid of the Palestinians and the Syrians." Allen then asked for a practical plan of action—a sign, Charles realized, that Reagan's foreign policy would be run directly out of the White House, bypassing the State Department. In parting, Allen said he would discuss the matter with the president, promising to keep Charles informed.[81]

When Charles returned to Beirut in late February, he immediately called Bashir, who, accompanied by two of his advisors, Zahi Boustani and Antoine Najm, met him at his house in Rabieh. Charles was full of enthusiasm, proposing a plan whereby the United States would guarantee the independence of Lebanon and the self-determination of its confessional communities. In return, Lebanon would evict international terrorists from its territory and permit the building of an American military base. Boustani, however, recommended that they wait to hear from the Israeli foreign minister, Yitzhak Shamir, who had promised to pursue a rapprochement between the Lebanese Front and the United States. Sure enough, the US ambassador to Lebanon, John Gunther Dean, soon met with Bashir, hand-delivering a secret document, dated March 9, 1981, entitled "Directives on Lebanon." In it, the Americans voiced their conviction that Lebanon's Palestinian problem would be solved in the context of the Camp David peace process. As for the Syrians, the Americans favored their total withdrawal from Lebanon. Finally, they encouraged Bashir to cooperate with the Sarkis government and enter into a dialogue with the Muslim and Druze communities.[82]

That spring, Charles went back to Washington to meet with Reagan administration officials and to sign a contract with the Catholic University of America. On April 2, he saw Secretary of State Alexander Haig, who was preparing to leave on a tour of Middle Eastern capitals.[83] No doubt they discussed the previous day's clash between the Lebanese Forces and the Syrians at Zahle, where Bashir had vowed to fight the Syrians to the last man. Now the Syrians were threatening to overrun Lebanese Forces positions on Mount Sannin, in the heart of Maronite territory. The day after his meeting with Haig, the *Washington Post* announced that Charles had been appointed to the new Jacques Maritain Distinguished Professorship in Moral and Political Philosophy at the CUA.[84] It was a fitting title for Charles, who had long admired the French Catholic philosopher and his contribution to the Universal Declaration of Human Rights. In fact, he had once asked Maritain for an autographed portrait "to keep as a precious souvenir of my high regard for you and my indebtedness to your thought."[85]

In June, Charles gave another speech at the Cosmos Club, entitled "The World Promise of America." That promise, he began, "is something providential.... America has been schooled and refined precisely for its world promise," which includes material abundance, the rule of law, social justice, trust, pluralism, and, above all, freedom. In this context, he invoked the name of his old friend John Foster Dulles, who

> once spoke of dissolving and rolling back—this is his phrase—the formidable glacier of slavery which is creeping upon the world. Who would dare mention "roll back" today, who would even dare to think of it?

As Charles well knew, Reagan and the Cold Warriors in his administration were talking about doing just that—rolling back the Soviet empire. To clinch his case, Charles quoted from Reagan's recent inaugural address: "Above all we must realize that no arsenal or no weapon in the arsenals of the world is so formidable as the will and moral courage of free men and women."[86]

Later that month, Charles joined Dory Chamoun at the annual convention of the American Lebanese League in Arlington, Virginia. One of the featured speakers was Senator Edward Kennedy of Massachusetts, who declared, "I am honored to be here with the outstanding Lebanese leader and statesman, Dr. Charles Malik."[87] For his part, Charles rejoiced that the United States "appears to be more involved in the Lebanese problem than it was in the recent past" (a reference to the disappointing Carter administration). He concluded with a tribute to the young Christian soldiers on the front line:

> Freedom, man, truth, the sanctity of the family, the sacred soil of Lebanon, the unbroken continuity of a 6,000-year heritage whose values are the very values you cherish most in America—this is the glorious burden for which these young men and women are fighting and dying, not only for themselves but for you in America and the free world. This fighting, unyielding, undaunted, believing, steadfast, rooted, self-denying spirit of the Lebanese Resistance is our greatest ground of hope. Long live the Lebanese Resistance![88]

And the undisputed leader of the Lebanese Resistance was his young protégé, Bashir Gemayel.

Ironically, the woman who followed Charles to the podium was one of Bashir's secret lovers, an ABC television producer named Barbara Newman. Newman was there to receive an award for "The Unholy War," an episode of the ABC television program *20/20* that had portrayed Bashir as a freedom fighter opposed to terrorism. As she later confessed in a memoir, Newman had fallen for Bashir the previous December, during her initial research trip to Beirut. The suggestion that she should interview Bashir had come from none other David Kimche, Bashir's Israeli handler, whom Newman had met in Tel Aviv just before flying to Beirut. Newman may not have been consciously working for Mossad, but her memoir leaves no doubt that her sympathies were with Israel and not with the "terrorists." In accepting her award, Newman spoke of Bashir as "that old-fashioned thing, a hero," concluding with a quotation from Ralph Waldo Emerson: "If a man hold his place and there abides, defying all odds, then the whole world will come round to him."[89]

In the fall of 1981, Charles inaugurated his visiting professorship at Catholic University with a remarkable lecture entitled "History-Making, History-Writing, History-Interpreting." At the age of seventy-five, he had lived long enough to read about himself in the history books—and the books got it all wrong. "If you had a hand ... in making history," he complained,

> and if you then read how the history you yourself helped shape has been actually written by historians, you begin to distrust the accounts of every book of history. What is written is either outright falsehood, or is partial and slanted, or has only the most tenuous resemblance to the truth.

The problem was that most "writers of history have never tasted historical responsibility and decision. How can they write on something which they really know nothing about?" He was forced to conclude that "history-writing ... is largely fiction: it is a species of art and literature."[90] If his nephew Edward had been in the audience that evening, he might have applauded Uncle Charles' seeming embrace of post-structuralism.

But Charles was no post-structuralist. As a history-maker, he knew the existential truths that could not be found in the history books. "I have known the anguish of deciding," he confessed. Then, venting his spleen against the campus radicals, he continued,

> I know the utter nonsense people indulge in when they ignorantly and externally and sometimes tendentiously attack, for example, the CIA or the

Pentagon or the State Department or what they call "the military-industrial complex," or this or that responsible person in the United States, when little do they know that the relative peace and security they enjoy, which enables them to indulge in the luxury of their armchair criticism, they owe wholly to the guilt-laden sufferings of these people, for the secret decision they made in their behalf.

Charles, of course, had been one of these responsible people, having suffered the guilt of his own secret decisions. "I have known," he admitted, "the full complement of human nature acting in the making of history; I have known it both in myself and in others. And believe me, the spectacle thus revealed is an awful mixture of good and evil."[91]

§

For good or for evil, Charles was not yet ready to give up history-making. In May 1982, he met with Howard Teicher and Geoffrey Kemp at the request of their boss, National Security Advisor William Clark. According to Teicher's weekly report to Clark, Charles "made an eloquent and impassioned plea for greater U.S. activism to save Lebanon." But surely Charles was anticipating, by then, that Lebanon's salvation would come from the Israel Defense Forces. That very week, Teicher also sat in meetings with Israeli defense minister Ariel Sharon, who had come to Washington to see Secretary of State Alexander Haig and Secretary of Defense Caspar Weinberger.[92] Teicher's report, however, mentioned nothing about Israeli military action in Lebanon, which suggests that he was not in the room when Haig gave Sharon his supposed "green light" to invade Lebanon. Now all that Sharon needed was a pretext, which arrived on June 3 when Ambassador Shlomo Argov was shot in the head outside the Dorchester Hotel in London.

The Israeli invasion of Lebanon came on June 6, 1982. Three days later, Charles attended a meeting of the Lebanese Front chaired by Camille Chamoun. Bashir Gemayel was also present. After the meeting, Chamoun read an official communique over the Phalange's radio station, the Voice of Lebanon. After blaming the Syrians for refusing to withdraw, the Palestinians for endangering security, and the Arab states for evading responsibility, the communique ended,

> Lebanon is pushed into a fierce war going on on its territory between the Israelis and the Palestinians and the Syrians and the Israelis. As we express our deepest regret in the face of this tragedy and the numerous victims which fall every minute, we pledge to do everything we can in order to turn these events in the favor of Lebanon and its people, and to secure Lebanon's total sovereignty, and the liberation of its territory from all foreigners without exception.

After Chamoun finished reading the communique, Bashir, who expected to be the next president of Lebanon, invited Lebanese Muslims to sit down with him and negotiate a new national charter.[93]

That summer, with Beirut surrounded by the Israeli army, Charles received a number of Israeli visitors, including Ariel Sharon himself. The source of this report was Etienne Sakr, aka "Abu-Arz," the leader of a small but fanatical Maronite militia known as the Guardians of the Cedars. According to Sakr,

> Defense Minister Ariel Sharon came to the home of Charles Malek [sic], and complained to him that Bashir was not cooperating with the Israelis. Sharon drove to look for Bashir at Lebanese Forces headquarters, but he wasn't there. He continued to Bikfaya, but he wasn't there. Bashir avoided the Israelis, including Sharon.[94]

Assuming that Sakr's story is accurate, it implies that Sharon had been apprised of the close relationship between Charles and Bashir. Certainly, Sharon was frustrated by Bashir's unwillingness to send his militia into battle, especially in West Beirut, where Sharon preferred not to risk his own troops. At one meeting early in the war, Sharon urged Bashir to get his men moving. "We're here with tanks!" he shouted. "*Do something!*"[95] But Bashir, fearing that his credibility as a presidential candidate would be ruined if he were seen as Sharon's lackey, demurred.

Another Israeli who came to visit Charles was Amos Perlmutter of American University in Washington, who interviewed him in his garden in Rabieh. As servants brought Turkish coffee and whiskey, Perlmutter offered Charles greetings from Abba Eban. "Ah, Eban," Charles reminisced. "Those metaphors. A man of imagery. . . . But I always had more metaphors than Eban." When Perlmutter mentioned Philip Habib, President Reagan's special envoy to the Middle East, Charles interrupted, "Habib, Habib, oh my God. He reminds me of some American Jew trying to make it into the Establishment." Insisting that "the PLO and the Syrians *must* get out," Charles added, "You know Begin. Send him a message. Tell him this is a golden opportunity for a new order in Lebanon." As for the current Lebanese government, it would have to go. "[Prime Minister] Wazzan is a weak man," Charles complained. "Sarkis is a lightweight." Playing devil's advocate, Perlmutter proposed a *coup d'etat*. But Charles shook his head. "There is a constitution. There are elections. . . . There are the Muslims. . . . And we can't take any action until Syria and the PLO are gone." On that note, the interview came to an end. "Give my regards to Begin," Charles said in parting. "He is a man of vision."[96]

Given the US alliance with Israel, it was inevitable that the AUB would become a target that summer. On July 19, Acting President David Dodge became the first American to be kidnapped in Beirut by Shia militants. Then, on August 4, the Israelis bombed and shelled West Beirut as Israeli columns advanced toward the Palestinian camps, encountering fierce resistance.[97] The next day, Marvine Howe of the *New York Times* visited Charles Malik at his hilltop villa overlooking the smoking ruins of West Beirut. Charles told her that Philip Habib faced an "impossible" task as he attempted to work out a solution to the Lebanese crisis. Unless the Americans and the Soviets convinced the Palestinian commandos, as well as the Syrian and Israeli armies, to leave Lebanon, he warned, Beirut would be totally destroyed. What the PLO needed was a "face-saving measure," a declaration that "after you have left Lebanon, and the departure of the Syrian and Israeli troops, we promise to take up seriously the Palestinian question."[98]

Eventually, Philip Habib and his intermediary, Saeb Salam, persuaded Yasir Arafat to leave Beirut for the sake of its residents. On August 21, the first PLO commandos sailed away as French peacekeepers came ashore, followed by Italian and American contingents. Two days later, Bashir Gemayel was elected president of Lebanon by the necessary two-thirds of the Chamber of Deputies. According to Schiff and Yaari, the decision to help Bashir secure the last seven or so votes he needed was recommended by a team of Israeli experts convened by the defense ministry in Tel Aviv. Begin's advisor on terrorism, Rafael Eitan, was sent to ask Camille Chamoun to come out for Bashir. The Israelis also warned deputies from southern Lebanon about the possible consequences of not showing up for the vote. In one case, according to Schiff and Yaari, "the IDF was solicitous enough to provide a helicopter to pluck one elderly delegate out of an isolated village in the Bekaa lest he be intimidated by the Syrians." Needless to say, millions of Lebanese pounds changed hands in the process of lining up the necessary votes for Bashir.[99]

Two weeks after Bashir's election, a reporter from the Israeli newspaper *Ha'aretz*, Roman Priester, interviewed Charles in his Rabieh home. Priester's lead is worth quoting:

> In his large library, on shelves crammed with the finest fruits of the tree of knowledge, a place of honor is reserved for the works of Aristotle, the Bible, the writings of the Rambam [Maimonides] and a full set of the Encyclopedia Judaica. Dr. Charles Malik, renowned man of letters and Christian statesman ranked among the top Lebanese politicians, enjoys being called "the modern Aristotle."

After coffee, brought by "a dark-skinned servant," Priester showed Charles and Eva the latest issue of the *Ha'aretz* weekend supplement, which featured a story on Bashir Gemayel, complete with photographs. The Maliks immediately spotted their son Habib in one of the photos, adding that he had recently returned to Harvard to finish his doctorate (and to help launch the Harvard-Radcliffe Conservative Club).

Inevitably, the interview turned to Bashir, who was preparing to take office at the end of September. "Most of the Muslim leaders are, in my eyes, like a fallow field," said Charles. "Bashir Jumayyil [sic] has the image of a fighter, but those close to him know that he [is] a man of great political wisdom." "His biggest test," Charles continued, "will be doing justice to all the social elements in the Lebanese society, even those who opposed him in the past. I believe he can stand up to the test." When Priester asked about the peace agreement that the Israelis were demanding of Bashir as the price of their support, however, Charles demurred. "What good would come out of open talks now?" he asked. "You are pushing for a peace agreement and I say: patience, patience." He proceeded to caution Israel against placing its trust in its military superiority rather than its spiritual values. "Even the most modern army," he chided, "cannot survive spiritual emptiness." Charles' words, Priester noted, "carry the sound of a prophetic warning."[100]

§

By the time Priester's interview with Charles was published in mid-September, Bashir was dead, the victim of a bomb planted in Phalange headquarters in East Beirut. According to

Etienne Sakr, Amin Gemayel announced his intention to succeed his younger brother at the funeral in Bikfaya with the full support of his father Pierre, who had always preferred Amin to the disobedient Bashir. Sakr himself was interested in the presidency, as he confided to Charles Malik and Camille Chamoun, who had already announced his own interest. A short while later, Sakr reported, some Mossad men came to his house in Baabda and informed him that the Israelis favored Amin in spite of the fact that, like his father, he had been wary of the Israeli connection from the beginning. Sakr warned his visitors, "Don't trust [Amin's] promises. He'll ruin you and us." He then rushed out to see Chamoun. Shortly thereafter, the Israelis arrived at Chamoun's house and asked him to withdraw in favor of Amin. According to Sakr, an angry Chamoun replied, "Je m'en fous."[101]

A week after Amin Gemayel's election as president of Lebanon, Charles received a visit from the new president of the AUB, Malcolm Kerr, who was living alone in Marquand House. Kerr described the visit in a letter to his family back in Los Angeles:

> Dr. Malik was fine and we had an interesting discussion about AUB's poor relationship with the Maronites … , but toward the end he began preaching about how only the Christians are capable of anything worthwhile and I felt irritated. But he and Mrs. M. were very friendly and asked repeatedly about Mother. Every time I've talked to Mrs. Malik for the past twenty years she has always begun by saying that the last time she saw me I was only four years old.[102]

No doubt they lamented the fate of Kerr's predecessor, David Dodge, who was still in captivity. Most likely they did not talk about Edward Said, whom Kerr had met at professional conferences.

Although Charles was not close to Amin Gemayel, he agreed to resume his role as an intermediary in Washington. On December 10, he attended a dinner party for Philip Habib at the Corcoran Gallery hosted by John Wallach, the foreign editor of the Hearst newspaper chain, and his wife Janet, a contributor to the *Washington Post*. The evening was a notable one, if only for the presence of both the Israeli ambassador, Moshe Arens, and the ambassadors of at least seven Arab nations. Before dinner, various tributes to Habib were read aloud, including notes from Ronald Reagan, Menachem Begin, Hosni Mubarak, King Hussein, and Henry Kissinger, who called Habib "Brooklyn's answer to Metternich and Bismarck." The note from Begin was curiously brief, having been censored by John Wallach, much to the annoyance of Ambassador Arens. Charles read a letter from President Gemayel, which he probably had a hand in drafting. "Greater than the tragedy of war," the letter read, "is the torment of a sham peace.... A way out must be found." "You can count on us," Habib replied.[103]

On April 18, 1983, a suicide bomber drove a van packed with explosives into the lobby of the US embassy in Beirut, killing sixty-three people, including most of the staff of the local CIA station. The following evening, Charles delivered a lecture on Lebanon at the University of Maryland.[104] He began by singing the praises of the Lebanese Forces and the Christians who had rallied behind them over the past decade. "The saga of the heroic Lebanese Resistance, and of the leadership of that Resistance," he proclaimed, "is one of the noblest—if so far least heralded and sung—episodes in human history." Thus did Charles transform the sordidness and brutality of the Lebanese Civil War into the stuff of epic poetry, going so far as to pose the question of whether Homer himself was of Phoenician origin. As for Lebanon's future, he acknowledged that "nothing can any longer be decided in and about this region against the will of Israel." That, he continued, is why the ongoing negotiations between President Gemayel and Israel must result in a peace agreement. He concluded by prophesying that peace will come to the eastern Mediterranean in fifty years—a "superhistoric achievement" in which "America appears to be destined to play a primary role."[105]

Sure enough, on May 17, 1983, Lebanese and Israeli negotiators signed an agreement that ended the official state of war between the two nations and provided for the eventual withdrawal of Israeli troops. Two months later, Charles was interviewed at his home in Rabieh by Claude Khoury of *Monday Morning*. With the US Marines in Beirut and Israeli troops continuing to occupy the Shouf region, Charles was still hopeful about the future. When Khoury asked him about Syrian demands that the May 17 agreement with Israel be abrogated, Charles replied, "If the Syrian demands really exist, I doubt that Lebanon would go along with them."[106] Soon after the interview appeared, however, Druze leader Walid Jumblatt announced the formation of a National Salvation Front to administer those areas of Lebanon occupied by the Syrian army. Joining Jumblatt in the Front were Suleiman Frangieh, who had broken with the Lebanese Front in 1978, and Rashid Karame, Charles' old nemesis from 1958.[107] The prospect of a new war between the Christians and the Druzes prompted the Israeli defense minister, Moshe Arens, to fly to Beirut, where he met with Pierre Gemayel, Camille Chamoun, and Charles Malik, urging them to reach an understanding with the Druzes before the IDF withdrew from the Shouf.[108]

§

On October 23, 1983, two truck-bombers drove into the barracks of the Multinational Force in Beirut, killing 240 American marines and 60 of their French counterparts. As with the embassy bombing in April, responsibility was claimed by Islamic Jihad. A few months later, the shadowy group struck again. On January 18, 1984, Malcolm Kerr was shot dead outside his office in College Hall. That Sunday, the Kerr family buried Malcolm's ashes under a banyan tree on the AUB grounds that he had loved to climb as a boy. A few days later, a memorial service was held in the old chapel on campus. As his wife Ann recalled,

> I requested the hymn, "A Mighty Fortress Is Our God," which I vividly remembered singing in the chapel at the memorial service of AUB President Stephen Penrose, who died the year Malcolm and I were students. Penrose was a hero of ours whose qualities and talents I believe Malcolm shared.[109]

As Malcolm's daughter Susan recalled, the rival warlords of Beirut had declared a period of mourning, which allowed Malcolm's friends and admirers—including, one assumes, the Maliks—to attend the service.[110]

Malcolm Kerr's murder marked the beginning of the end of Charles' dream of a Lebanon united under Amin Gemayel, allied with Israel, and safeguarded by the Americans. On February 5, Prime Minister Wazzan and his cabinet resigned amid heavy fighting between the Lebanese army and opposition militias. On February 6, the Shia Amal militia, supported by their Druze allies, drove the army from West Beirut. The neighborhood of Ras Beirut—the home of the AUB as well as those members of the Said, Cortas, and Makdisi families who had chosen to stay—was not spared. When Tom Friedman of the *New York Times* visited the neighborhood, he noted that artillery rounds had struck dormitories and a museum on the AUB campus.[111] On February 7, President Reagan announced that the Marines, who now found themselves in enemy territory, would withdraw to the safety of their ships. On February 10, unknown gunmen kidnapped AUB electrical engineering professor Frank Regier, the husband of Huda Said's cousin Mary Hanania.[112]

Charles flew to Washington to do what he could. In late February, he had a conversation with Reagan's UN ambassador, Jeane Kirkpatrick. A week later, Kirkpatrick defended aggressive displays of military force in testimony before a Senate subcommittee on foreign assistance. Such shows of force, she insisted, were "very frequently" necessary for effective diplomacy.

> I think, for example, of the Lebanon action of President Eisenhower, which the distinguished Lebanese scholar Dr. Charles Malik was reminding me of last week in a conversation.... There was the deployment of a large number of U.S. Marines at that time in Lebanon, many times the number that was deployed in this current operation.... No shots were fired, no lives were lost, and it was an example of where willingness to commit a large force may have prevented violence.[113]

The implication was that, if only President Reagan were willing to put more American boots on the ground, Lebanon might yet be pacified.

One consequence of the Marines' departure was President Gemayel's decision to abrogate the May 17 agreement with Israel, as Prime Minister Wazzan and Foreign Minister Elie Salem were counseling him to do. That done, he prepared to convene a National Dialogue Conference in Lausanne on March 12. According to Salem, Gemayel asked him to invite Charles Malik to draft an opening address for him to read at the conference. Charles asked to be left alone for an hour to pray about it. "I was sure he would accept," Salem recalled. "I was to be disappointed: Christ had apparently vetoed the idea." Salem then ventured a more secular explanation:

> Most likely Malik, like the hard-line Christian right, was not pleased with the rapprochement with Syria. Malik also felt that Jumayyil [sic] did not appreciate him enough and did not seek his counsel before. Malik was close to Bashir and was his intellectual mentor and was not enamoured of Amin. Amin knew that and kept Malik at a distance.[114]

It hardly mattered. Even before the delegates convened in Lausanne, the leaders of the Lebanese Forces had announced that they would not be bound by the conference's decisions.[115]

At the end of March, the *Wall Street Journal* carried an op-ed by Charles entitled "The West Misses Its Calling in Lebanon." "We witness today," he began, "a fateful confrontation between East and West in the Middle East." In the case of Lebanon, he continued, "the balance between East and West, as far as ground-fighting forces are concerned, is wholly unequal." Lebanon used to be "a land of freedom," he lamented, but now the forces of freedom are threatened "from every quarter." "The assassination of Malcolm Kerr," he warned, "is more than a political act: it bespeaks rejection of freedom of thought and learning," of

> a civilization constituted by Homer, Plato, and Aristotle, by the Old and New Testaments, by Cicero and Augustine, by Shakespeare and Goethe, by Newton and Einstein, by Pushkin and Dostoevski, and by the joy and zest and adventure and freedom of the great American experience.

Given the rejection of this civilization by the enemies of freedom, how could the West possibly hope to win its confrontation with the East? "Not by breeding 'Orientalists,'" Charles quipped. Only when the West decided to unleash its "supreme weapon"—namely, freedom itself—would the forces of slavery be defeated.[116]

Having imposed their will on President Gemayel, the Syrians were attempting to midwife a national unity government under Prime Minister Rashid Karame. By the end of April, Karame had succeeded in forming a government, with Camille Chamoun, Pierre Gemayel, Walid Jumblatt, and Nabih Berri—the head of Amal—all agreeing to serve in the cabinet. The leaders of the Lebanese Forces, however, were not happy with President Gemayel's rapprochement with Damascus and its Lebanese allies. According to Walid Phares, who later served on the executive committee of the Lebanese Forces, some thirty Christian leaders attended a meeting at LF headquarters that spring. The group appointed a commission, headed by Charles Malik, whose task was to "write a chart [sic] for the Lebanese Christian Resistance and to lay down proposals for the establishment of a national Christian Council." On June 1, the LF announced defiantly, "We will never drop any rights of the Christian people of Lebanon."[117]

In the meantime, more Americans had gone missing in Beirut. One of them was Rev. Benjamin Weir, a Presbyterian missionary who, along with his wife Carol, had lived in Lebanon for some three decades. Among those whom Carol consulted was Rev. Habib Badr, a colleague at the Near East School of Theology in Beirut. He was also the pastor of the National Evangelical Church, where his great-grandfather Youssef Badr had served. Badr advised Carol to see his uncle, Charles Malik, who was a friend of the Weirs. So one Sunday Carol drove across the dangerous Green Line dividing West Beirut, where the Weirs lived, from East Beirut, where the Maliks lived. "You or your church officials must go to your government," Charles told her. "Get an appointment with George Shultz [who had replaced Alexander Haig as Secretary of State]. Don't take no for an answer." Carol managed to get a meeting with Assistant Secretary of State for Near Eastern Affairs Richard W. Murphy. Unfortunately, Murphy didn't know who had kidnapped Weir or where he was.[118]

§

In March 1985, in what was called "The Movement of Christian Decision," Samir Geagea and his allies, Elie Hobeika and Karim Pakradouni, took over the Lebanese

Forces and called for the resignation of President Gemayel, whom they perceived as weak, a lackey of the Syrians. The rebellion was immediately endorsed by several of the veteran Lebanese Front intellectuals, including Fuad Bustani and Charles Malik.[119] Geagea lost credibility, however, when the LF failed to hold the Christian villages around Sidon once the Israelis had withdrawn from the area. Shortly thereafter, a fierce battle between the LF and Amal broke out along the Green Line dividing East from West Beirut. After a Lebanese Front meeting on May 7, Charles attributed the fighting to "a conspiracy against the Lebanese people."[120] Two days later, the Lebanese Forces replaced Geagea with Elie Hobeika, who, to the dismay of Geagea and his supporters, promptly closed the LF office in Israel and opened negotiations with Syria.

That June, Charles returned to San Francisco's Fairmont Hotel for the fortieth anniversary of the signing of the United Nations Charter. He was one of three surviving signers in attendance, the other two being Harold Stassen of the United States and Carlos Romulo of the Philippines. "We knew we were seeing the creation of an entirely new world order," Charles told the gathering, "in as much as what Uncle Sam and Uncle Joe agreed upon ultimately became world law. It has not changed so much since then." In fact, the speeches at the Fairmont included plenty of verbal sparring between the new US ambassador to the UN, Vernon Walters, and the Soviet deputy ambassador, Vsevolod Oleandrov. At one point, Oleandrov charged that the hostage crisis in Beirut was the result of American "support of Israeli arrogance."[121] The next day, speaking at a black-tie dinner for 1,500, Secretary of State Shultz demanded "the return of the hostages—all 46 of them—immediately, unharmed and unconditionally."[122]

Also present at the Fairmont was Herbert W. Armstrong, the nonagenarian founder of the Worldwide Church of God, who had covered the 1945 UN conference. A reporter for Armstrong's magazine, *The Plain Truth*, persuaded Charles to grant an interview. "You think the United Nations is going to bring about peace so long as the devil is around?" Charles asked.

> We had 1,000 people today at lunch, more than 1,000, maybe 1,500. I was sitting down and thinking all the time . . . what is going on in the minds of these people . . . with all their schemes, and ideas, and emotions, and aspirations, and plannings, and all kinds of things. The devil is at work.

"True words!" chimed the reporter, who went on to quote Brian Urquhart, the UN's Under Secretary General for Special Political Affairs. "There are moments," Urquhart admitted, "when I feel that the only thing that will restore the unanimity of the Security Council might be an invasion from outer space." The reporter agreed, noting that "Jesus Christ will come back from 'outer space'—heaven—to establish the kingdom of God to finally bring world peace."[123]

The following year, Charles Malik's last article, "The Drafting of the Universal Declaration of Human Rights," appeared in the UN's *Bulletin of Human Rights*. Drawing on his own diary and papers, he reviewed the ideological confrontations that had occurred in the Human Rights Commission over such issues as the metaphysical character of human rights, the proper hierarchy of rights, and the right to change one's religious beliefs. Then, noting that the UDHR was unique in human history, he declared that "in the Universal Declaration universal man is defining himself." "How much of man, how much of human dignity, how much of freedom there is in this or that nation or culture," he observed, "can be measured by the Universal Declaration itself."[124] By any measure, there was not much humanity left in Lebanon after a dozen years of brutal civil war. As for the taking of hostages, it was a blatant violation of Article 3: "Everyone has the right to life, liberty, and security of person."

On Sunday, November 2, one of those hostages—David Jacobsen, the director of the AUB Medical Center—was released by Islamic Jihad. On Monday, the reason for Jacobsen's release was revealed by the Beirut weekly *al-Shiraa*, which broke the story of the secret arms-for-hostages trades between the United States and Iran. That same week, a revived Lebanese Front met in the offices of Camille Chamoun's National Liberal Party in East Beirut. In addition to Chamoun and his son Dany, the participants included Dr. George Saadeh, the new leader of the Phalange; Samir Geagea and Karim Pakradouni of the Lebanese Forces; George Adwan of the *Tanzim*; and Etienne Sakr of the Guardians of the Cedars. Holdovers from the original Front included Shaker Abu Suleiman of the Maronite League, Fuad Bustani, Edward Honein, and Charles Malik.[125] One item on the agenda for future consideration, no doubt, was the recent rapprochement between the Lebanese Forces and the PLO, which had been sending cadres back to Lebanon with the consent of President Gemayel.

The architect of the LF-PLO alliance was Karim Pakradouni, the "Arabist" Phalange official who had often complained about Charles Malik's back-channel diplomacy. That May, Pakradouni had traveled to Tunis to meet with Yasir Arafat, who proposed that they form a common front in Beirut against the Syrians.[126] He even arranged for an interview with Arafat on the Lebanese Broadcasting Corporation, the Junieh-based television station of the Lebanese Forces, which aired on November 11. Arafat apologized to Lebanon's Christians for the "mistakes" his men had committed in the past. But the Palestinians and the Lebanese, he insisted, were the victims of the same conspiracy—which he attributed to Henry Kissinger—to divide Lebanon between the Israelis and the Syrians.[127] On orders from Damascus, Arafat claimed, Amal was attempting to "liquidate the camps under pretext of getting rid of the Arafatists."[128] That was exactly what the LF militias had tried to do between 1976 and 1982, starting with Tal al-Zataar. But the rise of the Shia militias, backed by Syria and Iran, had made allies of former enemies.

By the fall of 1987, Charles Malik was gravely ill, suffering from cancer and organ failure. Among those who visited him shortly before his death was Rev. Howard Schomer, his old Harvard friend, who had been his assistant on the Human Rights Commission.[129] After working for the World Council of Churches in Geneva, Schomer had returned to Chicago in 1959 to lead the Chicago Theological Seminary, where he became active in the civil rights movement. In 1963, he participated in the March for Freedom and Jobs in Washington, witnessing Dr. Martin Luther King's famous "I Have a Dream" speech. Two years later, in March 1965, he marched at King's side from Selma, Alabama, to the state capitol building in Montgomery, accompanied by twenty of his seminary students, including future civil rights leader Jesse Jackson.[130] No doubt Schomer was mystified by Charles' embrace of the Christian Right. But he had come to Beirut to pay his last respects to the philosopher who had been his mentor and icon.

By December, Syrian troops were rounding up young Maronites after the killing of a Syrian soldier, one of several recent attacks on Syrian soldiers and civilians. A group calling itself the "Lebanese Liberation Front" had taken responsibility for the attacks, but many suspected that the Lebanese Forces—headed once again by Samir Geagea, a bitter foe of Syria—were behind the violence. In any case, the Lebanese Front called for a general strike on Saturday, December 19, to protest the arrests.[131] By then, Charles Malik was dying, his legs amputated below the knees. On Christmas Eve, he was taken to a hospital in East Beirut, where he passed away on December 28. "With his death," read the obituary distributed by Lebanon's Christian news agency, "the Lebanese Front has lost one of its pioneer pillars." A funeral service was held that week at Saint Dimitri Orthodox Church in East Beirut.[132] If any of the Saids came to mourn the passing of Uncle Charles, it would have been Jean, the only member of the family still living in Beirut.

7

Edward Said: The Intellectual as Palestinian Nationalist, 1975–87

In spite of the street-fighting that had erupted in April 1975, the Saids flew to Beirut for their usual summer visit. Najla Said, who was just a year old at the time, later wrote of that summer:

> My brother and I apparently had a wonderful, magical time, while the adults' enjoyment was tainted by the political violence that was brewing. Skirmishes and gunfights had begun around the country in April, and though they were still few and far between, most people knew that something bigger and more dangerous was on the horizon.[1]

One of those people was Najla's aunt Jean, who started keeping a diary (the basis of her book *Beirut Fragments: A War Memoir*). The Saids also went to Cairo that summer—Edward's first visit in fifteen years. There he attended a dramatic production featuring Tahia Carioca, the famous belly-dancer and actress, whom he had last seen in 1950. Alas, both the play (a farce aimed at the Russians) and Tahia herself (who weighed 220 pounds) proved disappointing.[2]

That fall, the Saids moved temporarily to California, where Edward was to be a Fellow at Stanford's Center for Advanced Study in the Behavioral Sciences. First, however, he had a date in Washington with a subcommittee of the House Committee on International Relations, which was holding hearings on "The Palestinian Issue in Middle East Peace Efforts." Edward appeared as a witness on September 30, together with Ibrahim Abu-Lughod. Edward began by objecting to the reduction of the Palestinian to the category of "refugee" or "terrorist," declaring that "the Palestinian is a positive progressive challenge to any state policy that denies human rights," including that of the United States. From the Palestinian perspective, he explained, US policy means unrestricted aid to Israel and "total disregard in every possible way for the Palestinian as a real element in the contemporary Middle East." He concluded by calling for an immediate "foothold" in Palestine for a "national authority" and for the inclusion of Palestinians in future peace negotiations.[3]

After testifying in Washington, Edward returned to Stanford, where he set to work on *Orientalism*, destined to be his most influential book. Ironically, Yehoshafat Harkabi, whom Edward may or may not have confronted at Evanston in 1970, was also a Fellow at CASBS that year. Originally, Harkabi had intended to use his sabbatical to formulate a philosophy of international relations. "However," as he later explained, "the Arab-Israeli problem haunted me relentlessly."[4] As a result, he ended up writing yet another monograph on that problem, entitled *Arab Strategies and Israel's Response*. While there is no mention of Edward Said in its pages, Edward's presence at the Center surely contributed to Harkabi's "haunting" by the specter of the Arab. As Harkabi probably learned, Edward had condemned his 500-page dissertation, *Arab Attitudes to Israel*, at an AAUG conference the previous fall, dismissing it as an "artificially large collection of bias and racism dressed up as scholarship."[5]

Edward himself was haunted by the violence in Lebanon, which put the Said and Cortas families in constant danger. That fall, Mariam's sister-in-law, Asdghik Cortas, was shot in the leg by a sniper while crossing from PLO-controlled West Beirut to Christian East Beirut.[6] Meanwhile, arms flowed into Lebanon from a variety of sources. In November, the *Washington Post* reported that Saudi arms dealer Adnan Khashoggi—an alumnus of Victoria College in Alexandria—had been accused of selling weapons to the Phalangists with the help of a Lebanese associate, Samir Souki.[7] This was the same Sam Souki whose father had been Wadie Said's friend in Cairo, where Sam had befriended Kim Roosevelt during the Second World War.[8] Roosevelt had long since retired from the CIA and opened his own consulting business in Washington, representing corporations like Northrop, which had made a billion dollars in the Middle East thanks to his good offices. Roosevelt was still on friendly terms with Souki, whom he had recommended to Northrop as its regional representative. Souki, in turn, had recommended Khashoggi to Northrop as its agent in a sale of F-5E fighters to the Saudis.[9]

In December, Edward traveled to Los Angeles for a conference on the Middle East hosted by UCLA's Center for Arms Control and International Security. The featured speakers included Dr. Ashraf Ghorbal, the Egyptian ambassador to the United States, and General Aharon Yariv, a member of the Israeli Knesset.[10] After earning a PhD at Harvard in 1949, Ghorbal had joined the Egyptian delegation at the United Nations, where he had undoubtedly encountered Uncle Charles. Yariv had been Israel's representative at the disengagement talks with Egypt following the October War of 1973. Ironically, it was Yariv who, as Golda Meir's counterterrorism advisor, had overseen Operation Wrath of God, Israel's secret assassination campaign aimed at those who had plotted and executed the Munich massacre of 1972. Edward may not have known it, but the mild-mannered Yariv was apparently responsible for the death of his relative Kamal Nasir in April 1973.[11]

Edward's role at the conference was to participate in the concluding panel discussion, along with Yehoshafat Harkabi, Itamar Rabinovich of Tel Aviv University, and Malcolm Kerr of UCLA, whose father Stanley and mother Elsa had been Uncle Charles' colleagues at the AUB. Before she became Dean of Women at the AUB, Elsa taught mathematics at the American Junior College for Women, where her pupils included Edward's mother Hilda and his aunt Eva.[12] More importantly, Malcolm Kerr was a member of the Brookings Institution's Middle East Study Group, which had just completed a report entitled *Toward Peace in the Middle East*.[13] Among the report's recommendations were Israel's withdrawal to its pre-1967 boundaries and the establishment of a Palestinian entity in the West Bank, whether in the form of an independent state or in a federation with Jordan. Another member of the Brookings study group, former National Security Council staffer William Quandt, was also at the UCLA conference that December.

In January 1976, *New Outlook*—the Israeli journal devoted to reconciliation—carried a piece by Edward on the American perception of Arabs. "There is supposedly a group of so-called 'Arabists' in the American establishment," he noted, "whose role is to be a kind of Arab lobby in this country, to represent Arab interests." But even these professional Arabists, he complained, regard Arabs as simple, pastoral people with "certain habits of mind which various books have schematized." One of his examples was Edward Sheehan, a Fellow at the Center for International Affairs at Harvard, whose novel *Kingdom of Illusions* depicted Arabs as "wonderful, starry-eyed, dumb creatures." This belief that the Arab mind was fundamentally different from the Western mind, Edward continued, had "trickled down even to *Arab* Arabists." His evidence was an essay by Elie Salem, "Problems of Arab Political Behavior," published in *Tensions in the Middle East* in 1958. Salem, he noted sardonically, was now Dean of Arts and Sciences at the AUB, "half of whose budget is supplied by the U.S. State Department."[14] What he didn't say is that the introduction to *Tensions in the Middle East* had been written by none other than Uncle Charles, Salem's relative from Bterram.

§

Meanwhile, the violence in Beirut continued unabated. In April 1976, an artillery shell crashed into Samir and Jean Makdisi's dining room, leaving a gaping hole in the wall. A few days later, Samir's brother Nadim was kidnapped. Coincidentally, James Markham, the Beirut bureau chief of the *New York Times*, had been invited to lunch at Samir and Jean's apartment on the day of Nadim's disappearance. Markham recorded the event in his diary:

> Samir's brother (a Protestant) was kidnapped just before I arrived. Second time he's been kidnapped. We spent the somewhat frantic lunch calling everyone we knew who might help, and before dessert he was freed. The liberators came by with their AK-47s to say how happy they were that the brother was free and how helpful they'd been. Samir said he didn't realize at first that they wanted money. When he did, it cost him 400 Lebanese pounds, or about $200.[15]

This and other excerpts from Markham's diary were later published in the *Times*, where they were read, presumably, by Edward Said. Perhaps it was Edward who had told Markham to look up Samir and Jean in the first place.

That June, Edward's friend Shafiq al-Hout led a PLO delegation to the United Nations in New York, where the Security Council was due to vote on a committee report calling for a Palestinian state. Edward and Ibrahim Abu-Lughod arranged for the delegation to meet with Noam Chomsky and Eqbal Ahmad, who had nothing to lose by speaking freely about the PLO's shortcomings. As Ahmad recalled:

We both went and gave our critique of the movement—its preoccupation with armed struggle and its inability to focus American civil society. In very gentle terms, we offered that the United States is a complex society and should be reached in a variety of ways. We emphasized the importance of . . . talking to Israelis, including Israeli intellectuals, those who are questioning, doubting. We talked about the importance of talking to the leadership of the Jewish community here.

According to Ahmad, only Hout seemed receptive. "Chomsky felt particularly depressed by the encounter," he recalled. "I was beyond depression by that time. I had seen enough. They defeated themselves more than the Israelis did."[16] As for the UN committee report, the United States vetoed it, only to see the General Assembly endorse it anyway.[17]

With the Syrian army battling the PLO in Lebanon, the Saids decided not to go to Beirut that summer. Instead, Edward flew to Libya in late July for an "International Symposium on Zionism and Racism," inspired by the 1974 resolution in which the UN General Assembly had declared that "Zionism is a form of racism and racial discrimination." Among those who read papers at the symposium were Fayez Sayegh, who had introduced the UN resolution in 1974; Sami Hadawi, an expert on the dispossession of the Palestinians whose wife Nora was a cousin of Hilda Said's; and Abdullah Sharafuddin, the head of the Libyan Bar Association, who delivered the opening address, denouncing Zionism as a global Jewish menace.[18] Edward's paper, in contrast, represented Zionism as a product of European thought. "It is in the history of 19th-century European intellectual culture," he observed, "that one finds the common origins of imperialism and Zionism, origins that precede Herzl and the colonization of Palestine beginning in the 1880s."[19] Conference participants also had a chance to watch the premiere of *Muhammad, Messenger of God (The Message)*, Moustapha Akkad's controversial film starring Anthony Quinn.[20]

That same summer, a boat carrying a dozen Fatah officials from Sidon to Tripoli disappeared. Among the missing was Edward's friend Hanna Mikhail, with whom he had lost touch. In mid-August, John Cooley of the *Christian Science Monitor* reported the disappearance of the Fatah officials, naming Mikhail as "a key aide to Yasser Arafat." The twelve officials, Cooley reported, had "ended up as prisoners of the Lebanese rightists."[21] Cooley did not know who had intercepted the boat, but he noted that several of Lebanon's naval patrol vessels were now in the possession of the Christian militias, operating out of Junieh. More ominously, the Syrian navy had launched a blockade of Tripoli, which was held by Muslim and Leftist forces, and the Israeli navy had started to detain ships bound for the PLO-controlled ports of Sidon and Tyre. Whether or not Edward saw Cooley's story, he must have heard about Mikhail's disappearance from friends and family.

In September, Edward returned to the Mediterranean, this time to Cyprus, where he read a paper at a conference on the survival of small states. Among those he met in Cyprus was the journalist Christopher Hitchens of the *New Statesman*, whose description of Edward is worth quoting:

It was impossible not to be captivated by him. . . . When he laughed, it was as if he was surrendering unconditionally to some guilty pleasure. At first the very picture of professorial rectitude, with faultless tweeds, cravats, and other accoutrements (the pipe also being to the fore), he would react to a risqué remark, or a disclosure of something vaguely scandalous, as if a whole Trojan horse had been smuggled into his interior and suddenly disgorged its contents.[22]

Hitchens, who was on his way to Israel, asked Edward for some names to look up in the occupied West Bank. Edward recommended that he visit Birzeit, where Hanna Mikhail's cousin Hanan—who had recently married an artist from Jerusalem, Emil Ashrawi—was teaching English literature at Birzeit University.

In his conference paper, entitled "Visions of National Identity in Palestine and Lebanon," Edward declared that there are "two sorts of national self-definition—one backward-looking, the other future-oriented, one tied down to 'dark gods,' tribalism, atavism, mythology, the other committed to some sense of itself *in* the world." The first sort of nationalism, he implied, was on the rise in Lebanon, where old minority communities thought of themselves in mystical terms and closed themselves off from the world. As for the second sort of nationalism, the Palestinians were more or less its only exemplars in the Middle East, having "worked gradually out of the paranoia of backward-looking nationalism, of provincial ethnic and chauvinist, even xenophobic rejection of all that surrounds them."[23] Their progressive nationalism made them a threat not just to the Zionists, but also to so-called Arab nationalists like Hafez Assad, whose Lebanese policy was based not on Arab interests, but on *raisons d'état*. Hence Assad's tacit alliance with "Israel, whose patrol boats blockade the south Lebanese coast in conjunction with Syrian boats."[24]

After his return from Cyprus, Edward traveled to Washington for a conference on Arab and American cultures at the American Enterprise Institute, headed by Uncle Charles' old friend William Baroody, Sr.[25] Edward was one of four participants in a roundtable discussion entitled "Can Cultures Communicate?" The other participants were Samuel Huntington, Professor of Government at Harvard; Mustafa Safwan, an Egyptian psychoanalyst and man of letters who lived in Paris; and Laura Nader, Professor of Anthropology at Berkeley and the sister of Ralph Nader. Much of the discussion centered on the issues Edward was writing about in *Orientalism*—Western stereotypes, generalizations about "Islam" and the "Arab world," the politics of knowledge. At one point, the conversation turned to the belief that Arab societies are more religious than Western societies. "The religious coloration of Arab society has been overstated," Edward protested. "The same religious coloration can be found in other societies." As evidence, he pointed to "one of the major presidential candidates," who "certainly does not seem to think that revelation belongs to time past."[26] He was referring, of course, to Governor Jimmy Carter of Georgia, a devout Southern Baptist.

A few days before the AEI conference, another story about Hanna Mikhail's disappearance had appeared in the *Christian Science Monitor*. As reported by a correspondent from Athens, "Evidence from several sources suggests that at least some of the missing boat's 12 passengers have passed through the hands of both the Christian Phalangist Party and the Syrian military." As for Hanna Mikhail, the correspondent cited "an unconfirmed report that Mr. Mikhail was seen to be recovering from wounds in the hospital of the Syrian military prison of Mezze, outside Damascus, the Syrian capital."[27] Evidently, the *Monitor* story prompted a response from Mikhail's friends in the United States, who appealed to Charles Malik for help. It is conceivable that Edward, too, spoke with Uncle Charles, who was in Washington around the time of the AEI conference. In any event, Uncle Charles sent a telegram to Suleiman Frangieh, Camille Chamoun, and Pierre Gemayel requesting that they do everything possible to rescue Mikhail, who, he said, had been captured by Tony Frangieh's men.[28] Unfortunately, his telegram arrived too late. Most likely, Mikhail was already dead. His body was never found.

Hanna Mikhail's disappearance must have been a topic of conversation at the October convention of the Association of Arab-American University Graduates, which Edward attended. Symbolically, the convention took place in New York's Biltmore Hotel, where a 1942 Zionist congress had voted for a Jewish commonwealth in Palestine. Among those who spoke at the convention were Hanan Ashrawi and Shafiq al-Hout. "Perhaps the only serious solution that has been proposed for the Palestine problem," Hout said in his talk,

> is the one proposed by the Palestinian Arab and Jewish Communists. These Communists call for the partition of Palestine and the creation of two states on the soil of Palestine, one Jewish and the other Arab.

But was partition, Hout asked, any more realistic than a unitary state in all of Palestine? His answer was no, because the Zionists would regard partition as nothing more than a transitional step toward the establishment of a Jewish state in all of Palestine. "Let us replace the old Biltmore Programme," he concluded, "with a *new* Biltmore Programme: a secular democratic state for all Palestinian Arabs and all Israeli Jews."[29]

Spurred on, perhaps, by Shafiq al-Hout, Edward tried some private diplomacy with his former colleague Zbigniew Brzezinski, President-Elect Carter's choice for national security advisor. Brzezinski was one of the authors of the 1975 Brookings report calling for Israeli withdrawal from the occupied territories and the creation of a Palestinian entity. That report was expected to become the basis of Carter's Middle East policy. In mid-November, Edward sent a note to Brzezinski requesting a meeting with himself, Walid Khalidi, and possibly a visiting PLO official.[30] Khalidi had recently moved from Beirut to Boston, having accepted a two-year appointment at Harvard's Center for International Affairs. The PLO official was probably Hout, who, along with Farouk Kaddoumi—the head of the PLO's political office—was in New York for a UN debate on the Palestine question.[31] I do not know whether the meeting took place, but the idea of using Edward or Ibrahim Abu-Lughod as a back channel to the PLO was discussed by Brzezinski and his aides, notably William Quandt, who had met Edward at the UCLA security conference a year earlier. And Walid Khalidi continued to serve as a trusted intermediary between US officials and Arafat.[32]

§

It may have been Shafiq al-Hout who talked Edward Said and Ibrahim Abu-Lughod into joining the PNC, the parliament-in-exile of the Palestinian people. In any case, they flew to Cairo for the March 1977 session of the PNC, which had not met since 1974 because of the civil war in Lebanon. Because they belonged to none of the organizations that made up the PLO, Edward and Ibrahim were elected by the Council as independent members. They spent several days listening to speeches, including one in which Abu Mazen (Mahmoud Abbas) explained the difference between Zionists and Zionist dissidents, implicitly authorizing contacts with the latter.[33] In the end, the PNC reaffirmed some of its long-standing positions, refusing to recognize Israel's right to exist and vowing to continue the armed struggle. It also made some conciliatory gestures, calling for an independent state on "national soil," as opposed to land "liberated" from Israel, and agreeing to participate in a Middle East peace conference. Israeli prime minister Yitzhak Rabin was unimpressed, opining that "the only place the Israelis could meet the Palestinian guerrillas was on the field of battle."[34]

After his return from Cairo, Edward made a series of weekly trips to Princeton in order to deliver the Gauss lectures in criticism.[35] Coincidentally, three of his young Badr relatives from Beirut—Habib Badr, George Sabra, and Habib Malik—were all studying at Princeton that spring. Badr and Sabra were seminary students. Malik—the only child of Uncle Charles and Aunt Eva—had come to Princeton from the AUB for his senior year. Edward's former colleague Charles Issawi, the new Bayard E. Dodge Professor of Near Eastern Studies, was also in Princeton, as was the despised Bernard Lewis, the Cleveland E. Dodge Professor. Perhaps Edward's closest friend in Princeton was the legal scholar and progressive activist Richard Falk. It was Falk who introduced Edward to Fouad Ajami, a young professor of politics at Princeton, who had immigrated to the United States from his native Lebanon.[36]

That summer, Edward and his family flew to battle-scarred Beirut, where he saw his Badr relatives. Upon his return to New York, he published an uncharacteristically personal piece in the *New York Times*. "My natal connections," he admitted, "are principally with Lebanese Christians to some of whom I turn for explanations" of the bloodshed. "Yet everything I hear of Moslem savagery, Palestinian treachery, Communist conspiracy," he complained, "is unacceptably xenophobic," and "many relatives and old friends are unapproachable now." No doubt he was thinking of Uncle Charles, among others. Edward's primary motive for writing, however, was to put pressure on the Carter administration to include representatives of the PLO in a peace conference at Geneva. "The minority ideologies dominating Middle East political life have to be shed at Geneva," he asserted, "and replaced by a more generous conception of human variety." He did not name the "minority ideologies" in question, but they certainly included Zionism as well as Lebanese Christian nationalism.[37]

A few days after Edward's piece appeared, the *Times*' Sunday magazine carried a feature story by James Markham entitled "The War That Won't Go Away." Among those Markham interviewed in Beirut was Bashir Gemayel, who warned:

> Unless an honest solution can be found, we are not going to be quiet. We can also hijack airplanes and blow up embassies. And the world is going to face a new cause—the Lebanese cause.

Markham also went to visit Bashir's mentor, Charles Malik, at his home in Rabieh. Throwing caution to the wind, Uncle Charles spoke freely on the subject of Islam:

> "I don't think Islam has much to give the world, in terms of ultimate values, or to its own people," opined Charles Malik, the white-haired ideologue of the Christian right, chatting at his huge mansion, perched on a high hill with a panoramic view of Beirut. "If the Christian community can get away with it, it would prefer to live in peace by itself. The real problem is whether the Moslem world community . . . can tolerate the existence of a free, open and secure Christian community in the Middle East. . . . This may be the last stand of a free society in Asia or Africa. But it is a heroic fight."[38]

For Edward, Markham's story merely confirmed what he had just written about the "xenophobia" of his Lebanese Christian relatives.

That November, Edward hosted a forum at Columbia's School of International Affairs for Emile Habibi, the author of his favorite Palestinian novel, *The Secret Life of Saeed the Pessoptimist*.[39] The next day, President Anwar Sadat of Egypt, who was visiting Washington, told a group of congressmen that he wanted to go to Jerusalem, adding that he had solved the problem of Palestinian representation at Geneva:

> What about representing the Palestinians with an American professor of Palestinian origin? Would you or Israel consider him a terrorist? I have agreed with Arafat and sent this [proposal] to President Carter.

Speculation immediately centered on Ibrahim Abu-Lughod and Edward Said.[40] At first, both men declined to comment on the grounds that no one had asked them to participate in a peace conference. A couple of days later, however, Edward told the *Times*, "My inclination is to say no. . . . I'm principally a scholar and professor and not a full-time political person." He did allow, however, that he would consider an invitation if it came from the United States or the Soviet Union, or perhaps from the secretary-general of the United Nations, Kurt Waldheim.[41]

Then, on November 18, Edward led a delegation of AAUG members to Washington for a meeting with Cyrus Vance, the secretary of state, and Philip Habib, the under secretary of state for political affairs. According to Elaine Hagopian, who was part of the delegation, Edward had been approached by Vance's press spokesman, Hodding Carter III, a former Princeton classmate of Edward's. As Hagopian recalled, Vance left after a few minutes and turned the meeting over to Habib, who

> tended to berate whatever we raised with him. For example, I remember raising the issue of Israeli soldiers who were operating in Southern Lebanon, and Habib retorted that "the Christians invited them in." Edward saw which way it was going, and said very little. It seemed pointless. I recall that several of us caught a taxi after the meeting, and noted to each other that Vance and Habib had rejected outright the notion that the PLO should be a party to any negotiations. Edward commented wryly in the taxi, "All Arafat really wants is any piece of Israeli-occupied Palestinian land over which he can raise the Palestinian flag."[42]

Such remarks, made in private, foreshadowed Edward's future public criticism of Arafat.

One year later, in November 1978, Edward arranged to meet privately with Secretary Vance at the UN Plaza Hotel in New York. As he revealed years later, "I laid forth the Palestinian case to Vance as comprehensively and eloquently as I could, concentrating on my conviction that Arafat was, in fact, a man of peace." When he suggested that they invite his friend Shafiq al-Hout—who was staying at the same hotel—to join them, Vance declined, wary of violating the Kissinger ban on direct talks with the PLO. He did, however, offer to send a message to Arafat via Hout, who would soon be returning to Beirut. According to Edward, the message was the same one that President Carter had announced the previous year, namely, that the United States would open a dialogue with the PLO if Arafat would publicly accept UNSC Resolution 242. Knowing, however, that the PLO objected to 242 because it did not acknowledge the Palestinian right to self-determination, Vance said that Arafat could add a "reservation" to his acceptance. Edward then walked the message over to Hout for delivery to Arafat.[43]

§

After the shah of Iran was overthrown in January 1979, the *Boston Globe* published a profile of Edward under the title "A Palestinian hails Iran's revolution." Speaking to the *Globe*'s New York correspondent, Robert Lenzner, in his office at Columbia, Edward called the uprising in Iran "the greatest event of the 20th century since the Bolshevik Revolution of 1917," a "vast political upheaval which completely defies the stereotype of Islam as a passive tradition." Comparing Khomeini to Arafat as "a symbol of political survival without a state," he declared that events in Iran have given "a tremendous boost for the Palestinians." As for Palestinian violence against Israel, Lenzner found Edward to be "of two minds," opposing random terrorist bombings as "counterproductive" but defending them as "a response to Israeli terror." In addition to Edward himself, Lenzner spoke to Diana Trilling, who called Edward "a very attractive, mysterious man," as well as "a woman who has known Said 20 years," who told him that Edward was a romantic who identified with Joseph Conrad. Lenzner also dropped that Edward was about to fly to Paris at the invitation of Jean-Paul Sartre and Simone de Beauvoir, who were hosting a seminar on the Question of Palestine in mid-March.[44]

When he arrived in Paris, Edward learned that the seminar would be held at the apartment of Michel Foucault, who had just returned from Tehran, full of enthusiasm for the revolution. Edward recognized two of the other Palestinian participants— Ibrahim Dakkak, an engineer who had founded the National Guidance Committee to coordinate resistance in the West Bank, and Nafez Nazzal, a professor of political science at Birzeit University who had studied under Hisham Sharabi at Georgetown. For his doctoral dissertation, Nazzal had conducted fieldwork among Palestinian refugees with the assistance of Peter C. Dodd, a sociologist at the AUB, who had been a graduate student at Harvard at the same time as Edward.[45] Among the Israeli participants in the seminar, Edward recognized only Yehoshafat Harkabi, with whom he had formed a "polite but far from cordial" relationship at Stanford three years earlier. As Edward soon discovered, Harkabi was morphing into "Israel's leading establishment dove," an advocate of a Palestinian state, which he regarded as "a strategic advantage from Israel's point of view."[46]

What Edward didn't tell Sartre's other guests in Paris, presumably, is that he was carrying another message from Cyrus Vance to Yasir Arafat, who had never replied to the message he had sent through Shafiq al-Hout the previous autumn. Vance had called Edward and redictated the text of what Arafat was to say in order to earn US recognition of the PLO. After he got to Beirut, Edward went to Hout's house and asked him to arrange a meeting with Arafat, who arrived around midnight. To Edward's surprise, Arafat claimed that he had never received Vance's earlier message—a claim instantly contradicted by Hout, who reminded the Old Man that he had delivered the message himself. Sheepishly, Arafat told Edward that he would give him his answer the following night. Arriving at Hout's house after midnight, Arafat rejected Vance's terms, protesting that America was too close to Israel and that the PLO didn't need its recognition. Wishing he had never agreed to serve as a go-between, Edward returned home and broke the bad news to Vance.[47]

The following month, Shafiq al-Hout flew to the United States for a series of appearances Edward had arranged for him at Ivy League universities.[48] Afterwards, Edward flew to Los Angeles to read a paper at UCLA's Della Vida Conference on Islamic Studies, commemorating the noted Italian scholar Giorgio Levi Della Vida, who had once taught Arabic to Noam Chomsky at the University of Pennsylvania.[49] The guest of honor at the conference was Albert Hourani, who, coincidentally, had just reviewed *Orientalism* for the *New York Review of Books*, calling it a "powerful and disturbing book." Hourani was particularly disturbed by Edward's critique of two distinguished Orientalists he had known, Louis Massignon and Hamilton Gibb. "Can it be," Hourani asked, "that [Edward Said] himself has fallen into the trap which he has exposed, and has sunk human differences in an abstract concept called 'Orientalism'?" Hourani was willing to admit that politicians and colonial servants did conform, by and large, to the ideal type of the "Orientalist." Even in the case of a scholar like Gibb, who once claimed that the "Arab mind" was incapable of rational thought, Hourani acknowledged some "latent Orientalism." But he doubted that it had defined Gibb's work.[50]

The Della Vida Award was presented to Hourani by Malcolm Kerr, his former student, who had recently been elected to the AUB's board of trustees. In his presentation speech, Kerr noted that Islamic studies had come in for sharp criticism of late. "Indeed, to some critics," he observed,

> the Islamic studies or "Orientalist" tradition not only distorts its subject but even invents it out of whole cloth: the "Orient" as a coherent social, cultural, historical entity exists only in the minds of the Orientalists; "Islam" as a coherent phenomenon is an oversimplified construct; and the creators of these artificial ideas go on to force an entire system of interpretation, an entire world view, into a preconceived and undifferentiated mold.[51]

Kerr was referring, of course, to Edward, whose *Orientalism* had shaken the once-sleepy field of study out of its slumber. In his acceptance speech, Hourani also noted the challenge posed by Edward, which, he said, must be taken seriously.[52] Both Kerr and Hourani were ready to admit that the tradition of Islamic studies had its share of faults—exoticism, scholasticism, ulterior motives. But both maintained that these faults could be overcome through methodological self-consciousness and sympathetic imagination.

§

In the summer of 1979, Edward and his family vacationed in Andalusia before going on to Beirut, where they stayed with Mariam's widowed father Emile. (Her mother Wadad had died that spring, having entrusted the manuscript of her memoir to Edward during his last visit in March.[53]) Najla Said was only five years old at the time of this trip, but she retained vivid memories of the Golf Club, where her aunt Grace would take her and her brother Wadie to swim with their cousins Karim, Ussama, and Saree, the sons of Samir and Jean Makdisi. She also remembered several instances of the random violence that continued to plague the city. On one occasion, they heard shooting near the Golf Club and were quickly herded into the changing rooms by the lifeguards. When it was safe to return, they found bullets at the bottom of the pool. On another occasion, Najla injured her thumb and was taken by her mother to the AUB hospital, where she saw a woman with a serious head wound from a gunshot or bomb blast.[54]

Edward had another reason for going to Beirut that summer, namely, to launch a seminar on American foreign policy at the Institute for Palestine Studies. In one of his lectures, "The Palestine Question and the American Context," he undertook to remedy a serious flaw in the Palestinian national movement, namely, its lack of understanding of America. "No country," he cautioned his audience,

> not even a great imperial power like America, is simply a force for one thing or another. America ... is a society with its own history, its own peculiar institutions, forces, social and cultural formations which taken together act upon and in the world in many different, often confusing and contradictory ways.[55]

He went on to analyze America in Gramscian terms, drawing on his favorite Marxist theoretician, the Italian Antonio Gramsci. On the one hand, Edward explained, there is American political society, embodied in the state. On the other hand, there is American civil society, embodied in a host of private institutions—universities, churches, foundations, labor unions. It is in civil society, Edward insisted, that the strength of America is located, and it is there that the struggle for Palestine must be waged.

As a first step in this new strategy, Edward had persuaded the PLO to invite a delegation of American progressives and radicals to visit Lebanon that August and observe the destruction wrought by the Israelis in the southern part of the country. The group included a number of veteran civil libertarians and anti-war activists, notably former Attorney General Ramsey Clark, who had defended Eqbal Ahmad and the rest of the Harrisburg Eight at their conspiracy trial in 1972, and Movement lawyer David Dellinger, the editor of the radical magazine *Seven Days*. The group also included

Edward's friends Eqbal Ahmad and Fred Jameson, who had returned to Yale on the strength of his books *Marxism and Form* and *The Prison-House of Language*.[56] When he got back to the United States, Jameson published a piece in *Seven Days* in which he declared that "the Palestinians are the Blacks and Chicanos of the Israeli capitalist system."[57] For the moment, Edward's new American strategy seemed to be working.

§

If Edward happened to read the *New York Times* on September 11, 1979, he would have seen a story by Marvine Howe featuring an interview with Uncle Charles. Speaking for the Lebanese Front, Uncle Charles told Howe that the Front advocates "federalism based on the important religious communities," with a "politically neutral" central government. If Lebanon's Muslim community refuses to "give up their pan-Arab ideas," he warned, then the Christians "would go [their] own way." "We are determined," he explained, "to stay and maintain our identity and freedom and will never let go. Our militias are strong enough to defend us, even better than the Lebanese army before the war." Reminding her readers that the Christian militias had received arms and training from the Israelis, Howe noted that Dr. Malik "spoke openly of Israel as 'a friend.'"[58] A few days later, Howe filed another story from Beirut in which she quoted Uncle Charles as saying, "We are not fanatics but our religion is our nation because we are a minority and Islam is fanatical."[59]

That autumn, the Islamic revolution in Iran, which Edward had greeted with considerable enthusiasm, took an ominous turn. On November 4, student militants occupied the US embassy in Tehran, taking fifty-two Americans hostage. In desperation, American officials in Washington contacted PLO officials in Beirut, who were on friendly terms with the revolutionary government in Iran. One of the intermediaries was Walid Khalidi, who carried messages between Arafat and Ambassador John Gunther Dean in Beirut.[60] Another intermediary, it appears, was Edward Said, who told Arafat's British biographers, Andrew Gowers and Tony Walker, that he was asked by Cyrus Vance to seek Arafat's assistance in freeing the hostages. In response to these American overtures, Arafat sent Hani al-Hassan and Abu Walid (Saad Sayel), the PLO military commander, to Tehran. Although the Iranians refused to release all fifty-two hostages, they did agree to free thirteen blacks and five women in time for Thanksgiving.[61]

In March 1980, Edward traveled to Washington to participate in a forum sponsored by the Palestine Human Rights Campaign. Joining Edward were Dr. Ronald Walters of Howard University, who served as a liaison between the PHRC and the African American community; Dr. Israel Shahak, the Israeli human rights activist whom Edward had first met at the AAUG; and David Dellinger, who had traveled to Lebanon the previous summer.[62] A few days later, Edward flew to Beirut for a meeting on the curriculum of the planned Palestinian Open University, the brainchild of his old friend Ibrahim Abu-Lughod, who had secured the support of the PLO.[63] While there, Edward also moderated a symposium at the Institute for Palestine Studies featuring three prominent American radicals—Richard Barnet, David Dellinger, and Richard Falk. Although Falk was pessimistic about the prospect of reversing America's pro-

Israel policy, he acknowledged that "Edward Said, in particular, has begun to make a significant impact on at least intellectual public opinion, which has treated the Palestinian struggle like the dead fish in the centre of politics that you can smell, but can not talk about."[64]

That summer, Edward accompanied his friend Eqbal Ahmad, who knew something about guerrilla movements and army tactics, on a tour of PLO posts in southern Lebanon. Afterwards, Eqbal wrote up his findings for the PLO leadership. According to Edward, Eqbal not only predicted the Israeli invasion that was to come in 1982, but he also foresaw the result—a crushing defeat for the PLO.[65] That same summer, Eqbal introduced Edward to the Pakistani poet Faiz Ahmed Faiz, who was living in exile in Beirut. One evening, the three of them were dining out with a fourth friend, Nubar Hovsepian. As Eqbal recalled:

> Said was fully engaged as Faiz recited a poem—"Lullaby for a Palestinian Child." Just then a violent fire fight started nearby; the waiters scurried inside, leaving us the only diners in the courtyard. Instinctively, I stopped translating from Faiz's Urdu into English, and looked inquiringly at Nubar Hovsepian, who knew Beirut and its warriors well. "Go on," urged Said, as if nothing unusual was happening. We went on.[66]

Like Edward, Hovsepian had lived in Cairo before immigrating to the United States as an adolescent. After graduating from the University of Washington in 1972, he had enrolled at the AUB, where he studied with Walid Khalidi and joined the Palestinian resistance movement.[67]

At the end of August, Edward flew to Vienna for the second United Nations Seminar on the Question of Palestine, where he read a paper entitled "The Formation of American Public Opinion on the Question of Palestine." American attitudes toward the Palestinians, he observed, reflect "a rarely questioned consensus" dating from Puritan times. This American consensus does not operate mechanically, dictating what a reporter must say. Rather, it "sets limits and maintains pressures," with "little apparent admission or awareness that this is what in fact is being done." Thus Americans tend to identify with pioneering societies like Israel while viewing the Palestinians as pre-modern "savages" who have failed to put the land to good use. Edward's example of how this consensus is reinforced by the media was a September 1979 episode of ABC's *Issues and Answers* in which host Barbara Walters interviewed Yasir Arafat in Havana. Three times, Edward noted, Walters asked Arafat about the clause in the PLO Charter that called for the destruction of Israel, thereby "raising the specter of the Holocaust" and "exposing Arafat's latent Nazism to the world."[68]

That November, Edward's friend Sadik al-Azm submitted a manuscript to *Arab Studies Quarterly*, a new journal founded by Edward and Ibrahim Abu-Lughod. The manuscript was undoubtedly "Orientalism and Orientalism in Reverse," in which Azm took Edward to task for tracing European Orientalism all the way back to Homer. "It seems to me that this manner of construing the origins of Orientalism," Azm observed, "simply lends strength to the essentialistic categories of 'Orient' and 'Occident' . . . which Said's book is ostensibly set on demolishing." He also criticized Edward for understating the material causes of colonialism, implying that "the emergence of such observers, administrators, and invaders of the Orient as Napoleon, Cromer and Balfour was made inevitable by 'Orientalism.'"[69] Finally, he objected to Edward's criticism of Karl Marx for succumbing to Orientalist thinking. Marx's writings on British imperialism in India, Azm insisted, were consistent with his analysis of European capitalism and free from the taint of Orientalism.

Like Uncle Charles before him, Edward did not appreciate being on the receiving end of Azm's verbal assault. "Let me be honest with you as a friend, who as you know admires and loves you," Edward confided. He proceeded to object to the "narrowness and dogmatism" of Azm's recent work, including his critique of *Orientalism*. In making insinuations against "a polemicist like me," Edward added, you "lay yourself open to many worse insinuations, for example, to being (*literally*) a willing, silent servant of the Syrian regime, which currently employs you and demands your silence, a price which—as I have told you at least once—you have regrettably accepted to pay." Edward was referring to Azm's decision to take a faculty position at the University of Damascus, where the ruling Baathists screened and monitored the faculty and dismissed or arrested those who dared to criticize the regime, including Leftists like Azm.[70] "But I would never say that about you in print," Edward insisted: "that is the difference between us."[71]

That Azm declined to revise his essay can be inferred from a second, surprisingly conciliatory letter Edward wrote in mid-December, in which he promised to argue for the publication of the essay. He was even "prepared to concede that *Orientalism* is not really a very good book," although he defended his readings of Orientalist texts. He closed by offering to meet with Azm in Beirut in January.[72] If that meeting took place, it was evidently their last one. Azm ended up publishing his essay in the London-based journal *Khamsin*, a journal of "revolutionary socialists of the Middle East," whose editorial board included members of Matzpen, the Israeli Socialist Organization. Many years later, Azm recalled that his critique of *Orientalism* had cost him his friendship with Edward. "While it could have been a debate on friendly terms," he told an interviewer, "Said's flaw was that he was never good at taking others' criticism: we never spoke again."[73] It was a flaw he shared with Uncle Charles, whose own break with Azm had occurred a dozen years earlier.

§

In January 1981, Edward began a year-long sabbatical from teaching. According to a profile of him in *Broadway*, the magazine of the *Columbia Daily Spectator*, he worked on a number of projects that year, including *Covering Islam: How the Media and the Experts See the Rest of the World*, published that summer; a collection of his literary-critical essays for Harvard, published in 1983 under the title *The World, The Text, and the Critic*; a script for *The Shadow of the West*, a documentary about Palestine that he agreed to write and narrate for a BBC series entitled *The Arabs: A Living History*; and even a novel.[74] This last project may well have been the work of autobiographical fiction that eventually turned into his memoir, *Out of Place*. In any case, Edward's sabbatical began with a trip to Beirut, where his mother and two of his sisters, Jean and Grace, still lived. He also went to Amman, where he spoke with Dr. Hanna Nasir, the exiled president of Birzeit University, who had been deported by the Israelis in 1974.[75] Their conversation may have concerned the proposed Palestinian Open University, as Nasir was in charge of higher education for the PLO.

As Edward's sabbatical drew to a close that fall, he returned to Beirut, where he granted an interview to Mona es-Said of *Monday Morning*. The subject of the interview was the new Reagan administration, which Edward called "a very, very dangerous administration," perfectly "willing to spread military terror throughout the world." For that reason, he warned, the Arabs must be "extremely careful" in their dealings with it. At one point, Edward cautioned that the administration was likely to "make a concerted attempt to isolate the Palestinians" in the next few months. As evidence, he pointed to a recent article in the *New Republic* by Jeane Kirkpatrick, Reagan's ambassador to the UN, who praised the late Anwar Sadat for understanding "that dealing with the PLO cannot lead to a solution of the Palestinian problem."[76] Later in the interview, however, Edward reversed himself, opining that the administration was "likely" to open a dialogue with the PLO, if only to put pressure on the Israelis by playing "the Palestinian card."[77]

In January 1982, Edward traveled to South Lebanon with a camera crew to film scenes for *The Shadow of the West*. The film opens with footage of Arab inhabitants of East Jerusalem quarreling with Israeli soldiers as Edward provides the voice-over. We then see several old photographs of Edward's childhood as he tells us that he was born in Jerusalem. The scene then shifts to Edward's office in New York, where he confesses to his friend Ibrahim Abu-Lughod that, as a Palestinian, he is always angry these days. Later, the film takes us to South Lebanon. We visit Beaufort Castle, where we hear from a band of PLO soldiers guarding the old Crusader fortress, as well as a refugee camp, where Edward engages the residents in conversation. Toward the end of the film, we accompany Edward on a visit to Shafiq al-Hout, the PLO's representative in Lebanon.[78]

That spring, Edward returned to Beirut, where he met, once again, with Yasir Arafat. As he recalled a decade later:

> He [Arafat] was in bed. I went to visit him in one of his mysterious residences, and he seemed very, very ill and I said, you know it's quite clear to me that the Israelis are going to attack, and I'll never forget what he said. He said, if they want to attack, welcome to them, let them come.[79]

Arafat's reply was identical to what he told other visitors from New York that spring. One of them was John Edwin Mroz of the International Peace Academy, who had been approached by Arafat with a proposal for talks between the United States and the PLO. Mroz, in turn, had consulted the US State Department, which authorized him to meet with Arafat—as he did some fifty times between August 1981 and May 1982.[80] Another visitor was Stephen P. Cohen, who, after leaving Harvard, had founded the Institute for Middle East Peace and Development in order to continue his mediation work. He had been urged to see Arafat by Mordechai Gur, a Knesset member opposed to an Israeli invasion of Lebanon.[81]

All of these private efforts to avert war were in vain. On May 25, Secretary of State Alexander Haig gave Israeli defense minister Ariel Sharon a "green light" to invade Lebanon, or at least that is what Sharon concluded. A few days later, Edward arrived in Washington for a conference at Catholic University, where Uncle Charles was Maritain Professor of Moral and Political Philosophy. Entitled "Jerusalem, City of Peace: A National Conference on Biblical Foundations for Justice in the Holy Land," the conference was sponsored by a coalition of Christian and Arab American organizations, including two that Edward had supported since their inception—the Palestine Human Rights Campaign and the American Arab Anti-Discrimination Committee.[82] According to a reporter for a Jewish newspaper, Edward lamented the "crimes of silence" surrounding the "genocide" taking place in Palestine.[83] Unfortunately, it would appear that Uncle Charles was not there to hear him, having left town a few days earlier for a special centenary symposium on Jacques Maritain at the University of Notre Dame.[84]

Two weeks later, with Israeli troops surrounding Beirut, Edward published an op-ed in the *New York Times*. "The invasion," he announced, "has settled the long debate within Zionism as to the fate of the Palestinians who survived the destruction of their society in 1948." Those living in the occupied territories were to have, eventually, "autonomy without land on exclusively Israeli terms." The others, exiled Palestinians, were to be "exterminated," even if thousands of Lebanese civilians must die in the process.[85] Two days later, he told the *Times* that "the casualties in Beirut are uncountable," noting that "he was receiving information by telephone from relatives and friends in Beirut."[86] One of those friends was Ibrahim Abu-Lughod, who had arrived in Beirut just two days before the invasion to organize the Palestinian Open University. When the Israelis began to bomb and shell West Beirut, Ibrahim was forced to take refuge in Hilda Said's apartment, where he remained for the next two months. According to Edward, Ibrahim asked him, on behalf of Yasir Arafat, to serve as a "go-between" with the Reagan administration.[87] There is no indication, however, that he contacted administration officials at this time.

Later that month, the *New York Review of Books* carried a long essay by Bernard Lewis on "The Question of Orientalism," which offered a sharp, if belated, response to Edward's critique in *Orientalism*. Coinciding as it did with the Israeli invasion of Lebanon, the publication of Lewis' essay must have struck Edward as a declaration of academic war. As others had done, Lewis questioned Edward's decision to omit the German Orientalists—arguably more important than their French and British counterparts. The reason for the omission, Lewis speculated, was that a chapter on the Germans, who lacked an empire of their own, would have undermined Edward's thesis about the relationship between Orientalism and colonialism. He also wondered about Edward's omission of Russian Orientalism, which "comes closest—far more so than any of the British or French scholars whom he condemns—to precisely the kind of tendentious, denigratory writing that Mr. Said so much dislikes in others."[88] The reason for this omission, Lewis implied, was purely political: as a man of the Left, Edward was unwilling to criticize the Soviets.

In early July, Edward flew to London for an emergency gathering of forty prominent Palestinians who wanted to do something for their people in the wake of the invasion of Lebanon.[89] In addition to wealthy philanthropists like Hasib Sabbagh—a former student of Uncle Charles' at the AUB—the gathering included intellectuals like Walid

Khalidi, Hisham Sharabi, and Edward himself. Their meetings led to the creation of two new organizations: the Welfare Association, headquartered in Geneva, which dispensed emergency relief and development grants to Palestinians in Lebanon, the West Bank, Gaza, and Israel itself; and the American Middle East Peace Research Institute, intended to increase American understanding of the Palestinians. Edward served on the board of AMEPRI, which funded a number of research projects—including Rashid Khalidi's book on the invasion of Lebanon, *Under Siege*—until it ran out of money.[90] A young professor of political science at the AUB, Rashid Khalidi was himself a victim of the invasion, taking refuge in a vacant apartment on the AUB campus, courtesy of Malcolm Kerr.[91]

Among the organizations that took note of Edward's political activities during the summer of 1982 was the American Israel Public Affairs Committee, the influential Israel lobby in Washington. In an AIPAC report entitled *The Campaign to Discredit Israel*, the authors noted that Edward had participated in a pair of events in Washington organized by the American Arab Anti-Discrimination Committee. One was a "lobby-in" in support of the "Rahall Resolution," sponsored by Representative Nick Rahall of West Virginia, which called on the United States to suspend arms sales to Israel. The other was a "congressional seminar" led by Edward, Walter Fauntroy of the Congressional Black Caucus, and James Zogby of the ADC. That same summer, the report noted, Edward spoke at a teach-in at Manhattan's Town Hall organized by the November 29th Coalition, which took its name from the annual International Day of Solidarity with the Palestinian People.[92] Unfortunately, Edward's activities would soon draw the attention of Jewish groups more extreme than AIPAC.

§

In the fall of 1982, Edward taught a course on modern fiction at Columbia. One of his students was a senior political science major who dreamed of becoming a writer. His name was Barry Obama, and he would go on to become president of the United States. One of the other students in the class has claimed that he and Obama did not care for Professor Said's obsession with literary theory. Another of Obama's classmates, however, remembered the class quite differently. Professor Said's lectures, he recalled,

> were devoted to a careful analysis of the texts we were studying, without any reference to literary theory that I can recall. When Said lectured about Conrad's *Nostromo*, he dwelled on the meaning of the cracks in a vase. When he lectured on Kafka's *Metamorphosis*, he explained that the word that Kafka uses was the same word used in the gospels to describe Christ's transfiguration.

This sounds very much like the method of close reading Edward had learned from R. P. Blackmur at Princeton and Reuben Brower at Harvard. In any case, Obama was certainly not radicalized by Edward Said, who, according to both of Obama's classmates, never discussed politics in class.[93]

Outside of class, however, it was a different story. On September 11, Edward spoke at a rally at the White House organized by the November 29th Coalition. The Washington press corps hardly noticed the event, although it drew nearly 3,000 protesters representing some hundred organizations, including the PFLP, the Irish Republican Army, and the Workers World Party.[94] Then came the defining event of Ariel Sharon's war in Lebanon. After surrounding the Sabra and Shatila refugee camps in south Beirut, the IDF permitted the Lebanese Forces to enter in pursuit of "terrorists" who were said to have remained behind. The result was a massacre of Palestinian civilians that shocked the world, including the Israeli public. Asked to comment on what had taken place, Hisham Sharabi told the *New York Times* that "Israel is directly responsible, and moral responsibility, at one remove, rests with the U.S. Government." In the same story, Edward was quoted as saying that the massacre stemmed from Israel's "ideological policy from the beginning that, first, the Palestinians do not exist and, second, if they do, they are terrorists, two-legged beasts, as Begin has called them."[95]

A few days later, Edward offered a more considered response to the massacre, just days after a Peace Now demonstration had drawn a reported 400,000 Israelis into the streets of Tel Aviv to voice their displeasure with their government. "It is more rewarding to wonder at the process that is beginning among these courageous Israelis," Edward wrote, "than to add another expression of outrage to what has already been said about the massacres in Sabra and Shatila." "As Palestinians bury their dead," he concluded,

> the impulse is to endure the present tragedy in the hope that someday "they" will be paid back in kind. The question we must put to ourselves, however, is whether the real, cataclysmic events of the past should so relentlessly be repeated in the present and future. Perhaps this is a hopelessly difficult question to be asking now, but to risk another catastrophe is to risk too much.[96]

These lines could have been written by an apostle of nonviolence like Daniel Berrigan or Eqbal Ahmad, who urged the Palestinians to seize the moral high ground in their struggle for justice.

Just before Christmas, Edward and Ibrahim Abu-Lughod flew to Tunis, the new headquarters of the PLO, to meet with Arafat. Among those who saw Edward and Ibrahim in Arafat's office was Lally Weymouth, the daughter of Katherine Graham of the *Washington Post*, who was known for her interviews with heads of state. Also seated in Arafat's office, Weymouth reported, were Dr. Issam Sartawi, Dr. Nabil Shaath, and Dr. Ahmed Sidki Dajani, all high-ranking PLO moderates. Sartawi and Shaath had been talking to Israeli civilians for years—a fact that landed Sartawi on the hit list of Abu Nidal, Arafat's most brutal opponent in the Palestinian resistance movement.[97] As for Dajani, he had spoken casually with none other than Henry Kissinger—the author of the ban on direct talks with the PLO—in Rabat the previous month.[98] Arafat's interlocutors, it appears, were all urging him to recognize Israel—one of the American conditions for opening direct talks. Gesturing toward the other men in the room, Arafat told Weymouth that he preferred not to play the card of recognition, but "in spite of that, they are squeezing me."[99]

By the same token, Israel was unwilling to recognize the PLO, boycotting a UN conference on Palestine in Geneva that summer. Three Israeli speakers chose to go anyway: Uri Avnery and Matti Peled of the Council for Israeli-Palestinian Peace and Felicia Langer of the League for Human and Civil Rights. Edward went to Geneva, too, declaring that "the Palestinian people today are faced with nothing less than *ethnocide*." Israel, he charged, "has determined to reduce the Palestinians to a people without a narratable history." As evidence, he pointed to the fact that "Palestinian archives are either despoiled or stolen"—a reference to the removal of the files of the PLO Research Center during the Israeli occupation of Beirut. As for what the UN should do about this "ethnocide," Edward urged that "the production of concrete information" be its "first imperative," starting with a census of the Palestinian people. Sadly, both Israel and the Arab states had ignored a UN General Assembly resolution calling for a count.[100]

Meanwhile, Mariam Said and the children had flown from Paris to Beirut to visit Hilda Said and Mariam's father Emile. When Najla Said asked her mother why her father wasn't coming with them, Mariam replied, "It's not safe for him as a Palestinian." No sooner had their plane landed than an explosion near the runway jolted the passengers. Indeed, theirs was the last flight to arrive before the airport was closed due to heavy fighting between government forces and opposition militias. Once they made it safely to Emile's apartment in Ras Beirut, they spent much of their time in the building's dark stairwell as the shells fell all around them. One day, Mariam and Wadie were nearly killed by a shell as they walked to the building next door, where Samir and Jean Makdisi lived with their three sons. Finally, after a week or so, Emile was able to secure places for them on a crowded ferry to Cyprus. It would be almost a decade before the Said family returned to Beirut.[101]

That fall, Yasir Arafat returned to Tripoli, where his loyal cadres were battling Syrian-supported rebels within his own Fatah organization. In early November, Edward discussed the fighting in Tripoli and the question of Arafat's future on the *MacNeil/Lehrer Newshour*, a nightly television program aired nationwide on PBS. Joining the discussion from Atlanta was Dr. Landrum Bolling, a Quaker peacemaker who was participating in a high-level Middle East conference hosted by former presidents Gerald Ford and Jimmy Carter. Like Edward, Bolling served as an occasional back channel to Arafat, having seen him as recently as August. As the discussion unfolded, Edward and Bolling found themselves in complete agreement, defending Arafat as a moderate who understood that, in the wake of Lebanon, armed struggle must give way to negotiation. Arafat, they insisted, remained popular among ordinary Palestinians in the West Bank and elsewhere. They disagreed with US officials who hinted that the Palestinians would be better off without him.[102]

§

On January 18, 1984, after Malcolm Kerr was assassinated in Beirut, Eric Pace of the *New York Times* phoned Edward for a comment. "No one could doubt either his perceptiveness and knowledge or his understanding and genuine interest," Edward told Pace. "He was perhaps among the very few authentically informed students of Arab nationalism in its combative and tumultuous postwar years."[103] Less than a month later, President Reagan announced that the Marines would withdraw from Beirut. The following week, Edward penned an angry column about the breakdown of

Lebanon for the *Nation*. Denouncing US foreign policy as "willful and disingenuous," he declared, "We are witnessing a repetition of the policies the Carter administration followed in Iran prior to the revolution." President Gemayel, he predicted, "is on his way to becoming America's Lebanese shah," destined to be overthrown by his Muslim and Leftist opponents. At one point, Edward sounded like Uncle Charles, scolding Americans for not caring enough. "America presides over the cataclysm of a distant society," he lamented, "and just as the situation becomes unbearable, Reagan prepares to leave. No society deserves such a fate."[104]

In March, Edward addressed the annual convention of the Arab American Anti-Discrimination Committee in Washington. Among those who spoke were presidential candidates George McGovern and Jesse Jackson, whose campaign staff included James Zogby of the ADC.[105] Edward's role was to discuss "Media Perceptions of the Arab World" with Ted Koppel of ABC News, who prided himself on being independent, willing to give the Arabs a fair hearing. For Edward, however, that was beside the point. "On the one hand," he observed,

> Koppel wants to appear independent; on the other hand, he's part of a system, ABC, which is part of a bigger system, the network organization. And, on a third, strangely enough, he also represents the interests of the government. All of these journalists, particularly those on a national level—Brokaw, Jennings, Koppel, Rather—do not only give us the *news*, they also (usually unconsciously) represent what's happening from the standpoint of U.S. interests. Journalists internalize government norms to a degree that is quite frightening.[106]

The problem was not that Koppel failed to cover the Arab world; it was that he failed to reflect critically on whose interests that coverage served.

That autumn, Yasir Arafat and King Hussein prepared to convene the PNC in Amman for the first time since 1970. Unfortunately, the defection of the pro-Syrian members of the PNC made it difficult to assemble the necessary quorum. Arafat had to expend his personal capital to persuade reluctant members, such as Yusif Sayigh, to fly to Amman. Even though Sayigh favored reconciliation with Syria, Arafat called him in Oxford, pleading with him to come. Sayigh, in turn, phoned Khaled al-Fahoum, the Damascus-based speaker of the PNC who was boycotting the meeting, and told him he was going to Amman "because I believe in criticizing from inside rather than from the outside."[107] Edward himself had not attended a PNC meeting since 1977. But Arafat phoned him and Mariam "half a dozen times, begging us to show up in Amman together." Edward finally agreed to go, as did his friend Shafiq al-Hout. "Both Shafiq and I," Edward recalled, "were roundly denounced by Fatah dissidents now housed by the Assad government and threatened with death for our 'treasonous' rallying to Arafat."[108]

The Council opened in late November in a heavily guarded stadium, where King Hussein called on the membership to accept UNSC Resolution 242 as the basis for negotiations. That, it turned out, was further than most members were prepared to go. The Council did, however, strengthen Arafat's hand against his rivals in Damascus. One evening, after some sharp criticism, Arafat dramatically tendered his resignation, leaving it on the table all night. The next morning, he sat meekly in the third row as the Deputy Speaker pleaded with him to take it back. At that point, a group of traditionally dressed elders from the refugee camps entered the hall and carried him bodily back to the podium.[109] Perhaps the most important achievement of the Amman meetings, however, was to strengthen the PLO's standing with the inhabitants of the West Bank, who were able to watch the proceedings on Jordanian television. One West Bank resident who tuned in was Elias Freij, the mayor of Bethlehem, who told Tom Friedman, "I never met this Abu Iyad or Shafik al-Hout before, but when I heard them speak they were very moderate, very eloquent."[110]

Edward had to leave Amman early because he was due to speak at a conference at Rutgers University at the end of the month. The conference, entitled "Autonomy and the Other: A Conceptual Approach to the Israeli-Palestinian Question," brought Israeli and Palestinian academics together in a series of panels, with a keynote address by Jean-Francois Lyotard, the author of *La Condition Postmoderne* (1979). Edward's panel included Matti Peled, the former Israeli general turned literature professor and peace activist, who had participated in the Geneva conference on Palestine in the summer of 1983. Peled's paper focused on images of Israel and Israelis in post-1967 Palestinian writing. Edward's paper analyzed the "ideology of difference" on which the state of Israel depends—the difference between Jew and non-Jew. His argument was that it ought to be possible to think about difference more creatively, acknowledging the many distinctions between Jews and Palestinian Arabs without privileging the experience of either side.[111]

The following spring, the so-called War of the Camps exploded in Beirut as Amal—the Shia militia of Nabih Berri—battled the PLO, whose rival factions put aside their differences for the time being.[112] On May 24, Edward and his friends Ibrahim Abu-Lughod and Eqbal Ahmad addressed a mailgram to President Assad of Syria, pleading with him to put an end to the bloodshed.[113] Three days later, the *MacNeil/Lehrer NewsHour* invited Edward to discuss the Palestinian-Shia conflict on air with Fouad Ajami, himself a Lebanese Shia. The two friends took opposing sides, with Ajami blaming the conflict on Arafat, whom he called "an actor without a stage" who longed to return to his "glory days" in West Beirut. Edward blamed the conflict on Amal's sponsor Syria, which was "bleeding" all of the combatants "in order to take over the country." As for the role of the United States, Edward claimed that the Americans "encouraged this kind of intersectarian fighting" in order to postpone "any resolution of the fundamental problem, which is the problem of Palestine." Ajami complained that "the U.S. has abdicated its role" in Lebanon, leaving Syria the dominant power.[114]

That July, the *London Review of Books* published an essay in which Edward celebrated pre-war Beirut, which had provided him and other exiles with "a substitute home." Now, alas, Beirut was engaged in a process of "self-dismantling—much of it performed on prime-time television." As for the cause of this self-dismantling, Edward pointed to "the insidious role played by religious and sectarian conviction."

> I'm ashamed to admit that a great many of my early memories of friends and family expressing religious opinions are harsh and unpleasant. "Moslems," I was told in 1954 by a great friend of my father's, "are dust. They should be blown

away." Another wise man, a prominent philosopher and former Lebanese foreign minister, frequently denounced Islam and the Prophet Mohammed to me, using such words as "lechery," "hypocrisy," "corruption," and "degeneracy."[115]

By 1985, most readers of the *London Review* were probably unable to identify this "prominent philosopher and former Lebanese foreign minister." But Edward could not forget Uncle Charles' religious bigotry, real or imagined.

Meanwhile, Islamic Jihad was proving Edward's point about the insidious role of sectarian conviction. By summer, the shadowy organization had taken a number of American and European hostages from the streets of Beirut, including Rev. Benjamin Weir and William Buckley, the CIA's Beirut station chief, who later died in captivity. One of their captors took charge of their political reeducation, bringing them English books to read. As Ben Weir recalled:

> Some of the books were about the Iranian revolution, others about the history and development of Shiite religious thought. One book, by a Columbia University professor, dealt with the misunderstanding of Islam in the West. . . . We read all these books. Some I pondered for days at a time.[116]

The book by the Columbia University professor was undoubtedly *Covering Islam*, by Edward Said, whom Weir would meet in person after his release. Edward may have had no use for terrorism, but the terrorists—some of whom were university students and graduates—had found a use for his books.

§

On October 1, 1985, the Israelis bombed PLO headquarters outside Tunis, killing some seventy Palestinians and Tunisians. That evening, the *MacNeil/Lehrer NewsHour* invited Edward to debate the bombing raid with Amos Perlmutter, who had visited Uncle Charles in Beirut back in 1982. Israel's UN ambassador, Benjamin Netanyahu, was defending the raid as a response to the recent murder of three Israelis by Palestinian hijackers on a yacht in Cyprus.[117] Edward rejected that explanation, noting that the hijackers had denied any connection to the PLO and that, in any case, the raid in Tunisia was out of all proportion to the Cyprus hijacking. The real purpose of the Israeli raid, he implied, was to scuttle the peace process. "For the last eight or nine months," he pointed out, "there's been unmistakable evidence . . . that the PLO is in fact interested in peace—there's the Jordanian-Palestinian peace agreement." Perlmutter, however, dismissed Edward's talk of peace as "interesting propaganda." The PLO, he declared, has "demonstrated clearly that it is a terrorist organization. It is not interested in peace; it is not interested in negotiations." The one point Perlmutter and Edward agreed on was that the Israeli raid on Tunisia had "buried the peace process."[118]

Later that month, the Harvard *Crimson* broke the story of the CIA's funding of a conference on "Islam and Politics in the Contemporary Arab World" organized by Nadav Safran, the director of Harvard's Center for Middle Eastern Studies. After the story broke, about half of the 100 or so invitees decided not to attend the conference.[119]

One of them was Fouad Ajami, who had been urged by Edward and Eqbal Ahmad to stay away. It was not long, however, before Ajami started having second thoughts. On October 21, he wrote an anguished letter to his two old friends, regretting that he had not gone to the Harvard conference to support Safran, whom he considered a friend. He admitted that he could not get over the deaths of his mother's Lebanese relatives at the hands of the PLO. He complained that Edward had not phoned him when he was seriously ill or congratulated him when he was awarded a MacArthur Fellowship.[120] It was, in effect, a good-bye letter. Henceforth, Ajami would join Bernard Lewis and Martin Peretz as an object of Edward's spleen.

In November, Edward journeyed to a Presbyterian retreat center in Montreat, North Carolina, to give one of the keynote addresses at a Middle East peacemaking conference. The first speaker was his former Columbia colleague Arthur Hertzberg, who, although he regarded Zionism itself as non-negotiable, continued to advocate a two-state solution. Edward did not disagree, but he insisted that the Israelis, as the stronger party, must make a gesture toward the Palestinians. As the weaker party, the Palestinians should not be expected to make all the concessions. The conference organizers were also pleased to welcome Ben and Carol Weir as late additions to the program. In addition to sharing his experience as a hostage in Lebanon, Weir advised US officials to address the root causes of the conflict, be prepared to negotiate, and refrain from retaliation.[121] He also mentioned that he had read one of Edward's books while he was in captivity.[122]

Edward was never a hostage like Weir, but he, too, had to live with the constant threat of violence. That winter, vandals broke into his office at Columbia as well as the apartment building where he lived. An FBI agent was assigned to the case. The culprits, Edward was told, were associated with the Jewish Defense League, whose cofounder, Rabbi Meir Kahane, was the spiritual leader of Israel's ultra-nationalist *Kach* party.[123] At the time of the vandalism, the JDL was being investigated by the journalist Robert I. Friedman. Among the JDL partisans who agreed to speak to Friedman was one Victor Vancier, who had already served time for setting fire to eleven Egyptian properties on the East Coast. Vancier claimed not to know who had broken into Edward's office, but he praised them as "Jewish patriots." "I think the man is a monster," he said of Edward. "And that means anything goes. I believe Arabs are the new Nazis, the heirs of the Third Reich." "If you think the Shi'ites in Lebanon are capable of fantastic acts of suicidal terrorism," he boasted, "the Jewish underground will strike targets that will make Americans gasp: 'How could Jews do such things?'"[124]

At some point in the winter of 1985–6, Edward flew to Tunis and checked into the Hilton Hotel, where he cooled his heels until Yasir Arafat could see him. At the time, Ambassador Richard W. Murphy, Assistant Secretary of State for Near Eastern Affairs, was attempting to negotiate the terms of a peace conference with Arafat through King Hussein.[125] Meanwhile, unbeknownst to the Americans and the Jordanians, Arafat was pursuing his own secret talks with the Israelis. Edward may have guessed as much when he bumped into Stephen P. Cohen in the Tunis Hilton. As Cohen recalled,

> when Said found out that I had been granted an audience, he was just furious. He obviously did not know what my meeting was about, but he very much resented

that Arafat would choose to speak with a Jew from America over an important Palestinian figure like himself. It was, I believe, among the early seeds of Edward Said's alienation from Arafat.[126]

More plausibly, it was the seed of Edward's alienation from Steve Cohen and his mentor Herb Kelman, in whose problem-solving workshops he had participated at Harvard.

Coincidentally, Kelman invited Edward to a meeting of the International Society of Political Psychology (ISPP) in Amsterdam that summer, where he staged a "fishbowl" workshop between Israelis and Palestinians.[127] In addition, he asked Edward and Mordechai Bar-On, one of the founders of Peace Now, to join him in the presidential session. As soon as Edward started speaking, however, it was obvious that he was going to challenge the validity of Kelman's workshop methodology, which prescribed equal numbers of Israelis and Palestinians at the seminar table, along with a smaller number of third-party observers. Even Kelman's protocol for the very session in which they were speaking, Edward noted, assumes "that outside the fateful circle of Palestinians and Israelis stands a group of people less involved and less affected than the main parties . . . , able to legislate, inform, and perhaps even achieve a totally distinct and other point of view." But "there can be no neutrality or objectivity about Palestine," he cautioned. Even "to place the Palestinian and Israeli sides . . . on what appears to be an equal, opposite, and symmetrical footing is also to reduce the claims of the one by elevating the claims of the other."[128]

Edward's paper was, in effect, his letter of resignation from Kelman's workshops. Years later, he explained that, while Kelman himself was "undoubtedly an idealist,"

> there was always some governmental interest in what he and others did who sponsored dialogues of this kind. Often there were U.S. State Department officials present, one of whom I recall was the author of an article provocatively entitled "Foreign Policy According to Freud." One of the underlying assumptions seemed false to me, that the struggle over Palestine was not a real or material one, but was largely the result of a . . . psychological misunderstanding. In any case I also felt that the idea of an American sponsor or referee who somehow stood outside the conflict and could either manage or observe it calmly was also an ideological fiction.[129]

The State Department official in question was Joseph Montville, a contemporary of Edward's who had studied at Harvard and Columbia before joining the Foreign Service. It was in his Freud article that Montville and his coauthor, the psychiatrist William Davidson, had coined the term "Track Two Diplomacy," referring to unofficial dialogues like those hosted by Kelman.[130]

§

In September 1986, Edward's book *After the Last Sky* was published. It was his most personal book to date, a meditation on what it means to be Palestinian in the form of a commentary on the photographs of Jean Mohr. His book tour included a stop in

London, where he was interviewed by Salman Rushdie before a live audience at the Institute for Contemporary Arts. "For those of us who see the struggle between Eastern and Western descriptions of the world as both an internal and an external struggle," Rushdie began, "Edward Said has been for many years an especially important voice." After introducing Edward, Rushdie opened the conversation by asking him whether things were getting better or worse for him, as a Palestinian, in New York. "Well," Edward reflected, "I think it is getting worse." It was not just the threats from the Jewish Defense League, which Rushdie had mentioned. It was that he had been "tokenized, so that whenever there is a hijacking or some such incident, I get phone calls from the media asking me to come along and comment. It's a very strange feeling to be seen as a kind of representative of terrorism."[131]

In November, the *Guardian* published Edward's review of Bernard Lewis' *Semites and Anti-Semites*.[132] At the time, Edward was busy preparing for his much-anticipated debate with Lewis at the Middle East Studies Association convention in Boston, which took place on November 22. The organizer of the debate was Leila Fawaz, a Lebanese professor of Middle Eastern history at Tufts University, whose background was similar to Edward's. Like the Saids, her family (the Tarazis) had summered in Dhour el Shweir in the 1950s and 1960s. In the 1960s, she had studied at the AUB at the same time as Edward's sister Joyce. After moving to the United States, she had earned a PhD from Harvard, traveling to Oxford to consult with Albert Hourani.[133] For better or for worse, the MESA debate she organized resembled a duel, with a principal and a second on each side. Lewis' second was Leon Wieseltier of the *New Republic*, whose publisher, Martin Peretz, loathed Edward. Edward's second was his friend Christopher Hitchens, whose reputation as a champion debater had been earned at the Oxford Union.

As Edward recalled, some 3,000 people showed up to watch the debate on "Scholars, Media, and the Middle East." After an opening plea for civility by Lewis, Edward launched into his familiar critique of American media coverage of the Middle East, noting that its six main themes—terrorism, Islamic fundamentalism, tribalism, and so on—"coincide almost perfectly with current U.S. policy." Then he turned to his real target—Middle East scholars who serve as "resources" for the media and the government, "whose political sympathies are clearly inscribed in what they write," but who "persist in characterizing what they do as impartial, detached, or expert." He even produced a list, starting with Bernard Lewis himself. In his rebuttal, Lewis accused Edward of using "smear tactics," of attributing motives to his opponents and implying that they "constitute one homogeneous, centrally directed, conspiratorial whole." Edward denied that the scholars he had named "were all directed by some outside source—far from it." But he offered to demonstrate, case by case, that the same six themes kept showing up in their work.[134]

In April 1987, Edward flew to Algiers for the eighteenth session of the PNC.[135] The main business was the reunification of the PLO, which had been divided ever since the PFLP, the DFLP, and the other "rejectionists" had boycotted the last session in Amman in 1984. In exchange for their return to the fold, the Damascus-based leftist fronts demanded concessions from Arafat, notably the official cancellation of his December 1984 agreement with King Hussein—already a dead letter—and a resolution affirming that future relations between the PLO and Egypt must be based on previous PNC resolutions, including a 1983 resolution condemning Egypt for signing the Camp David Accords. When the resolution passed, the official Egyptian observers walked out in protest and President Hosni Mubarak ordered the closure of the PLO's offices in Egypt. On the other hand, the leftists did agree to a resolution insisting that an international peace conference include the PLO on an "equal basis," leaving the door open to a joint Arab delegation. The session ended with Council members joining hands and dancing to chants of "Unity! Unity!" and "Yas-ser Ar-a-fat!"[136]

The month of June found Edward in London, where he called on one of his intellectual and political heroes, the eighty-six-year-old West Indian revolutionary historian C. L. R. James.[137] James lived modestly in Brixton, which happened to be one of the districts featured in a novel Edward's friend Salman Rushdie was writing. Not long after his meeting with James, Rushdie invited Edward to celebrate the Fourth of July at the London home he shared with the American novelist Marianne Wiggins. In Rushdie's study, Edward spotted the manuscript of his new novel and asked him what it was about. It's about Islam, Rushdie replied, and "the Muslims are going to be very angry." Intrigued, Edward asked if he could read it. A week or two later, a typescript of the novel was delivered to Edward's apartment in Manhattan. It was called *The Satanic Verses*. Edward was busy, however, and didn't have time to read it. So he gave it to his colleague Akeel Bilgrami, a young Indian professor of philosophy at Columbia.[138]

On December 9, the first *Intifada*—a spontaneous mass uprising against the Israeli occupation—began in Gaza. The next day, BBC Two aired an episode of the television series *Thinking Aloud* on the question "Has Zionism become its own worst enemy?" Joining host Michael Ignatieff were two friends of Israel, Conor Cruise O'Brien and Amos Elon, and two of its most vocal critics, Patrick Seale and Edward Said. Seale, who had written a glowing review of *Orientalism* back in 1979, was married to Rana Kabbani, the Syrian ex-wife of Edward's friend Mahmoud Darwish.[139] During the discussion, Ignatieff asked Seale to explain the basis of the charge that Zionism is racism. Seale responded by quoting derogatory comments about Arabs made by Menachem Begin and Rafael Eitan. Elon retorted that he could quote other "loudmouth generals" in Israel who had said outrageous things. Then he blamed the attitudes of Begin and his generals on Arab extremists, claiming that Israel had been "infected" by their brutality. At that point Edward intervened, noting that, were the United States to permit only White Anglo-Saxon Protestants to immigrate to America, then Elon would cry racism. In Israel, however, racial discrimination was enshrined in the Law of Return.[140]

Just after Christmas, Uncle Charles died in Beirut. Edward may have learned of it from the obituary in the *New York Times*, written by Ihsan Hijazi, the paper's Beirut correspondent. Dr. Malik, Hijazi recalled, "was regarded as a friend of the United States and the West."

> A Greek Orthodox Christian, he also played a major role in Lebanese politics, defending a system that divides power among Christian and Moslem groups in such a way that guarantees Christians a dominant role in key government institutions. In 1958, when he was Foreign Minister, he was a key defender of his Government's decision to invite the United States to land its Marines to end a period of civil unrest that had been led by Lebanese Moslems.

Later, Hijazi added, Malik "was a member of the Lebanese Front, an all-Christian grouping that led a political campaign against the presence in Lebanon of Palestine Liberation Organization guerrillas and Syrian troops."[141] The news of Uncle Charles' death must have elicited a combination of regret and bewilderment from Edward—regret over their broken relationship, bewilderment that an intellectual of Charles Malik's stature should have so betrayed his calling.

8

Edward Said: The Intellectual in Exile, 1987–2003

Not long after Uncle Charles was buried, Edward published his first commentary on the *Intifada* in the *New York Times*. "Anyone who has watched TV coverage of the kickings and beatings of young Palestinians by Israeli troops," he wrote,

> must have gathered that what is at stake is no mere episode of law and order but a national conflict in which one side, now in power, has little interest in sharing or dividing Palestine but in making sure that the other side remains a permanent underclass.

And for such "daily inhumanity," he complained, "America cannot reward Israel enough." The settlements in the West Bank and Gaza, he reminded his readers, "are in effect funded by America, as is the Israeli military, at an annual rate of $9,750 per soldier."[1] Perhaps it was Edward's op-ed in the *Times* that moved Rabbi Douglas Krantz to invite him to attend a Sabbath service and give a talk at Congregation B'nai Yisrael in Armonk. It was Edward's first visit to a synagogue. "I was moved," he told Dinitia Smith of *New York* magazine. "I appreciated the gesture very much."[2]

Meanwhile, Ian Black of the *Guardian* reported that Yasir Arafat had named three Palestinians to meet with Secretary of State George Shultz, who was flying home following talks in Jerusalem and Amman. They were Edward Said, Ibrahim Abu-Lughod, and Akram Haniya, a newspaper editor from Ramallah who had recently been deported by the Israelis.[3] Before the month was out, State Department spokeswoman Phyllis Oakley—whose husband Robert had been Walid Khalidi's back channel to Henry Kissinger in the early 1970s—announced that Shultz would meet with Edward and Ibrahim in Washington on Saturday, March 26.[4] The meeting was promptly denounced by Israeli Prime Minister Yitzhak Shamir, who charged that it violated the Kissinger ban on negotiating with the PLO. Oakley, however, insisted that "there is no change in U.S. policy on negotiating with or recognizing the PLO," of which Edward and Ibrahim were not members. Asked to comment, Edward told the *Washington Post* that he welcomed the meeting with Shultz as "a move off dead center." He added that he had notified Yasir Arafat about the meeting.[5]

After the Shultz meeting, Marvine Howe of the *New York Times* interviewed Edward at his home in Manhattan. The first topic broached by Shultz, Edward told her, was the state of their alma mater, Princeton University. After the pleasantries, Shultz had handed over the text of his peace plan, which called for talks between the Israelis and a mixed delegation of Palestinians and Jordanians, who would report to an international conference hosted by the five permanent members of the UN Security Council. Edward and Ibrahim "came away with the feeling that Secretary Shultz is serious about going forward with his peace effort," even though the plan had several shortcomings, notably its failure to affirm the Palestinian right to self-determination and to specify a role for the PLO. Edward also confided that Arafat had asked him to protest the Justice Department's recent order to close the PLO's mission at the UN, as mandated by Congress in an anti-terrorism bill signed by President Reagan.[6]

Within days of Edward and Ibrahim's meeting with Shultz, Benjamin Netanyahu announced his resignation as Israel's ambassador to the United Nations.[7] On April 10, Edward appeared with Netanyahu and Henry Kissinger on ABC News' *This Week with David Brinkley*, where they were questioned separately by Brinkley, Sam Donaldson, and George Will. Brinkley began by asking Edward what would happen in the Middle East tomorrow if he had his way. "The end of the occupation," Edward replied. Brinkley followed up by asking whether a withdrawal from the occupied territories would be the first step on the road to the "obliteration" of Israel. "Absolutely not," Edward replied, citing a recent *New York Times* interview with Yasir Arafat in which the PLO chairman had declared his readiness to make peace.[8] George Will pointed out that whenever Arafat affirmed UNSC Resolution 242, he did so in conjunction with the other relevant UN resolutions, the "composite effect" of which was to "deny the legitimacy of the state of Israel." Edward disputed Will's reading of the resolutions, adding that it is Israel, not the PLO, that rejects 242.[9]

After Kissinger's segment, it was Netanyahu's turn. "You've just had Mr. Said on this program saying that the PLO has accepted the State of Israel," Netanyahu told Brinkley.

> That's not true. Yasser Arafat recently, just a few weeks ago, said the aim is Jaffa, Jerusalem, Tel Aviv, Haifa, everything.

Sam Donaldson interjected that you make peace with your enemies, not your friends. Netanyahu retorted that the PLO "is not an enemy you can make peace with." Then he trotted out the Hitler-Arafat comparison:

> Hitler didn't go as far as Arafat. He didn't say, Britain shouldn't exist. He didn't say, I'm going to destroy Britain. That's what Arafat says. He says it maybe not through ... English speaking spokesmen like Edward Said, but he says it daily in the Arab Middle East.[10]

Had Edward been allowed to respond, he would have reminded Netanyahu that it was the Palestinians who were the victims of Israeli aggression. Unlike the British, they had lost not only the war but also their land.

There was an ironic sequel to Edward's appearance with Netanyahu on the Brinkley show. Later that month, Edward found himself sitting directly behind Netanyahu on an airplane bound for Europe. As he recounted the story to Jim Naughton of the *Washington Post*, Netanyahu "started fidgeting."

> He got up, went to the bathroom, came back. It was only about an hour after we had left and when he was sitting down, he saw me. He sat down for a second, he gathered together his handbag and everything. He got up. I was sitting on the left side of the plane near the front and he went and sat in the back on the right side as far away from me as possible.[11]

I am not sure whether this encounter took place before or after the assassination of Abu Jihad, the number two man in Fatah, in his home in Tunis on April 16. It was a classic Israeli operation, modeled on the 1973 Beirut raid that had liquidated Kamal Nasir and two other top PLO officials. Reportedly, the Tunis raid was directed by the leader of the Beirut hit team, Ehud Barak.[12]

Later that spring, Edward flew to Cairo, which he had started to write about in a retrospective vein. His visit may have had something to do with his effort to get more contemporary Arab novelists published in New York. Naguib Mahfouz, for example, had sold the English translation rights to his novels to the American University in Cairo. When Jacqueline Kennedy Onassis took an interest in publishing Mahfouz's *Cairo Trilogy* with Doubleday, she turned to Edward for assistance (or perhaps he turned to her).[13] Another Egyptian novelist who interested him was Gamal al-Ghitani, whose *Zayni Barakat* was published by Viking that year with an introduction by Edward. On his way back from Cairo, Edward stopped in Rome to interview the Italian director Gillo Pontecorvo, whose *Battle of Algiers* Edward considered the greatest political film ever made. His ulterior motive, it seems, was to persuade Pontecorvo to make a film about the *Intifada*. Pontecorvo assured him that he supported the Palestinians, but, alas, he expressed no interest in making a film about them.[14]

§

In late August 1988, Edward flew to Tunis for a meeting with Yasir Arafat. Earlier that month, King Hussein had renounced his claim to the West Bank. The next move belonged to Arafat, and Edward hoped that the PNC would announce the formation of a Palestinian state. Edward had another reason for visiting Arafat, however—he wanted to profile him for a popular American audience. Arafat was enthusiastic about the idea, and the profile was published in *Andy Warhol's Interview* a few months later under the title "A Meeting with the Old Man." What impressed Edward was Arafat's "microscopic" grasp of politics, his mastery of the region's ever-shifting alliances. "As we spoke," Edward noted,

> there was a sort of objective alliance between Arafat and the Lebanese Forces (a radical right-wing Christian group opposed to Amin Gemayel and the Phalange Party, also right-wing Christian) since both were opposed to Syria; the Lebanese Forces had been allies of Israel, so the volte-face was bewildering.

Arafat defended the alliance with the Lebanese Forces on the grounds that he had to play all of his cards, just as the Arab nations were willing to play the Palestinian card whenever it served their interests.[15]

That November, Edward hosted a seminar for twenty Palestinian intellectuals in New York. The seminar, which took place on the eve of the much-anticipated meeting of the PNC in Algiers, was organized by the American Council for Palestine Affairs, which Edward and Ibrahim Abu-Lughod had set up with the consent of the PLO executive committee.[16] In addition to Edward and Ibrahim, the Council's board included Rashid Khalidi of the University of Chicago and Fouad Moughrabi of the University of Tennessee at Chattanooga. Its director was Nubar Hovsepian, then teaching at Hunter College in Manhattan. Most of the participants in the seminar were professors from American universities, but several came all the way from the West Bank—Mamdouh al-Aker, Ibrahim Dakkak, and Hanan Ashrawi.[17] Aker and Ashrawi were the organizers of the "Political Committee," a group of West Bank academics, professionals, and faction leaders who served as the diplomatic arm and public voice of the *Intifada*.[18]

After the seminar, Edward, Ibrahim, and two other PNC members flew to Algiers, where the PNC was expected to announce the creation of a Palestinian state. Hitherto a back-bench spectator at PNC sessions, Edward was determined to play an active role this time. Late on the evening of his arrival, he went to see Arafat, who handed him Mahmoud Darwish's Arabic draft of the declaration of statehood, which the Council adopted a few days later. Edward's task was to translate it into English. The next day, after the opening ceremony, the Council divided itself into a Political Committee and an *Intifada* Committee. Edward sat in the Political Committee, chaired by Uncle Charles' former AUB colleague Nabil Shaath, where the most important speeches were delivered by George Habash of the PFLP and Abu Iyad of Fatah. Habash opposed acceptance of UNSC Resolution 242 on the grounds that it implied recognition of Israel; Abu Iyad argued for it. Habash lost the argument, and a resolution accepting 242 was approved by an overwhelming majority of the delegates, including Edward.[19]

After the historic Algiers session, Yasir Arafat applied for a visa so that he could address the United Nations General Assembly in early December. But Secretary of State Shultz rejected Arafat's application, even though Farouk Kaddoumi, the PLO's "foreign minister," had already received a visa. The reason, according to Shultz's statement, was that Arafat "knows of, condones, and lends support" to acts of terrorism against Americans. Sources told the *Washington Post* that Shultz was incensed by Arafat's toleration of Abul Abbas, whose men had recently hijacked the *Achille Lauro* cruise ship and dumped Leon Klinghoffer, an elderly American Jew, into the sea.[20] Shultz's decision forced the United Nations to move its planned General Assembly session on Palestine to Geneva, where Arafat finally said what Shultz wanted to hear—that he "renounced" terrorism, that he did not insist upon "self-determination" as a condition for a peace conference, and that he recognized Israel's right "to exist in peace and security." Within hours of Arafat's statement, Shultz announced the opening of a dialogue with the PLO in Tunis.[21]

§

In January 1989, Dinitia Smith of *New York* magazine profiled Edward in a story entitled "Arafat's Man in New York: The Divided Life of Columbia Professor Edward Said." Edward was not happy with the title—he was nobody's man—but the story was part of the American public relations campaign he had been authorized to launch in order to humanize the Palestinian struggle. In addition to providing plenty of biographical details, he allowed the magazine to print photographs of his grandfather Ibrahim, his parents, and his childhood. Unfortunately, he left Smith with the impression that he and his family had lived in Jerusalem until he was twelve, not moving to Cairo until the end of 1947. Inevitably, Smith also asked him about terrorism, noting that he had sat in the same meeting room as Abul Abbas in Tunis. Abbas is "a shit, a degenerate," Edward told Smith, admitting that "in the conditions of exile politics, very strange things occur." He reminded her that Menachem Begin and Yitzhak Shamir had themselves been involved in terrorism in the 1940s.[22]

In March, Edward joined a number of PLO and Israeli Knesset members for a three-day "Road to Peace" conference at Columbia's School of International and Public Affairs, cosponsored by the American Council for Palestine Affairs. The State Department issued visa waivers for three PLO members, including Nabil Shaath, who were judged to have had no "personal involvement in terrorist activity." It also granted a visa to Faisal Husseini, the director of the Arab Study Center in Jerusalem, whom the Israelis had just released from administrative detention for his "illegal" activities on the West Bank. The Israeli delegation included Knesset members Shulamit Aloni and Yair Tsabon as well as former member Mordechai Bar-On of Peace Now.[23] Another Israeli "dove" in attendance was Yehoshafat Harkabi, whom Edward had known for some fifteen years. Unfortunately, they were constrained by an Israeli law forbidding "direct contact" between Israeli citizens and the PLO, which forced them to address their remarks to the audience, rather than to their PLO counterparts. Outside the building, behind a police barricade, protesters voiced their opposition to any dialogue between Israel and the PLO.[24]

That fall, Edward was interviewed in New York by Hisham Milhim of *al-Qabas* ("The Torch"), an Arabic newspaper published in Kuwait and London. When Milhim asked him to assess the US-PLO dialogue, Edward replied:

> the United States is assuming the role of spokesman for Israel and is defending Israel's interests. I have read the minutes of the meetings. These meetings have not served our interests.

Later, Milhim asked him about the PLO's failure to present its case "cleverly and logically" in the United States. "There is no excuse for this situation," Edward admitted.

> We who live in the United States—and here I speak on my own behalf and that of my colleague Ibrahim Abu-Lughod—because we feel totally disgusted by the negligence, corruption, and incompetence of Palestinian performance in this

country. Supposedly, as we are told, there is a committee called the U.S. Committee within the PLO. I know that this committee has never met in Tunis. It includes people who have never visited the United States and have no understanding of this complex and powerful society.[25]

He didn't mention it, but the American Council for Palestine Affairs was capable of filling the void, if only the leadership in Tunis would listen to it.

Edward's criticism drew an immediate response from Yasir Abd Rabbo (Abu Bashar), the head of the PLO Information Department and Arafat's designated negotiator with the Americans in Tunis. Rabbo agreed that the Palestinian performance in the United States had been shoddy. The solution, he continued, lay in the hands of Edward Said and other members of "the Palestinian community which lives day to day in the U.S. society." "Leaders of the PLO and its factions are not sociologists specializing in U.S. society," he noted, nor are they "required to be so." What is required of them is "something completely different," namely, to pursue dialogue "in a manner which serves the interests of the Palestinian national struggle." In Rabbo's opinion, Edward's advice—such as his suggestion that Arafat refuse to visit the United Nations without a formal invitation from the United States—did not always serve those interests. "In other words," Rabbo concluded, "what is required is to 'Palestinize' the Palestinian community in the United States, not to 'Americanize' the Palestinian leadership in Tunis."[26]

After this exchange, Edward was invited to Tunis to clear the air with the PLO leadership. One of the targets of Edward's criticism was Hassan Abdul Rahman, the head of the Palestine Affairs Center in Washington, whom he regarded as ineffective. Edward had known Rahman since the early 1970s, when he was employed in the PLO office on Park Avenue in Manhattan. In October 1974, just before Arafat's controversial appearance at the United Nations, Rahman was alone in the office when it was attacked by three young men wearing the insignia of the Jewish Defense League. The men trashed the office and beat Rahman with a lead pipe, which did not stop him from chasing after them.[27] Now, however, Edward wanted Rahman replaced by Fouad Moughrabi, his colleague in the American Council for Palestine Affairs. Arafat and Rabbo objected to Moughrabi, but they did attempt to mollify Edward by sending Rahman into temporary exile in Canada. They also agreed to send Shafiq al-Hout to New York as their new US spokesman and senior official. Edward assured Josh Friedman of *Newsday* that Moughrabi and Hout "are both quite different from the run-of-the-mill types the PLO has had working in the various offices in this country."[28]

§

On August 2, 1990, Saddam Hussein, having accused Kuwait of stealing Iraqi oil, sent his army to plunder the defenseless emirate. In response, the United States initiated a blockade of Iraq and announced that American ground troops would be stationed in Saudi Arabia in an operation dubbed "Desert Shield." Among those who refused to condemn the Iraqi invasion were King Hussein and Yasir Arafat, both of whom were on friendly terms with Saddam. As for Edward Said, his opinion of Saddam was evident in the opening sentence of a commentary he wrote for the *Guardian* ten days after the invasion. "Saddam Hussein," he admitted, "is an appalling dictator whose rule in Iraq has turned the place into a graveyard for democracy." And yet "the events now unfolding" in the Gulf, he added, "are not a mere matter of good and evil." To be sure, Kuwait did not deserve to be invaded. But Edward was ambivalent about its rulers, who "gave considerable help to the Palestinian movement," but whose oil production was "geared not to Arab requirements but to American needs." As for Saddam, he must be seen as a product of his environment—an environment that has "been shaped to a considerable degree by US Middle East policies."[29]

On the same Sunday that Edward's commentary appeared in the *Guardian*, the *Independent* published one of his occasional essays on contemporary Arab writing. Although the essay was commissioned before the invasion of Kuwait, Edward attempted to draw a connection between the impending war in the Gulf and the West's neglect of Arab writers. "I write these lines," he concluded,

> as the international American-led campaign against Iraq increases the likelihood of horrific violence and waste in the near future. Is it too much to connect the stark political and military polarisation with the cultural abyss that exists between the Arabs and the West?[30]

One Arab writer who took offense at these remarks was "Samir al-Khalil," the pseudonymous author of *The Republic of Fear*, which offered Western readers a startling look at the horror of Saddam's Iraq. Khalil did not go so far as to accuse Edward of endorsing Saddam's annexation of Kuwait. But Edward's reader, he complained, "ends up not even being sure what he thinks on the issue of the hour while at the same time not being left in any doubt about how culpable the West always is."[31] Khalil's point was a fair one. But it was obvious that he had not read—or preferred not to acknowledge—Edward's unambiguous condemnation of Saddam and his invasion of Kuwait in the *Guardian*.

Edward responded to Khalil in kind, denying that he supported Saddam Hussein, charging him with ignoring "Western racism and jingoism," and accusing him of cowardice. "Unlike Mr. al-Khalil," he pointed out,

> I do not hide behind a pseudonym. Surely everyone who writes or speaks freely about Middle Eastern politics is exposed to threats, abuse or, possibly, death. This has certainly been my experience, but it hasn't deterred and will not intimidate me into not using my name.[32]

It didn't take long for Edward to discover Khalil's true identity. He was none other than Kanan Makiya, the former student radical whom he had met at the Harvard-MIT Arab Club in the early 1970s. Like Ahmad Chalabi and Edward's friend Sami al-Banna, Makiya was an alumnus of Baghdad College, the prestigious Jesuit high school. After graduating from MIT, he had rejoined his family in London, where he fell in with the Trotskyites and wrote for *Khamsin*—the socialist journal in which Sadik al-Azm had published his critique of *Orientalism*—under a pseudonym. In time, a series of debacles in the Middle East—the Lebanese Civil War, the Khomeini revolution,

Saddam's repression of the Kurds and the Shia—led him to break with his colleagues on the Left.[33]

When Saddam failed to meet the January 15, 1991, deadline for withdrawal from Kuwait, Congress authorized President Bush to go to war in Iraq. A few weeks later, Edward participated in a teach-in on the war, which drew an overflow crowd to Columbia's Altschul Auditorium. "We are in an extremely bloody moment in our history as a superpower," Edward announced. He went on to ask "why the television networks never linger on the suffering of Arabs the way they linger on the pain of the Jews." He was joined by his faculty colleague Roger Hilsman, former assistant secretary of state for Far Eastern Affairs, who had resigned in 1964 over his disagreement with Lyndon Johnson's strategy in Vietnam. "If things go reasonably well," Hilsman warned,

> American casualties will be in the tens of thousands. Hussein will become a hero to the Arabs. For every one we kill, five will emerge more committed. It is a lesson I thought we learned in Vietnam.[34]

Misled by the Vietnam analogy, Hilsman overestimated the military prowess and fighting spirit of the Iraqi army. Saddam Hussein, however, did become a hero in the eyes of many Palestinians—including Yasir Arafat, much to Edward's chagrin.

Later that month, the *London Review of Books* published a long commentary by Edward on what he called "The Arab-American War." "It is my supposition," he wrote,

> that Iraq is being destroyed today, not because of its aggression against Kuwait, which could have been reversed patiently, regionally, economically, and politically, but because the United States wants a physical presence in the Gulf, wants to have direct leverage on oil to affect Europe and Japan, because it wishes to set the world agenda, because Iraq was perceived as a threat to Israel.

But his primary target, as usual, was American media coverage of the war, particularly the role played by "academic experts on the Arab mind." Among the experts he criticized by name was his former friend Fouad Ajami, whom he took to task for dismissing Iraq as "a brittle land, a frontier country between Persia and Arabia, with little claim to culture and books and grand ideas." As for Michael Walzer's perplexing pronouncement that the war was "just," if not "prudent," it was a reminder that "words are the first casualty in any conflict."[35]

Unfortunately, Edward lapsed into conspiracy theory at one point, appearing to question the veracity of reports that Saddam's forces had used chemical weapons against Iraqi Kurds. Here is the passage in question:

> The claim that Iraq gassed its own citizens has often been repeated. At best, and according to U.S. official sources, this has sometimes seemed uncertain, depending not on truth or principle, but on the policy of the moment. There is at least one War College report, done while Iraq was a U.S. ally, which claims that the gassing of the Kurds in Halabja was done by Iran. Few people mention such reports in the media today, although references to them turn up occasionally in the alternative

press. Now, the "gassing of his own citizens" has become a fact about Saddam, elevated into one of the proofs that the United States should destroy him.[36]

Perhaps Edward only meant to say that American officials were spinning the chemical weapons story differently now that Saddam had become the enemy. But there was plenty of evidence that Iraq had used such weapons, some of which was unearthed by his friend Christopher Hitchens.[37]

§

In May 1991, Edward made his first trip to South Africa, where he delivered a lecture entitled "Identity, Authority, and Freedom" at the University of Cape Town. He began by noting that the phrase "academic freedom" had been appropriated by conservatives calling for the depoliticization of the university and a return to "courses, ideas, and values that derived exclusively from the mainstream European thinkers—Plato, Aristotle, Sophocles, Descartes, Montaigne, Shakespeare, Bacon, Locke, and so on." Uncle Charles, of course, had been one of those conservatives, a strident critic of the academic Left and a staunch defender of the Western canon. Needless to say, Edward found the "academic freedom" of the conservatives to be a politicized concept in its own right and an unattractive limitation on the curriculum. By the same token, he repudiated the doctrinaire nationalism that limited academic freedom at state-controlled universities in the Arab world and elsewhere. Authority and identity, he proclaimed, are the enemies of academic freedom, for which the best model is the migrant or traveler. "Inside the academy," he insisted, "we must be able to discover and travel among other selves, other identities, other varieties of human adventure."[38]

While Edward was in South Africa, he visited the headquarters of the African National Congress in Johannesburg. There he met Nelson Mandela and other leaders of the ANC, including Walter Sisulu and Mendi Tsimang, who represented the ANC in the UK. Edward asked Sisulu—who, like Mandela, had been imprisoned for decades on Robben Island—how the ANC had managed to turn defeat into victory. The key, said Sisulu, was the ANC's realization that its only hope was to organize on the international stage. "Every victory that we registered in London, or Glasgow, or Iowa City, or Toulouse, or Berlin, or Stockholm," he told Edward,

> gave the people at home a sense of hope, and renewed their determination not to give up the struggle. In time we morally isolated the South African regime and its policy of apartheid so that even though militarily we could not do much to hurt them, in the end they came to us, asking for negotiations.

Inspired by what he had seen and heard in South Africa, Edward asked Nubar Hovsepian of the American Council for Palestine Affairs to organize a seminar in London for "every leading Palestinian activist-intellectual that I knew."[39]

The seminar, which took place in early September, came at a decisive juncture in the history of the Palestinian national movement. US secretary of state James Baker's patient effort to bring the Israelis and their Arab neighbors, including the Palestinians, to the conference table was about to bear fruit in Madrid. Before that, in late September, the PNC was scheduled to meet in Algiers to approve the arrangements for the Madrid conference. Edward believed that closed-door negotiations must be accompanied by an ANC-like publicity campaign designed to humanize the Palestinians and expose Israeli "apartheid." To that end, he invited Mendi Tsimang, with whom he had shared his return flight from Johannesburg, to address the London seminar, which included several figures who would play important unofficial roles in Madrid, including Nabil Shaath, Faisal Husseini, and Hanan Ashrawi. More importantly, he wanted to hammer out an agreement on the conditions under which the Palestinians would agree to participate in the Madrid conference. According to Edward, the seminar participants agreed, for example, that an end to Israeli occupation and settlement of the West Bank and Gaza must be guaranteed by the Americans.[40]

Just before the seminar's final session, Edward phoned Mariam from Nubar Hovsepian's hotel room. He received the shock of his life. His doctor, suspecting that he had leukemia, wanted to see him as soon as he returned to New York. Visibly shaken, Edward asked Hovsepian not to tell anyone and returned to chair the final session of the seminar. "Everyone noticed the change in his demeanor," Hovsepian recalled. "He seemed preoccupied, a bit resigned. Everyone was perplexed."[41] After he got home, he received a pastoral visit from his friend Cornel West, Professor of Religion and Director of African American Studies at Princeton, who brought two of his friends—Rev. James Forbes, the pastor of Riverside Church, and James Melvin Washington, a professor at Union Theological Seminary—to pray with Edward.[42] Around the same time, he resigned from the PNC, along with Ibrahim Abu-Lughod, Mahmoud Darwish, and Abdul Mohsen Qattan, a wealthy Palestinian businessman from Kuwait, who called Arafat's support for Saddam Hussein "a serious strategic error."[43] Later, Edward explained that his decision to resign from the PNC was motivated by Arafat's failure to heed the negotiating conditions recommended by his London seminar.[44]

§

In June 1992, Edward returned to Palestine for the first time in nearly thirty years, accompanied by Mariam, Wadie, and Najla (who was about to join her brother at Princeton). They were met at the airport in Tel Aviv by Mohammed Miari, a Palestinian member of the Israeli Knesset, and Rashid Khalidi, then teaching at the University of Chicago. Edward was carrying two documents sent to him by his cousin Yousif Said— the title deed to the Boulos Said house in Jerusalem, where Edward had been born, and a map drawn from memory. One day, the Saids set out to find the house, accompanied by a photographer from the *Observer*, which had commissioned Edward to chronicle his journey. Their guide was an elderly Jerusalemite named George Khodr, the former accountant of the Palestine Educational Company, who had been a classmate of Uncle Charles' at the AUB. Two years earlier, Harold Veeser had traveled to Jerusalem and interviewed Khodr, who remembered Edward as a boy.[45] With Khodr's help, they finally located the house, which, to Edward's dismay, now housed the "International Christian Embassy." That did not stop him from posing in front of the house for a photograph, which was duly published in the *Observer*, along with the first installment of Edward's narrative.[46]

In addition to visiting the places he remembered from his youth—including his grandfather's Baptist church in Nazareth—Edward met with a number of Palestinian leaders involved with the bilateral talks in Washington, including Faisal Husseini, Raja Shehadeh, and Haidar Abdel Shafi. His meeting with Dr. Shafi took place in Gaza, where, as he wrote in the *Observer*, "my recent memories of a trip to South Africa kicked in with considerable force." He was also introduced to Um Mohammed, who turned out to be the sister of Yusif Najjar, the PLO leader who had been assassinated, along with Kamal Nasir, in Beirut in 1973. A few days later, Edward paid a visit to Birzeit University near Ramallah, where he spoke in Kamal Nasir Hall. Responding to questions from the student body, he denounced Saddam Hussein as "a dictator and a fool," blasted the American-led war against Iraq, and defended his friend Salman Rushdie, still living in London under police protection. Edward also criticized political Islam "somewhat impetuously," knowing that the Islamists had become a militant presence on the Birzeit campus. Afterwards, he was introduced to two of their leaders. Instead of shouting at him or threatening him, they thanked him for his honesty and invited him back.[47]

From the West Bank, the Saids crossed the Allenby Bridge into Jordan. Yasir Arafat happened to be in Jordan at the time, recovering from an operation in one of King Hussein's palaces. So Edward brought his family to meet the Old Man and pay their respects. By chance, it was the day of the Israeli elections, which Arafat was monitoring on television, staking his future on Yitzhak Rabin and the Labor party (which won a majority, ending Likud's six years in power.) In her memoir, Najla Said offers an amusing account of this visit:

> Arafat kissed me heartily on each cheek, and I wiped my hand across my face in disgust. Daddy had often asked me why I disliked Arafat so much, since he was "the only leader we have." I am sure he suspected it was because I just wanted to hate everything about Palestine, but when I told him, honestly, "When I look at him the way Americans do, he looks like a stupid idiot," Daddy laughed. He had never been a big fan himself.... He always acted civil and respectful, but, I noticed, he couldn't help but smile as I wiped Arafat's slobbery kisses off my face without even pretending to be deferential in the company of a world leader.[48]

From Jordan, the Saids flew to Beirut, where Mariam's father Emile still lived. It was Edward's first visit since 1982, the year of the Israeli invasion.[49]

Upon their return to the States, Edward and Mariam drove Najla to Princeton for the beginning of her freshman year. She would be living in Forbes College, formerly the Princeton Inn, where Edward's parents had stayed when they took him to Princeton back in 1953. When her residential advisor introduced himself to Najla, he exclaimed, "Oh my God. Hey! I didn't know that Edward Said was your dad!" The next day, Najla and the rest of the freshman class attended a lecture by Cornel West, whom Najla knew as "Brother Cornel." Needless to say, Najla's classmates were impressed when Professor West caught sight of her, pulled her up on the stage, and gave her a hug. As she recalls in her memoir:

I knew who Cornel West was because I had met him in my apartment when I was in seventh grade. He was a student of my dad's, and had come over to see him, but my dad had forgotten about the appointment.[50]

That would have been in the mid-1980s, when West was teaching at Yale. He had never been a full-time student at Columbia, but he did audit at least one of Edward's courses in the late 1970s, when he was teaching at Union Theological Seminary.[51]

§

On November 3, 1992, Bill Clinton defeated George Bush in the US presidential election, becoming the first Democrat to occupy the White House since Jimmy Carter. For his part, Edward was cautiously optimistic. A week and a half later, he addressed the annual convention of the Association of Arab-American University Graduates in Washington. The Reagan and Bush administrations, he complained, had done nothing "to promote democracy, human, women's or minority rights at all in any Arab state." But the election of Bill Clinton, he suggested, affords a new opportunity "to those Arabs and Arab Americans searching for a more democratic vision of the future. It is up to Arab-American professionals and intellectuals to seize this opportunity to insert ourselves in an organized way into the national agenda through writing, speaking out, and political action."[52] Alas, Clinton would prove to be another disappointment, putting Martin Indyk and Dennis Ross—who had studied with Malcolm Kerr at UCLA—in charge of the Middle East peace process. Edward regarded both of them as pro-Israel.

The following May, Edward traveled to Tampa, Florida, the headquarters of United States Central Command, which coordinated military operations in the Middle East, including the recent Gulf War. He had been invited to speak at CENTCOM's second annual Southwest Asia Symposium. At first, he was reluctant to meet with the "enemy," as he put it. But his friend Eqbal Ahmad, who had been invited to speak at West Point during the Vietnam War, persuaded him to go. In Tampa, he was reunited with an old classmate from Princeton—General Hank Stackpole, the commander of Marine Forces in the Pacific—who had flown in from Honolulu to hear him. He also chatted with General Joseph Hoar, the Commander of CENTCOM, and other officers. According to Edward, the military men agreed with everything he had to say about the Middle East. It was the politicians in Washington, they complained, who made them do "all these terrible things."[53]

The keynote speaker at the symposium was Chas Freeman, the US ambassador to Saudi Arabia, and the banquet speaker was Prince Bandar bin Sultan, the Saudi ambassador to the US. A panel on Iran featured Edward's colleague Gary Sick, who had famously accused the Reagan campaign of making a secret deal with Iran to delay the release of the American hostages until after the 1980 election.[54] A panel on humanitarian crises featured the State Department's Robert Oakley, just back from Somalia. Joining Edward on a panel devoted to "Political Islam" was Dr. Sami al-Arian, a professor of computer engineering at the University of South Florida.[55] Arian, whose parents had settled in Kuwait after fleeing Palestine in 1948, had recently founded a charity, the Islamic Concern Project, and a think-tank, the World and Islam Studies

Enterprise, which would soon be investigated as possible fronts for Islamic Jihad. After September 11, 2001, he would be fired by the university and indicted on terrorism-related charges. Two years later, Edward's son Wadie would agree to represent one of the defendants in the case of *US v. Al-Arian*.[56]

After the CENTCOM symposium, Edward traveled to London to give the BBC's annual Reith Lectures and to hear Daniel Barenboim, the famous Israeli conductor and pianist, play with the London Symphony Orchestra. He and Barenboim happened to be staying at the same hotel, and they ended up spending much of the weekend in an Arab restaurant, deep in conversation. After the concert, Edward went backstage to congratulate his new friend and noticed a copy of *The Question of Palestine* standing open on his practice piano.[57] It was the beginning of a musical collaboration and peace initiative that resulted, some years later, in the formation of the West-Eastern Divan Orchestra, which brings promising young Arab and Israeli musicians to Europe each summer for workshops and a concert tour. Edward's grand-nephew Karim Said, a pianist from Amman, was among the first young prodigies to attend the workshops.

In early July, Edward returned to Birzeit University, where Ibrahim Abu-Lughod was now a vice president, having resigned from Northwestern in order to return to the land of his birth. Ibrahim had organized a special meeting of the AAUG and arranged for Edward to receive an honorary doctorate from Birzeit, whose president, Hanna Nasir, had recently been allowed to return after two decades in exile. For his part, Edward kept his promise to spend more time with Birzeit's Islamist student leaders, sitting down with four young men representing Hamas and Islamic Jihad. He found them accepting of "the truths of modern science," "hopelessly reductive in their views of the West," and "irrefragably opposed to the existence of Israel." When the conversation turned to the fate of Salman Rushdie, Edward informed them that Rushdie was a good friend whose writings he fully endorsed. The young men from Islamic Jihad insisted that Rushdie must be killed as an apostate; those from Hamas thought that severe punishment would suffice. Edward concluded that Hamas and Islamic Jihad had little to offer the majority of Palestinians and "no great base of support."[58]

That same summer, the Arab press, followed by the Western press, reported that Israel and the PLO had been holding secret back-channel talks in Oslo and were close to an agreement on a Palestinian Authority in Gaza and the West Bank. In exchange for limited self-rule in Gaza and Jericho, it was reported, Yasir Arafat and his negotiators had agreed to suspend their claim to East Jerusalem and their demand that the Israelis withdraw immediately from all of the West Bank. Washington was taken by surprise, as were the official Palestinian delegates to the bilateral talks and most members of the PLO's executive committee in Tunis. Indignant at being kept in the dark, Faisal Husseini, Hanan Ashrawi, and Saeb Erekat offered to resign from the delegation. Mahmoud Darwish resigned from the executive committee, vowing to devote himself to poetry, and Shafiq al-Hout suspended his membership, saying, "The perception of the people is that the leadership is giving concessions, so where's the reward? If you ask any Palestinian in the occupied territories or outside he will tell you that."[59]

When Edward learned of the secret deal, he was just as skeptical as his friends. On September 7, he told a reporter, "I think it's a step forward that Israel is about to recognize the P.L.O." But, he continued,

> There is still a dominant and a subordinate relationship. You can't have peace between a servant and a master. I've always believed in equality. This is a peace of the weak. It strikes me as a quick, easy solution for the current Palestinian leadership. It's disastrous in many ways. I'm very disturbed.[60]

Two days later, his critical reading of the Oslo peace plan, known as the "Declaration of Principles," appeared in the *Guardian* and in *al-Ahram*'s new English-language weekly, published in Cairo. The Israelis, he noted, would retain control of the land, the water, the overall security, and the foreign affairs of the autonomous Palestinian zones. The Palestinians would take over policing, health and sanitation, education, the postal service, and tourism. In short, "the PLO has transformed itself from a national liberation movement into a kind of small-town government, with the same handful of people still in command."[61]

A few days later, Yasir Arafat and Yitzhak Rabin came to Washington for a signing ceremony on the White House lawn, presided over by President Clinton. The audience was full of dignitaries and celebrities, including former presidents Jimmy Carter and George Bush. Hanan Ashrawi was there, desperately negotiating last-minute changes to the text with the help of the lead American negotiator, Dennis Ross. Her old friend and former employer Peter Jennings was also there, covering the ceremony for ABC News.[62] Even Christopher Hitchens was there. But Edward refused to come, even though both Arafat and Clinton wanted him to. Clinton advisor George Stephanopoulos—a 1982 Columbia graduate—phoned Hitchens more than once, pleading with him to persuade Edward to attend the ceremony. "The feedback we get from Arab-American voters," Stephanopoulos told Hitchens, "is this: If it's such a great idea, why isn't Said signing off on it?" When Hitchens called Edward in New York, he was, as Hitchens recalled, "grudging and crabby." "The old man has no right to sign away land," Edward complained.[63]

That fall, Edward agreed to write a regular column for *al-Hayat*, an Arabic daily owned by Prince Khalid bin Sultan of Saudi Arabia, edited in London, and published in Arab as well as Western capitals. It was the second incarnation of *al-Hayat*, which, as noted earlier, had been founded in Beirut by Kamel Mroueh, the pro-Western publisher whom Charles Malik had admired. After Mroueh's assassination by Nasserites in 1966, his widow Salma published the paper until 1975, when the Lebanese Civil War forced her into exile. In 1988, her sons revived *al-Hayat* in London with the help of Prince Khalid, who gave them complete editorial freedom—except when it came to criticizing the Saudi royals. The editor-in-chief was the Lebanese journalist Jihad el-Khazen, an AUB graduate who, as the editor of Mroueh's *Daily Star* newspaper, had come to know Uncle Charles quite well and published him on occasion. In fact, Khazen remembered debating Dr. Malik at Marquand House, the home of President Kirkwood, during one of the student strikes of the early 1970s.[64] Now it was his privilege to publish Dr. Malik's equally opinionated nephew.

In early October, *al-Hayat* published Edward's second broadside against the Oslo agreement. The English version appeared a week later in the *London Review of Books* under the title "The Morning After." It was, in effect, a declaration of rhetorical war on Arafat and the PLO leadership:

> The vulgarities of the White House ceremony, the degrading spectacle of Yasir Arafat thanking everyone for what, in fact, was the suspension of most of his people's rights, and the fatuous solemnity of Bill Clinton's performance—like a twentieth-century Roman emperor shepherding two vassal kings through rituals of reconciliation and obeisance—all these only temporarily obscure the truly astonishing proportions of the Palestinian capitulation.

"So first of all," he continued, "let us call the agreement by its real name: an instrument of Palestinian surrender, a Palestinian Versailles." But Edward vowed to fight on. Calling for "optimism of the will," he proposed a number of specific steps: a census of Palestinians worldwide, a demand for reparations, nonviolent resistance to Israeli occupation and settlements, and, last but not least, reform of the PLO itself.[65]

Hamas and Islamic Jihad also rejected the Oslo agreement, vowing to continue the armed struggle. But Edward downplayed their importance in an essay he published in the Sunday magazine of the *New York Times* that November, entitled "The Phony Islamic Threat." He began by reviewing the signs of "extraordinary social and political ferment in the Arab Islamic world," from the violent Islamist opposition to the Mubarak regime in Egypt to the emergence of Hezbollah as the sole armed faction in Lebanon. But he did not find these signs particularly worrisome. "I am not alone," he claimed, "in believing that the prospects of an Islamic takeover are highly unlikely, and therefore grotesquely exaggerated in the West." "What interests me," he continued, "is the opposition: the forces of resistance to Islam." He proceeded to recount his travels in the region during the last two summers, quoting a number of secular intellectuals who opposed the Islamists, if not Islam itself. Ibrahim Abu-Lughod told him that Hamas and Islamic Jihad "are losers and in the end have nothing to offer."[66]

§

In March 1994, Edward began the first of many rounds of chemotherapy at Long Island Jewish Hospital under the direction of Dr. Kanti Rai. Shortly thereafter, he began writing his memoir.[67] Meanwhile, he continued to write his regular column for *al-Hayat* and *al-Ahram*. In June, he penned a tribute to Hanna Mikhail, his PLO friend who had disappeared in Lebanon nearly two decades earlier. "Hanna Mikhail," he concluded, "was a true intellectual."

> As an intellectual should, he lived according to his ideas and never tailored his democratic, secular values to suit new masters and occasions. For all Palestinians today, and in stark contrast to the great sell-out and abject surrender of our leaders, he represents a distinguished role model, a man who did not debase himself or his people. He *lived* his ideas, and died for them. It is as simple as that. By his example Hanna Mikhail admonishes those who have outlived him for a while.[68]

Yasir Arafat, in contrast, had debased both himself and his people by selling their birthright for a mess of pottage known as the Palestinian Authority. In fact, just two days after Edward's column appeared in *al-Ahram*, Arafat returned to Gaza to take charge of his new rump state.

That fall, Edward's son Wadie, who had just graduated from Princeton, traveled to Cairo to study Arabic at the American University. A year later, in the fall of 1995, he moved to the West Bank to work as a volunteer at the Democracy and Workers' Rights Center in Ramallah. The following March, Edward and Mariam went to visit him despite a warning from Haider Abdel Shafi not to come. Wadie himself advised his father not to make any public pronouncements. Reluctantly, Edward agreed. When they got to East Jerusalem, they checked into their favorite hotel, the American Colony. As Edward later admitted:

> Jerusalem has never been especially attractive to me, although I was born there, as were my father, his father, and several generations before them. There is something ungenerous and unyielding about the place that encourages intolerance, given that all sorts of ultimate religious and cultural claims emanate from the city, most of them essentially denying or downgrading the others.

The "something" Edward disliked about the city was the same thing he saw in the faces of the Christian tourists wandering the streets, "transporting dreadful little brown crosses in their hands with a look of rapt vacancy."[69]

Visiting Birzeit one day, Edward learned from Hanan Ashrawi and other friends that he had been denounced on Arafat's Voice of Palestine that morning by someone who dismissed him as an "Orientalist" and accused him of lying about the PA's persecution of journalists. Edward decided to take it as a compliment, proof that people were listening to what he had to say. He also decided to go see Yasir Abd Rabbo, the PA Minister of Information and Culture, whom he had known for two decades. When Edward asked him what it was like to work for Arafat, Rabbo replied,

> Dreadful. . . . Everything must be approved by him. . . . He's absolutely fixated on his various security organizations. . . . Beyond that, the man has no vision, no idea of where we are going, no plan, no sense of direction. All he deals with are the details, and he loves those because they assure him of complete control.[70]

Later, Edward kicked himself for not asking Rabbo why he didn't resign in protest.

By the time Edward's chronicle of his trip was published in the *London Review of Books* that September, it carried a postscript in which he described a second visit to Palestine in early July. Members of Arafat's "entourage," he reported, had left phone messages for him, trying to get him to reconcile with Arafat.

> I refused to speak to them or to see him. Two weeks ago security men appeared in all Gaza and West Bank bookshops (by order of the Minister of Information, Abd Rabbo) and confiscated every one of my books. I am now banned in Palestine for having dared to speak against our own Papa Doc.[71]

Edward's books were still available in East Jerusalem, presumably, where Israeli law applied. It was there that Ahmad Muna had opened his Educational Bookshop in the former location of the Palestine Educational Company, near the Muslim Quarter of the Old City.

That October, Salman Rushdie came to Columbia to read from his new novel, *The Moor's Last Sigh*, and participate in a discussion with his friend Edward. Although the government of Iran was no longer actively pursuing Rushdie, there was still a bounty on his head, and security at the theater was tight. His visit had not been publicized, attendance was by invitation only, and identification was checked at the door. New York City police patrolled the sidewalks, Columbia security guards were posted in the building, and private bodyguards watched the audience from the wings. After the reading, Edward joined Rushdie on stage, fondly recalling a time "when it was possible to write books without them incurring lethal wrath or having them banned." He was thinking of his own books, no doubt, as well as Rushdie's. Rushdie labeled Iran "the most treacherous nation in the world," complaining that other nations had been too lenient with the Ayatollah.[72]

Meanwhile, Edward's friends in Beirut were planning a conference in his honor for the summer of 1997. Called "For a Critical Culture," it featured thirty invited scholars and writers from around the world, including good friends like Eqbal Ahmad, Tariq Ali, and Elias Khoury. Edward's contribution was to read excerpts from the Arabic version of his memoir.[73] He also revisited Dhour el Shweir for the first time, perhaps, since 1970. As he wrote in *Out of Place*:

> I went to Dhour to see what was still there. Still a Syrian army stronghold with soldiers and officers billeted there, it is one of the few popular summer places that has not been rebuilt and filled with new residents flocking there after the civil war.... My sister Jean and her husband and sons have bought and refurbished a house in Shweir, next door to where, forty-three years ago, I had my geography tutorials.[74]

No doubt he also remembered his walks with Uncle Charles and his stimulating talk of philosophy and literature, which had opened a world of books and ideas to him. Certainly his memories of Uncle Charles were finding their way into the memoir he was writing.

§

In February 1998, Edward rose from his sickbed and journeyed to Bethlehem, where he delivered the keynote address at the third international conference of the Sabeel Ecumenical Liberation Theology Center. On the third day of the conference, participants were transported by bus to pray at "contemporary stations of the cross"— checkpoints, demolished houses, expropriated land, and other sites of injustice. Afterwards, they returned to Bethlehem for Edward's address. He began by thanking the founder of Sabeel, Rev. Naim Ateek of St. George's Cathedral. "I am a child of the Anglican community here," Edward told the overflow crowd.

> I have to tell you I am a lapsed child. I was baptized at St George's by Rev. Mamoura [*sic*], whom some of you may remember. His son Michael was my teacher at St

George's, and later became my friend in Toronto. Anyway, I feel that Rev. Ateek represents what has so often been left out of Christianity, namely Christianity: dedication, the total absence of any egotistical, or personal arrogance of any kind."[75]

It was the same Christianity he had admired in his friend Hanna Mikhail, whose sister Jean Zaru also spoke at the Sabeel conference.

In May, Edward flew to Paris to participate in a conference hosted by *Le Monde Diplomatique* and the *Revue d'Études Palestiniennes*. The purpose of the conference was to bring the "new" or "revisionist" Israeli historians into dialogue with their Palestinian counterparts. On the Israeli side were Benny Morris, Ilan Pappe, Itamar Rabinovich, and Zeev Sternhall, author of *The Founding Myths of Israel*, a book Edward admired. Joining Edward on the Palestinian side were Elie Sanbar, the editor of the *Revue*, who had participated in the bilateral negotiations in Washington, and Nur Masalha, a London-based historian and editor. Referring to the Israeli historians, Edward observed that "only Ilan Pappe was open in his espousal of the Palestinian point of view. . . . For the others, in varying degrees, Zionism was seen as a necessity for Jews." Even so, Edward recommended that the work of the Israeli historians be translated into Arabic as soon as possible. Then he went one step further, calling on Arab intellectuals to invite the Israelis to speak in their countries and even to lecture in Israel themselves. "What have years of blanket refusal to deal with Israel done for us?" he asked. "Nothing at all, except to weaken us and weaken our perception of our opponent."[76]

Later that same month, Edward went to Chicago to speak at a banquet hosted by a local community organization, the Arab American Action Network. Among the AAAN's projects were the Women and Children's Well-Being Project, which offered immigrant women access to interpreters, language classes, and domestic violence counseling, among other services. Seated with Edward and Mariam at the head banquet table were their friends Rashid Khalidi, who had recently joined the faculty of the University of Chicago, and his wife Mona, who sat on the board of the AAAN. Also seated at the table were the Khalidis' new Hyde Park neighbors, Barack and Michelle Obama. Obama—who no doubt reminisced about the modern fiction course he had taken from Edward at Columbia—was in his first term as an Illinois state senator. A decade later, when Obama was running for president, photographs of the AAAN banquet were circulated by right-wing and pro-Israel propagandists as proof of Obama's radicalism. The irony was that, by 2008, Obama was under fire from Palestinian activists for courting the Israel lobby and wealthy Zionist donors.[77]

According to Ray Hanania, who attended the AAAN banquet, Edward complained that Israeli settlements were being built by Palestinian workers. He called for an unemployment fund "to prevent or at least discourage Palestinians from taking these jobs" in order to feed their families. "We are not in a position to engage in violent struggle," Edward admitted. Instead, he called for "a sustained series of peaceful marches on settlements . . . to impede construction." He also called for a program to assist Palestinians in rebuilding homes demolished by the Israelis. As for Arafat's Palestinian Authority, he accused it of employing 100,000 people "who are doing absolutely nothing. Their loyalty is being bought." During the question-and-answer time following his talk, a young man declared that the Palestinian cause was an Islamic cause. Respectfully, Edward warned him that to build an Islamic state in Palestine would be to "fall into the trap of Zionism." The only basis for a Palestinian state, he insisted, is a secular one guaranteeing the right of all individuals to practice their religion.[78]

In January 1999, Edward published another essay in the Sunday magazine of the *New York Times*, entitled "The One-State Solution." In it, he pronounced the Oslo peace process dead and returned to the vision of Palestine he had embraced as a young radical after 1967. "It is my view," he announced,

> that the peace process has in fact put off the real reconciliation that must occur if the hundred-year war between Zionism and the Palestinian people is to end. Oslo set the stage for the separation, but real peace can come only with a binational Israeli-Palestinian state.

The state of Israel, he reminded readers, was based on the principle of separation between Jews and others. Yet "the effort to separate," he pointed out, "has occurred simultaneously and paradoxically with the effort to take more and more land, which has in turn meant that Israel has acquired more and more Palestinians." As a result, the two peoples have remained so closely intertwined that "clean separation" simply won't work. The way to peace, therefore, lies in the concept of citizenship for members of both communities.[79]

That August, just before the publication of *Out of Place*, a legal scholar named Justus Reid Weiner, writing in the neoconservative magazine *Commentary*, accused Edward of lying about his past. In May 1998, for example, Edward had written in the *London Review of Books*, "I was born in Jerusalem and spent most of my formative years there and, after 1948, when my entire family became refugees, in Egypt." As Weiner pointed out, this statement was largely false: Edward did not spend most of his formative years in Jerusalem, and he had resided in Egypt since 1935, not 1948. By means of such exaggerations, according to Weiner, Edward had invented "a parable of Palestinian identity" in order to burnish his moral authority. As for *Out of Place*, Weiner acknowledged that it "thoroughly revises the personal tale Said has been reciting all these years, bringing it into greater conformity with the truth while at the same time ignoring his 30 years of carefully crafted deception."[80] It may well have been his own research into Edward's past, Weiner added, that had motivated him to come clean in his memoir.

Edward responded to Weiner's attack in predictable fashion, pointing out his factual errors and accusing *Commentary* of perpetuating the "Zionist Big Lie," namely, that "the dispossession of Palestinians is an ideological fiction."[81] Disingenuously, Weiner had ignored the multitude of true statements Edward had made about his past prior to the publication of *Out of Place*. In a 1997 essay for *House & Garden* called "Cairo Recalled," for example, Edward wrote, "We gave up Cairo in 1963 as a family resident in it for three decades, two parents and their five children."[82] He went on to paint a colorful portrait of the upper-class, cosmopolitan Cairo he had known as a boy, from the Gezira Club to Victoria College to Ignace Tiegerman, his revered Polish-Jewish piano teacher. With essays like "Cairo Recalled" in the public record, it was unfair to charge him with "30 years of carefully crafted deception." As for Weiner's hunch that his investigation was responsible for Edward's decision to publish a memoir, the opposite was more plausible—that *Commentary* had timed Weiner's essay to coincide with the release of *Out of Place*.

§

On June 28, 2000, Edward delivered an oration that Uncle Charles had delivered many times before him—the annual commencement address at the American University of Beirut.[83] What they needed most, Edward told the young graduates, was "critical intelligence," which is "skeptical of most orthodoxy and dogma, whether that be nationalist, religious, or philosophical."

> Human history is first and foremost a human effort of overcoming obstacles and making institutions. These are brought about not by dogma, nor by eternal laws, but rather by human labor, human will, human rationality. They always confront the forces of superstition, organized ignorance and unjust authority.

When he heard these words, Uncle Charles must have rolled over in his grave. Here was his own nephew preaching secular humanism straight out of Vico on the hallowed ground where Daniel Bliss had built the first and finest Christian college in the Near East. It was the revenge of the atheist intellectuals, of the Roland Puccettis and Sadik al-Azms.

In passing, Edward celebrated a recent and rare victory in the struggle against Zionism. Just a month earlier, in May 2000, Israel had withdrawn the last of its troops from Lebanese soil—the result, in large measure, of the heavy toll exacted by Hezbollah, which had replaced the PLO as the greatest military threat to Israel inside Lebanon. "Being Arab or American or Chinese is less important," he reminded the students, "than being able to exchange ideas as equals involved in the same struggle for human liberation as your fighters have been in the South." As if to prove his point, Edward paid a visit to Sheikh Hassan Nasrallah, the secretary general of Hezbollah, while he was in Beirut. Nasrallah told him he must go and see the newly liberated land along the Israeli border.[84] When he got there, he joined the struggle for human liberation by tossing a stone in the direction of an Israeli border post.[85]

A photograph of Edward in the act of tossing the stone soon appeared in the world press, raising howls of protest from his critics, some of whom read his gesture as proof of what they had believed all along—that he wished for the destruction of Israel. When Ari Shavit of *Haaretz* came to New York to interview Edward that August, he started by asking about the infamous stone-throwing incident. Edward explained that he and his party had gone to a place on the border known as Fatma Gate, where hundreds of tourists had gathered to throw stones. No Israelis were visible—just barbed wire and a distant tower. His son Wadie threw the first stone, prompting his daughter Najla to ask, "Daddy, can you throw a stone as far as Wadie?" So he gave it his best shot. "What I regret in all this," Edward told Shavit, "is that the comic quality of the situation did not come out." The atmosphere at Fatma Gate, he said, was carnivalesque, anarchic, and triumphant. "For the first time in my life, and in the lives of the people gathering at Fatma Gate, we won. We won one."[86]

More shocking than his stone-throwing, however, was Edward's praise of Sheikh Nasrallah, whom he told Shavit, "I found to be a remarkably impressive man."

> A very simple man, quite young, absolutely no bullshit. A man who adopted a strategy toward Israel quite similar to that of the Vietnamese against the Americans: We cannot fight them because they have an army, a navy, and a nuclear option, so the only way we can do it is to make them feel it in body bags. . . . We agreed that as far as reclaiming Palestinian rights, the Oslo accord was a total mess.[87]

It was not surprising to find Edward celebrating Nasrallah less than a decade after his very public break with Yasir Arafat over Oslo. Nasrallah's frankness must have seemed refreshing after so many year of Arafat's "bullshit." The primary difference between the two men, however, was simply that Nasrallah was a winner and Arafat a loser. Nasrallah had refused to concede a single hectare of Lebanese soil to the Israelis, whereas Arafat had ceded large portions of the West Bank in exchange for a petty fiefdom which he could rule like a feudal lord.

§

In the wake of al-Qaeda's attack on the World Trade Center on September 11, 2001, Edward had unusually kind words for Rudy Giuliani, the Mayor of New York, who "has rapidly attained Churchillian status." What struck him about the media coverage of the attack, however, was

> how little time is spent trying to understand America's role in the world and its direct involvement in the complex reality beyond the two coasts that have for so long kept the rest of the world extremely distant and virtually out of the average American's mind. You'd think that "America" was a sleeping giant rather than a superpower almost constantly at war, or in some sort of conflict, all over the Islamic domains.

As for those who celebrated Osama bin Laden and the suicide-hijackers, Edward lamented that

> the poor and the desperate are often conned into the magical thinking and quick bloody solutions that such appalling models provide, wrapped in lying religious claptrap. This remains true in the Middle East generally, in Palestine in particular, but also in the United States, surely the most religious of all countries.[88]

With the born-again George W. Bush beating the drum of war, Edward feared a new Crusade against the infidels.

Shortly thereafter, Edward accepted an invitation to deliver the commencement address at his alma mater, the Northfield Mount Hermon School, in June 2002. As the date approached, however, Edward found himself confined to his bed because of illness. So his son Wadie went to Northfield in his place, reading his father's speech in the first person. Alluding to 9/11 and the invasion of Afghanistan, he cautioned the 362 graduates:

> Many would have you believe that it is a dangerous world . . . and that we alone are fighting the good fight against terrorism, since we keep being reminded that we are being threatened by people who hate us and that the war against terrorism must go on and on.

But America, he insisted,

> is far too powerful and developed in the best sense to be threatened by murderous fanaticism, and the world . . . is far too full of human potential and hope to be turned into armed camps of zealous warriors eager to go out and confront, dehumanize, and demonize foreign enemies.

The strength of America, he continued, is to be found not in its "bloated defense budget" but in its rich diversity—a diversity now well represented at Mount Hermon, in contrast to his experience of the school in early 1950s, when there were only two black students and he himself felt lonely and far from home.[89]

That November, Edward taped his "Last Interview" over the course of three days with documentary filmmaker Mike Dibb. The instigator and producer of the film was an old friend, D. D. Guttenplan, a London-based writer and lecturer who had studied with Edward at Columbia in the mid-1970s. The interviewer was another old friend, the journalist Charles Glass, who, like quite a few other Westerners, had been held hostage in Beirut in the summer of 1987 before his miraculous escape. In the film, Edward appears haggard, with a gray beard covering his sunken cheeks, like a man who does not have terribly long to live. His mind and his tongue, however, are as sharp as ever. At the beginning of the interview, he tells Glass that he has finally accepted the fact that he will not overcome his illness the way he has mastered the other challenges in his life—through sheer will and determination. He also laments the recent passing of his closest friends, most notably Eqbal Ahmad and Ibrahim Abu-Lughod. As the interview proceeds, however, Edward warms up, his passion, charm, and wit on full display.[90]

In the long run-up to the March 2003 invasion of Iraq, dubbed "Operation Iraqi Freedom," Edward issued a spate of public denunciations of the war in *al-Ahram*, *al-Hayat*, and British and American newspapers. In January, for example, he thundered in the *Guardian*:

> The clash of civilizations that George W. Bush and his minions are trying to fabricate as a cover for a preemptive oil and hegemony war against Iraq is supposed to result in a triumph of democratic nation-building, regime change,

and forcible modernization *à l'américain*. Never mind the bombs and the ravages of the sanctions, which are unmentioned. . . . Iraqis, we are told by the Iraqi dissidents, will welcome their liberators and perhaps forget entirely about their past sufferings. Perhaps.

He proceeded to name those scholars and intellectuals who were helping to fabricate the cover for the war, including Bernard Lewis (a "tireless mediocrity" peddling "recycled Orientalist clichés") as well as Fouad Ajami and Kanan Makiya ("academics whose very language reeks of subservience, inauthenticity, and a hopelessly stilted mimicry").[91]

One intellectual Edward did not mention was his old friend Christopher Hitchens, who had come out in favor of the invasions of Afghanistan and Iraq. For whatever reason—possibly sheer exhaustion—Edward refrained from attacking Hitchens in print the way he pummeled former friends like Fouad Ajami. As for Hitchens, he, too, managed to hold his tongue, knowing that Edward was fighting for his life. But then in September 2003, a few weeks before Edward's death, Hitchens decided to criticize his old friend in a reconsideration of *Orientalism* for *The Atlantic*. Among other complaints, he chastised Edward for neglecting Turkish imperialism and for blaming the Americans for the looting of Baghdad's libraries and museums in the early days of the occupation. He also objected to Edward's "repeated and venomous attacks on Ahmed Chalabi and Kanan Makiya," both of whom Hitchens knew and admired.[92] When Edward died later that month, Hitchens was accused of having attacked his old friend on his deathbed.

Five days after Edward's death, a memorial service was held in the monumental Riverside Church near the Columbia campus. Nearly 2,000 of his friends, relatives, colleagues, and admirers filled the church's huge nave, including Noam Chomsky, Susan Sontag, and Peter Jennings.[93] Although Riverside pastors James Forbes and James Fitzgerald officiated, it was Rev. Fuad Bahnan—Hilda Said's old pastor from Beirut—who preached the sermon in Arabic, voicing his hope that Edward would one day be buried in Jerusalem. Edward's son Wadie spoke about his father, and his daughter Najla read his favorite poem, Cavafy's "Waiting for the Barbarians." Daniel Barenboim—Edward's collaborator in the West-Eastern Divan Orchestra—played Bach, Mozart, and Brahms on the piano. A month later, the family took Edward's ashes to his great-grandfather's church in Beirut, where hundreds of mourners came to pay their last respects. Then they buried the urn in the Protestant cemetery in Brumanna, Mariam Said's home village.[94] Edward had refused to be laid to rest in the United States, a final gesture of imperial defiance.

Conclusion

The Intellectual and Power

In June 1993, Edward Said delivered the BBC's annual Reith lectures, following in the footsteps of such thinkers as Bertrand Russell, who inaugurated the series in 1948, and Arnold Toynbee, whose 1952 lectures on "The West and the World" he recalled listening to on the radio.[1] Said's topic was "Representations of the Intellectual," by which he meant both images of the intellectual as a member of a distinct tribe and truths represented by the intellectual to the public by means of words. For Said, the intellectual was an *exile*, an expatriate or marginal figure, an outsider, a dissenter from the status quo. "Never solidarity before criticism" was the intellectual's motto. Furthermore, the intellectual was an *amateur* whose representations are motivated by love and care, not a professional who performs specialized intellectual work for hire, much less a paid consultant. Finally, and most importantly, the intellectual *speaks truth to power*, siding with the weak and unrepresented against governments, armies, and the corporate media.[2]

Said's portrait of the intellectual brought out a number of traits commonly found in representatives of the class. Intellectuals are idealists who believe in "universal principles" of freedom and justice, refusing to bow to practical considerations. They are "thoroughgoing individuals with powerful personalities." They can never be mistaken for "anonymous functionaries or careful bureaucrats." They are eccentrics, with "a quite peculiar, even abrasive style of life and social performance that is uniquely theirs."[3] They are both bold and vulnerable. They are often lonely even as they voice the aspirations of many. They use language well and know just when to use it. They are not motivated by profit or reward. They are skeptical, constantly questioning orthodoxy and dogma. They are stubborn and uncompromising. They are detached and ironic, but never cynical. They can be dyspeptic and curmudgeonly, but they need not be humorless. They live by their wits. Needless to say, Said's portrait of the intellectual was a self-portrait, his *Apologia Pro Vita Sua*.

Charles Malik shared many of these same traits. He had a strong personality, and he was both stubborn and curmudgeonly. What prevented him from being an intellectual in Said's sense, however, was that he put solidarity before criticism. Given the choice between universal principles of freedom and justice and solidarity with his land and his people—with the Christians of Lebanon—Malik had chosen solidarity. Of course, Malik might have questioned the need for such a stark choice. Solidarity with your people did not require you to refrain from criticizing them on the basis of universal principles. On the contrary, solidarity was what required them to take your criticism seriously. The Chamouns and the Gemayels of the world were never going to listen to the criticism of deracinated intellectuals like Edward Said. But they listened to Charles Malik, who was one of their own. To this argument, Said might have replied that the Chamouns and the Gemayels had crossed a line that made solidarity morally impossible. Solidarity with such men of power required too much compromise, too much complicity. Better to make a clean break, to go into exile.

There was another reason why Malik was not an intellectual in Said's sense. According to Said, "the true intellectual is a secular being." This did not mean that intellectuals must be atheists. "In and of itself," he allowed,

> religious belief is to me both understandable and deeply personal: it is rather when a total dogmatic system in which one side is innocently good, the other irreducibly evil, is substituted for the process, the give-and-take of vital interchange, that the secular intellectual feels the unwelcome and inappropriate encroachment of one realm on another. Politics becomes religious enthusiasm ... with results in ethnic cleansing, mass slaughter and unending conflict that are horrible to contemplate.[4]

From Said's point of view, the problem was not that Malik was a devout Christian. It was that he had allowed his religious devotion to encroach upon his politics, turning the preservation of Christian Lebanon into a sacred cause and America into God's chosen instrument to save the world.

It was the strength of Malik's religious conviction that enabled him to persist in his faith in America in the face of constant disappointment. The truth is that America had let Malik down over and over again by refraining from using its power in the Middle East. First came Truman's abandonment of the Palestinian Arabs and his recognition of the State of Israel. Then came Eisenhower's decision to rescue President Nasser in the Suez War of 1956 and his approval of General Chehab in Lebanon in 1958. Then came Johnson's failure to force the Israelis to return Gaza and the West Bank after the 1967 war, followed by Nixon's failure after the 1973 war. Then came the negligence of Gerald Ford and Jimmy Carter as Lebanon slipped into chaos in 1975-6 and was trampled under the boots of the PLO and the Syrians. Then came Reagan's failure to follow up on the expulsion of the PLO from Lebanon by ejecting the Syrians. Why, Malik wondered, was the world's strongest nation, the leader of the free world, so hesitant to use its power? The answer could only be that America had lost faith in itself, thanks to its intellectuals.

Malik's idea of the intellectual derived from his reading of nineteenth-century Russian novelists, particularly Dostoevsky, his favorite. This is evident, for example, from a radio address he gave in 1951 as part of the United Nations "Price of Peace" series. "Is it an accident," he asked,

> that it is never the poor and dispossessed in the under-developed countries who first disturb the peace, but always the intellectuals? It is these intellectuals, living amidst real situations of injustice, but at the same time filled with hatred and

nihilism and a false view of human nature, who are the real cause of unrest in the world today.

The price of peace, therefore, must include justice. But while justice may be necessary, it is not sufficient to satisfy the intellectuals. What the intellectuals need most of all, Malik declared, is love. For "when man is not loved . . . , he will rise in rebellion against the whole universe which has brought him into existence only to make a mockery of him."[5] Like Dostoevsky's character Ivan Karamazov, he will choose to return his ticket.

It was this existential rebellion, combined with the poverty of the masses, that left the intellectuals vulnerable to Communism. For this sorry state of affairs, Malik blamed the West. As he wrote in *Life* magazine in 1952:

> The state of mind of Asia's intellectuals today is not a happy commentary on the West's influence to date. Many of them, devoting years to learning in European or American universities, returned to Asia afflicted with a great intellectual restlessness. Some of these sincerely thought they found solace only in Marxism; others were the clever, self-seeking intellectual radicals familiar enough in the West.[6]

Five years later, not long after he had become Lebanon's foreign minister, *U.S. News & World Report* asked Malik, "How is it that the Communists make their impression upon the intellectuals in your part of the world?" He replied:

> Because the intellectuals have nothing else to believe in; because they can't live in an intellectual and spiritual vacuum; because their old systems of thought and life and of feeling and of hope have crumbled, and because their contact with the Western world during the last 50 to 80 years—and education through books, through magazines, through all that sort of thing—has not filled their souls. Into this vacuum comes Communism![7]

The challenge of the West, therefore, was to fill the souls of the Arab intellectuals with a system of thought and life superior to Communism.

The irony was that Russia, the locus of International Communism, no longer had any use for its intellectuals. As Malik observed in his famous 1949 UN speech on war and peace:

> The tragic fate of intellectuals, scientists, poets and musicians under Communist rule—whether of those who heroically remain loyal to their best lights at the risk of liquidation, or those who disgracefully retrace their steps and make public retractions—is not surprising. The Communist state—or, at least, the dictatorship of the proletariat—like any other form of totalitarianism, necessarily suffocates spontaneity, inner dynamism, freedom and diversity. The spirit of man, which can be itself and its best self only in freedom and love and genuine communion, is choked and annihilated by totalitarianism.[8]

And nowhere was this desire for communion more evident than in nineteenth-century Russian literature. "A clearly discernable motif," Malik informed his fellow ambassadors,

> is the mystical quest for wholeness, completeness, unity. There is the mystical burning for absorption and reconciliation, a self-projection onto an ultimate universal harmony. The Russian soul at its best is consumed by a mystical flame of the purest type.[9]

It was this mystical quest for unity, Malik explained, that had allowed the Communists to foist themselves on Russia in the first place. In the end, however, nothing would satisfy the Russian soul but the mystical unity of the Orthodox Church.

§

In his third Reith lecture, Said singled out two exiled European intellectuals as "marvels of adjustment" in their new country:

> The United States today is in the unusual position of having two extremely high former officers in recent presidential administrations—Henry Kissinger and Zbigniew Brzezinski—who were (or still are, depending on the observer's outlook) intellectuals in exile, Kissinger from Nazi Germany, Brzezinski from Communist Poland. . . . Yet both Kissinger and Brzezinski seem on the surface at least to have contributed their talents entirely to their adopted country, with results in eminence, material rewards, national, not to say worldwide, influence that are light-years away from the marginal obscurity in which Third World exile intellectuals live in Europe or the U.S.[10]

Said went on to contrast these marvelously adjusted exiles with two of his intellectual heroes, Theodor Adorno and C. L. R. James, who not only remained marginal figures in exile, but who also embraced the position of marginality. Renouncing power, Adorno and James managed to transform exile into "a model for the intellectual who is tempted, and even beset and overwhelmed, by the rewards of accommodation, yea-saying, settling in."[11] Kissinger and Brzezinski, in contrast, were happy to accept such rewards as their due.

As it happened, both Kissinger and Brzezinski were still teaching at Harvard when Said arrived there as a graduate student in the fall of 1958. Kissinger was a protégé of Professor William Yandell Elliott, the conservative Cold Warrior whose friendship with Charles Malik dated from the late 1940s. It was Elliott who had helped Kissinger raise funds for his International Seminar, which brought future world democratic leaders from around the world to Harvard each summer for a crash course in American government and culture. No doubt it was Elliott who had recommended Malik as a potential contributor to *Confluence*, the journal Kissinger launched in 1952.[12] I am not sure when Kissinger and Malik first met, but it was probably no later than the summer of 1960, when Kissinger was conducting his International Seminar and Malik was teaching at the Harvard Summer School. By that time, Kissinger had become Associate Director of Harvard's new Center for International Affairs. As for Brzezinski, he was moving to New York that summer in order to direct the new Research Institute on Communist Affairs at Columbia.

Three years later, Edward Said followed Brzezinski from Harvard to Columbia. At the time, Brzezinski was hawkish on Vietnam, taking a leave of absence in 1966 and 1967 to join the State Department's Policy Planning Staff in Washington. In January 1968, he was invited to join the presidential campaigns of both Governor Nelson Rockefeller—Kissinger's longtime patron—and Vice President Hubert Humphrey. A lifelong Democrat, Brzezinski opted for Humphrey. As for Rockefeller, he was destined to lose the Republican nomination, once again, to Richard Nixon. That is why, in the spring of 1968, Kissinger reportedly offered to hand Rockefeller's "black book" on Nixon to Brzezinski. By the time Brzezinski got around to asking for it, however, Kissinger had agreed to join the Nixon camp.[13] Then, in December 1968, Kissinger accompanied Brzezinski and a hundred other intellectuals to Princeton for the inaugural conference of the International Association for Cultural Freedom (as the Congress for Cultural Freedom was renamed after the exposure of its CIA funding.) When asked what the incoming Nixon administration should do about foreign policy, Brzezinski replied, "The first order of business will be to see whether the war in Vietnam can be terminated on terms acceptable to the American people."[14]

In January 1969, Kissinger became Richard Nixon's National Security Advisor. The following year, Charles Malik came to the White House for a meeting with Nixon regarding the upcoming Lebanese presidential election. After Suleiman Frangieh won that election, Malik began to send memoranda to Kissinger and met with him at Frangieh's request in the summer of 1973. He did not see Kissinger again until the fall of 1976, when the Lebanese Front sent him to Washington to seek assurances of US support. Unfortunately, Kissinger's assurances did not mean much after Gerald Ford was defeated by Jimmy Carter in the November presidential election. So the Lebanese Front sent Malik back to Washington to make contact with the incoming Carter administration. Fortunately, Under Secretary of State Philip Habib, to whom he had been introduced by Kissinger, had been asked to stay on by Cyrus Vance, the new secretary of state. Malik met with both Habib and Vance, but not, apparently, with Zbigniew Brzezinski, whom Carter had named—against Kissinger's advice—as his National Security Advisor.[15]

By then, Brzezinski had been Edward Said's colleague at Columbia for more than a decade. Said would have remembered at least one campus incident involving Brzezinski. On November 6, 1969, students from the Revolutionary Youth Movement, which had called for the closure of Columbia's School of International Affairs, led a piglet on a rope to Brzezinski's office building, chanting, "A pig for Professor Zbig."[16] The irony was that Brzezinski had already changed his mind about the Vietnam War, having joined Clark Kerr's Committee for a Political Settlement of the War in Vietnam and traveled to Saigon to plead for a cease-fire.[17] Then, after Israel's hard-won victory in the October 1973 war, Brzezinski came out in favor of an autonomous Palestinian state, federated with Jordan, in the pages of the liberal magazine *New Leader*.[18] Brzezinski's plan served as the blueprint for the 1975 Brookings study, which called for Palestinian autonomy but stopped short of recommending that the PLO represent the Palestinians in negotiations. As soon as Carter was elected president in November 1976, Said wrote to Brzezinski, offering to arrange a meeting for him with Walid Khalidi and a representative of the PLO. Carter, however, decided to honor the Kissinger ban on direct talks with the PLO, preferring, like Kissinger, to rely on private intermediaries.

One of those intermediaries was Dr. Landrum Bolling, the Quaker peacemaker who had traveled extensively in the Middle East on behalf of the American Friends Service Committee. Among those Bolling consulted was his friend Charles Malik, whose "heroic vision" of a Middle East confederation embracing both Israel and the Palestinians he found inspiring.[19] On September 6, 1977, Bolling met with Brzezinski in Washington before traveling to Beirut to meet with Yasir Arafat and his lieutenants. If Arafat would offer a qualified endorsement of UNSC Resolution 242, Brzezinski said, the United States would open direct talks with the PLO. Arafat replied that he could only issue such a statement if the United States were to guarantee, in return, a Palestinian state led by the PLO. Unwilling to offer such a guarantee, the Carter administration abandoned its pursuit of direct talks with the PLO and turned instead to the question of Palestinian representation at an international peace conference in Geneva.[20] That is how Edward Said's name entered the conversation as a possible delegate. But Anwar Sadat's surprise visit to Israel on November 19 opened the door to a bilateral alternative to a comprehensive Middle East peace. "Bye-bye PLO" was the way Brzezinski put it, much to the chagrin of Edward Said.[21]

Looking back on their careers, Said found little to choose between Kissinger and Brzezinski. Both were Harvard intellectuals and veteran Cold Warriors who sought and acquired power in Washington, but neither was able to exercise it on behalf of the Palestinians. It was not that they denied the validity of Palestinian claims or refused to talk with the PLO. As hard-headed foreign policy realists, they knew that peace in the Middle East required a measure of justice for the Palestinians, and that it was better to deal with Arafat than to drive him into the arms of the rejectionists. The problem was that their power to aid and even negotiate with the Palestinians was limited, constrained by the political influence of the Israel lobby, by the sincere commitment of US presidents and political parties to the "special relationship" with Israel, and by the internal disagreements of the Palestinians themselves. These constraints explain why Kissinger signed the secret September 1975 memorandum prohibiting the United States from recognizing or negotiating with the PLO until it affirmed Israel's right to exist and accepted UNSC Resolutions 242 and 338—a policy that even Charles Malik, who hated the PLO, disputed. For Said, the careers of Kissinger and Brzezinski illustrated what happens when intellectuals are too eager to enter the halls of power— they soon forget what it's like to be an exile.

§

If Said blamed Kissinger and Brzezinski for succumbing to the temptation of power, he faulted other intellectuals for holding themselves aloof from power. A prime example was his friend Noam Chomsky, whose 1967 manifesto "The Responsibility of the Intellectuals" had done much to rally academics to the anti-war movement. Much of the appeal of Chomsky's manifesto lay in its simplicity. "It is the responsibility of the intellectual," Chomsky proclaimed, "to speak the truth and to expose lies."[22] This he proceeded to do in books like *Peace in the Middle East?*, which included his contribution to the 1970 conference of the Association of Arab-American University Graduates in Evanston, where he had shared the stage with Edward Said and Eqbal Ahmad. On that occasion, Ahmad had voiced skepticism regarding Chomsky's prescription for Palestine, namely, two federated republics, one Jewish, one Arab. But the two men remained friends. When Ahmad was arrested two months later, accused of plotting to kidnap Henry Kissinger, Chomsky was the second person to fly to Chicago to see him, the first being Richard Falk.[23]

When *Peace in the Middle East?* was published in 1974, Chomsky was severely criticized by pro-Israel reviewers like Michael Walzer, who dismissed Chomsky's ideal of a socialist, binationalist Palestine as antiquated and impractical.[24] In his own review of the book, entitled "Chomsky and the Question of Palestine," Said defended his friend, accusing Walzer of "blind ethnocentric ignorance."[25] Yet he did not hesitate to spell out his own disagreements with Chomsky. For one thing, he regretted that Chomsky's knowledge of the Palestinians, and of the Arab world in general, was so thin. This criticism was related to another, namely, that Chomsky assigned the determining role in Arab history to outside powers like the United States, ignoring the internal dynamics of Arab societies. On the level of theory, Said noted that Chomsky's "anarcho-socialism" made him suspicious of the state, leading him to reject recent calls for a Palestinian state. He also lamented Chomsky's lack of sympathy for the PLO. Said himself was unwilling to give up on the PLO or to renounce the armed struggle. "What violence, what arms, what force are we to advocate, employ, or discover," he asked, "if the best goals for the area are to be realized?"[26] He did not attempt to answer the question, but it was evident that he did not share Chomsky's near-pacifism.

A decade later, Said reviewed *The Fateful Triangle*, Chomsky's account of the 1982 Israeli invasion of Lebanon. While praising his old friend for marshaling the *facts* of Israeli cruelty and US complicity, he noted that the book lacked something more essential than facts, namely, an imaginatively and ideologically compelling *narrative*. "Facts do not at all speak for themselves," he emphasized, "but require a socially acceptable narrative to absorb, sustain, and circulate them."[27] Without such a narrative, facts were too easy to deny, suppress, or ignore. As far as Said was concerned, the missing narrative was none other than the Palestinian national narrative, ending with a homeland for the exiles of 1948. It was not that he disagreed with Chomsky's new prescription for Palestine, namely, partition into two separate states. The difficulty, rather, was that Chomsky had failed to weave the two-state solution into a narrative capable of displacing the "official" narrative repeated by the supporters of Israel.

Said lodged other complaints against Chomsky's analysis as well. Chomsky, he thought, was too pessimistic in concluding that it was too late for a reasonable settlement of the conflict over Palestine. "Perhaps giving up is the rational thing to do," Said admitted, "yet ... injustice is injustice, and no one should acquiesce in it." He also thought that Chomsky was too unreflective, too isolated a thinker. "His isolation from the actual arena of contest, his distance from power as a fiercely uncompromising intellectual," Said feared, had allowed Chomsky to imagine that he was a simple reporter of facts, free from the taint of ideology. As far as Said was concerned, however, no one is ever free from ideology. In Chomsky's case, that ideology was "history-transcending universal rationalism." That is why it is the responsibility of intellectuals to reflect on what they are doing—to formulate "a theory of perception," "a theory of intellectual activity," and "an epistemological account of ideological structures." The difficulty is that "none of these things is within the capacity of a solitary individual to produce, and none is possible without some sense of communal or collective commitment," a commitment that "national narratives authorize and represent."[28]

Such criticisms notwithstanding, Said stood shoulder to shoulder with Chomsky against those intellectuals who had sold out to power—the Kissingers and the Brzezinskis. No doubt he applauded the invitation to Chomsky to address a rally at Columbia in April 1977 organized by the Kissinger Statement Committee, a faculty group opposed to President William J. McGill's effort to endow a chair for Henry Kissinger. Asked about the accusation that the committee was violating academic freedom, Chomsky called it "fraudulent," asserting that "the universities have never been committed to academic freedom." As proof, he pointed to the complicity of the School of International Affairs in the Vietnam War effort, which included the training and recruitment of officers for the State Department and, more quietly, the CIA. "How many people in SIA were advisors to the National Liberation Front?" Chomsky asked rhetorically.[29] Kissinger soon abandoned the idea of going to Columbia, choosing to remain at Georgetown, closer to the corridors of power. Four years later, after Jimmy Carter's defeat, he was joined by his old Harvard colleague Zbigniew Brzezinski.

§

One intellectual whom Said never criticized was his martyred friend Hanna Mikhail. In July 1994, when Yasir Arafat returned to Gaza to take charge of the Palestinian Authority, Said was moved to pay homage to Mikhail, who had been dead for nearly twenty years. "Hanna Mikhail," he proclaimed,

> was a true intellectual. . . . He retained his original Quaker modesty and plainness. But as an intellectual should, he lived according to his ideas and never tailored his democratic, secular values to suit new masters and occasions. For all Palestinians today, and in stark contrast to the great sell-out and abject surrender of our leaders, he represents a distinguished role model, a man who did not debase himself or his people. He lived his ideas, and died for them. It is as simple as that.[30]

This remarkable tribute suggests that Mikhail had become Said's alter ego—an intellectual who sacrificed the comforts and rewards of academic life in the West and took up arms against the principalities and powers of this world. After all, Said and Mikhail were the same age; they were raised in pious Christian homes; they left home to study at elite US universities; they married Euro-American women, divorced them, and remarried Arab women; they abandoned the Christian faith and embraced secularism; they became men of the Left and dedicated themselves to the Palestinian cause.

A graduate of the Friends School in Ramallah, Mikhail arrived in the United States in 1952 to attend Haverford College, one of the country's leading Quaker institutions. Already studying at Haverford was another future friend of Edward Said's, Fred Jameson, who had attended the nearby Moorestown Friends School. As Said recalled, he first met Mikhail in the 1950s, when they were still undergraduates. It is conceivable that they were introduced by Charles Malik, whose appointment calendar records a meeting with one "John Mikhail" in May 1954, near the end of Said's first year at Princeton.[31] In those days, Ambassador Malik was often approached by Arab students seeking scholarships and fellowships. Two years later, Mikhail received a Danforth Graduate Fellowship, which enabled him to pursue graduate study in political science at Harvard. As a student in Harvard's Government department, Mikhail encountered Malik's friend William Y. Elliott as well as junior professors like Henry Kissinger and Zbigniew Brzezinski. He also took courses in Middle Eastern Studies, where he met his first wife. His doctoral dissertation, on the medieval Islamic scholar Mawardi, was supervised first by H. A. R. Gibb and then, after Gibb was disabled by a stroke, by Nadav Safran.[32]

According to Said, he lost touch with Mikhail after the latter took a job at the University of Washington in 1967. In the summer of 1970, however, he bumped into Mikhail again in Amman, by which time his friend had abandoned his academic career in order to join Fatah full-time, adopting "Abu Omar" as his nom de guerre. One person who knew his true identity was Seattle journalist Shelby Scates, who went to Amman to look for him that spring. On May 27, 1970, Scates took a taxi to PLO headquarters, where he was locked in a holding cell by the *fedayeen*. Once his identity was confirmed, he was ushered into Mikhail's office. "I am John Mikail [sic]," his host freely admitted, asking Scates for news of his friends back in Seattle. Scates then asked him about the May 22 bombing of an Israeli school bus near the Lebanese border, which had killed a dozen children. "Would you, and others of course, bother to come here if we did not commit such acts?" Mikhail replied.

> No, I admitted. He had made his point, yet he betrayed it with a flash look of distress. For a moment I felt sorry for the man, overwhelmed by the tragedy. John Mikail-Abu Omar did not murder children. History did.

Following the interview, Scates was allowed to leave after promising not to reveal the true identity of Abu Omar—a promise he kept for thirty years.[33]

Not long after his meeting with Shelby Scates in Amman, Mikhail flew to Los Angeles for the taping of *The Advocates*—the public television program in which he was interrogated by Harvard's Alan Dershowitz. By August, Mikhail was back in Amman, where Edward Said encountered him. In September, during King Hussein's bloody crackdown on the PLO, Mikhail was interviewed by another American journalist, Edward R. F. Sheehan. "Since the [Jordanian] government has accepted the Rogers peace plan in July," he told Sheehan,

> there has been a concerted effort to recognize Israel behind her old frontiers and to liquidate the Palestinian revolution. The Americans—and I mean particularly the

C.I.A.—are pushing the King to do this, as the price he must pay for winning back the west bank of the Jordan.[34]

Then, in October, Mikhail appeared at a press conference following a meeting between the king's negotiator, Wasfi al-Tal, and Yasir Arafat. He was recognized by the political officer at the US embassy in Amman, Hume Horan, who had studied with Mikhail at Harvard in the early 1960s. "I looked up and there was Hanah [sic] Mikhail," Horan recalled. "I thought I better play it cool." As the PLO contingent was leaving, Mikhail paused in front of Horan, and they shook hands and exchanged greetings. Horan never saw him again.[35]

By then, Said knew what Shelby Scates and Hume Horan knew—that Hanna Mikhail had transformed himself into Abu Omar. That is how he was known to Jean Genet, to whom he had been introduced in the spring of 1970 by Genet's friend Mahmoud Hamshari, the PLO representative in Paris (later assassinated by an Israeli hit squad). When Genet traveled to Jordan in the early 1970s, it was Mikhail who served as his guide and interpreter, introducing him to Arafat and other PLO officials.[36] By the time Said arrived in Lebanon in the summer of 1972 for his sabbatical, Mikhail had relocated to Beirut, where he worked at the PLO's Research Center and Planning Center while serving as a member of the Organizing Committee for the Occupied Territories. It was in October 1972 that Mikhail brought Genet to Said's quarters in Beirut, where they talked into the wee hours of the morning. Unfortunately, Genet failed to mention Said in his book about the Palestinians, *Un Captif amoureux*, which Said praised in a review of Barbara Bray's 1989 English translation.[37] But the fact that the great French writer was a friend of Abu Omar's cast Hanna Mikhail in a whole new light for Said.

In the early 1970s, Mikhail led a dissident Leftist faction within Fatah—one that looked to the North Vietnamese and the Viet Cong for inspiration. In the fall of 1975, shortly after the fall of Saigon, he traveled to Vietnam, where he spent a few months in cadre training while touring the country and writing poetry. On his fortieth birthday, he lamented the time he had wasted:

> Marching on a path not mine,
> Moved by a spirit sublime
> Yet by thoughts unscientific
> Served in essence bourgeois schemes
> Offering masses mere dreams.

Now that he was finally on the right path, however, he was confident of the ultimate victory of the masses:

> My greatest wish
> We not desist
> What counts is will
> To still persist.[38]

Said, too, counted on the will of the Palestinian people to persist in their struggle—not to mention his own will, which was strong, indeed.

Upon Mikhail's return from Vietnam, he told Said about his experiences there. Shortly thereafter, in July 1976, Mikhail disappeared during his ill-fated boat trip to northern Lebanon. Among those who appealed to the US State Department for assistance in locating him was his sister Joyce Hanna, a US citizen who had lived in New York for twenty years. Joyce's appeal was taken up by none other than Henry Kissinger, who immediately asked the US embassies in Beirut and Damascus to pursue any leads. If Kissinger remembered Mikhail from Harvard, his message contained no hint of it.[39] In mid-December, the US ambassador to Syria, Richard Murphy, reported that, according to the Damascus representative of the Red Cross, Mikhail was almost certainly dead.[40] However, reports that Mikhail was still alive in a Damascus prison surfaced again in 1977, and the following year Talcott Seelye, who had succeeded Murphy as US ambassador to Syria, raised the Mikhail case with the Syrian Ministry of Foreign Affairs.[41] But nothing came of it, and Mikhail's name was added to the long list of martyrs to the Palestinian cause.

Nearly twenty years passed before Edward Said penned his tribute to Mikhail, prompted by the publication of Mikhail's Harvard dissertation, for which he wrote a preface, and by the writing of his own memoir, *Out of Place*. That Mikhail was a saintly figure seems beyond dispute—selfless, gentle, incorruptible, viscerally pained by suffering and violence. The question remains, however, of whether he was a true intellectual, in Said's sense, or rather an ideologist, a self-appointed member of a revolutionary vanguard whose task was to indoctrinate the cadres. His belief in a science of revolution, his contempt for the bourgeoisie, and his celebration of the masses implied that he had become a Marxist, as Said admitted. To be sure, Said admired independent Marxist intellectuals like his friend Fred Jameson, another former Quaker. But one senses that Said was uncomfortable with Mikhail's conversion to Marxism, dismissing it in a single sentence ("I think by that time he had become a Marxist, but how different from his colleagues in the progressive movement he was!").[42] In the final analysis, it was not so much the power of Mikhail's ideas that Said admired as the purity of his character—a testimony to his Quaker upbringing.

§

In his final Reith lecture, "Gods That Always Fail," Said described an Iranian émigré who, in his opinion, had chased after false political gods, losing his critical detachment and thereby betraying the high calling of the secular intellectual. He did not name the intellectual in question, but he was easily identifiable as Mansour Farhang, a professor of politics at Bennington College in Vermont, who had staunchly opposed the shah's corrupt and brutal regime—as well as American imperialism—in the 1970s. When the shah was overthrown in 1979, Farhang offered his services to the new revolutionary government, serving as the Islamic Republic's first UN ambassador until he resigned over Khomeini's refusal to free the American hostages. He then returned to Iran as an advisor to President Abolhassan Bani Sadr, only to flee the country the following year, fearing for his life after Bani Sadr's fall from power. Exiled once again, Farhang became a vocal critic of the Khomeini regime. After Iraq invaded Kuwait in 1990, however, he spoke out in defense of President Bush's decision to expel the Iraqis in Operation Desert Storm—a war Said opposed.[43]

From an intellectual standpoint, what disturbed Said about Farhang's political journey was its religious overtones. "The story of my Iranian friend's pilgrimage back to Islamic theocracy and out of it," he observed, "is about a quasi-religious conversion, followed by what appeared to be a very dramatic reversal in belief, and a counterconversion." The problem was that Farhang had put too much faith in Khomeini. He had then compounded his original sin by putting too much faith in the Americans, whose imperialism he had previously denounced. "I am against conversion to and belief in a political god of any sort," Said declaimed. "I consider both as unfitting behavior for the intellectual." How, then, had his own behavior differed from that of Farhang? After all, he, too, had welcomed the Iranian revolution, only to be disappointed. "I was never particularly taken with Khomeini himself," he recalled.[44] More importantly, he had never compromised with American imperialism, even though, had there been no Operation Desert Storm, Saddam Hussein would have been left in control of Kuwait.

Interestingly, Said did not criticize Ali Shariati, the religious intellectual who did as much as anyone to inspire the revolutionaries who overthrew the shah in 1979. On the contrary, he praised Shariati for "provocatively disturb[ing] the monumental calm and inviolate aloofness of the [Islamic] tradition."[45] Yet it was that very tradition—the tradition of Shia Islam—that made Shariati's work so popular in the bazaars as well as the universities. Iran had plenty of Communists and other secular leftists, but their appeal was neither as wide nor as deep as Shariati's reinterpretation of Shiism as a theology of the oppressed. As Mansour Farhang noted in *Race & Class* in 1979: "More than 80 per cent of the books on display on the pavements of Iranian cities are the writings of Ali Shariati." For those who couldn't read, cassette tapes of his lectures were just as widely available.[46] Arguably, Shariati did exactly what Said reprimanded Farhang for doing—converting politics into religious enthusiasm. The difference was that Shariati had died in exile in 1977, before he could witness the revolution he inspired.

It would be an exaggeration to call Charles Malik the Ali Shariati of the Lebanese Christian resistance. The militant monks of Kaslik, who challenged the traditional conservatism of the Maronite Patriarchate, had a better claim to that title. Just as Shariati drew on Shia tradition, so they drew on Maronite tradition, which also embodied the historical memory of an oppressed minority. Although he was not a Maronite himself, Malik understood the power of the tradition and made effective rhetorical use of it, as in his 1980 "Letter to the Maronites":

> Is there anyone among the enemies of Lebanon and its freedoms and values who does not act with hostility toward the Maronites or seek to dishonor and divide them? This is an honor for the Maronites. . . . Despite all adversaries, they stand their ground, defying and resisting like a mountain that even the strongest winds cannot shake![47]

Of course, Malik's vision of a free and just society was a far cry from Shariati's. But he, too, summoned legendary heroes and holy martyrs to battle.

For Malik, the hero and martyr of the Lebanese Christian resistance was Bashir Gemayel. It is hard to fathom what the old philosopher saw in the young thug, who did not hesitate to use violence to crush his rivals. Here is what Malik's relative Elie Salem, the AUB professor who served as foreign minister under Amin Gemayel, wrote about Bashir:

> Napoleon first attained fame by shooting at the Paris mob. He did not waver, did not compromise and certainly did not negotiate. Bashir admired Napoleon, and if he read at all, his reading was probably limited to biographies of great military leaders—men whose rise to power involved the ruthless deployment of the bayonet.

After Salem was threatened by Bashir in the spring of 1982, he boldly asked to see the young warlord in person. In the course of that meeting, his opinion of the young man began to change:

> Unconsciously, I assumed a fatherly role. I love this guy, I thought. I like his style. He did not have much intellectual discipline, but passion he had in abundance. Here was good material, I thought. Perhaps it can be molded. I was the inveterate teacher, the hidden Messianic, the counsellor.[48]

No doubt Charles Malik also looked upon Bashir through the eyes of a teacher, believer, and counsellor, as Aristotle once looked upon Alexander.

One might draw a parallel between Malik's relationship with Bashir Gemayel and Said's relationship with Yasir Arafat, another freedom fighter with blood on his hands. Of course, the age difference between Arafat and Said was much smaller and the geographic distance much greater, with Said living on the far side of the Atlantic Ocean. Nevertheless, Said spent many hours attempting to educate Arafat, to explain how democratic nations like America and Israel work, to make a statesman of him. He even stooped to public relations in an effort to burnish Arafat's image. In his 1988 profile of Arafat for *Andy Warhol's Interview*, he did his best to humanize the PLO chairman, describing a typical day in the life of the "Old Man," starting with a bowl of cornflakes soaked in hot tea. He even tried to rehabilitate Arafat's notoriously unkempt appearance:

> Palestinians are a messy and uneven people, and finally, perhaps, Arafat—stubbly face, small, slightly overweight body, overarticulate eloquence, and all—has led and represented us for so long because he has never lost touch with who we are.[49]

Perhaps Said's own sartorial splendor marked him as less authentically Palestinian than the Old Man.

Five years later, Said broke with the Old Man over the signing of the Oslo Accord, which he denounced as a betrayal of Palestinian hopes and dreams. Did the example of Charles Malik play any part in Said's decision to part ways with Arafat and the PLO after twenty-five years? Like Said, Malik had started out his public life as a champion of the Palestinian Arabs, only to end it as an apologist for the reprehensible Lebanese Forces, torn by internal dissension, restricted to the parcel of land left to it by the Syrian occupation. Perhaps the parallels to what the PLO had become were too obvious not to be noticed. Perhaps Said looked into his own diminishing future and saw another Uncle Charles, a man whom history would forget because he had attached himself to violent, narrow-minded men and hopeless sectarian causes. Perhaps he had come to see in Malik's life a warning to intellectuals who place too much faith in men of power, who trade their independence for a seat at the table. Perhaps that was what he meant when he called Malik's trajectory "the great negative intellectual lesson of my life."

§

A year before he died, Edward Said wrote in *al-Hayat*, "The intellectual's role is to speak the truth, as plainly, directly, and as honestly as possible. No intellectual is supposed to worry about whether what is said embarrasses, pleases, or displeases people in power."[50] Certainly that is how Charles Malik understood his role. Throughout his life, he prided himself on his single-minded devotion to truth. It was his calling as a Christian philosopher to speak truth to the Arabs. In order to speak truth, however, one needed to be free to speak the truth. And the Arab nations were not free. You could not speak truth in Cairo or Damascus; only in Beirut were you free to do so. But Lebanon was powerless to defend its freedom. Without outside help, it would inevitably be enslaved by its more powerful neighbors—if not by Israel, then by Egypt and Syria, directed by Moscow. That help could come only from the Christian nations of the West. With France and Britain in decline, Lebanon had no choice but to rely on American power. But would the Americans understand that it was their moral duty to guard Lebanon and other free nations? As a diplomat, Malik's calling was to speak truth to America—to persuade the Americans that their own cherished traditions and values obligated them to use their power to defend the Free World.

Understandably, Malik longed to rid his beloved Lebanon of the foreign armies that threatened its sovereignty, namely those of Arafat and Assad. But he was wrong to hitch his wagon to the militias of Chamoun and Gemayel, which were just as brutal as the *fedayeen* and soldiers they fought. Similarly, Malik was wrong to put his faith in American presidents like Nixon and Reagan, whose misguided prosecution of the Cold War resulted in thousands of unnecessary deaths abroad—particularly in Vietnam—and implicated them in the abuse of power at home. Intellectuals should have no truck with butchers and war criminals. Unfortunately, Malik could not take the imaginative leap that was necessary to see himself through the eyes of Lebanon's others—the Shia *fellahin* or the Palestinian refugees. Nor could he see the power of the United States through the eyes of black South Africans or Nicaraguan *campesinos*. Historically, it was Christians like Malik who had benefited the most from French colonialism in the Levant. And it was autocrats like the king of Saudi Arabia and the shah of Iran who benefited the most from US neocolonialism in the Middle East.

If Malik was able to identify imaginatively with any of the non-Christian peoples of the Middle East, it was the Jews of Israel. He regarded the Hebrew Scriptures as divinely inspired, admired the philosophical writings of Maimonides and Martin Buber, and experienced first-hand the anti-Semitism of Nazi Germany. At the United Nations, he learned to admire Israeli diplomats like Gideon Rafael and Abba Eban even as he debated them in the most vigorous terms. Like him, they were the beneficiaries of European culture, having studied at elite universities in Berlin and Cambridge. Like Lebanon, Israel was an outpost of modern, Western civilization in the vast Islamic desert. Thus it was natural for Malik, along with Camille Chamoun and other leaders of the Christian community in Lebanon, to turn to Israel in their hour of need. As for the Zionist organizations in the United States, they no longer shunned Malik as they had done in the 1940s and 1950s, when he thundered against Israel. On the contrary, they welcomed him as a new ally in their never-ending battle with the Palestinians, with confrontationist Arab states like Syria, Libya, and Iraq, and with Shia terrorists supported by Iran. But Israel was bound to let him down just as the United States had done—by leaving Lebanon before the job was done.

If Malik's imaginative identification with the Jews of Israel was the end product of a natural evolution, the same was true of Edward Said's. Like Malik, he was raised in a Christian home in which the Old Testament was read and revered as Holy Scripture. In Zamalek, many of his classmates, neighbors, and childhood friends were Jewish. At clubby, Waspy Princeton, he befriended Jewish students like Ralph Schoenman as fellow outsiders. His most influential professors and mentors were Jewish—Arthur Szathmary at Princeton, Harry Levin at Harvard, Lionel Trilling at Columbia. His close friends at Columbia included Jewish colleagues like Robert Alter, Sidney Morgenbesser, and Michael Rosenthal. His intellectual heroes included Jewish thinkers like Auerbach, Lukacs, and Adorno. As early as 1973, Said was writing of Arabs and Jews that "each is the other." By the end of his life, he was boasting to Ari Shavit of *Ha'aretz*:

> I'm the last Jewish intellectual. You don't know anyone else. All your other Jewish intellectuals are now suburban squires. From Amos Oz to all these people here in America. So I'm the last one. The only true follower of Adorno. Let me put it this way: I'm a Jewish-Palestinian.[51]

To be a "Jewish" intellectual and a follower of Adorno was to be homeless, an exile, a wanderer. It was to be forced to invent oneself and to regard all power and authority with a critical eye.

Charles Malik may have been an intellectual who admired the Jews, but he was not a "Jewish" intellectual. He had a home, and he would do whatever was necessary to protect it from alien intruders, refusing the safety of exile in the West. It was not that he lacked sympathy for the dispossessed Palestinians, many of whom were his students and colleagues. But his hospitality faltered when Lebanon's guests began to make themselves obnoxious, threatening to stay forever and send their hosts packing, as the Israelis had done to them. That is what made Said's identification with the Jews of Israel so remarkable. They had taken over his family's beautiful old house in Jerusalem and banished its rightful owners. But he had no desire to live in that house again, to indulge the fantasy of a triumphant return. Not only was such a return impossible, but it would also be wrong to perpetuate the tragic cycle of injustice and violence in Palestine. Better to persuade both sides to share their ancestral home, as Christians and Muslims had been forced to do, for better or for worse, in Lebanon. That, too, may have been no more than a fantasy, but at least it was a fantasy of peace and justice, not blood and retribution.

Said may have been a "Jewish" intellectual, but he had no use for Judaism or other religions, which he associated, in good Enlightenment fashion, with fatalism, dogma, and holy wars. For him, the intellectual was by definition a secular being, if not a crusading atheist like his friends Christopher Hitchens and Salman Rushdie. On the other hand, Said was perfectly willing to make common cause with religious friends who shared his commitment to justice in Palestine, from Daniel Berrigan to Cornel West to Sari Nusseibeh, the Oxford-educated Muslim philosopher and Palestinian activist. Surely these men qualify as intellectuals, as do a surprising number of modern French religious thinkers: Emmanuel Levinas, Paul Ricoeur, Rene Girard, Mohammed Arkoun. It ought to be possible, therefore, to combine the spiritual yearning and even the theological orthodoxy of a Charles Malik with the critical acumen and political dissent of an Edward Said, even if they themselves could not imagine it.

§

As Edward Said noted in his Reith lectures, one hallmark of the intellectual is a belief in universal principles of freedom and justice, principles that must be vindicated in the face of power. Certainly Charles Malik believed in such principles, as embodied in the Universal Declaration of Human Rights, which he helped to draft and steer through the ideological cross-currents of the United Nations. Largely ignored for half a century, Malik's contribution to human rights was celebrated in December 1998 with an international conference at the American University of Beirut on the fiftieth anniversary of the UDHR. Among the featured speakers was Mary Ann Glendon of the Harvard Law School. Subsequently, Malik's son Habib edited a volume of his father's speeches and writings under the title *The Challenge of Human Rights: Charles Malik and the Declaration*, with an introduction by Glendon.[52] Glendon's own book on the UDHR, *A World Made New: Eleanor Roosevelt and the Universal Declaration of Human Rights*, came out in 2001. Historians of human rights may not share Glendon's reverence for Charles Malik as a Christian philosopher and statesman, but they can no longer ignore his role in the post–Second World War human rights movement.

That movement has been criticized of late by revisionist historians such as Samuel Moyn, who, in *Christian Human Rights*, laments what he sees as the appropriation of secular human rights by Christians like Malik.[53] Another revisionist, Andrew Arsan, takes a different tack, situating Malik's turn to human rights, as well as his pro-Americanism, in the context of his overriding concern for the fate of his beloved Lebanon. According to Arsan, it was the threat to Lebanese sovereignty posed by Zionism, Arab Nationalism, and Communism that eventually drove a reluctant Malik into the arms of the United States. As evidence of Malik's early pessimism concerning the US role in the Middle East, Arsan quotes a confidential report that Malik had sent to the Lebanese ministry of foreign affairs in February 1949. Of the three great Western powers, Malik warned, only France could be counted on to come to Lebanon's aid in a crisis. France had a sentimental attachment to Lebanon, whereas US political leaders were too sympathetic to Israel and too dependent on Jewish voters.[54] Malik's report was republished in 2003 by Ghassan Tueni, a former protégé of Malik's who had come to admire the work of Edward Said. Said's copy of the report is now located in the Edward Said Reading Room at Columbia University, which houses his personal library.

Had he lived longer, Said would no doubt have welcomed these revisionist critiques of the human rights movement. Indeed, he anticipated them. In 1992, Said was one of a group of leading philosophers and literary theorists—including Jacques Derrida—who were invited to deliver the Oxford Amnesty Lectures. In his lecture, "Nationalism, Human Rights, and Interpretation," Said complained that the language of human rights had been made to serve national interests—in particular, those of the United States, which denounced the oppressive regime of Saddam Hussein, for example, while ignoring human rights violations in Kuwait and Saudi Arabia. His response was not to abandon the language of human rights but to contest the US interpretation of those rights by exposing its contradictions.[55] In fact, he continued to advocate for universal human rights throughout his life, praising the work of organizations like Amnesty International. In one of his last lectures, "Memory, Inequality, and Power: Palestine and the Universality of Human Rights," delivered at the American University in Cairo on the eve of the US invasion of Iraq in March 2003, he declared, "Even if such terrible abstractions as national interest, national unity, and national security are affirmed as being more important than individual rights, I don't think they are; I think exactly the opposite."[56] In effect, he was reaffirming the hierarchy of rights defended by Charles Malik half a century earlier.

Malik believed that of all the nations of the Middle East, Lebanon was uniquely devoted to the rights of the individual. Just before Christmas 1980, the Lebanese Front—the political leadership of the Christian mini-state that formed after the outbreak of civil war in 1975—issued a manifesto entitled "The Lebanon We Want To Build." It was signed by, among others, Camille Chamoun, Pierre Gemayel, and Charles Malik, its primary author. "In the determination of the principles of its existence," the Front promised, "Lebanon will be guided by the terms of the Universal Declaration of Human Rights, especially with regard to the fundamental rights and freedoms of man." In the same document, however, the Front declared its opposition to the settlement of Palestinians in Lebanon, calling for the abrogation of land sales to Palestinians as well as the illegal acquisition of Lebanese citizenship.[57] The question is whether such state actions would have violated the UDHR. Article 14 specifies that "everyone has the right to seek and to enjoy in other countries asylum from persecution." Article 15 states that "everyone has the right to a nationality," and Article 17 that "everyone has the right to own property." The UDHR does not distinguish between nationals and resident aliens, but the United Nations Declaration on the Human Rights of Individuals Who are not Nationals of the Country in which They Live (1985) asserts the right of aliens to own property, "subject to domestic law."[58]

It was the apparent contradiction between Malik's belief in universal human rights and his sectarian understanding of Lebanese national identity that Edward Said found so perplexing. It was not that Malik denied that the Palestinians had human rights. It was that, in the context of Lebanon, the granting of equal rights to the Palestinians, including citizenship, would have meant the end of Lebanon's confessional political system, which ensured the minority Christians a disproportionate share of political power. The same sectarian logic dictated the Israeli denial of citizenship to the residents of Gaza and the West Bank, which would mean the beginning of the end of the Jewish state. As far as Said was concerned, it was religion that was the bane of the Palestinians—Judaism in Israel, Christianity in Lebanon, Islam in Gaza. What the Palestinians needed, he believed, was a secular state—if not one they could share with the Israelis, then one of their own. Unfortunately, what they got instead was a "National Authority" with an established religion. Article 4 of the Basic Law of the Palestinian Authority states that "Islam is the official religion in Palestine" and that "the principles of Islamic *Sharia* shall be a principal source of legislation."[59] Although the Basic Law also guarantees freedom of worship to adherents of other faiths, Said had no desire to live in such a state.

Said would also be alarmed by the current state of human rights in the United States, where Christian human rights are on the verge of a surprising revival. In July 2019, Secretary of State Mike Pompeo, an evangelical Christian, announced that Mary Ann Glendon would chair a new Commission on Unalienable Rights whose purpose is to advise the secretary on "international human rights matters" and to "provide fresh thinking about human rights discourse where such discourse has departed from our nation's founding principles of natural law and natural rights."[60] Certainly Charles Malik, as a follower of Aristotle and Aquinas, believed in natural law and natural rights, to which positive law and declarations of rights ought to conform. And he would have agreed that contemporary rights discourse has departed from the natural law tradition. The practice of abortion, for example, was to his mind a violation of the natural right to life of all humans, including the unborn. That is why he had proposed to insert the phrase "from the moment of conception" into the right to life article of the UDHR.[61] And he was appalled by the decision of some universities, in the 1980s, to include "sexual orientation" in their nondiscrimination statements.[62] It remains to be seen whether Pompeo and Glendon, who share Malik's conservative moral opinions, will succeed in bringing US human rights policy back into line with Catholic and Evangelical teaching.

Notes

Introduction

1 Edward W. Said, *Out of Place* (New York: Alfred A. Knopf, 1999), 265-6.
2 Ibid., 264.
3 Ibid., 265.
4 Ibid., 267.
5 Ibid., 265.
6 Ibid., 280.
7 Ibid., 268.
8 Ibid.
9 Stephen B. L. Penrose, Jr., *That They May Have Life: The Story of the American University of Beirut, 1866-1941* (Princeton: Princeton University Press, 1941), 13.
10 Brian VanDeMark, *American Sheikhs: Two Families, Four Generations, and the Story of America's Influence in the Middle East* (Amherst and New York: Prometheus Books, 2012), 79.
11 *Foreign Relations of the United States: The Paris Peace Conference, 1919* (Washington: US Government Printing Office, 1946), Vol. 11, 66-7.
12 Joseph L. Grabill, *Protestant Diplomacy and the Near East: Missionary Influence on American Policy, 1810-1927* (Minneapolis: University of Minnesota Press, 1971), 83.
13 Makram Rabah, *A Campus at War: Student Politics at the American University of Beirut, 1967-1975* (Beirut: Dar Nelson, 2009), 23-4.
14 Philip J. Baram, *The Department of State in the Middle East, 1919-1945* (Philadelphia: University of Pennsylvania Press, 1978), 130.
15 Stephen C. Schlesinger, *Act of Creation: The Founding of the United Nations* (Boulder: Westview Press, 2003), 201.
16 Irene L. Gendzier, *Notes from the Minefield: United States Intervention in Lebanon and the Middle East, 1945-1958* (New York: Columbia University Press, 2006), 304-10.
17 Rabah, *Campus*, 105-6.
18 Zeev Schiff and Ehud Yaari, *Israel's Lebanon War*, ed. and trans. Ina Friedman (New York: Simon and Schuster, 1984).
19 Bob Woodward, *Veil: The Secret Wars of the CIA, 1981-1987* (New York: Simon and Schuster, 1987).
20 Moshe Arens, *In Defense of Israel* (Washington: Brookings Institution Press, 2018), 76. Ambassador Arens, who was in the room with Haig and Sharon, maintains that Haig opposed Sharon's military plans.
21 Schiff and Yaari, *Israel's Lebanon War*, 230-2.
22 Hugh Wilford, *America's Great Game: The CIA's Secret Arabists and the Shaping of the Modern Middle East* (New York: Basic Books, 2013), 139.
23 Matthew F. Holland, *America and Egypt: From Roosevelt to Eisenhower* (Westport, CT: Praeger, 1996), Chapter 3.

24 John S. Badeau, interview by Dennis J. O'Brien, February 25, 1969, John F. Kennedy Presidential Library, https://archive1.jfklibrary.org/JFKOH/Badeau,%20John%20S/JFKOH-JSB-01/JFKOH-JSB-01-TR.pdf.
25 Patrick Tyler, *A World of Trouble: The White House and the Middle East from the Cold War to the War on Terror* (New York: Farrar Strauss Giroux, 2009), 64–106.
26 Avi Shlaim, *Lion of Jordan: The Life of King Hussein in War and Peace* (New York: Alfred A. Knopf, 2008), 328–9.
27 Edward W. Said, *The Politics of Dispossession: The Struggle for Palestinian Self-Determination, 1969-1994* (New York: Vintage Books, 1994), xxi–xxii.
28 Ibid., 145–51.
29 Edward W. Said, *Peace and Its Discontents* (New York: Vintage Books, 1996), xxviii, 7.
30 Charles H. Malik, "The World Promise of America," *Vital Speeches of the Day* 47, no. 17 (June 15, 1981): 538.
31 Mary Ann Glendon, *A World Made New: Eleanor Roosevelt and the Universal Declaration of Human Rights* (New York: Random House, 2001).
32 Glenn Mitoma, "Charles H. Malik and Human Rights: Notes on a Biography," *Biography* 33, no. 1 (Winter 2010): 222–41.

Chapter 1

1 "People of Bterram," accessed September 14, 2019, http://www.bterram.com/people.html.
2 Charles Malik, "A Near Eastern Witness to Christian Missions," *Theology Today* 5, no. 4 (1949): 527–32.
3 Donald M. Reid, *The Odyssey of Farah Antun* (Minneapolis: Bibliotheca Islamica, 1975).
4 Beth Baron, *The Women's Awakening in Egypt* (New Haven: Yale University Press, 1997), 25–6.
5 Afif I. Tannous, *Village Roots and Beyond* (Beirut: Dar Nelson, 2004), 94.
6 Daniel B. Leavitt, *Cogwheeling with History* (Jaffrey, NH: Savron Graphics, 2000), 141–2.
7 William Nesbitt Chambers, *Yoljuluk: Random Thoughts on a Life in Imperial Turkey* (London: Simpkin, Marshall Ltd., 1928).
8 Laurens Hickok Seelye, "An Experiment in Religious Association," *Journal of Religion* 2, no. 3 (May 1922): 309.
9 *Students Union Gazette*, Christmas Issue 1927, 17, http://ddc.aub.edu.lb/projects/jafet/gazette/1927/.
10 Ibid., 23.
11 Yoram Kahati, "The Role of Education in the Development of Arab Nationalism in the Fertile Crescent during the 1920s," in *Political Thought and Political History: Studies in Memory of Elie Kedourie*, ed. Moshe Gammer (London: Frank Cass, 2003), 25.
12 "Outspoken Arab Orator: Ahmad Shukairy," *New York Times*, November 5, 1960, 4.
13 Wadad Khuri Mackdisi to Charles Malik, March 20, 1928, Box 52, Folder 7, Charles Habib Malik Papers, 1888-1994, Manuscript Division, Library of Congress.
14 Wadad Makdisi Cortas, *A World I Loved* (New York: Nation Books, 2009), 46.
15 "Dr. Malik," *New Yorker*, December 9, 1950, 32.

16 *YMCA Cairo Central Branch Annual Report 1930*, Box 8, Cairo Central Branch Annual Reports, 1929–31, YMCA International Work in Egypt, Kautz Family YMCA Archives, University of Minnesota.
17 Ibid.
18 James K. Quay, "Service in Egypt from 1919 to 1948," September 1975, Box 8, Cairo 1919–48, Kautz Archives.
19 *YMCA Cairo Central Branch Annual Report 1931*, Box 8, Cairo Central Branch Annual Reports, 1929–31, Kautz Archives.
20 Heather J. Sharkey, *American Evangelicals in Egypt: Missionary Encounters in an Age of Empire* (Princeton: Princeton University Press, 2008), 162.
21 Said, *Out*, 264.
22 A. J. Russell, *For Sinners Only* (London: Hodder and Stoughton, 1932), 339.
23 Ibid., 303.
24 "The New Bishop in Jerusalem," *London Times*, March 30, 1932, 13.
25 Malik, "Near Eastern Witness," 51.
26 Charles Malik, "An Appreciation of Professor Whitehead," *The Journal of Philosophy* 45, no. 21 (1948): 573.
27 Bertrand Russell to Charles Malik, January 26, 1932, Box 52, Folder 10, Malik Papers.
28 Ray Monk, *Bertrand Russell: The Spirit of Solitude, 1872-1921*, vol. 1 (New York: Free Press, 1996), 350.
29 Charles Malik to Laurens Seelye, February 17, 1932, Box 43, Folder 1, Malik Papers.
30 Charles Malik to Stephen Penrose, August 25, 1932, Box 52, Folder 11, Malik Papers.
31 Laurens Seelye to Charles Malik, August 31, 1932, Box 43, Folder 1, Malik Papers.
32 Charles Malik, "A Tribute to a Friend Departed," March 6, 1964, Box 223, Folder 3, Malik Papers.
33 "James Roosevelt Addresses 2000," *Boston Globe*, April 3, 1933, 16.
34 Malik, "An Appreciation," 573.
35 Donald Vandenberg, "Harry Broudy and Education for a Democratic Society," *Journal of Aesthetic Education* 26, no. 4 (Winter 1992): 5.
36 J. Seelye Bixler, *German Recollections* (Waterville: Colby College, 1985), 21.
37 William Ernest Hocking, "Palestine—An Impasse?" *Atlantic Monthly*, July 1930, 129.
38 "Failure of British Rule Foreseen in Palestine," *Harvard Crimson*, March 22, 1935, http://www.thecrimson.com/article/1935/3/22/failure-of-british-rule-foreseen-in/.
39 Daniel Sack, *Moral Re-armament: The Reinventions of an American Religious Movement* (New York: Palgrave Macmillan, 2009), 32–3.
40 Mitoma, "Charles H. Malik," 231.
41 "Five-Hour Session for Ford Hall Folk," *Boston Globe*, April 8, 1935, 3.
42 Charles H. Malik, "A Christian Reflection on Martin Heidegger," *Thomist* 41, no. 1 (1977): 7.
43 Charles Malik to William Ernest Hocking, February 1, 1936, Box 54, Folder 3, Malik Papers.
44 Glendon, *World*, 126.
45 Charles Malik to Laurens Seelye, October 7, 1936, Box 43, Folder 1, Malik Papers.
46 Howard Schomer, "In Homage to My Icons and Mentors," Outlook Club of Berkeley, February 20, 1992, bMS 551/23 (7b), Howard Schomer Papers, 1928–2001, Andover-Harvard Theological Library, Harvard Divinity School.
47 Allen W. Dulles to Charles Malik, March 10, 1937, Box 54, Folder 6, Malik Papers.

48 Report on Five-Year Stabilization Fund by Tamblyn and Brown, March 1938, Box 1, Folder 10, Near East College Association Records, Burke Library, Union Theological Seminary.
49 Makram Rabah, *A Campus at War: Student Politics at the American University of Beirut, 1967-1975* (Beirut: Dar Nelson, 2009), 24–5.
50 Todd Thompson, "Albert Hourani, Arab Christian Minorities and the Spiritual Dimension of Britain's Problem in Palestine, 1938-1947," in *Christians in the Middle East Conflict*, ed. Paul S. Rowe, John H. A. Dyck, and Jens Zimmermann (London: Routledge, 2014), 68–9.
51 Albert Hourani, "Patterns of the Past," in *Paths to the Middle East: Ten Scholars Look Back*, ed. Thomas Naff (Albany: SUNY Press, 1993), 31.
52 Charles Malik to Philosophy Circle, June 8, 1939, Box 56, Folder 1, Malik Papers.
53 *American University of Beirut Directory of Alumni, 1870-1952* (Beirut: Alumni Association, 1953).
54 Rosemary Sayigh, ed., *Yusif Sayigh: Arab Economist, Palestinian Patriot* (New York: American University of Cairo Press, 2015), 110.
55 Fouad Ajami, *The Dream Palace of the Arabs* (New York: Vintage, 1999), 53.
56 Salim Mujais, *Antoun Saadeh: A Biography*, vol. 2 (Beirut: Kutub, 2009), 111.
57 Sayigh, *Yusif Sayigh*, 111.
58 Kamal Maalouf Abu-Chaar, *Memoirs of Grandma Kamal* (Beirut: World Book Publishing, 1999), 94.
59 Charles Malik, "The Problem of Lebanon: An Interpretation," Box 1, File 1, Sir Iltyd Clayton Collection, Middle East Centre Archive, St. Antony's College, Oxford.
60 Howard Schomer, "Culture and Religion in the New Germany," April 1, 1938, bMS 551/3(18), Schomer Papers.
61 An English translation of Saadeh's letter can be found in Edmond Melhem, *Antun Saadeh: National Philosopher* (Beirut: Dar Fikr, 2010), 373–6.
62 Franck Salameh, *Language, Memory, and Identity in the Middle East: The Case for Lebanon* (Lanham: Lexington Books, 2010), 132.
63 Sayigh, *Yusif Sayigh*, 119–20.
64 Abu-Chaar, *Memoirs*, 94.
65 Sahar Hamouda and Colin Clement, eds., *Victoria College: A History Revealed* (Cairo: American University in Cairo Press, 2002), 89. Hamouda mistakes Charles Malik, whom Issawi did not name in his letter to Reed, for Albert Hourani.
66 Charles Malik to C. H. Barlow, April 25, 1939, Box 26, Folder 1, Malik Papers.
67 George Scherer to Charles Malik, May 29, 1939, Box 56, Folder 1, Malik Papers.
68 Labib Zuwiyya Yamak, *The Syrian Social Nationalist Party: An Ideological Analysis* (Cambridge: Center for Middle Eastern Studies, 1966), 60.
69 Thompson, "Albert," 74.
70 Michael E. Marmura, "George Fadlo Hourani," *Journal of the American Oriental Society* 105, no. 1 (1985): 3–6.
71 Cecil Hourani, *An Unfinished Odyssey* (London: Weidenfeld and Nicolson, 1984), 77.
72 Leslie Leavitt to Charles Malik, December 16, 1939, Box 56, Folder 4, Malik Papers.
73 Charles Malik to Costi Zurayk and Najla Cortas, December 30, 1939, Box 56, Folder 4, Malik Papers.
74 Sayigh, *Yusif Sayigh*, 123.
75 John McManus, "Feastday Speech for Brother Francis," *Mancipia: The Report of the Crusade of Saint Benedict Center*, November/December 2009, 4.

76 Hisham Sharabi, *Embers and Ashes: Memoirs of an Arab Intellectual*, trans. Issa J. Boullata (Northampton: Olive Branch Press, 2008), 55.
77 Baram, *The Department of State in the Middle East, 1919-1945*, 130.
78 Albert Hourani to Charles Malik, November 15, [1941], Box 57, Folder 7, Malik Papers.
79 George Said to Charles Malik, December 7, 1941, Box 57, Folder 7, Malik Papers.
80 Elsa Kerr to Charles and Eva Malik, July 27, 1941, Box 57, Folder 7, Malik Papers.
81 Hazem Zaki Nusseibeh, *Jerusalemites: A Living Memory* (Nicosia: Rimal Publications, 2009), 437.
82 Ibid., 93.
83 Enaya Hammad Othman, *Negotiating Palestine: Encounters between Palestinian Women and American Missionaries, 1880s-1940s* (Lanham: Lexington Books, 2016), 178.
84 Kamal B. Nasir to Dr. Charles Malik, August 7, 1942, Box 58, Folder 3, Malik Papers.
85 Kenneth Cragg, *Faith and Life Negotiate* (Norwich: Canterbury Press, 1994), 96–107.
86 Sayigh, *Yusif Sayigh*, 138.
87 George Said to Charles Malik, September 16, 1942, Box 53, Folder 4, Malik Papers.
88 Monty Noam Penkower, *Decision on Palestine Deferred: America, Britain, and Wartime Diplomacy, 1939-1945* (Abingdon: Routledge, 2013), 149.
89 Notes, November 14, 1942 to March 1, 1943, Box 5, Harold B. Hoskins Papers, 1822–1982, Public Policy Papers, Department of Rare Books and Special Collections, Princeton University Library.
90 Osamah F. Khalil, *America's Dream Palace: Middle East Expertise and the Rise of the National Security State* (Cambridge: Harvard University Press, 2016), 118.
91 Notes, November 14, 1942 to March 1, 1943, Box 5, Hoskins Papers.
92 Meir Zamir, *The Secret Anglo-French War in the Middle East: Intelligence and Decolonization, 1940-1948* (Abingdon: Routledge, 2015), 37.
93 Khalil, *America's Dream*, 119.
94 Shlomo Aronson, *Hitler, the Allies, and the Jews* (Cambridge: Cambridge University Press, 2004), 98–9.
95 Wilford, *America's Great Game*, 36.
96 Albert Hourani, "Great Britain and Arab Nationalism," *Islamic Movements in the Arab World, 1913-1966*, vol. 3, ed. Anita L. P. Burdett (London: Archive Editions, 1998), 411, 449.
97 Malik, "Problem," Part 1.
98 Ibid., Part 2.
99 Sir Edward Spears, *Fulfilment of a Mission* (London: Archon Books, 1977), 237.
100 Mary Borden, *Journey Down a Blind Alley* (New York: Harper, 1946), 307.
101 Charles Malik to Brigadier I. N. Clayton, January 11, 1944, Box 1, Folder 1, Clayton Collection.
102 Charles Malik to Brigadier I. N. Clayton, March 22, 1944, Box 1, Folder 1, Clayton Collection.
103 Cecil Hourani to Charles Malik, March 21, 1944, Box 21, Folder 4, Malik Papers.
104 Charles Malik to George Said, April 19, 1944, Box 58, Folder 10, Malik Papers.
105 Charles H. Malik, "Freedom of Thought," May 1944, Box 208, Folder 4, Malik Papers.
106 Cecil Hourani, *Unfinished*, 45. Tragically, Kraus would hang himself in the flat that fall, leaving his body to be discovered by the Houranis.

107 "The Idea of an Arab Academy," Box 59, Folder 3, Malik Papers.
108 Charles Malik to George Said, August 7, 1944, Box 44, Folder 10, Malik Papers.
109 Zamir, *Secret*, 85.
110 Glendon, *World*, 126–7.
111 Bertram Thomas to Charles Malik, December 24, 1944, Box 109, Folder 2, Malik Papers.
112 Charles Malik to Bertram Thomas, February 8, 1945, Box 109, Folder 2, Malik Papers.
113 Zamir, *Secret*, 119.
114 "Syria and Lebanon Get U. S. Minister," *New York Times*, September 20, 1944, 11.
115 "Wants Syria, Lebanon at Parley," *New York Times*, March 16, 1945, 8.
116 Hani J. Bawardi, *The Making of Arab Americans: From Syrian Nationalism to U.S. Citizenship* (Austin: University of Texas Press, 2014), 249.
117 Kamal S. Salibi, "Recollections of Lebanon in the 1940s and 1950s," *Bulletin of the Royal Institute for Inter-Faith Studies* 5, no. 2 (Autumn/Winter 2003): 126.
118 E. J. Kahn, "Talk of the Town," *New Yorker*, December 9, 1950, 33.

Chapter 2

1 Sharabi, *Embers and Ashes*, 25.
2 Laura Z. Eisenberg, *My Enemy's Enemy: Lebanon in the Early Zionist Imagination, 1900-1948* (Detroit: Wayne State University Press, 1994), 198.
3 "Dulles Drops Duties with Just-Peace Unit," *New York Times*, April 12, 1945, 12.
4 Schlesinger, *Act of Creation*, 166.
5 Virginia Crocheron Gildersleeve, *Many a Good Crusade* (New York: Macmillan, 1954), 333.
6 Eliahu Elath, *Zionism at the UN* (Philadelphia: Jewish Publication Society of America, 1976), 98–9.
7 Charles Malik to William Ernest Hocking, October 8, 1945, Box 20, Folder 12, Malik Papers.
8 *FRUS*, 1945, Vol. 8, 766–9.
9 Avery Dulles, "Leonard Feeney: In Memoriam," *America*, February 25, 1978, http://www.americamagazine.org/content/article.cfm?article_id=10724.
10 Fakhri Malouf to Charles Malik, January 1, 1946, Box 33, Folder 9, Malik Papers.
11 "In Memoriam," AUB *MainGate*, Summer 2004, http://www.wwwlb.aub.edu.lb/~webmgate/summer04/in_memoriam.html.
12 "Arab Envoys Affirm Palestine Defiance," *New York Times*, May 3, 1946, 3.
13 C. A. Hourani, Letter to the Editor, *New York Times*, May 8, 1946, 24.
14 "U.S. Assures Arabs of Consultation," *New York Times*, May 11, 1946, 10.
15 "United Nations: Progress Report," *Time*, November 18, 1946, 32.
16 "Unesco Gets Classics," *New York Times*, December 6, 1946, 18.
17 *Guide to the Stephen B. L. Penrose, Jr. Papers, 1908-1990*, http://archiveswest.orbiscascade.org/ark:/80444/xv75253/pdf.
18 Glendon, *World*, 33.
19 Ibid., 39–40.
20 Sharabi, *Embers*, 50–3.
21 "Near Eastern Culture and Society," *Princeton Alumni Weekly*, March 21, 1947, 7.

22 *Near Eastern Culture and Society* (Princeton: Princeton University, 1947), 26–7.
23 Glendon, *World*, 53, 69–70.
24 *FRUS*, 1947, Vol. 5, 1176–7.
25 Michael J. Cohen, "William A. Eddy, the Oil Lobby and the Palestine Problem," *Middle Eastern Studies* 30, no. 1 (1994): 168.
26 Robert Vitalis, *America's Kingdom: Mythmaking on the Saudi Oil Frontier* (Palo Alto: Stanford University Press, 2006), is convinced that Eddy was CIA. Thomas W. Lippman, *Arabian Knight: Colonel Bill Eddy USMC and the Rise of American Power in the Middle East* (Vista, CA: Selwa Press, 2008) is more circumspect, quoting friends and relatives who insisted that Eddy was never on the CIA's payroll.
27 "Partition Called Fair," *New York Times*, November 17, 1947, 19.
28 "Questions Put to Dr. Charles Malik, Minister of Lebanon in the United States, by Mrs. Franklin D. Roosevelt on the American Broadcasting System's 'World Security Workshop' program from New York on Sunday, November 16, 1947, at 12:30–1:00 P.M., EST," Box 209, Folder 5, Malik Papers.
29 Howard Schomer, "From 'Just War' to 'Just Peace': CPS and War Resistance Among Congregationalists," *Mennonite Quarterly Review* 66, no. 4 (October 1992): 610.
30 Glendon, *World*, 89.
31 Charles Malik to Costi Zurayk, April 9, 1948, Box 52, Folder 3, Malik Papers.
32 Charles Malik to Stephen Penrose, February 23, 1949, Box 119, Folder 3, Malik Papers.
33 Cecil Hourani, *Unfinished*, 61.
34 Gildersleeve, *Many*, 409.
35 Jack Werkley, "New Committee Opposes U.N.'s Palestine Plan," *New York Herald Tribune*, March 3, 1948.
36 Wilford, *America's Great Game*, 91–2.
37 "Statement Made by Dr. Charles Malik, Representative of Lebanon, in the Second Special Session of the General Assembly, in the Political and Security Committee, on April 23, 1948," Box 209, Folder 7, Malik Papers.
38 Sasson Sofer, *Zionism and the Foundations of Israeli Diplomacy* (Cambridge: Cambridge University Press, 1998), Chapter 18.
39 "Excerpts from Plea by Lebanese Delegate," *New York Times*, May 29, 1948, 3.
40 Hannah Arendt, "Peace or Armistice in the Middle East?" *Review of Politics* 12, no. 1 (1950): 72–3.
41 Gendzier, *Notes*, 78.
42 Tom Segev and Haim Watzman, *A State at Any Cost: The Life of David Ben-Gurion* (New York: FSG, 2019), 313.
43 G. Ruffer to M. Shertok, May 29, 1948, *Documents on the Foreign Policy of Israel*, ed. Yehoshua Freundlich, vol. 1 (Jerusalem: Israel State Archives, 1981), 98.
44 Glendon, *World*, 119–20.
45 Ibid., 149–53.
46 William Ernest Hocking to Charles Malik, March 21, 1949, Box 40, Folder 12, Malik Papers.
47 See Archie Roosevelt, *For Lust of Knowing: Memoirs of an Intelligence Officer* (Boston: Little, Brown, 1988), Chapter 22.
48 Wilford, *America's Great Game*, 115–16.
49 Eyal Zisser, *Lebanon: The Challenge of Independence* (London: I. B. Tauris, 2000), 168–9.
50 Avi Shlaim, "Husni Zaim and the Plan to Resettle Palestinian Refugees in Syria," *Journal of Palestine Studies* 15, no. 4 (1986): 31–2.

51 Wilford, *America's Great Game*, 99–109.
52 "Excerpts from Statements by Malik and Eban on Israel's Membership Application to the U.N.," *New York Times*, May 6, 1949, 14.
53 Prior to the admission of Ireland and Italy in December 1955, the Israeli ambassador sat between Iraq and Lebanon on the floor of the General Assembly.
54 Hisham Sharabi to Charles Malik, May 28, 1949, Box 43, Folder 6, Malik Papers.
55 Sharabi, *Embers*, 140–81.
56 Arthur Szathmary to Charles Malik, August 6, 1949, Box 174, Folder 2, Malik Papers.
57 Albion Ross, "Grant Aids Study of Modern Arabs," *New York Times*, July 1, 1949, 8.
58 Dr. Charles Malik, *War and Peace* (New York: National Committee for A Free Europe, n.d.), 25.
59 "Shift to Offensive in 'Cold War' Urged," *New York Times*, December 14, 1949, 3.
60 Charles Malik, "The Cultural Aspects of International Cooperation," Box 211, Folder 3, Malik Papers.
61 William Y. Elliott to Charles Malik, January 10, 1950, Box 150, Folder 4, Malik Papers.
62 Sigmund Diamond, *Compromised Campus: The Collaboration of Universities with the Intelligence Community, 1945-1955* (New York: Oxford University Press, 1992), 145.
63 *FRUS*, 1950, Vol. 5, 1100–6.
64 Charles Malik, "The Near East Between East and West," in *The Near East and the Great Powers*, ed. Richard N. Frye (Port Washington: Kennikat Press, 1969), 22–3.
65 Eleanor Roosevelt to President Truman, May 27, 1951, Harry S. Truman Presidential Library, http://www.trumanlibrary.org/eleanor/1951.html.
66 Wilford, *America's Great Game*, 136.
67 Cornelius Van H. Engert to Charles Malik, June 24, 1951, Box 101, Folder 4, Malik Papers.
68 Wilford, *America's Great Game*, 118–21.
69 Charles Malik, "A New Dawn in the East," *Vital Speeches of the Day* 18, no. 1 (October 1, 1951): 29–32.
70 Charles Malik, interview by R. Bayly Winder, August, 27, 1964, Box 3, John Foster Dulles Oral History Collection, 1964–1967, Public Policy Papers, Department of Rare Books and Special Collections, Princeton University Library.
71 Charles Malik, "The Near East: The Search for Truth," *Foreign Affairs* 30, no. 2 (January 1952): 257–9.
72 Charles Malik, "From a Friend of the West," *Life*, March 31, 1952, 59–60.
73 Charles Malik to Nelson Rockefeller, July 12, 1950, Box 39, Folder 6, Malik Papers.
74 Dr. Charles Malik, Untitled Statement, *World Neighbors: Working Together for Peace and Plenty* (Washington: n.p., 1952), 24.
75 Zisser, *Challenge*, 237.
76 *FRUS*, 1952–1954, Vol. 9, 1001–2.
77 Charles Malik to John Shope, Executive Secretary of AFME, October 13, 1952, Box 101, Folder 4, Malik Papers.
78 Edward L. R. Elson, *Wide Was His Parish* (Wheaton, Illinois: Tyndale House, 1986), 75.
79 Charles Malik, "Middle Eastern-American Relations," *Proceedings of the First Annual Conference of the American Friends of the Middle East, Inc.* (New York: AFME, 1953), 106–8.
80 Charles Malik, "The Historic Moment," *Harvard Alumni Bulletin*, July 5, 1953, 768.
81 Charles Malik, "Facing the Future: Some Issues for Americans," *Virginia Quarterly Review* 30, no. 2 (1954): 165–7.

82 Zachary Karabell, *Architects of Intervention: The United States, the Third World, and the Cold War, 1946-1962* (Baton Rouge: LSU Press, 1999), 154–5.
83 Charles Malik, Speech on the Missionary Movement in the Middle East, December 4, 1953, Box 215, Folder 1, Malik Papers.
84 Raymond Close, "Hard Target," *Washington Post*, August 30, 1998, C1.
85 Charles Malik, Appointment Calendar, February 26, 1954, Box 262, Folder 4, Malik Papers.
86 Wilford, *America's Great Game*, 115–16.
87 Costi Zurayk to Charles Malik, December 14, 1954, Box 52, Folder 3, Malik Papers.
88 Albert Hourani to Eva Malik, January 23, 1955, Box 61, Folder 2, Malik Papers.
89 *World-Wide Spiritual Offensive: Addresses Given at a Joint Meeting of National Religious Broadcasters, Inc. and International Christian Leadership, Inc., Mayflower Hotel, Washington, D.C., February 3–4, 1955* (National Religious Broadcasters, 1955).
90 "Dedicatory Prayer Breakfast," 101 *Congressional Record* 1212 (February 4, 1955).
91 *FRUS*, 1955–57, Vol. 13, 172.
92 Ibid., 27.
93 Wilbur Crane Eveland, *Ropes of Sand: America's Failure in the Middle East* (New York: Norton, 1980), 124.
94 *FRUS*, 1955–57, Vol. 21, 82–4.
95 Roland Burke, *Decolonization and the Evolution of International Human Rights* (Philadelphia: University of Pennsylvania Press, 2010), 20–5.
96 Mohammed Fadhel Jamali, "Experiences in Arab Affairs 1943-1958," http://phys4.harvard.edu/~wilson/Fadhel.html.
97 *FRUS*, 1955–57, Vol. 21, 95–8.
98 Bonnie F. Saunders, *The United States and Arab Nationalism: The Syrian Case, 1953-1960* (Westport: Praeger, 1996), 44.
99 Charles Malik, Appointment Calendar, May 1955, Box 262, Folder 4, Malik Papers.
100 Eveland, *Ropes*, 113–14.
101 Andrew Rathmell, *Secret War in the Middle East: The Covert Struggle for Syria, 1949-1961* (London: I.B. Tauris, 1995), 99–100.
102 Secretary Dulles, "The Middle East," *Department of State Bulletin*, September 5, 1955, 378–80.
103 Harold Hoskins to Secretary of State, January 10, 1957, Box 2, Folder 9, Hoskins Papers.
104 "Maliks Honored," *Washington Post*, August 31, 1955, p. 54.
105 Cary Reich, *The Life of Nelson A. Rockefeller: Worlds to Conquer, 1908-1958* (New York: Doubleday, 1996), 559.
106 Nelson Rockefeller to Charles Malik, September 20, 1955, Box 39, Folder 6, Malik Papers.
107 Bayard Dodge, *American University of Beirut* (Beirut: Khayat's, 1958), 102.
108 Dana Adams Schmidt, "40 Colleges Join U.S. Technical Aid to 26 Countries," *New York Times*, October 18, 1954, 1.
109 Cabell Phillips, "The Super-Cabinet for Our Security," *New York Times Sunday Magazine*, April 4, 1954, 14.
110 Charles Malik, Speech at Al Kataib Party Annual Convention, Beirut, November 20, 1955, Box 216, Folder 3, Malik Papers.
111 "Memorial Service," *al kulliyah*, January 1956, 6.
112 Charles H. Malik, "What One Learns," *Middle East Forum* 31 (February 1956): 14–15.
113 Samuel P. Huntington, *The Clash of Civilizations and the Remaking of World Order* (New York: Simon and Schuster, 1996).

114 William Eddy to Cita, March 25, 1956, Box 6, Folder 6, William Alfred Eddy Papers, 1859-1978, Public Policy Papers, Department of Rare Books and Special Collections, Princeton University Library.
115 Carl Bernstein, "The CIA and the Media," *Rolling Stone*, October 20, 1977, 55-67.
116 In *Out of Place*, Edward named Sam's father Philip, an AUB alumnus, as a bridge-playing friend of Wadie Said's. For Sam's alleged CIA connection, see Eveland, *Ropes*, 165.
117 Philip Wylie, *The Innocent Ambassadors* (New York: Rinehart, 1957). To conceal his identity, Wylie referred to Fistere as "Doc."
118 Caroline Attie, *Struggle in the Levant: Lebanon in the 1950s* (London: I.B. Tauris, 2004), 107.
119 Francis Kettaneh to Allen W. Dulles, April 20, 1955, Freedom of Information Act Reading Room, Central Intelligence Agency, http://www.foia.cia.gov/sites/default/files/document_conversions/5829/CIA-RDP80R01731R000500540002-0.pdf.
120 Charles Malik, "Call to Action in the Near East," *Foreign Affairs* 34, no. 4 (1956), 638.
121 Ibid., 652.
122 Michael Doran, *Ike's Gamble: America's Rise to Dominance in the Middle East* (New York: Free Press, 2016), 168.
123 *FRUS*, 1955-57, Vol. 16, 184-5.
124 Gendzier, *Notes*, 214-15.
125 John Fistere to Charles Malik, December 5, 1956, Box 16, Folder 9, Malik Papers.
126 Alwyn Van der Merwe, ed., *Old and New Questions in Physics: Essays in Honor of Wolfgang Yourgrau* (New York: Plenum Press, 1983), 20.
127 Kai Bird, *Crossing Mandelbaum Gate* (New York: Scribner, 2010), 280.
128 "Lebanese in Paris," *New York Times*, January 12, 1957, 6.
129 Eveland, *Ropes*, 242.
130 *FRUS*, 1955-57, Vol. 13, 200-3.
131 Eveland, *Ropes*, 227.
132 Sam Pope Brewer, "U.S., Britain and France Linked by Syrian Lawyer to Conspiracy," *New York Times*, February 2, 1957, 3.
133 "The Eisenhower Doctrine, 1957," Office of the Historian, US Department of State, https://history.state.gov/milestones/1953-1960/eisenhower-doctrine.
134 "United States Policy in the Middle East," February 14, 1957, Council on Foreign Relations Digital Sound Recordings, Box 733, Public Policy Papers, Department of Rare Books and Special Collections, Princeton University Library.
135 Charles Malik, Appointment Calendar, April 1957, Box 263, Folder 4, Malik Papers.
136 Eveland, *Ropes*, 249-50.
137 Ibid., 251-2.
138 Joseph Alsop, "Evening with Charles Malick [sic]," *Washington Post*, June 7, 1957, A21.
139 "Lebanese Editor Set at Liberty," *Times*, July 22, 1957, 6.
140 Norman Polmar and Thomas B. Allen, *Spy Book: The Encyclopedia of Espionage* (New York: Random House, 1998), 169.
141 Said Taky Deen, *Bridge Under the Water* (Beirut: n.p., 1957), 15-19.
142 Alexander Cockburn, *The Golden Age Is in Us: Journeys and Encounters* (London: Verso, 1996), 327.
143 *FRUS*, 1955-1957, Vol. 13, 712-13.
144 Tyler Abell, ed., *Drew Pearson Diaries, 1949-1959* (New York: Holt Rinehart Winston, 1974), 393-4.
145 Sam Pope Brewer, "Lebanon Affirms Support of West," *New York Times*, November 27, 1957, 6.

146 Karabell, *Architects*, 160.
147 Attie, *Struggle*, 159, 179.
148 "Lebanese Mourn Murdered Editor," *New York Times*, May 10, 1958, 6.
149 Ray Close, "Swamp Speak: Then and Now," *Nieman Reports*, Summer 2007, http://www.nieman.harvard.edu/reportsitem.aspx?id=100222.
150 Erika Alin, "U.S. Policy and Military Intervention in the 1958 Lebanon Crisis," in *The Middle East and the United States*, ed. David W. Lesch, 3rd ed. (Boulder: Westview, 2003), 157.
151 "Army Moves in Tripoli," *New York Times*, May 31, 1958, 5.
152 "Lebanon Bids U.N. Check Incursions," *New York Times*, June 7, 1958, 1.
153 "U. N. May Receive Troop Plan Today," *New York Times*, July 15, 1958, 1.
154 Harry J. Almond, *Iraqi Statesman: A Portrait of Mohammed Fadhel Jamali* (Salem: Grosvener Books, 1993), 140–1. In fact, Jamali was in hiding. He was soon arrested and spent the next three years in prison.
155 Wilford, *America's Great Game*, 288.
156 Lippman, *Arabian Knight*, 283.
157 "Trouble-Shooter Murphy Sent by Ike to Beirut," *Boston Globe*, July 17, 1958, 1.
158 *FRUS*, 1958–1960, Vol. 11, 335.
159 John Fistere to Charles Malik, July 21, 1958, Box 16, Folder 9, Malik Papers.
160 Lippman, *Arabian Knight*, 284–5.
161 Sam Pope Brewer, "Lebanon Elects a New President," *New York Times*, August 1, 1958, 1.
162 "Beirut Rebel Here as U.N. 'Observer,'" *New York Times*, August 21, 1958, 9.
163 "Nixon Defends U.S. Policy," *New York Times*, September 7, 1958.
164 Charles H. Malik, "A Job for the Businessman," *Fortune*, November 1958, 120–1.
165 Eveland, *Ropes*, 303.
166 Jack O'Connell, *King's Counsel: A Memoir of War, Espionage, and Diplomacy in the Middle East* (New York: W. W. Norton, 2011), 14.
167 Michael James, "Malik and French Talk on Algeria," *New York Times*, October 31, 1958, 1–2.
168 Cecil Hourani to Charles Malik, April 3, 1958, Box 21, Folder 4, Malik Papers.
169 Charles Malik to Albert Hourani, January 5, 1959, Box 21, Folder 3, Malik Papers.
170 Baheej Malik to Charles Malik, January 15, 1959, Box 61, Folder 8, Malik Papers.
171 Miles Copeland, *The Game Player: The Confessions of the CIA's Original Political Operative* (London: Aurum, 1989), 111.
172 Charles Malik to McGeorge Bundy, February 27, 1959, Box 149, Folder 2, Malik Papers.
173 Brendan M. Jones, "Mideast Amity Marks Opening of Trade Fair Here," *New York Times*, May 9, 1959, 1.
174 "Malik Explains Picture at Fair," *New York Times*, May 11, 1959, 2.
175 "Lebanon Excludes Dr. Malik," *New York Times*, September 9, 1959, 15.

Chapter 3

1 Eva Malik to Charles Malik, February 17, 1960, Box 61, Folder 9, Malik Papers.
2 "Panel Offers Advice for President-To-Be," *Hartford Courant*, April 10, 1960, 1A.
3 Lyman B. Kirkpatrick, Jr., *The Real CIA* (London: Macmillan, 1968), 209.

4 Charles Malik, *Will the Future Redeem the Past?* (Richmond: Virginia Commission on Constitutional Government, 1960), 14, 19.
5 *Colonial Williamsburg: The President's Report* (Williamsburg: Colonial Williamsburg Foundation, 1960), 40.
6 Richard Nixon to Charles Malik, September 9, 1960, Box 473, Pre-Presidential Papers, General Correspondence, Series 320, Richard Nixon Presidential Library.
7 "New Leader Is Urged," *New York Times*, June 14, 1960, 40.
8 "Conference Studies U.S. Cultural Aid," *Harvard Crimson*, August 4, 1960, https://www.thecrimson.com/article/1960/8/4/conference-studies-us-cultural-aid-pa/.
9 Charles H. Malik, "The World Looks at the American Program," *Annals of the American Academy of Political and Social Science* 335 (1961): 140.
10 Charles Malik to John Case, November 19, 1960, Box 119, Folder 6, Malik Papers.
11 Hisham Sharabi to Charles Malik, November 17, 1960, Box 147, Folder 2, Malik Papers.
12 John M. Munro, *A Mutual Concern* (Delmar, NY: Caravan Books, 1977), 136.
13 On July 30, 1953, Charles dined with David Rockefeller in New York. The following day, he sent him a copy of the address he had delivered at Harvard that June. Charles Malik to David Rockefeller, July 31, 1953, Box 39, Folder 5, Malik Papers.
14 Charles Habib Malik, "The Individual in Modern Society," in *The One and the Many: The Individual in the Modern World*, ed. John Brooks (New York: Harper and Row, 1962), 135–56.
15 Adel Beshara, *Lebanon: The Politics of Frustration—The Failed Coup of 1961* (New York: Routledge, 2005), 127.
16 *FRUS*, 1961–3, Vol. 17, 449.
17 H. B. Sharabi, *Governments and Politics in the Middle East in the Twentieth Century* (Princeton: Van Nostrand, 1962), 137.
18 It is now located in the Centre for Palestine Studies at Columbia University.
19 Charles Habib Malik, *Man in the Struggle for Peace* (New York: Harper and Row, 1963), xiii, 230.
20 Leonard Binder, ed., *Politics in Lebanon* (New York: John Wiley and Sons, 1966), ix.
21 Sharabi, *Embers*, 32.
22 Malcolm Kerr, "Political Decision Making in a Confessional Democracy," in *Politics in Lebanon*, ed. Binder, 206.
23 Timothy Mitchell, "The Middle East and the Past and Future of Social Science," in *The Politics of Knowledge: Area Studies and the Disciplines*, ed. David L. Szanton (Berkeley: University of California Press, 2004), 88–9.
24 Manfred Halpern, *The Morality and Politics of Intervention* (New York: Council on Religion and International Affairs, 1963), 12.
25 Sadik Jalal al-Azm, *Ces Interdits Qui Nous Hantent* (Marseilles: Editiones Parentheses, 2008), 23–9.
26 *Proceedings of the CIOS XIII International Management Congress* (New York: Council for International Progress in Management, 1963).
27 Charles H. Malik, "Ideals for Export," *Harvard Business Review* 40, no. 1 (January–February 1964): 59.
28 Jack Raymond, "President to See Birmingham Team," *New York Times*, September 22, 1963, 71.
29 Charles Malik to Robert F. Kennedy, October 4, 1963, Box 26, Folder 4, Malik Papers.
30 Robert F. Kennedy, *Just Friends and Brave Enemies* (New York: Harper and Row, 1962), 13–14.

31 Hugh D. Auchincloss to John F. Kennedy, October 4, 1963, Papers of John F. Kennedy, Presidential Papers, President's Office Files, Special Correspondence, Auchincloss, Hugh D., Jr., March 1961–September 1963, John F. Kennedy Presidential Library.
32 Charles Malik, "The Struggle for Peace," *BYU Studies* 8, no. 4 (1968): 8.
33 Dr. Robert Hickson, "Father Malachi Martin's Visit to the Senate and Our Lady of Fatima," May 16, 2016, http://catholicism.org/father-malachi-martin-and-our-lady-of-fatima.html. Hickson heard this story from Fakhri Maalouf, who heard it from Malik himself.
34 "The Meeting of Pope Paul VI and Ecumenical Patriarch Athenagoras in Jerusalem, Jan. 5–6, 1964," YouTube video, posted by the Greek Orthodox Archdiocese of America, https://www.youtube.com/watch?v=4DuNJ9g4RFA.
35 Nixon's Handwritten Notes, Box 4, Trip File, Asia Trip 1964, Wilderness Years Series II, Richard Nixon Presidential Library.
36 *The Conservative Papers* (New York: Doubleday-Anchor, 1964), vii.
37 Winston W. Ehrmann and Jordan E. Kurland, 'Academic Freedom and Tenure: Two Cases of Excessive Probation,' *AAUP Bulletin*, vol. 52, no. 1 (Mar. 1966), 40.
38 Julius Duscha, "President Rebukes Alliance Alarmists," *Washington Post*, December 4, 1964, 1.
39 Charles Malik, "The Metaphysics of Freedom," in *Freedom and Man*, ed. John Courtney Murray (New York: P. J. Kennedy and Sons, 1965), 196.
40 Peter C. Moore, ed., *Youth in Crisis* (New York: Seabury Press, 1966), 21, 47.
41 Charles Malik, "Reflections on the Great Society," *Saturday Review*, August 6, 1966, 14.
42 Charles Malik to Courtney Brown, March 18, 1966, Box 138, Folder 3, Malik Papers.
43 Ashbel Green, ed., *My Columbia: Reminiscences of University Life* (New York: Columbia University, 2005), 361.
44 Thomas F. Brady, "Problems Plaguing American University of Beirut," *New York Times*, June 28, 1966, 6.
45 Charles Malik to W. W. Rostow, September 10, 1966, Box 184, Folder 5, Malik Papers.
46 Jonathan V. Marshall, *The Lebanese Connection: Corruption, Civil War, and the International Drug Traffic* (Stanford: Stanford University Press, 2012), 54–5.
47 Hisham Sharabi, "The Transformation of Ideology in the Arab World," in *A Middle East Reader*, ed. Irene L. Gendzier (New York: Pegasus, 1969), 87–8.
48 Charles Malik to Hisham Sharabi, August 2, 1966, Box 43, Folder 5, Malik Papers.
49 Hans Küng, *Disputed Truth: Memoirs II* (London: Continuum, 2007), 33–4.
50 "University Professor in Beirut Leaves Lebanon as Aquinas Text Stirs Dispute," *New York Times*, March 20, 1966.
51 Dr. Charles Habib Malik, "Faith, Truth, Freedom," in *Addresses Delivered at the Centennial Day Convocation, December 3, 1966* (Beirut: AUB, 1966), 14.
52 Tex DeAtkine, "Great Days in Beirut and the American University of Beirut," January 19, 2013, http://memoriesandreflections.wordpress.com/2013/01/19/great-days-in-beirut-and-the-american-university-of-beirut/.
53 David Egee, *Wake Up Running* (Bayside, CA: Editons Tilleul, 2014).
54 S. M., "Speak History," AUB *MainGate*, Summer 2010, 46–9.
55 Joseph J. Malone, "A Hundred Years of Change and Progress," in *Addresses Delivered*, 26–7.
56 Thomas F. Brady, "American University of Beirut Marks 100th Year," *New York Times*, December 4, 1966, 2.
57 Charles Malik to Doug Coe, January 30, 1967, Box 10, Folder 10, Malik Papers.

58 "Address by Charles Habib Malik at the American University of Beirut," 113 *Congressional Record* S7488 (March 21, 1967).
59 Fouad Ajami, *The Vanished Imam: Musa Al Sadr and the Shia of Lebanon* (Ithaca: Cornell University Press, 1986), 113–14.
60 Here I rely on Malik's summary of Sadr's paper in his introduction to the conference proceedings, *God and Man in Contemporary Islamic Thought*, ed. Charles Malik (Beirut: AUB, 1972), 79–83.
61 Sadik J. al-Azm, "Scientific Culture and the Poverty of Religious Thought," *Critique of Religious Thought*, trans. George Stergios and Mansour Ajami (Berlin: Gerlach Press, 2015), 17–75.
62 Azm, *Ces Interdits*, 42.
63 Ibid., 42–3.
64 Munro, *Mutual*, 160.
65 "A 20-Year Story," *Near East Report Special Survey*, October 1964, B13–B22.
66 "Heard in Washington," *Near East Report*, May 2, 1967, 35–6.
67 Visser 't Hooft, "The Contemporary Church," in *God and Man in Contemporary Christian Thought*, ed. Charles Malik (Beirut: American University of Beirut, 1970), 10.
68 Hans Küng, "The Church and Sincerity," ibid., 38–54.
69 John Wild, "Philosophy and Christian Faith in an Age of Science," ibid., 65–77.
70 Sadik al-Azm, "Analysis and Critique of A.U.B.'s Centennial Symposium on God and Man in Contemporary Christian Thought," May 19, 1967, Box 184, Folder 8, Malik Papers.
71 "About His Eminence," accessed December 12, 2006, http://www.metropolitanphilip.com/book/export/html/198.
72 Malik, "Struggle for Peace," 8.
73 "Alte Kameraden," *Der Spiegel*, July 31, 1967, 71.
74 "Closer Ties for Catholic, East Orthodox Group Seen," *Washington Post*, April 6, 1968, E10.
75 Lyndon B. Johnson, "Remarks at the Presidential Prayer Breakfast," February 1, 1968, American Presidency Project, University of California, Santa Barbara, http://www.presidency.ucsb.edu/ws/?pid=29060.
76 For Adair's reference to Charles' visit to Washington, see *The Foreign Assistance Act of 1968* (Washington: U.S. Government Printing Office, 1968), 259.
77 Sadik al-Azm, *Self-Criticism After the Defeat*, trans. George Stergios (London: Saqi, 2011), 111.
78 Munro, *Mutual*, 160–1.
79 "Arabs Hope Nixon Will Bring Change," *New York Times*, November 8, 1968, 23.
80 Charles Malik to Richard M. Nixon, December 2, 1968, Box 42, Folder 1, White House Special Files Collection, Richard Nixon Presidential Library. The handwritten annotations on the letter indicate that H. R. Haldeman, Nixon's chief of staff, asked him to reread it two years later—not for Malik's dire warning about the Middle East, but for his request that Nixon set aside two days per week for rest and reflection.
81 Lowell Thomas to Charles Malik, December 16, 1968, Box 48, Folder 3, Malik Papers.
82 "Universal Declaration of Human Rights: Twentieth Anniversary Observed," *U.N. Monthly Chronicle*, January 1969, 31.
83 In *White House Sermons*, ed. Ben Hibbs (New York: Harper and Row, 1972), 87.
84 Ibid., 88.
85 For a comprehensive review of the al-Azm affair by a contemporary witness, see Stefan Wild, "Gott und Mensch im Libanon," *Der Islam* 48, no. 2 (1972): 206–53.

86 Sadek Jalal al-Azm and Abu Fakhr, "Trends in Arab Thought: An Interview with Sadek Jalal al-Azm," *Journal of Palestine Studies* 27, no. 2 (Winter 1998): 73.
87 Charles Malik to Mary Regier, January 14, 1970, Box 11, Folder 7, Malik Papers.
88 Jean Said Makdisi, *Teta, Mother and Me* (London: Saqi, 2005), 30–1.
89 Tamara Chalabi, *Late for Tea at the Deer Palace* (New York: HarperCollins, 2011), 178, 335.
90 James R. Stocker, *Spheres of Intervention: US Foreign Policy and the Collapse of Lebanon, 1967-1976* (Ithaca: Cornell University Press, 2016), 79.
91 Harold Saunders, Memorandum to Henry Kissinger, April 17, 1970, Box 621, Folder Lebanon Vol. II, February 1, 70–December 31, 70, NSC Country Files-ME, Richard Nixon Presidential Library.
92 Meir Zamir, "The Lebanese Presidential Elections of 1970," *Middle Eastern Studies* 16, no. 1 (1980): 52.
93 Dwight J. Porter, interview by Horace G. Torbert, November 5, 1990, Foreign Affairs Oral History Collection of the Association for Diplomatic Studies and Training, http://memory.loc.gov/ammem/collections/diplomacy/.
94 *State Department executive secretary Theodore Eliot, Jr. provides National Security Adviser Henry Kissinger with a 51-page document from former Lebanese Foreign Minister Charles Malik*, August 1, 1970, U.S. Declassified Documents Online, http://tinyurl.galegroup.com/tinyurl/BYZ6c3.
95 Jonathan C. Randal, *Going All the Way: Christian Warlords, Israeli Adventurers, and the War in Lebanon* (New York: Vintage, 1984), 127.
96 Hisham Sharabi, *The Peaceful Solution: Illusions and Realities* (Beirut: Fifth of June Society, 1971).
97 Sharabi, *Ashes*, 18.
98 A copy of Kirkwood's letter to Sharabi, dated May 15, 1971, is in the Malik Papers, Box 43, Folder 5.
99 "Lodge Shouted Down by Antiwar Hecklers," *Los Angeles Times*, January 12, 1971, 3.
100 Charles H. Malik, "The United Nations as an Ideological Battleground," in *The United Nations in Perspective*, ed. E. Berkeley Tompkins (Stanford: Hoover Institution Press, 1972), 27.
101 Betty S. Anderson, "Voices of Protest: Arab Nationalism and the Palestinian Revolution at the American University of Beirut," *Comparative Studies of South Asia, Africa, and the Middle East* 28, no. 3 (2008): 401.
102 Rabah, *Campus*, 56.
103 David C. Gordon, *Lebanon: The Fragmented Nation* (Stanford: Hoover Institution Press, 1980), 193.
104 "Interview of Dr. Charles Malik of Lebanon," 117 *Congressional Record* S47393-95 (December 16, 1971).
105 Charles Malik, Untitled Memorandum for Richard Nixon, December 4, 1971, Box 36, Malik Papers.
106 Rabah, *Campus*, 61–2.
107 Henry Kissinger, Memorandum for Richard Nixon, August 31, 1972, Box 621, Folder Vol. II, 1 February 70–31 December 70, to Vol III, January 71–October 73, NSC Country Files-ME, Richard Nixon Presidential Library.
108 "Remarks by Dr. Charles Malik from Lebanon at the Meeting of the Westinghouse Developing Nations Advisory Committee on Wednesday, November 1, 1972," Box 188, Folder 2, Malik Papers.

109 Nissim Rejwan, "Dr. Charles Malik on Israel: A Recent Arab Reappraisal," *New Outlook* 16, no. 4 (May 1973): 19–22.
110 Rabah, *Campus*, 87.
111 *Inventory to the Edward J. Rozek Papers*, Hoover Institution Archives, http://www.oac.cdlib.org/findaid/ark:/13030/c8jq14b7/entire_text/.
112 Secretary of State to American Embassy in Beirut, June 26, 1973, Electronic Telegrams, January 1, 1973–December 31, 1973, Central Foreign Policy Files, Record Group 59, National Archives, http://aad.archives.gov/aad/createpdf?rid=30042&dt=2472&dl=1345.
113 Harold Saunders and William Quandt, Memorandum for Henry Kissinger, July 12, 1973, Box 621, Folder Lebanon Vol. II February 1–December 31, 70, to Vol III January 71–October 73, NSC Country Files-ME, Richard Nixon Presidential Library.
114 "Citations for the Ten Honorary Degrees," *Daily Princetonian*, June 18, 1952, 2.
115 Harold H. Saunders, interview by Thomas Stern, November 24, 1993, Association for Diplomatic Studies and Training, Foreign Affairs Oral History Project, http://www.adst.org/OH%20TOCs/Saunders,%20Harold%20H.toc.pdf.
116 Trip Itinerary, November 8–December 12, 1973, Box 265, Folder 7, Malik Papers.
117 "Sakharov Tells of New Threat," *Milwaukee Journal*, November 29, 1973, 10.
118 "Richardson Says Press Was Unfair in Agnew Inquiry," *New York Times*, December 7, 1973, 20.
119 Kathleen Teltsch, "Rights Manifesto Is Hailed at U.N.," *New York Times*, December 11, 1973, 6.
120 See Rabah, *Campus*, Chapter VI.
121 Charles Malik to Nelson Rockefeller, May 8, 1974, Box 39, Folder 7, Malik Papers.
122 Charles H. Malik, "My Philosophy," in *Qualities of Life: Critical Choices for Americans*, vol. 7 (Lexington: D. C. Heath, 1976), 399.
123 "Critical Choices Debate Quality of Life Meaning," *New York Amsterdam News*, June 22, 1974, C15.
124 Charles Malik, "Continuity of US Policy," *Journal of Palestine Studies* 4, no. 1 (Autumn 1974): 161.
125 Charles Malik to Nelson Rockefeller, September 8, 1974, Box 39, Folder 7, Malik Papers.
126 Charles Malik to William J. Baroody, Jr., September 16, 1974, Box 5, Folder 5, Malik Papers.
127 Charles H. Malik, "Christian Reflections on Martin Heidegger," *The Thomist* 41, no. 1 (January 1977): 8, 61.
128 Untitled memorandum, January 6, 1975, Box 145, Folder 7, Malik Papers.
129 "8 Guerrillas Killed in Clashes with Lebanese Villagers," *New York Times*, March 26, 1970, 5.
130 Shafiq al-Hout, *My Life in the PLO*, ed. Jean Said Makdisi and Martin Asser and trans. Hader al-Hout and Laila Othman (London: Pluto Press, 2011), 104–5.
131 Israel Mowshowitz, *A Rabbi's Rovings* (Hoboken: Ktav Publishing House, 1985), 288.
132 Norman Cousins, "Last Chance for Peace in the Middle East?" *Saturday Review*, March 22, 1975, 16.
133 Charles Malik, "Text Prepared for *Monday Morning*," February 21, 1975, Box 39, Folder 7, Malik Papers.
134 Charles Malik to Nelson Rockefeller, March 11, 1975, Box 39, Folder 7, Malik Papers.
135 Nelson Rockefeller to Charles Malik, April 24, 1975, Box 39, Folder 7, Malik Papers.

Chapter 4

1. Said, *Out of Place*, 6–11.
2. Said Makdisi, *Teta*, 290–1.
3. Daniel Lançon, *Jabès L'Egyptien* (Paris: Jean-Michel Place, 1998), 66.
4. Samir Raafat, "Zionist Heyday on Zamalek's Al-Kamel Mohammed Street," *Egyptian Mail*, September 11, 1993, http://www.egy.com/judaica/93-09-11.php.
5. Said, *Out of Place*, 25.
6. For his involvement with the PPS, see Nadim's doctoral dissertation, "The Syrian National Party: A Case Study of the First Inroads of National Socialism in the Arab World" (PhD diss., American University, 1960).
7. Salim Majais, *Antoun Saadeh: A Biography*, Vol. 2 (Beirut: Kutub, 2009), 105.
8. *Central Branch Cairo Summary Report 1944*, Box 3, "Reports and Correspondence, 1944–June 1945," Kautz Archives.
9. John S. Badeau, *The Middle East Remembered* (Washington: Middle East Institute, 1983), 118.
10. Said, *Out of Place*, 95.
11. W. A. Said to Charles Malik, October 27, 1944, Box 109, Folder 1, Malik Papers.
12. W. A. Said to Charles Malik, December 28, 1944, Box 59, Folder 3, Malik Papers.
13. Patrick Carey, "Avery Dulles, St. Benedict's Center, and No Salvation Outside the Church," *Catholic Historical Review* 93, no. 3 (July 2007): 553–75.
14. W. A. Said to Charles Malik, June 23, 1945, Box 44, Folder 10, Malik Papers.
15. Edward W. Said, "Paradise Lost," in *Best American Travel Writing 2001*, ed. Paul Theroux (Boston: Houghton Mifflin, 2001), 276–85.
16. Said, *Out of Place*, 83.
17. Sharabi, *Embers*, 56.
18. Habib C. Malik, "Kierkegaard's Reception in the Arab World," in *Kierkegaard's International Reception, Tome III: The Near East, Asia, Australia, and the Americas*, ed. Jon Stewart (Farnham: Ashgate, 2009), 74–80.
19. "*Commentary* 'Scholar' Deliberately Falsified Record in Attack on Said," *Counterpunch*, September 1, 1999, http://www.counterpunch.org/1999/09/01/c ommentary-scholar-deliberately-falsified-record-in-attack-on-said/.
20. Said, *Out of Place*, 113.
21. Edward Said, "Keynote Address," in *Jerusalem Today*, ed. Ghada Karmi (Reading: Ithaca Press, 1996), 4.
22. Said, *Out of Place*, 238.
23. W. A. Said to Charles Malik, May 22, 1948, Box 44, Folder 10, Malik Papers.
24. Said, *Out of Place*, 145.
25. Alain de Botton, interview by Robert Chalmers, *The Independent*, March 25, 2012, http://www.independent.co.uk/news/people/profiles/alain-de-botton-my-father-was-physically-quite-violent-he-would-destroy-the-house-7580958.html.
26. Edward Said, *Edward Said: The Last Interview*, DVD (London: Institute of Contemporary Arts, 2005).
27. Said, *Out of Place*, 223–4.
28. *Year Book of Prayer for Missions 1949* (New York: Presbyterian Church in the United States, 1949), 170.
29. For Jessup's account of the ordination, see *The Presbyterian Monthly Record of the Presbyterian Church in the United States of America* 23 (1872): 273.

30 Said, *Out of Place*, 233.
31 Bishara's 1949 letter to Senator Pat McCarran of the Senate Judiciary Committee was published in *Displaced Persons: Hearings Before the Subcommittee on Amendments to the Displaced Persons Act* (Washington: US Government Printing Office, 1950), 378.
32 "Threat to Use Force in Palestine Decried," *New York Times*, May 31, 1948, 10.
33 Said, *Out of Place*, 241–2.
34 Miles Copeland, *The Game Player* (London: Aurum Press, 1989), Chapter 15.
35 Wilford, *America's Great Game*, Chapter 10.
36 Said Makdisi, *Teta*, 84.
37 Said, *Out of Place*, 245.
38 Ibid., 246.
39 Farhad Kazemi, "Richard Bayly Winder," *Middle East Studies Association Bulletin* 22, no. 2 (December 1988): 310–12.
40 Samir W. Raafat, *Maadi 1904-1962: Society and History in a Cairo Suburb* (Cairo: Palm Press, 1994), 221.
41 Copeland, *Game Player*, 161.
42 Wilford, *America's Great Game*, 153.
43 Said, *Out of Place*, 224.
44 Mohammed Rustom, "In Memoriam Michael E. Marmura, 1929-2009," *Arabic Sciences and Philosophy* 20, no. 1 (2010): 177–84.
45 *Colloquium on Islamic Culture in its Relation to the Contemporary World* (Princeton: Princeton University Press, 1953).
46 Charles Malik to Garland Evans Hopkins, January 11, 1954, Box 21, Folder 1, Malik Papers.
47 Said, *Out of Place*, 276–7.
48 Ibid., 178.
49 Kennett Love, "Nasser Censures Moslem Fanatics," *New York Times*, August 22, 1954, 22.
50 Edward Said, "My Guru," *London Review of Books*, December 13, 2001, http://www.lrb.co.ok/v23/n24/edward-said/my-guru.
51 Eva Malik, Appointment Calendar, January 1955, Box 262, Folder 4, Malik Papers.
52 Said, *Out of Place*, 280.
53 Kennett Love, "Naguib Is Deposed as Coup Plotter by Egypt's Junta," *New York Times*, November 14, 1954, 1.
54 Charles H. Malik, "The Peace of God and the Peace of Man," *Princeton Seminary Bulletin* 49, no. 2 (October 1955): 7–8.
55 Bernard Lewis, "Arabs Hit 'Imperialism' While Russia Sneaks In," *Los Angeles Times*, December 6, 1955, A4.
56 *Princeton University Weekly Bulletin*, April 7, 1956.
57 "Smith Assails Hiss Bid," *New York Times*, April 17, 1956, 12.
58 "Two Chaplains Criticize Halton's Remarks, Acts," *Daily Princetonian*, April 24, 1956, 1.
59 "Hiss Dismisses Fears of New Red Scare," *Columbia Daily Spectator*, April 10, 1980, 1.
60 Merrill Noden, "The (Un)Silent Generation Speaks Again," *Princeton Alumni Weekly*, July 18, 2007, http://www.princeton.edu/paw/archive_new/PAW06-07/15-0718/features_unsilent.html.
61 Edward W. Said, "Nasser and His Canal," *Daily Princetonian*, October 11, 1956, 2.
62 Said Makdisi, *Teta*, 105–7.
63 Frank H. Epp, *The Palestinians: Portrait of a People in Conflict* (Scottdale, PA: Herald Press, 1976), 48.

64 Said Makdisi, *Teta*, 379.
65 Charles Malik to Bruce McClellan, November 16, 1956, Box 44, Folder 10, Malik Papers.
66 *Princeton University Weekly Bulletin*, February 9, 1957.
67 Fayez A. Sayegh, "Some Observations on the Eisenhower Doctrine," Sayegh Collection, http://content.lib.utah.edu/cdm/compoundobject/collection/uu-fasc/id/862/rec/15.
68 Edward Said, "The Moral Vision: André Gide and Graham Greene" (BA thesis, Princeton University, 1957).
69 "Honorary Degrees Awarded to Dulles '14, Parrott '88," *Daily Princetonian*, June 18, 1957, 1.
70 Said, *Out of Place*, 284.
71 Edward W. Said, "Desert Flowers," *Middle East Forum* 35, no. 9 (1959): 32.
72 Said, *Out of Place*, 267, 292.
73 See Jonathan Dimbleby's profile of Bulos in *The Palestinians* (New York: Quartet Books, 1980), 209–11.
74 Edward W. Said, *Peace and Its Discontents: Essays on Palestine in the Middle East Peace Process* (New York: Vintage Books, 1996), 77–8.
75 Said, *Out of Place*, 283.
76 Eric Rouleau, "Cairo: A Memoir," *Cairo Review of Global Affairs* (Summer 2012), www.thecairoreview.com/essays/cairo-a-memoir.
77 John Paul Russo, *The Future Without a Past: The Humanities in a Technological Society* (Columbia: University of Missouri Press, 2005), 284.
78 Charles Malik, "Christian Morals in International Affairs," *Harvard Divinity School Bulletin* 24, no. 1 (1960): 4.
79 Said, *Out of Place*, 288–9.
80 Said Makdisi, *Teta*, 116.
81 Ibid., 115.
82 Said, *Out of Place*, 290.
83 Edward Said to Eva Malik, December 14, [1961], Box 44, Folder 10, Malik Papers.
84 "News of the Week," *Great Britain and the East*, February 15, 1934, 124.
85 "Rev. Dr. Fuad J. Bahnan," accessed August 12, 2016, obitservices.com/obits.php?ID=1455.
86 Said Makdisi, *Teta*, 118–19.
87 Robert L. Tignor, "In the Grip of Politics: The Ford Motor Company of Egypt, 1945-1960," *Middle East Journal* 44, no. 3 (1990): 383–98.
88 Said, *Out of Place*, 255–6.
89 Maire Jaanus, *She* (New York: Dial Press, 1984), 201.
90 Said, *Out of Place*, 255.
91 Lewis Leary to Charles Malik, June 1, 1953, Box 138, Folder 3, Malik Papers.
92 Michel Oksenberg, "In Memory of A. Doak Barnett," *China Quarterly* 158 (June 1999): 484–7.
93 Susanne Klingenstein, *Enlarging America: The Cultural Work of Jewish Literary Scholars, 1930-1990* (Syracuse: Syracuse University Press, 1998), 281–2.
94 "Open Letter to President Johnson on Vietnam," *New York Times*, February 28, 1964, E10.
95 Z. Brzezinski, "Another View of Trip of Kosygin to Hanoi," *New York Times*, February 16, 1965, 34.
96 Stanford N. Sesser, "Will Russia Play Brzezinski Chess Game in Asian War?" *Columbia Daily Spectator*, March 4, 1965, 1.

97 Hilda Said to Edward Said, June 29, [1965,] Box 28, Folder 16, Edward W. Said Papers, Columbia University.
98 Hilda Said to Edward Said, December 4, 1965, Box 28, Folder 16, Said Papers.
99 "On Vietnam," *New York Times*, June 5, 1966, 207–9.
100 Said Makdisi, *Teta*, 336.
101 "Labib and Joyce Nasir, Builders from Ashes," *United Church Herald* 11, no. 12 (1968): 40.
102 Edward W. Said, "The Franco-American Dialogue: A Late Twentieth-Century Assessment," in *Traveling Theory: France and the United States*, ed. Ieme van der Poel and Sophie Bertho (Cranbury, NJ: Associated University Presses, 1999), 134–56.
103 Najla Said, *Looking for Palestine: Growing Up Confused in an Arab-American Family* (New York: Riverhead Books, 2013), 10.

Chapter 5

1 "The Long Accounting," *New York Times*, June 6, 1967, 19.
2 "To Uphold Our Own Honor," *New York Times*, June 7, 1967, 35.
3 "Professors Call Upon United States to Safeguard Israel's Integrity," *New York Times*, June 9, 1967, 42–3.
4 "An Interview with Edward Said," in *The Edward Said Reader*, ed. Moustafa Bayoumi and Andrew Rubin (New York: Vintage, 2000), 422.
5 Edward Said to Charles Malik, June 19, 1967, Box 44, Folder 10, Malik Papers.
6 Ibid.
7 Charles Malik to Edward Said, July 12, 1967, Box 44, Folder 10, Malik Papers.
8 "Interview," *Edward Said Reader*, 423.
9 Drew Pearson, "The Reluctant Dragons at State," *Washington Post*, May 3, 1965, D13.
10 Cecil Hourani, "The Moment of Truth," *Encounter*, November 1967, 4.
11 Robert Alter, "Israel and the Intellectuals," *American Reactions to the Six Day War* (New York: American Jewish Committee, 1967), 8.
12 "A Call for Respect and Humanity in the Middle East Crisis," *New York Times*, November 22, 1967, 34.
13 Edward Said to Robert Alter, December 12, 1967, Box 28, Folder 22, Said Papers. The letter appears not to have been mailed, however.
14 Said Makdisi, *Teta*, 124.
15 In the summer of 1968, Edward told Jonathan Arac that his sister was more involved in the Palestinian movement than he was. See Arac's lecture "What Can We Learn from Uniqueness?" November 9, 2013, YouTube video, posted by boundary 2, https://www.youtube.com/watch?v=mqdC-A64jms&list=PLA-JcpetpbiPCcdODkVs8h9ZbEQaa4_Px&index=9&t=0s.
16 Grace Said to Charles Malik, November 30, 1967, Box 44, Folder 10, Malik Papers.
17 Said, *Out of Place*, 268.
18 Edward Said, Curriculum Vitae, Box 28, Folder 11, Said Papers.
19 J. Hillis Miller, *For Derrida* (New York: Fordham University Press, 2009), 261.
20 Edward W. Said, Foreword to *The American Mystery*, by Tony Tanner (Cambridge: Cambridge University Press, 2000), ix.
21 Edward Said to Lewis Leary, February 29, 1968, Box 28, Folder 11, Said Papers.

22 Edward W. Said, *Power, Politics, and Culture: Interviews with Edward W. Said*, ed. Gauri Viswanathan (New York: Vintage, 2001), 166.
23 Edward Said, Norms Paper, Box 168, Folder 7, Said Papers.
24 Like Malik, Cordier was an active churchman. In 1960, they had both attended a conference on Christianity and culture at Hanover College in Indiana. See Frank S. Baker, ed., *Christian Perspectives in Contemporary Culture* (New York: Twayne, 1962).
25 Said, "My Guru."
26 "Princeton Pervaded by Wars, Past and Present," *New York Times*, June 10, 1967, 35.
27 Edward Said, "The Arab Portrayed," *Arab World* 14, nos. 10–11 (October–November 1967): 5.
28 Michael Walzer and Martin Peretz, "Israel Is Not Vietnam," *Ramparts*, July 1967, 11–14.
29 H. Aram Veeser, *Edward Said: The Charisma of Criticism* (New York: Routledge, 2010), 59–60.
30 Stephen P. Cohen, *Beyond America's Grasp: A Century of Failed Diplomacy in the Middle East* (New York: FSG, 2009), 263.
31 Said, *Peace*, 32.
32 Arthur Hertzberg, *A Jew in America* (New York: HarperCollins, 2003), 370–1. Hertzberg wrote that the seminar took place in the fall of 1967, but other participants place it, correctly, in 1969.
33 "Hussein and Fatah's Leader Meet in Amman," *New York Times*, February 18, 1969, 5.
34 Said, *Politics*, 23.
35 Georgie Anne Geyer, *The New 100 Years War* (New York: Doubleday, 1972), 116.
36 "Shows Arsenal High Explosives to 'Blow Up Half of Jerusalem,'" Jewish Telegraphic Agency, March 7, 1969, http://www.jta.org/1969/03/07/archive/shows-arsenal-high-explosives-to-blow-up-half-of-jerusalem.
37 Edward W. Said, "A Palestinian Voice," *Columbia University Forum*, Winter 1969, 27.
38 Ibid., 27.
39 Ibid., 24.
40 The issue is in Box 138, Malik Papers.
41 Said, "Palestinian Voice," 29.
42 "400 Stage Sit-In at Uris," *Columbia Daily Spectator*, March 16, 1970, 1.
43 Edward W. Said, "On Genet's Late Works," *Grand Street* 36 (November 1990): 28.
44 Paul Auster, *Hand to Mouth: A Chronicle of Early Failure* (New York: Picador, 1997), 60.
45 "What Future for the Palestine Arabs?" *War/Peace Report*, June–July 1970, 7, 11.
46 "New Jordan Regime Eases Guerrilla Policy," *Los Angeles Times*, June 28, 1970, 6.
47 O'Connell, *King's*, 103–4.
48 Said Makdisi's *Teta, Mother and Me* includes a family photograph taken during this reunion.
49 Mariam C. Said, Introduction to *A World I Loved*, by Wadad Cortas, xxiii.
50 Wadad Cortas' *A World I Loved* includes a photograph of Wadad and Mona, who was her cousin as well as her sister-in-law.
51 Said, *Peace*, 78–80.
52 Azm, *Ces Interdits*, 45.
53 Hisham Ahmed-Fararjah, *Ibrahim Abu-Lughod: Resistance, Exile, and Return* (Birzeit: Birzeit University, 2003), 115–16.
54 Paul Thomas Chamberlin, *The Global Offensive: The United States, The Palestine Liberation Organization, and the Making of the Post-Cold War Order* (New York: Oxford University Press, 2012), 115.

55 Paul Berman, *Power and the Idealists* (New York: Soft Skull Press, 2005), 176.
56 Edward W. Said, "Palestinian Liberation," *Columbia Daily Spectator*, October 9, 1970, 4.
57 John S. Badeau, "Muzzling Free Discussion," *Columbia Daily Spectator*, October 13, 1970, 4.
58 Edward W. Said, "Unsolicited Sermon," *Columbia Daily Spectator*, October 16, 1970, 4.
59 Edward W. Said, "A Palestinian Perspective," in *The Arab World: From Nationalism to Revolution*, ed. Abdeen Jabara (Wilmette: Medina University Press International, 1971), 198.
60 Stuart Schaar, *Eqbal Ahmad: Critical Outsider in a Turbulent Age* (New York: Columbia University Press, 2015), 49.
61 Justin Jackson, "Kissinger's Kidnapper: Eqbal Ahmad, the U.S. New Left, and the Transnational Romance of Revolutionary War," *Journal for the Study of Radicalism* 4, no. 1 (2010): 75–119.
62 Ahmed-Fararjah, *Ibrahim*, 112–13.
63 M. Cherif Bassiouni, "The AAUG: Reflections on a Lost Opportunity," *Arab Studies Quarterly* 29, nos. 3–4 (2007): 29–30.
64 Martin Peretz, "Debating the Legacy of Edward Said," *The New Republic* (blog), May 24, 2008, http://www.tnr.com/blog/the-spine/debating-the-legacy-edward-said.
65 Marie Syrkin, "The Arabs' Modest Proposal," *Jewish Frontier* 38, no. 1 (January 1971): 14–18.
66 Najla Said, *Looking*, 7–9.
67 Said Makdisi, *Teta*, 356–61.
68 Said, *Out*, 267.
69 Mariam C. Said, Introduction to *World*, by Wadad Cortas, xxiii–xxiv.
70 Edward W. Said, *From Oslo to Iraq and the Road Map* (New York: Vintage Books, 2005), 233.
71 Edward Said, "The Palestinian Situation Today," Harvard-MIT Arab Club, May 1, 1971, Box 118, Folder 2, Said Papers.
72 Edward Said to Sami al-Banna, July 31, [1971?], Box 30, Folder 6, Said Papers. The letter's date contains no year, but internal evidence suggests that it was written in 1971.
73 Said, *Politics*, 25–6.
74 Joseph F. McDonnell, SJ, *Jesuits by the Tigris* (Boston: Jesuit Mission Press, 1994).
75 Sami al-Banna, "The Arab-Persian Gulf: A Political Analysis," in *The Arabs Today*, ed. Edward Said and Fuad Suleiman (Columbus: Forum Associates, 1973), 99.
76 Sadik al-Azm, "The Palestinian Resistance Movement Reconsidered," ibid., 134.
77 Edward Said, "Living in Arabic," *Al-Ahram Weekly*, February 12–18, 2004, http://weekly.ahram.org.eg/prit/2004/677/cu15.htm.
78 Torgeir Norling, "A View from the East: Sadik al-Azm," *Global Knowledge*, August 11, 2006, http://www.siu.no/nor/Front-Page/Global-knowledge/Issues/No-1-2006/A-View-from-the-East-Sadik-al-Azm.
79 Peter Lancelot Mallios, "What Is Contrapuntalism? An Interview with Edward Said on Joseph Conrad," *Culture.pl*, December 1, 2017, https://culture.pl/en/article/what-is-contrapuntalism-an-interview-with-edward-said-on-joseph-conrad.
80 Louis Fournier, *F.L.Q.: The Anatomy of an Underground Movement*, trans. Edward Baxter (Toronto: NC Press, 1984), 207.
81 Glendon, *World*, 149.

82 Tariq Ali, *Street Fighting Years* (London: Verso, 2018), 193.
83 Said, *Politics*, 215–16.
84 Irene Tucker, "LaRouche: Every Which Way But Ours," *Broadway*, April 24, 1984, 1.
85 Noam Chomsky, *Keeping the Rabble in Line: Interviews with David Barsamian* (Monroe, ME: Common Courage Press, 1994), 142–3.
86 Hermyle Golthier, Jr., "Why the CIA Often Succeeds," *The Campaigner*, Winter 1972–3, 23.
87 Juan de Onis, "A Palestinian Leader Promises More Terrorism," *New York Times*, September 29, 1972, 18.
88 Hout, *My Life*, 107.
89 Said, *Peace*, 81–2.
90 Edward Said to Monroe Engel, November 29, 1972, Box 5, Folder 3, Said Papers.
91 Edward Said, "Fire and Steel," *The Observer*, March 19, 1989, 49.
92 Charles Glass, "Teacher Bridged Diverse Worlds," *Baltimore Sun*, October 5, 2003, 4.
93 "Nixon Resumes All-Out Bombing," *Los Angeles Times*, December 18, 1972, 1.
94 Edward Said to Ferial Ghazoul, January 6, 1973, Box 5, Folder 4, Said Papers.
95 David C. Gordon, *Lebanon: The Fragmented Nation* (New York: Routledge, 2016), 195.
96 Edward Said to Sami al-Banna, February 7, [1973], Box 5, Folder 5, Said Papers.
97 Azm, *Ces Interdits*, 45.
98 Said Makdisi, *Teta*, 129.
99 A flyer advertising both of Edward's 1973 appearances at the Beirut College for Women is in Box 29, Folder 19, Said Papers.
100 Charles Glass, "A Passionate Reading," *Times Literary Supplement*, February 16, 1996, 15.
101 Edward W. Said, *The World, the Text, and the Critic* (Cambridge: Harvard University Press, 1983), 2. The friend in question may have been Norman Augustine, Edward's Princeton classmate, who worked in the Office of the Secretary of Defense in the late 1960s.
102 Said, *Edward Said: The Last Interview*. Edward's memory of this sequence of events may have been faulty; his sister Jean reports that Aunt Nabiha died in May 1973, not April (Said Makdisi, *Teta*, 366).
103 Juan de Onis, "Lebanese Break Up Anti-U.S. Protest," *New York Times*, April 12, 1973, 14.
104 Juan de Onis, "Slain Guerrillas Buried in Lebanon," *New York Times*, April 13, 1973, 1.
105 Georgie Anne Geyer, *Buying the Night Flight: The Autobiography of a Woman Foreign Correspondent* (Chicago: University of Chicago Press, 2001), 203–5. In fact, the blond woman was an Israeli soldier—possibly Lt. Col. Ehud Barak, the mission's commander—wearing a wig.
106 Edward W. Said, *On Late Style* (New York: Random House, 2006), 78.
107 Auster, *Hand to Mouth*, 82.
108 Edward W. Said, "Arab and Jews: 'Each Is the Other,'" *New York Times*, October 14, 1973, 217.
109 Edward W. Said, "Arab and Jews," *Journal of Palestine Studies* 3, no. 2 (1974): 6–9.
110 Father Daniel Berrigan, "The Middle East: Sane Conduct?" in *The Great Berrigan Debate* (New York: Committee on New Alternatives in the Middle East, 1974), 1–8.
111 Rabbi Arthur Hertzberg, "Response to Dan Berrigan," ibid., 12.

112 Edward W. Said, "Getting to the Roots," *American Report*, November 26, 1973, 1, 10–12.
113 See Asad AbuKhalil, "Honoring Samir Khalaf at the AUB," *Angry Arab News Service* (blog), June 4, 2014, http://angryarab.blogspot.com/2014/06/honoring-samir-khalaf-at-aub.html.
114 Edward Said to Costi Zurayk, February 18, 1974, Box 30, Folder 5, Said Papers.
115 Walter N. Rothschild III, "Professors' Israel Tour Plumbs Leaders' Opinions," *Harvard Crimson*, February 9, 1974, http://www.thecrimson.com/article/1974/2/9/professors-israel-tour-plumbs-leaders-opinions/.
116 V. S. Naipaul, *The Return of Eva Peron* (New York: Vintage Books, 1981), 233.
117 Najla Said, *Looking*, 31.
118 Hout, *My Life*, 120–6.
119 Kai Bird, *The Good Spy: The Life and Death of Robert Ames* (New York: Crown, 2014), 154.

Chapter 6

1 Eveland, *Ropes*, 334–5.
2 Juan de Onis, "22 Palestinians Killed in Beirut," *New York Times*, April 14, 1975, 1.
3 Eveland, *Ropes*, 336–7.
4 Clay F. Richards, "Rockefeller's Day," *Mansfield News-Journal*, May 19, 1975, 3.
5 Clifford Hansen to Charles Malik, November 19, 1975, Box 182, Folder 6, Malik Papers; Charles Malik to Nelson Rockefeller, January 7, 1976, Box 39, Folder 7, Malik Papers.
6 Charles Malik to George McGovern, January 7, 1976, Box 182, Folder 6, Malik Papers.
7 "Preparation of a talking paper for Vice President Rockefeller's 12/10/75 meeting with Lebanese statesman Charles Malik," December 8, 1975, *U.S. Declassified Documents Online*, GALE|CK2349290484.
8 Godley to Secretary of State, December 24, 1975, Electronic Telegrams, January 1, 1975–December 31, 1975, Central Foreign Policy Files, Record Group 59, National Archives, http://aad.archives.gov/aad/createpdf?rid=61407&dt=2476&dl=1345.
9 Godley to Secretary of State, December 31, 1975, ibid., https://aad.archives.gov/aad/createpdf?rid=62658&dt=2476&dl=1345.
10 Randal, *Going*, 12, 94.
11 "Statement," January 31, 1976, Box 145, Folder 7, Malik Papers.
12 American Embassy Beirut to Secretary of State, February 2, 1976, Electronic Telegrams, January 1, 1976–December 31, 1976, Central Foreign Policy Files, Record Group 59, National Archives, http://aad.archives.gov/aad/createpdf?rid=62658&dt=2476&dl=1345.
13 Schiff and Yaari, *Israel's Lebanon War*, 11–14.
14 "Fundamental Positions," April 2, 1976, Box 145, Folder 8, Malik Papers.
15 Jack Foisie, "Lebanese Statesman Accuses U.S. of 'Don't-Give-a-Damn' Attitude," *Los Angeles Times*, April 4, 1976, 4.
16 Dr. Charles Malek [sic], "The Impossible and the Possible," *Monday Morning*, May 17, 1976, 16–18.
17 Henry Tanner, "P.L.O. Urges Syria to Quit Lebanon," *New York Times*, May 15, 1976, 1.

18 Schiff and Ya'ari, *Israel's Lebanon War*, 19-20.
19 Secretary of State to White House, July 18, 1976, Electronic Telegrams, January 1, 1976-December 31, 1976, Central Foreign Policy Files, Record Group 59, National Archives, http://aad.archives.gov/aad/createpdf?rid=157538&dt=2082&dl=1345.
20 Charles Malik, "Why You Are Fighting," Kataeb Rally in Beirut, August 29, 1976, Box 228, Folder 3, Malik Papers.
21 American Embassy in Beirut to Secretary of State, September 1, 1976, Electronic Telegrams, January 1, 1976-December 31, 1976, Central Foreign Policy Files, Record Group 59, National Archives, http://aad.archives.gov/aad/createpdf?rid=347179&dt=2082&dl=1345.
22 Itamar Rabinovich, *The War for Lebanon, 1970-1985*, Revised Edition (Ithaca: Cornell University Press, 1985), 70-1.
23 Charles Malik to Pierre Gemayel and the Three Presidents, October 2, 1976, Box 145, Folder 8, Malik Papers.
24 "Prospectus for a Public Affairs Program for Free Lebanon," Martin Ryan Haley and Associates, October 11, 1976, Box 145, Folder 8, Malik Papers.
25 Charles Malik to Lebanese Front leaders, October 27, 1976, Box 145, Folder 8, Malik Papers.
26 The Secretary and Ambassador Dinitz, October 27, 1976, Kissinger Telephone Conversations, 1969-1977, Digital National Security Archive, https://search.proquest.com/docview/1679164244?accountid=14784.
27 Charles Malik to President Sarkis, Suleiman Frangieh, Camille Chamoun, Pierre Gemayel, and Father Kassis, October 30, 1976, Box 145, Folder 8, Malik Papers.
28 Laurence Stern, "Carter Taps Establishment for Brain Trust," *Washington Post*, May 8, 1976, 5.
29 American Embassy in Beirut to Secretary of State, November 20, 1976, Electronic Telegrams, January 1, 1976-December 12, 1976, Central Foreign Policy Files, Record Group 59, National Archives, http://aad.archives.gov/aad/createpdf?rid=280343&dt=2082&dl=1345.
30 "Leadership Group to Open Convention," *Washington Post*, January 29, 1949, 9.
31 J. Brooks Frippen, *Jimmy Carter, the Politics of Family, and the Rise of the Religious Right* (Athens: University of Georgia Press, 2011), 113.
32 Secretary of State to USDEL Secretary, December 9, 1976, Electronic Telegrams, 1976, Central Foreign Policy Files, Record Group 59, National Archives, https://aad.archives.gov/aad/createpdf?rid=68082&dt=2082&dl=1345.
33 "Free Lebanon," Revised Version, December 30, 1976, Box 145, Folder 9, Malik Papers.
34 "Israel Secretly Joins the War in Lebanon," *Time*, September 13, 1976, 13-14.
35 Karim Pakradouni, *Le Paix Manquée: Le Mandat D'Elias Sarkis, 1976-1982*, 2nd ed. (Beirut: Éditions FMA, 1984), 96.
36 Memorandum from the Lebanese Front to Cyrus R. Vance, February 18, 1977, Box 146, Folder 1, Malik Papers.
37 American Embassy in Beirut to Secretary of State, February 24, 1977, Electronic Telegrams, January 1, 1977-December 31, 1977, Central Foreign Policy Files, Record Group 59, National Archives, http://aad.archives.gov/aad/createpdf?rid=42534&dt=2532&dl=1629.
38 Pakradouni, *Le Paix*, 96-7.
39 American Embassy in Beirut to Secretary of State, April 25, 1977, Electronic Telegrams, January 1 -December 12, 1977, Central Foreign Policy Files, Record

Group 59, National Archives, http://aad.archives.gov/aad/createpdf?rid=92973&dt=2532&dl=1629.

40 Charles Malik, "Between Hope and Despair," May 11, 1977, Box 146, Folder 1, Malik Papers.
41 Camille Chamoun, *Mémoires et souvenirs du 16 juillet 1977 au 24 décembre 1978* (Beyrouth: Impremerie Catholique, 1979), 21.
42 Untitled typescript, June 22, 1977, Box 146, Folder 1, Malik Papers.
43 Unsigned notes, August 8, 1977, Box 146, Folder 1, Malik Papers.
44 David Kimche, *The Last Option* (New York: Charles Scribner's Sons, 1991), 132.
45 Richard B. Parker, interview by Charles Stuart Kennedy, April 21, 1989, Foreign Affairs Oral History Collection of the Association for Diplomatic Studies and Training, https://www.adst.org/OH%20TOCs/Parker,%20Richard%20B.toc.pdf?_ga=2.45854883.601391173.1568398291-1105999933.1560288919.
46 Jimmy Carter, National Prayer Breakfast Remarks at the 26th Annual Breakfast, February 2, 1978, American Presidency Project, http://www.presidency.ucsb.edu/wa/?pid=30006.
47 Sharlet, *Family*, 24.
48 National Prayer Breakfast Schedule for Charles Malik, February 1–3, 1978, Box 183, Folder 4, Malik Papers.
49 Sharlet, *Family*, 215–16, 246–52.
50 "American University of Beirut," 116 *Congressional Record* S39258 (December 1, 1970).
51 Jonathan C. Randal, "Lebanese Christians Fight 'War' of Vengeance," *Washington Post*, June 23, 1978, 25.
52 William Claiborne, "Jerusalem Sees Threat to Mideast Balance," *Washington Post*, July 7, 1978, 1.
53 "13 Protesters Arrested in Lebanese Demonstration," *Washington Post*, July 6, 1978, 12. The paid ad appears on p. 15.
54 "A Note," July 14, 1978, Box 146, Folder 2, Malik Papers.
55 "Statement of Hon. Charles Malik," in *Lebanon: Hearing Before the Subcommittee on Near Eastern and South Asian Affairs of the Committee on Foreign Relations*, August 16, 1978 (Washington: US Government Printing Office, 1978), 8–9.
56 American Embassy Beirut to Secretary of State, August 25, 1978, Electronic Telegrams, January 1, 1978–December 31, 1978, Central Foreign Policy Files, Record Group 59, National Archives, http://aad.archives.gov/aad/createpdf?rid=211274&dt=2694&dl=2009.
57 Secretary of State to American Embassy Beirut, August 26, 1978, Electronic Telegrams, January 1, 1978–December 31, 1978, Central Foreign Policy Files, Record Group 59, National Archives, http://aad.archives.gov/aad/createpdf?rid=211783&dt=2694&dl=2009.
58 "Gemayel May Tap Ex-Utican's Son," *Utica Observer-Dispatch*, October 21, 1982, 19.
59 "Ex-Lebanese Aide Describes Hopes for His Divided Land," 124 *Congressional Record* H28243 (September 6, 1978).
60 Edward Cody, "U.S. Lebanese Start New Organization to Press Views on War," *Washington Post*, October 20, 1978, 13.
61 "Interreligious Affairs Commission Dinner," October 26, 1978, Series D, Box 55, Folder 1, Rabbi Marc H. Tannenbaum Collection, American Jewish Archives, Cincinnati, Ohio.

62 Jimmy Carter, "National Prayer Breakfast Remarks at the Annual Breakfast," January 18, 1979, American Presidency Project, http://www.presidency.ucsb.edu/ws/?pid=32335.
63 Jimmy Carter, "Tehran, Iran Toasts of the President and the Shah at a State Dinner," December 31, 1977, American Presidency Project, http://www.presidency.ucsb.edu/ws/?pid=7080.
64 Flo Conway and Jim Siegelman, *Holy Terror: The Fundamentalist War on America's Freedoms* (New York: Doubleday, 1982), 148. Charles is misidentified as "Jacob Malik," the former Soviet ambassador to the UN.
65 Jeannine Guttman, "Man of God—Man of the World," *San Bernardino Sun*, February 8, 1979, B6.
66 Charles Malik, "Ultimate Questions of the Middle East," *New York Times*, February 17, 1979, 21.
67 Charles Malik, "The Problem of the West," *Vital Speeches* 45, no. 15 (May 15, 1979): 459–60.
68 Ibid., 459.
69 "Dr. Charles Malik Addresses the Cosmos Club," 125 *Congressional Record* S7530-32 (April 5, 1979).
70 Jacqueline Trescott, "Dinner for Dissidents," *Washington Post*, June 13, 1979, E1.
71 John F. MacArthur, Jr., "The Rise and Fall of the World, Part 2," December 2, 1979, https://www.gty.org/library/print/sermons-library/27-09.
72 Charles Malik, "Much Is Required," *Al-Fusul Al-Lubnaniya* 3 (Summer 1980): 24–34, http://www.maroniteacademy.com/uploads/courses/Charles%20Malek's%20letter%20to%20the%20Maronites.pdf.
73 Charles H. Malik, "The Two Tasks," *Journal of the Evangelical Theological Society* 23, no. 4 (December 1980): 294–5.
74 Alain Ménargues, *Les Secrets De La Guerre Du Liban* (Paris: Albin Michel, 2004), 11–19.
75 Cecil Hourani to Charles Malik, December 9, 1980, Box 21, Folder 4, Malik Papers.
76 Christopher S. Wren, "Lebanon Hills Echoing with Gospel Tunes," *New York Times*, August 15, 1980, 10.
77 Lauren F. Winner, "Reaganizing Religion: Changing Political and Cultural Norms Among Evangelicals in Ronald Reagan's America," in *Living in the Eighties*, ed. Gil Troy and Vincent J. Cannato (New York: Oxford University Press, 2009), 188.
78 A transcript of the interview is appended to Doug Wead and Bill Wead, *Reagan in Pursuit of the Presidency, 1980* (Plainfield, NJ: Haven Books, 1980), 177.
79 Peggy L. Shriver, *The Bible Vote: Religion and the New Right* (New York: Pilgrim Press, 1981), 14.
80 "The Lebanon We Want to Build," December 23, 1980, http://www.aramaic-dem.org/English/politik/97.htm.
81 Ménargues, *Secrets*, 96–9.
82 Ibid., 99–101.
83 "U.S. Reaction to the Escalation of Violence in Lebanon," April 3, 1981, *American Foreign Policy Current Documents: 1981* (Washington: Department of State, 1984), 777–8.
84 "Former U.N. President Is Named to Newly Established Chair at CU," *Washington Post*, April 3, 1981, C3.
85 Linde Lindqvist, *Religious Freedom and the Universal Declaration of Human Rights* (Cambridge: Cambridge University Press, 2017), 46.

86 Malik, "World Promise," 538–42.
87 "Support for Diplomatic Efforts to Resolve Current Crisis in Lebanon," 127 *Congressional Record* S6954-59 (June 25, 1981).
88 Charles Malik, "Signs of Hope," June 20, 1981, Box 102, Folder 1, Malik Papers.
89 Barbara Newman with Barbara Rogan, *The Covenant: Love and Death in Beirut* (London: Bloomsbury, 1991), 113.
90 Charles Malik, "History-Making, History-Writing, History-Interpreting," *Center Journal* 1, no. 4 (Fall 1982): 28–9.
91 Ibid., 22–3.
92 "National Security Council (NSC) staff member Howard Teicher provides National Security Advisor William Clark with his weekly report," May 28, 1982, *U.S. Declassified Documents Online*, GALE|CK2349662905.
93 "Lebanese Front Discusses Israeli Invasion," Voice of Lebanon, June 9, 1982, *BBC Summary of World Broadcasts*, July 11, 1982, ME/7049/A/3, LexisNexis Academic.
94 Mordecai Nisan, *The Conscience of Lebanon: A Political Biography of Etienne Sakr (Abu-Arz)* (London: Frank Cass, 2003), 64.
95 Schiff and Ya'ari, *Israel's Lebanon War*, 189.
96 Amos Perlmutter, "Glimpses of War," *Encounter*, November 1982, 90–1.
97 Thomas L. Friedman, "Beirut Is Pounded," *New York Times*, August 5, 1982, 1.
98 Marvine Howe, "Lebanese Conveys Doubts on Accord," *New York Times*, August 6, 1982, 4.
99 Schiff and Ya'ari, *Israel's Lebanon War*, 231.
100 Roman Priester, "Notables Interviewed on Future, Relations with Israel," *Ha'aretz Weekend Supplement*, September 17, 1982, 7–9.
101 Nisan, *Conscience*, 67.
102 Susan van de Ven, *One Family's Response to Terrorism: A Daughter's Memoir* (Syracuse: Syracuse University Press, 2008), 128.
103 Elisabeth Bumiller, "The Art of Diplomacy," *Washington Post*, December 11, 1982, C1; Stephen S. Rosenfeld, "Strife of the Party," *Washington Post*, December 17, 1982, 21.
104 In dating the lecture to April 19, 1983, I follow Mammy Helou, "Contingency Planning for Systems Evolution after Crisis," *Journal of Contingencies and Crisis Management* 3, no. 3 (September 1995): 149–64.
105 Charles Malik, "Lebanon and the World," in *Lebanon and the World in the 1980s*, ed. Edward E. Azar and Robert F. Haddad (College Park: Center for International Development, University of Maryland, 1983), 1–22.
106 Claude Khoury, "Talk to Syria and the PLO!" *Monday Morning*, July 18–24, 1983, 26–31.
107 Ihsan A. Hijazi, "3 Lebanon Leaders Form an Alliance for Separate Rule," *New York Times*, July 24, 1983, 1.
108 Moshe Arens, *In Defense of Israel: A Memoir of a Political Life* (Washington: Brookings Institution Press, 2018), 102.
109 Ann Zwicker Kerr, *Come with Me from Lebanon* (Syracuse: Syracuse University Press, 1994), 17.
110 van de Ven, *One Family's Response*, 3.
111 Thomas L. Friedman, "Life in West Beirut Comes Full Circle," *New York Times*, February 8, 1984, 8.
112 Con Coughlin, *Hostage* (London: Warner Books, 1993), 58.

113 *Foreign Assistance and Related Programs Appropriations for Fiscal Year 1985*, Part 1 (Washington: U.S. Government Printing Office, 1984), 133.
114 Elie A. Salem, *Violence and Diplomacy in Lebanon: The Troubled Years, 1982-1988* (London: I.B. Tauris, 1995), 144, 157.
115 J. Michael Kennedy, "Lebanon Foes Declare Truce," *Los Angeles Times*, March 14, 1984, 6.
116 Charles Malik, "The West Misses Its Calling in Lebanon," *Wall Street Journal*, March 28, 1984, 32.
117 Walid Phares, *Lebanese Christian Nationalism: The Rise and Fall of an Ethnic Resistance* (Boulder: Lynne Rienner, 1995), 147.
118 Ben and Carol Weir, *Hostage Bound, Hostage Free* (Philadelphia: Westminster Press, 1987), 85-6.
119 *Middle East Contemporary Survey* 9 (1984-85), ed. Itamar Rabinovich and Haim Shaked (Tel Aviv: Tel Aviv University, 1987), 539.
120 "Gemayel Told to Quit After Latest Beirut Fighting," *Guardian*, May 8, 1985, 6.
121 Randy Shilts, "Ceremony in S.F. Today Honors U.N.," *San Francisco Chronicle*, June 26, 1985, 1.
122 Randy Shilts, "U.N. Has Disappointed the U.S., Shultz Says," *San Francisco Chronicle*, June 27, 1985, 1.
123 Gene H. Hogberg, "The United Nations After 40 Years," *Plain Truth*, October 1985, 2-4, 39.
124 Charles Malik, "The Drafting of the Universal Declaration of Human Rights," *UN Bulletin of Human Rights* 86/1 (1986), 24.
125 "Re-formed Lebanese Front Discusses New Charter," BBC Summary of World Broadcasts, November 7, 1986, ME/8410/A/1, LexisNexis Academic.
126 Karim Pakradouni, *Le Piège: De la malédiction libanaise à la Guerre du Golfe* (Paris: Bernard Grasset, 1991), 188-9.
127 For more on the Kissinger conspiracy theory, see André Sleiman, "'Zionising' the Middle East: Rumours of the 'Kissinger plan' in Lebanon, 1973-1982," in *Conspiracy Theories in the United States and the Middle East*, ed. Michael Butter and Maurus Reinkowski (Berlin: De Gruyter, 2014), 76-99.
128 David Hirst, "Arafat Wants United Front Against Assad," *Guardian*, November 13, 1986, 10.
129 Schomer, "In Homage," 23.
130 Howard Schomer, "Martin Luther King," *Chicago Theological Seminary Register*, Spring 1996, 1-4.
131 Ihsan A. Hijazi, "Syrians Seize Scores of Christians in Crackdown in North Lebanon," *New York Times*, December 17, 1987, 12.
132 Rodeina Kenaan, "Former Lebanese U.N. General Assembly President Dies," Associated Press, December 28, 1987, https://www.apnews.com/32f70967f3ad92a5e7f74b2b364b9d01.

Chapter 7

1 Najla Said, *Looking*, 31.
2 Edward W. Said, *Reflections on Exile and Other Essays* (Cambridge: Harvard University Press, 2000), 351-2.

3 *The Palestinian Issue in Middle East Peace Efforts* (Washington: U.S. Government Printing Office, 1976), 28–31.
4 Yehoshafat Harkabi, *Arab Strategies and Israel's Response* (New York: Free Press, 1977), ix.
5 Edward W. Said, "Shattered Myths," in *Middle East Crucible*, ed. Naseer H. Aruri (Wilmette: Medina University Press International, 1975), 436.
6 Wadad Cortas, *World*, 177.
7 Joseph Fitchett, "$2.5 Million Deal Reported," *Washington Post*, November 24, 1975, 1.
8 Samyr Souki, *Middle Eastern Tales* (New York: Vantage Press, 1994), 37–41.
9 Jim Hoagland, "Princely Perks on Wheel of Fortune," *Washington Post*, October 14, 1975, 17.
10 *Proceedings from a Conference on Problems of War and Peace in the Middle East* (Los Angeles: Center for Arms Control and International Security, 1976).
11 Simon Reeve, *One Day in September* (New York: Arcade Publishing, 2000), 160.
12 "Elsa Reckman Kerr, Ex-Dean of Women at School in Beirut," *New York Times*, March 24, 1985, 36.
13 *Toward Peace in the Middle East* (Washington: Brookings Institution, 1975).
14 Edward Said, "American Perception of Palestinians and Arabs," *New Outlook* 19, no. 1 (January 1976): 27–30.
15 James M. Markham, "Lebanon: The Insane War," *New York Times Magazine*, August 15, 1976, 6.
16 Eqbal Ahmad, *Confronting Empire: Interviews with David Barsamian* (Cambridge: South End Press, 2000), 34.
17 "U.S. Vetoes Measure on Palestine at U.N.," *Washington Post*, June 30, 1976, A14.
18 Pierre-André Taguieff, *Rising from the Muck: The New Anti-Semitism in Europe*, trans. Patrick Camiller (Chicago: Ivan R. Dee, 2004), 68.
19 Edward W. Said, "Intellectual Origins of Imperialism and Zionism," in *Zionism and Racism* (London: Billing and Sons, 1977), 125.
20 Khalid Fattah Griggs, "Islamic Party in North America: A Quiet Storm of Political Activism," in *Muslim Minorities in the West: Visible and Invisible*, ed. Yvonne Yazbeck Haddad and Jane I. Smith (Walnut Creek: Altamira Press, 2002), 99.
21 John K. Cooley, "The Secret War Off Lebanon," *Christian Science Monitor*, August 16, 1976, 2.
22 Christopher Hitchens, *Hitch-22: A Memoir* (New York: Twelve, 2010), 383.
23 Edward W. Said, "Visions of National Identity in Palestine and Lebanon," in *Small States in the Modern World*, ed. Peter Worsley and Paschalis Kitromilides, Revised Edition (Nicosia, 1979), 141.
24 Ibid., 132.
25 Uncle Charles had known Baroody since the mid-1960s, if not longer. After Nixon's election in 1968, Charles had asked Baroody to deliver congratulatory letters to several Nixon appointees, including Secretary of Defense Melvin Laird. Charles Malik to William Baroody, Sr., December 19, 1968, Box 101, Folder 1, Malik Papers.
26 *Can Cultures Communicate?* (Washington: American Enterprise Institute, 1976), 15.
27 "Palestinian Leaders Now Secret Prisoners?" *Christian Science Monitor*, September 20, 1976, 6.
28 Charles Malik to Frangieh, Chamoun, and Gemayel, September 30, 1976, Box 145, Folder 8, Malik Papers.

29 Shafiq al-Hout, "Toward a Unitary Democratic State," *Journal of Palestine Studies* 6, no. 2 (Winter 1977): 9–11.
30 Edward Said to Zbigniew Brzezinski, November 15, 1976, Box 29, Folder 26, Said Papers.
31 Peter Grose, "P.L.O. Says It Would Take Over from Israel in West Bank, Gaza," *New York Times*, November 18, 1976, 4.
32 Jorgen Jensehaugen, *Arab-Israel Diplomacy Under Carter: The US, Israel and the Palestinians* (London: I.B. Tauris, 2018), 47.
33 Edward Said, "A Road Map to Where?" *London Review of Books*, June 19, 2003, 3–5.
34 "Palestinians Back Peace Parley Role," *New York Times*, March 21, 1977, 1.
35 Mariam C. Said, Preface to *Counterpoints: Edward Said's Legacy*, ed. May Telmissany and Stephanie Tara Schwartz (Newcastle: Cambridge Scholars Publishing, 2010), xi.
36 Richard Falk, "Remembering Fouad Ajami," July 9, 2014, http://richardfalk.wordpress.com/2014/07/09/1628/.
37 Said, *Politics*, 30–2.
38 James M. Markham, "The War That Won't Go Away," *New York Times Magazine*, October 9, 1977, 33f.
39 Jim Khatami, "Palestinian National Calls PLO 'Sole Rep,'" *Columbia Daily Spectator*, November 15, 1977, 2.
40 Dusko Dodor, "Sadat Proposes U.S. Professor as Palestinian Envoy," *Washington Post*, November 13, 1977, 1.
41 Pranay Gupte, "2 Professors Deny They Received Offers to Represent Palestinians," *New York Times*, November 16, 1977, 14.
42 Elaine C. Hagopian, "Ibrahim and Edward," *Arab Studies Quarterly* 26, no. 4 (Fall 2004): 8–9.
43 Said, *Politics*, xxi–xxii.
44 Robert Lenzner, "A Palestinian Hails Iran's Revolution," *Boston Globe*, March 1, 1979, 6.
45 Nafez Nazzal, *The Palestinian Exodus from Galilee 1948* (Beirut: Institute for Palestine Studies, 1978).
46 Edward Said, "My Encounter with Sartre," *London Review of Books*, June 1, 2000, 42–3.
47 Said, *Politics*, xxii.
48 Hout, *My Life*, 136f.
49 "Noam Chomsky, MIT," *The Linguist List*, accessed September 13, 2019, http://linguistlist.org/studentportal/linguists/chomsky.cfm.
50 Albert Hourani, "The Road to Morocco," *New York Review of Books*, March 8, 1979, 29–30.
51 Malcolm H. Kerr, "Presentation of Award to Seventh Recipient, Albert Hourani," in *Islamic Studies: A Tradition and its Problems*, ed. Malcolm H. Kerr (Malibu: Undena Publications, 1980), 1.
52 Albert Hourani, "Islamic History, Middle Eastern History, Modern History," ibid., 9.
53 Mariam Said, "Introduction," Wadad Cortas, *World*, xxvi.
54 Najla Said, *Looking*, 36–40.
55 Edward W. Said, *The Palestine Question and the American Context* (Beirut: Institute for Palestine Studies, 1979), 7.
56 Kathleen Teltsch, "P.L.O.'s New York Office Glows in Post-Young Spotlight," *New York Times*, September 8, 1979, 2.

57 Fred Jameson, "But Their Cause Is Just: Capitalism, not Zionism, Is the Problem's Real Cause," *Seven Days*, September 28, 1979, 19–21.
58 Marvine Howe, "Lebanon's Struggling Christians Are Determined to Stay," *New York Times*, September 11, 1979, 21.
59 Marvine Howe, "Christians of the Mideast Uneasy Among Moslems," *New York Times*, September 15, 1979, 2.
60 John Gunther Dean, interview by Charles Stuart Kennedy, September 6, 2000, The Foreign Affairs Oral History Collection of the Association for Diplomatic Studies and Training, http://adst.org/wp-content/uploads/2012/09/Dean-John-Gunther.pdf.
61 Andrew Gowers and Tony Walker, *Behind the Myth: Yasser Arafat and the Palestinian Revolution* (New York: Olive Branch Press, 1992), 182–3.
62 *Human Rights Internet Newsletter* 5, no. 8 (April–May 1980): 63.
63 Elaine C. Hagopian, "Reversing Injustice: On Utopian Activism," *Arab Studies Quarterly* 29, nos. 3–4 (Summer/Fall 2007): 68.
64 "Symposium: US Foreign Policy in the Middle East," *Journal of Palestine Studies* 10, no. 4 (Autumn 1980): 20.
65 Edward W. Said, Foreword to *Confronting*, by Eqbal Ahmad, xxi.
66 Eqbal Ahmad, Introduction to *The Pen and the Sword: Conversations with David Barsamian*, by Edward W. Said (Monroe, Maine: Common Courage Press, 1994), 8.
67 Youssef M. Ibrahim, "The Middle East Talks," *New York Times*, October 30, 1991, 12.
68 Edward W. Said, "The Formation of American Public Opinion on the Question of Palestine," in *The Second United Nations Seminar on the Question of Palestine*, Vienna, August 25–29, 1980, United Nations Division for Palestinian Rights, http://unispal.un.org/UNISPAL.NSF/0/7057B228AE31A9E9852574C9004EE90D.
69 Sadik J. al-Azm, "Orientalism and Orientalism in Reverse," *Secularism, Fundamentalism and the Struggle for the Meaning of Islam*, Vol. 3 (Berlin: Gerlach, 2014), 29, 31.
70 *Human Rights in Syria* (New York: Human Rights Watch, 1990), 120.
71 Edward Said to Sadek al-Azm, November 10, [1980], Box 30, Folder 15, Said Papers.
72 Edward Said to Sadek al-Azm, December 15, 1980, Box 30, Folder 15, Said Papers.
73 Adam Century, "Visiting Prof Is 'Voltaire of Arab World,'" *Williams Record*, October 28, 2009.
74 Michael Waldman, "The Question of Edward Said," *Broadway*, March 4, 1982, 6.
75 Edward Said to Hanna Nasir, February 5, 1981, Box 6, Folder 3, Said Papers.
76 Jeane Kirkpatrick, ""Dishonoring Sadat," *New Republic*, November 11, 1981, 16.
77 Mona es-Said, "The Dangerous President of the United States," *Monday Morning*, December 7–13, 1981, 50–7.
78 Edward W. Said, *The Shadow of the West*, directed by Geoff Dunlop (Falls Church, VA: Landmark Films, 1985), VHS.
79 Tariq Ali, *Conversations with Edward Said* (London: Seagull Books, 2006), 79.
80 Gowers, *Behind*, 187–9.
81 Stephen P. Cohen, *The Go-Between: A Century of Failed Diplomacy in the Middle East* (New York: Farrar Straus Giroux, 2009), 26.
82 Marjorie Hyer, "CU Conference Focuses on Problems of Arab Christians in Israel Today," *Washington Post*, May 29, 1982.
83 Joseph Polakoff, "Ramsey Clark, Mark Lane Attack Israel at Conference," *The Southern Israelite*, June 4, 1982, 24.
84 "The Jacques Maritain Centenary Symposium," *Cross Currents*, Fall 1981, 47.
85 Edward W. Said, "Begin's Zionism Grinds On," *New York Times*, June 11, 1982, 31.

86 "Casualties Are Hard to Determine," *New York Times*, June 13, 1982, 12.
87 Said, "My Guru," 19–20.
88 Bernard Lewis, "The Question of Orientalism," *Islam and the West* (New York: Oxford University Press, 1993), 112.
89 Edward W. Said, "There Are Tears in Things," in *Hasib Sabbagh: From Palestinian Refugee to Citizen of the World*, ed. Mary-Jane Deeb and Mary E. King (Lanham, MD: University Press of America, 1996), 53–6.
90 Walid Khalidi, "Hasib," ibid., 34–52.
91 van de Ven, *One Family's Response*, 117.
92 Amy Kaufman Goott and Steven Rosen, *The Campaign to Discredit Israel* (Washington: American Israel Public Affairs Committee, 1983), 52, 81.
93 Michael Iachetta, "Reconstructing Obama's Columbia Transcript," February 11, 2013, https://theobamahustle.wordpress.com/tag/edward-said/.
94 Goott, *Campaign*, 82.
95 "Palestinians in U.S. Denounce Israel," *New York Times*, September 25, 1982, 5.
96 Edward W. Said, "'Purifying,' Israelis Called It," *New York Times*, September 29, 1982, 27.
97 Gowers, *Behind*, 134–5.
98 Jim Hoagland, "Kissinger Met with PLO Official," *Washington Post*, April 7, 1983, 1.
99 Lally Weymouth, "Arafat Says Only PLO Can Represent Palestinians in Peace Talks," *Washington Post*, December 22, 1982, 16.
100 *Compilation of Statements Made by Eminent Persons at the International Conference on the Question of Palestine*, Geneva, August 29–September 7, 1983, United Nations Division for Palestinian Rights, https://www.un.org/unispal/document/auto-insert-201568/.
101 Najla Said, *Looking*, 91–7.
102 *MacNeil/Lehrer NewsHour*, November 8, 1983, PBS, American Archive of Public Broadcasting, http://americanarchive.org/catalog/cpb-aacip_507-959c53fn2k.
103 Eric Pace, "Malcolm Kerr, Expert on the Arabs," *New York Times*, January 19, 1984, 8.
104 Said, *Politics*, 269–72.
105 "Palestine in Public Debate," *Journal of Palestine Studies* 13, no. 4 (Summer 1984): 189–90.
106 Said, *Power*, 44.
107 Sayigh, *Yusif*, 265–6.
108 Said, *Politics*, xxv–xxvi.
109 Gowers, *Behind*, 242–3.
110 Thomas L. Friedman, "West Bank Arabs Give Mixed Reviews to Palestinian Parley," *New York Times*, December 1, 1984, 6.
111 "The Palestine Problem in Public Debate," *Journal of Palestine Studies* 14, no. 2 (Winter 1985): 244–45.
112 Ihsan A. Hijazi, "2 Moslem Groups Battle in Beirut," *New York Times*, May 21, 1985, 1.
113 Edward Said et al. to President Assad, May 24, 1985, Box 8, Folder 8, Said Papers.
114 *The MacNeil/Lehrer NewsHour*, May 27, 1985, PBS, American Archive of Public Broadcasting, http://americanarchive.org/catalog/cpb-aacip_507-rn3028q93v.
115 Edward Said, "Edward Said Reflects on the Fall of Beirut," *London Review of Books*, July 4, 1985, 3–4.
116 Weir, *Hostage*, 156.
117 "Peace Process Jolted by Raid Against PLO," *Wall Street Journal*, October 2, 1985, 35.

118 Amritjit Singh and Bruce G. Johnson, eds., *Interviews with Edward W. Said* (Jackson: University of Mississippi Press, 2004), 39–44.
119 Colin Campbell, "Harvard Widens Inquiry in C.I.A. Aid to Professor," *New York Times*, October 20, 1985, 54.
120 Fouad Ajami to Eqbal Ahmad and Edward Said, October 21, 1985, Box 8, Folder 17, Said Papers.
121 "Palestine in Public Debate," *Journal of Palestine Studies* 15, no. 2 (Winter 1986): 206–7.
122 Said, *Power*, 333.
123 Said, *Power*, 422.
124 Robert I. Friedman, "Nice Jewish Boys with Bombs," *Journal of Palestine Studies* 15, no. 4 (Summer 1986): 193–7.
125 Shlaim, *Lion of Jordan,* 438.
126 Cohen, *Go-Between*, 33.
127 Herbert C. Kelman, "Interactive Problem Solving in the Israeli-Palestinian Case," in *Paving the Way: Contributions of Interactive Conflict Resolution to Peacemaking*, ed. Ronald J. Fisher (Lanham, MD: Lexington Books, 2005), 49.
128 Edward W. Said, "The Burdens of Interpretation and the Question of Palestine," *Journal of Palestine Studies* 16, no. 1 (Autumn 1986): 30–1.
129 Said, *Peace*, 35–6.
130 William D. Davidson and Joseph V. Montville, "Foreign Policy According to Freud," *Foreign Policy* 45 (Winter 1981–82): 145–57.
131 Said, *Politics*, 107, 113.
132 Ibid., 337–40.
133 Leila Fawaz, "Swimming Against the Tide: Personal Passions and Academic Fashions," *Middle East Studies Association Bulletin* 31, no. 1 (Summer 1998): 2–10.
134 "Scholars, Media, and the Middle East," in *Power*, by Edward W. Said, 291–312.
135 Singh, *Interviews*, xxxi.
136 Michael Ross, "Arafat Bows to Radicals, Hits Egypt," *Los Angeles Times*, April 26, 1987, 1.
137 Edward W. Said, *Culture and Imperialism* (New York: Vintage, 1993), 247.
138 Akeel Bilgrami, "A Dialogue with Edward Said," YouTube video, *Midnight's Children* Festival, Columbia University, March 5, 2003, posted by Columbia University, April 30, 2010, https://www.youtube.com/watch?v=gb9Ny-41C_I.
139 Patrick Seale, "Eastern Reproaches," *Observer*, January 28, 1979, 34.
140 *Thinking Aloud*, "Has Zionism Become Its Own Worst Enemy?" BBC Two, December 10, 1987, BBC Broadcast Archive, https://www.gettyimages.com/detail/video/has-zionism-become-its-own-worst-enemy-michael-ignatieff-news-footage/BBC_NBSF806W.
141 Ihsan A. Hijazi, "Charles H. Malik of Lebanon," *New York Times*, December 29, 1987, 19.

Chapter 8

1 Edward W. Said, "Some Satisfactions for the Palestinians," *New York Times*, January 8, 1988, A31.
2 Dinitia Smith, "Arafat's Man in New York: The Divided Life of Columbia Professor Edward Said," *New York*, January 23, 1989, 43.

3   Ian Black, "PLO Names Three to Meet Shultz," *Guardian*, March 1, 1988, 10.
4   Timothy Naftali, *Blind Spot: The Secret History of American Counterterrorism* (New York: Basic Books, 2005), 74–5.
5   David B. Ottaway, "Shultz to Meet Members of PLO Legislative Unit," *Washington Post*, March 26, 1988, A21.
6   Marvine Howe, "For Edward Said, Shultz Session Proved Collegial and Constructive," *New York Times*, March 28, 1988, A12. The PLO had refused the order to close its mission, and a lawsuit had just been filed in US District Court in Manhattan. A few months later, thanks to Ramsey Clark and other lawyers representing the PLO, the government lost its case, argued by US Attorney Rudolph Giuliani ("Judge: U.S. Has No Right to Close PLO's U.N. Post," *Washington Post*, June 30, 1988, A17).
7   Masha Hamilton, "Israelis Quits to Protest Shultz Talks," *Washington Post*, April 1, 1988, A15.
8   Anthony Lewis, "Arafat on Peace," *New York Times*, March 13, 1988, E27.
9   *This Week with David Brinkley*, ABC, April 10, 1988, Henry A. Kissinger Papers, Yale University Library, http://findit.library.yale.edu/catalog/digcoll:558441.
10 Ibid.
11 Jim Naughton, "The Emerging Voices of the Palestinians," *Washington Post*, June 7, 1988, D1.
12 Dan Fisher and John Broder, "Killing of Wazir Ruthless and Efficient," *Los Angeles Times*, April 22, 1988, 4.
13 Edward Said, "Naguib Mahfouz and the Cruelty of Memory," *Counterpunch*, December 15, 2001, http://www.counterpunch.org/2001/12/15/naguib-mahfouz-and-the-cruelty-of-memory/.
14 Said, *Reflections*, 282f.
15 Edward Said, "Meeting with the Old Man," *Andy Warhol's Interview*, December 1988, 194.
16 Hout, *My Life*, 211.
17 American Council for Palestine Affairs, "The Palestinian Perspective on Peace in the Middle East," *Journal of Palestine Studies* 18, no. 2 (Spring 1989): 181–2.
18 Hanan Ashrawi, *This Side of Peace* (New York: Touchstone, 1996), 50.
19 Edward Said, "*Intifada* and Independence," *Social Text* 22 (Spring 1989): 23–9.
20 Don Oberdorfer, "U.S. Denies Entry Visa to Arafat," *Washington Post*, November 27, 1988, 1.
21 Robert Pear, "Getting Arafat to Say the Magic Words," *New York Times*, December 18, 1988, E1.
22 Smith, "Arafat's Man," 42.
23 Norman Kempster, "3 PLO Aides Get U.S. Visas but 3 Latin Mayors Do Not," *Los Angeles Times*, March 9, 1989, 10.
24 Celestine Bohlen, "U.S. Plan Faulty, a P.L.O. Aide Says," *New York Times*, March 13, 1989, A6.
25 "Edward Said's Interview on PLO Dealings with the U.S., *Al-Qabas*, Kuwait, 7 October 1989," *Journal of Palestine Studies* 19, no. 2 (Winter 1990): 146–51.
26 "Yasir 'Abd Rabbu's Response to Edward Said," ibid., 151–4.
27 Judith Cummings, "Aide Beaten at Palestinian Office Here," *New York Times*, October 30, 1974, 19.
28 Josh Friedman, "PLO Seeks Fresh Image in U.S.," *Newsday*, ed. Nassau and Suffolk, February 3, 1990, 6.
29 Edward Said, "Fueling the Arab Fire Next Time," *Guardian*, August 12, 1990, 12.

30 Edward Said, "Tragically, a Closed Book to the West," *Independent on Sunday*, August 12, 1990, SR28.
31 Samir al-Khalil, "Second Thoughts," *Independent*, August 25, 1990, 28.
32 Edward W. Said, "Ideas Massacred in Thuggish Tirade," *Independent*, September 4, 1990, 18.
33 Lawrence Weschler, "Oedipus in Samara: Kanan Makiya In and Out of Iraq," in *Calamities of Exile* (Chicago: University of Chicago Press, 1998), 1–61.
34 Michael Specter, "Return of the Teach-In," *Washington Post*, February 9, 1991, D1, 9.
35 Said, *Politics*, 299, 302–3.
36 Ibid., 300–1.
37 Hitchens, *Hitch 22*, 293. In 1991, Hitchens visited Halabja and was photographed next to an unexploded chemical bomb with Iraqi Air Force markings.
38 Said, *Reflections*, 390, 403.
39 Edward W. Said, *The End of the Peace Process: Oslo and After* (New York: Vintage, 2110), 195–6.
40 "Interview," *Edward Said Reader*, 438.
41 Nubar Hovsepian, "Edward W. Said: A Tribute," *Middle East Report*, Winter 2003, 2–3.
42 Cornel West, "The Legacy of Edward Said," October 1, 2015, https://www.thejerusalemfund.org/5327/the-2015-edward-said-memorial-lecture-with-dr-cornel-west.
43 Kim Murphy, "Arafat Is Under Siege by Radicals, Moderates Alike," *Los Angeles Times*, October 3, 1991, VYA1.
44 "Interview," *Edward Said Reader*, 438–9.
45 Veeser, *Edward*, 161–4.
46 Edward Said, "Holy Land of My Fathers," *Observer*, November 1, 1992, 49–50.
47 Said, *Politics*, 175–99.
48 Najla Said, *Looking*, 179–80.
49 "Interview," *Edward Said Reader*, 420.
50 Najla Said, *Looking*, 191–2.
51 Veeser, *Edward*, 209.
52 Catherine M. Willford, "Arab American Activism," *Washington Report on Middle East Affairs*, December 1992–January 1993, 69.
53 Singh, *Interviews*, 106.
54 Gary Sick, *October Surprise: America's Hostages in Iran and the Election of Ronald Reagan* (New York: Times Books, 1992).
55 *Challenges to Security in Southwest Asia* (Tampa: United States Central Command, 1993). Unfortunately, Said's paper was not included in the published proceedings.
56 Wadie E. Said, *Crimes of Terror: The Legal and Political Implications of Federal Terrorism Prosecutions* (New York: Oxford University Press, 2015).
57 Edward W. Said, "Bonding Across Cultural Boundaries," *New York Times*, February 27, 2000, AR43.
58 Said, *Politics*, 403–4.
59 Youssef M. Ibrahim, "Palestinian Critics Accuse Arafat of Secret Concessions to Israelis," *New York Times*, August 25, 1993, A1.
60 Don Terry, "Accord a Bittersweet Occasion for Arabs in U.S.," *New York Times*, September 8, 1993, A1.
61 Edward Said, "The Lost Liberation," *Guardian*, September 9, 1993, 20.
62 Ashrawi, *This Side*, 263.
63 Hitchens, *Hitch 22*, 395.

64. Jihad el-Khazen, "Read with Me," *al-Hayat*, September 10, 2013, www.alhayat.com/Ayoon+Wa+Azan+(+Read+With+Me+).-a0342440125.
65. Said, *Peace*, 7–20.
66. Edward W. Said, "The Phony Islamic Threat," *New York Times Sunday Magazine*, November 21, 1993, 62–5.
67. Said, *Out of Place*, ix.
68. Said, *Peace*, 84.
69. Said, *End*, 79.
70. Ibid., 98–9.
71. Ibid., 107.
72. Eli Sanders, "Rushdie Speaks on Miller Stage," *Columbia Spectator*, October 10, 1996, 1, 7.
73. Mona Takieddine Amyuni, "Tribute to Edward Said," *Al-Raida* 14, no. 78 (Summer 1997): 46.
74. Said, *Out of Place*, 270.
75. Edward W. Said, "Keynote Address," in *Holy Land, Hollow Jubilee: God, Justice and the Palestinians*, ed. Naim Ateek and Michael Prior (London: Melisende, 199), 17–18.
76. Said, *End*, 274, 276.
77. Ali Abunimah, "How Barack Obama Learned to Love Israel," March 4, 2007, https://electronicintifada.net/content/how-barack-obama-learned-love-israel/6786.
78. Ray Hanania, "'Unemployment Fund Needed," *Arab American News*, June 12, 1988, 2.
79. Edward Said, "The One-State Solution," *New York Times Sunday Magazine*, January 10, 1999, 36–9.
80. Weiner, "Beautiful," 24–5.
81. Edward Said, "Defamation, Zionist-Style," *al-Ahram Weekly*, August 26–September 1, 1999, http://weekly.ahram.org.eg/Archive/1999/444/op2.htm.
82. Said, *Reflections*, 268.
83. Edward W. Said, Commencement Speech, American University of Beirut, June 28, 2000, http://www.aub.edu.lb/activities/public/graduation/ed-said.html.
84. Said, *Power*, 445.
85. "Metro Briefing," *New York Times*, July 17, 2000, B4.
86. Said, *Power*, 446.
87. Ibid., 445.
88. Said, *From Oslo*, 107–11.
89. "Said: 'Human Beings Make Their History,'" *Brattleboro Reformer*, June 3, 2002, 1.
90. Said, *Edward Said: The Last Interview*.
91. Said, *From Oslo*, 246–7.
92. Christopher Hitchens, *Arguably: Essays by Christopher Hitchens* (New York: Twelve, 2011), 511.
93. Najla Said, *Looking*, 241.
94. Andrew N. Rubin, "Edward," *Alif* 25 (2005): 15–17.

Conclusion

1. Edward W. Said, *Representations of the Intellectual* (New York: Pantheon, 1994), ix.
2. Ibid., 32.
3. Ibid., 5, 7, 13, 14.

4 Said, *Representations*, 113-14.
5 Charles Malik, "The Price of Peace," *U.N. Bulletin* 10, no. 9 (May 1, 1958): 459.
6 Malik, "From a Friend of the West," 64.
7 Malik, "How to Beat Communism," 90.
8 Malik, *War and Peace*, 22-3.
9 Ibid., 28.
10 Said, *Representations*, 50-1.
11 Ibid., 63.
12 Kissinger to Malik, December 2, 1953, Box 149, Folder 1, Malik Papers.
13 Terence Smith, "Kissinger Role in '68 Race Stirs Conflicting Views," *New York Times*, June 13, 1983, B6.
14 Israel Shenker, "6 Experts, Interviewed in Princeton, Urge Complete Review of U.S. Foreign Policy," *New York Times*, December 8, 1968, 76.
15 Justin Vaisse, *Zbigniew Brzezinski: America's Grand Strategist* (Cambridge: Harvard University Press, 2018), 272.
16 Ibid., 109.
17 Ibid., 113.
18 Zbigniew Brzezinski, "A Plan for Peace in the Middle East," *New Leader*, January 7, 1974, 7-9.
19 Landrum R. Bolling, "A Middle East Confederation," *Friends Journal*, October 1, 1983, 7-8.
20 William B. Quandt, *Camp David: Peacemaking and Politics* (Washington: Brookings Institution, 1986), 101-2.
21 Said, *Question of Palestine*, 194.
22 Noam Chomsky, "The Responsibility of the Intellectuals," *New York Review of Books*, February 23, 1967, https://chomsky.info/19670223/.
23 Eqbal Ahmad, *Confronting Empire* (Cambridge: South End Press, 2000), 27.
24 Michael Walzer, Review of *Peace in the Middle East?* and *Between Enemies*, *New York Times*, October 6, 1974, 356.
25 Said, *Peace*, 326.
26 Ibid., 336.
27 Ibid., 254.
28 Ibid., 267-8.
29 "Chomsky Attacks Henry Kissinger for Crowd of 400," *Columbia Daily Spectator*, April 27, 1977, 3.
30 Said, *Peace*, 84.
31 Charles Malik, Appointment Calendar, May 1, 1953, Folder 3, Box 263, Malik Papers.
32 Hanna Mikhail, *Politics and Revelation: Mawardi and After* (Edinburgh: Edinburgh University Press, 1995).
33 Shelby Scates, *War and Politics by Other Means: A Journalist's Memoir* (Seattle: University of Washington Press, 2000), 141-50.
34 Edward R. F. Sheehan, "In the Flaming Streets of Amman," *New York Times Sunday Magazine*, September 27, 1970, 111.
35 John Wallach and Janet Wallach, *The New Palestinians* (Rocklin, CA: Prima Publishing, 1992), 22-3.
36 Edmund White, *Genet: A Biography* (New York: Alfred A. Knopf, 1993), 554.
37 Edward Said, "Fire and Steel," *Observer*, March 19, 1989, 49.
38 Hanna Mikhail, "On Reaching Forty," http://www.abu-omar-hanna.info/spip/spip.php?article60.

39 Kissinger to American Embassy Beirut, November 1, 1976, Electronic Telegrams, 1976, Central Foreign Policy Files, Record Group 59, National Archives, https://aad.archives.gov/aad/createpdf?rid=275995&dt=2082&dl=1345.
40 American Embassy Damascus to Secretary of State, December 16, 1976, Electronic Telegrams, 1976, Central Foreign Policy Files, Record Group 59, National Archives, https://aad.archives.gov/aad/createpdf?rid=70943&dt=2082&dl=1345.
41 American Embassy Damascus to Secretary of State, August 29, 1978, Electronic Telegrams, 1978, Central Foreign Policy Files, Record Group 59, National Archives, https://aad.archives.gov/aad/createpdf?rid=213018&dt=2694&dl=2009.
42 Said, *Peace*, 80.
43 Said, *Representations*, 103–5.
44 Ibid., 107–9.
45 Ibid., 37.
46 Mansour Farhang, "Resisting the Pharoahs: Ali Shariati on Oppression," *Race & Class* 21, no. 1 (1979): 31.
47 Malik, "Much Is Required."
48 Salem, *My American*, 233–4.
49 Said, "Meeting," 115.
50 Said, *End*, 283.
51 Said, *Power*, 458.
52 *The Challenge of Human Rights: Charles Malik and the Universal Declaration*, ed. Habib C. Malik (Oxford: Charles Malik Foundation and Centre for Lebanese Studies, 2000).
53 Samuel Moyn, *Christian Human Rights* (Philadelphia: University of Pennsylvania Press, 2015).
54 Andrew Arsan, "'A Unique Little Country': Lebanese Exceptionalism, Pro-Americanism and the Meanings of Independence in the Writings of Charles Malik, c. 1946-1962," in *Decolonization and the Cold War*, ed. Leslie James and Elisabeth Leake (London: Bloomsbury, 2015), 107–21.
55 Edward W. Said, "Nationalism, Human Rights, and Interpretation," in *Freedom and Interpretation: The Oxford Amnesty Lectures 1992*, ed. Barbara Johnson (New York: Basic Books, 1993), 175–205.
56 Edward W. Said, "Memory, Inequality, and Power: Palestine and the Universality of Human Rights," *Alif* 24 (2004): 18.
57 "Lebanon We Want."
58 Declaration on the Human Rights of Individuals Who are not Nationals of the Country in which They Live (1985), Human Rights Library, University of Minnesota, http://hrlibrary.umn.edu/instree/w4dhri.htm.
59 2003 Amended Basic Law, https://www.palestinianbasiclaw.org/basic-law/2003-amended-basic-law.
60 "Department of State Commission on Unalienable Rights," *Federal Register*, May 30, 2019, https://www.federalregister.gov/documents/2019/05/30/2019-11300/department-of-state-commission-on-unalienable-rights.
61 John P. Humphrey, *Human Rights and the United Nations: A Great Adventure* (Dobbs Ferry, NY: Transnational Publishers, 1984), 45.
62 Charles H. Malik, "Faith and Reason in the University," *Modern Age* 28, no. 4 (Fall 1986): 316.

Selected Bibliography

Archival Collections

Eqbal Ahmad Papers, Hampshire College
Allen W. Dulles Papers, Princeton University
John Foster Dulles Papers, Princeton University
William Alfred Eddy Papers, Princeton University
William Ernest Hocking Papers, Harvard University
Harold B. Hoskins Papers, Princeton University
Kautz Family YMCA Archives, University of Minnesota
John F. Kennedy Presidential Library
Henry A. Kissinger Papers, Yale University
Charles Habib Malik Papers, Library of Congress
Middle East Centre Archive, St. Antony's College, Oxford
Near East College Association Records, Union Theological Seminary
Richard M. Nixon Presidential Library
Stephen B. L. Penrose, Jr. Papers, Whitman College
Ronald Reagan Presidential Library
Edward Said Papers, Columbia University
Fayez A. Sayegh Collection, University of Utah

Published Archives

Access to Archival Databases, US National Archives and Records Administration
CIA Freedom of Information Act Electronic Reading Room
Digital National Security Archive
Foreign Relations of the United States
US Declassified Documents Online

Newspapers

The Boston Globe
The Columbia Daily Spectator
The Harvard Crimson
The Guardian
The Independent
The New York Times
The Observer

The Princetonian
The Times of London
The Washington Post

Oral Histories

Association for Diplomatic Studies and Training Foreign Affairs Oral History Project
John Foster Dulles Oral History Collection, Princeton University

Secondary Sources

Abu-Chaar, Kamal Maalouf. *Memoirs of Grandma Kamal*. Beirut: World Book Publishing, 1999.
Abu Fakhr, Saqr. "Trends in Arab Thought: An Interview with Sadek Jalal al-Azm." *Journal of Palestine Studies* 27, no. 2 (Winter 1998): 68–80.
Ahmad, Eqbal. *Confronting Empire: Interviews with David Barsamian*. Cambridge, MA: South End Press, 2000.
Ahmed-Fararjah, Hisham. *Ibrahim Abu-Lughod: Resistance, Exile, and Return*. Birzeit: Birzeit University, 2003.
Ajami, Fouad. *The Dream Palace of the Arabs*. New York: Vintage, 1999.
Ajami, Fouad. *The Vanished Imam: Musa Al Sadr and the Shia of Lebanon*. Ithaca: Cornell University Press, 1986.
Ali, Tariq. *Conversations with Edward Said*. London: Seagull Books, 2006.
Ali, Tariq. *Street Fighting Years: An Autobiography of the Sixties*. New ed. London: Verso, 2018.
Alin, Erika. "U.S. Policy and Military Intervention in the 1958 Lebanon Crisis." In *The Middle East and the United States*, edited by David W. Lesch, 3rd ed., 155–62. Boulder: Westview, 2003.
Almond, Harry J. *Iraqi Statesman: A Portrait of Mohammed Fadhel Jamali*. Salem, OR: Grosvener Books, 1993.
Alter, Robert. "Israel and the Intellectuals." In *American Reactions to the Six Day War*, 7–14. New York: American Jewish Committee, 1967.
al-Azm, Sadik J. *Ces Interdits Qui Nous Hantent*. Marseilles: Editiones Parentheses, 2008.
al-Azm, Sadik J. *Critique of Religious Thought*. Translated by George Stergios and Mansour Ajami. Berlin: Gerlach, 2015.
al-Azm, Sadik J. *Secularism, Fundamentalism and the Struggle for the Meaning of Islam*. Berlin: Gerlach, 2014.
al-Azm, Sadik J. *Self-Criticism After the Defeat*. Translated by George Stergios. London: Saqi, 2011.
al-Azm, Sadik J. "The Palestinian Resistance Movement Reconsidered." In *The Arabs Today*, edited by Edward Said and Fuad Suleiman, 121–35. Columbus: Forum Associates, 1973.
American University of Beirut Directory of Alumni, 1870–1952. Beirut: Alumni Association, 1953.
Anderson, Betty S. "Voices of Protest: Arab Nationalism and the Palestinian Revolution at the American University of Beirut." *Comparative Studies of South Asia, Africa, and the Middle East* 28, no. 3 (2008): 390–403.

Arendt, Hannah. "Peace or Armistice in the Middle East?" *Review of Politics* 12, no. 1 (1950): 56–82.
Arens, Moshe. *In Defense of Israel: A Memoir of a Political Life*. Washington: Brookings Institution Press, 2018.
Aronson, Shlomo. *Hitler, the Allies, and the Jews*. Cambridge: Cambridge University Press, 2004.
Arsan, Andrew. "'A Unique Little Country': Lebanese Exceptionalism, Pro-Americanism and the Meanings of Independence in the Writings of Charles Malik, c. 1946-1962." In *Decolonization and the Cold War*, edited by Leslie James and Elisabeth Leake, 107–21. London: Bloomsbury, 2015.
Ashrawi, Hanan. *This Side of Peace*. New York: Touchstone, 1996.
Attie, Caroline. *Struggle in the Levant: Lebanon in the 1950s*. London: I.B. Tauris, 2004.
Auster, Paul. *Hand to Mouth: A Chronicle of Early Failure*. New York: Picador, 1997.
Badeau, John S. *The Middle East Remembered*. Washington: Middle East Institute, 1983.
al-Banna, Sami. "The Arab-Persian Gulf: A Political Analysis." In *The Arabs Today*, edited by Edward Said and Fuad Suleiman, 93–108. Columbus: Forum Associates, 1973.
Baram, Philip J. *The Department of State in the Middle East, 1919–1945*. Philadelphia: University of Pennsylvania Press, 1978.
Baron, Beth. *The Women's Awakening in Egypt*. New Haven: Yale University Press, 1997.
Bassiouni, M. Cherif. "The AAUG: Reflections on a Lost Opportunity." *Arab Studies Quarterly* 29, no. 3–4 (2007): 21–32.
Bawardi, Hani J. *The Making of Arab Americans: From Syrian Nationalism to U.S. Citizenship*. Austin: University of Texas Press, 2014.
Berman, Paul. *Power and the Idealists*. New York: Soft Skull Press, 2005.
Beshara, Adel. *Lebanon: The Politics of Frustration—The Failed Coup of 1961*. New York: Routledge, 2005.
Binder, Leonard, ed. *Politics in Lebanon*. New York: John Wiley and Sons, 1966.
Bird, Kai. *Crossing Mandelbaum Gate*. New York: Scribner, 2010.
Bird, Kai. *The Good Spy: The Life and Death of Robert Ames*. New York: Crown, 2014.
Bixler, J. Seelye. *German Recollections*. Waterville, ME: Colby College, 1985.
Bolling, Landrum R. "A Middle East Confederation." *Friends Journal*, October 1, 1983, 7–8.
Borden, Mary. *Journey Down a Blind Alley*. New York: Harper, 1946.
Brzezinski, Zbigniew. "A Plan for Peace in the Middle East." *New Leader*, January 7, 1974, 7–9.
Burke, Roland. *Decolonization and the Evolution of International Human Rights*. Philadelphia: University of Pennsylvania Press, 2010.
Carey, Patrick. "Avery Dulles, St. Benedict's Center, and No Salvation Outside the Church." *Catholic Historical Review* 93, no. 3 (July 2007): 553–75.
Chalabi, Tamara. *Late for Tea at the Deer Palace*. New York: HarperCollins, 2011.
Chamberlin, Paul Thomas. *The Global Offensive: The United States, The Palestine Liberation Organization, and the Making of the Post-Cold War Order*. New York: Oxford University Press, 2012.
Chambers, William Nesbitt. *Yoljuluk: Random Thoughts on a Life in Imperial Turkey*. London: Simpkin, Marshall Ltd., 1928.
Chamoun, Camille. *Mémoires et souvenirs du 16 juillet 1977 au 24 décembre 1978*. Beyrouth: Impremerie Catholique, 1979.
Chomsky, Noam. *Keeping the Rabble in Line: Interviews with David Barsamian*. Monroe, ME: Common Courage Press, 1994.

Chomsky, Noam. "The Responsibility of the Intellectuals." *New York Review of Books*, February 23, 1967, https://chomsky.info/19670223/.
Cockburn, Alexander. *The Golden Age Is in Us: Journeys and Encounters*. London: Verso, 1996.
Cohen, Michael J. "William A. Eddy, the Oil Lobby and the Palestine Problem." *Middle Eastern Studies* 30, no. 1 (1994): 166–80.
Cohen, Stephen P. *Beyond America's Grasp: A Century of Failed Diplomacy in the Middle East*. New York: Farrar Straus Giroux, 2009.
Colloquium on Islamic Culture in Its Relation to the Contemporary World. Princeton: Princeton University Press, 1953.
"Commentary 'Scholar' Deliberately Falsified Record in Attack on Said," *Counterpunch*, September 1, 1999, http://www.counterpunch.org/1999/09/01/commentary-scholar-deliberately-falsified-record-in-attack-on-said/.
Compilation of Statements Made by Eminent Persons at the International Conference on the Question of Palestine, 29 August–7 September 1983, https://www.un.org/unispal/document/auto-insert-201568/.
The Conservative Papers. New York: Doubleday, 1964.
Copeland, Miles. *The Game Player: The Confessions of the CIA's Original Political Operative*. London: Aurum, 1989.
Cortas, Wadad Makdisi. *A World I Loved*. New York: Nation Books, 2009.
Coughlin, Con. *Hostage*. London: Warner Books, 1993.
Cousins, Norman. "Last Chance for Peace in the Middle East?" *Saturday Review*, March 22, 1975, 10–19.
Cragg, Kenneth. *Faith and Life Negotiate*. Norwich: Canterbury Press, 1994.
DeAtkine, Tex. "Great Days in Beirut and the American University of Beirut," January 19, 2013, http://memoriesandreflections.wordpress.com/2013/01/19/great-days-in-beirut-and-the-american-university-of-beirut/.
Deeb, Mary-Jane, and Mary E. King, eds. *Hasib Sabbagh: From Palestinian Refugee to Citizen of the World*. Lanham, MD: University Press of America, 1996.
Diamond, Sigmund. *Compromised Campus: The Collaboration of Universities with the Intelligence Community, 1945–1955*. New York: Oxford University Press, 1992.
Dimbleby, Jonathan. *The Palestinians*. London: Quartet Books, 1980.
Dodge, Bayard. *American University of Beirut*. Beirut: Khayat's, 1958.
Doran, Michael. *Ike's Gamble: America's Rise to Dominance in the Middle East*. New York: Free Press, 2016.
"Dr. Malik." *New Yorker*, December 9, 1950, 32.
Dulles, Avery. "Leonard Feeney: In Memoriam." *America*, February 25, 1978, http://www.americamagazine.org/content/article.cfm?article_id=10724.
"Edward Said's Interview on PLO Dealings with the U.S., *Al-Qabas*, Kuwait, 7 October 1989." *Journal of Palestine Studies* 19, no. 2 (Winter 1990): 146–51.
Eisenberg, Laura Z. *My Enemy's Enemy: Lebanon in the Early Zionist Imagination, 1900–1948*. Detroit: Wayne State University Press, 1994.
Elath, Eliahu. *Zionism at the UN*. Philadelphia: Jewish Publication Society of America, 1976.
Elson, Edward L. R. *Wide Was His Parish*. Wheaton, IL: Tyndale House, 1986.
Epp, Frank H. *The Palestinians: Portrait of a People in Conflict*. Scottdale, PA: Herald Press, 1976.
Eveland, Wilbur Crane. *Ropes of Sand: America's Failure in the Middle East*. New York: Norton, 1980.

Friedman, Robert I. "Nice Jewish Boys with Bombs." *Journal of Palestine Studies* 15, no. 4 (Summer 1986): 193-7.

Frippen, J. Brooks. *Jimmy Carter, the Politics of Family, and the Rise of the Religious Right.* Athens: University of Georgia Press, 2011.

Gendzier, Irene L. *Notes from the Minefield: United States Intervention in Lebanon and the Middle East, 1945-1958.* New York: Columbia University Press, 2006.

Gildersleeve, Virginia Crocheron. *Many a Good Crusade.* New York: Macmillan, 1954.

Glass, Charles. "A Passionate Reading." *Times Literary Supplement,* February 16, 1996, 15.

Glass, Charles. "Teacher Bridged Diverse Worlds." *Baltimore Sun,* October 5, 2003, 4.

Glendon, Mary Ann. *A World Made New: Eleanor Roosevelt and the Universal Declaration of Human Rights.* New York: Random House, 2001.

Goott, Amy Kaufman, and Steven Rosen. *The Campaign to Discredit Israel.* Washington: American Israel Public Affairs Committee, 1983.

Gordon, David C. *Lebanon: The Fragmented Nation.* Stanford: Hoover Institution Press, 1980.

Grabill, Joseph L. *Protestant Diplomacy and the Near East: Missionary Influence on American Policy, 1810-1927.* Minneapolis: University of Minnesota Press, 1971.

Gowers, Andrew, and Tony Walker. *Behind the Myth: Yasser Arafat and the Palestinian Revolution.* New York: Olive Branch Press, 1992.

Green, Ashbel, ed. *My Columbia: Reminiscences of University Life.* New York: Columbia University, 2005.

Hagopian, Elaine C. "Ibrahim and Edward." *Arab Studies Quarterly* 26, no. 4 (Fall 2004): 3-22.

Hagopian, Elaine C. "Reversing Injustice: On Utopian Activism." *Arab Studies Quarterly* 29, no. 3-4 (Summer/Fall 2007): 57-73.

Halpern, Manfred. *The Morality and Politics of Intervention.* New York: Council on Religion and International Affairs, 1963.

Hamouda, Sahar, and Colin Clement, eds. *Victoria College: A History Revealed.* Cairo: American University in Cairo Press, 2002.

Harkabi, Yehoshafat. *Arab Strategies and Israel's Response.* New York: Free Press, 1977.

Hertzberg, Arthur. *A Jew in America.* New York: HarperCollins, 2003.

Hitchens, Christopher. *Arguably: Essays by Christopher Hitchens.* New York: Twelve, 2011.

Hitchens, Christopher. *Hitch-22: A Memoir.* New York: Twelve, 2010.

Hocking, William Ernest. "Palestine—An Impasse?" *Atlantic Monthly,* July 1930, 121-32.

Holland, Matthew F. *America and Egypt: From Roosevelt to Eisenhower.* Westport, CT: Praeger, 1996.

Hourani, Albert. "Great Britain and Arab Nationalism." In *Islamic Movements in the Arab World, 1913-1966,* edited by Anita L. P. Burdett, vol. 3, 407-56. London: Archive Editions, 1998.

Hourani, Albert. "The Road to Morocco." *New York Review of Books,* March 8, 1979, 29-30.

Hourani, Cecil. *An Unfinished Odyssey.* London: Weidenfeld and Nicolson, 1984.

Hourani, Cecil. "The Moment of Truth." *Encounter,* November 1967, 3-14.

al-Hout, Shafiq. *My Life in the PLO.* Edited by Jean Said Makdisi and Martin Asser. Translated by Hader Al-Hout and Laila Othman. London: Pluto Press, 2011.

al-Hout, Shafiq. "Toward a Unitary Democratic State." *Journal of Palestine Studies* 6, no. 2 (Winter 1977): 9-11.

Hovsepian, Nubar. "Edward W. Said: A Tribute." *Middle East Report,* Winter 2003, 2-3.

Howe, Marvine. "For Edward Said, Shultz Session Proved Collegial and Constructive." *New York Times,* March 28, 1988, A12.

Humphrey, John P. *Human Rights and the United Nations: A Great Adventure*. Dobbs Ferry, NY: Transnational Publishers, 1984.
Huntington, Samuel P. *The Clash of Civilizations and the Remaking of World Order*. New York: Simon and Schuster, 1996.
Jaanus, Maire. *She*. New York: Dial Press, 1984.
Jackson, Justin. "Kissinger's Kidnapper: Eqbal Ahmad, the U.S. New Left, and the Transnational Romance of Revolutionary War." *Journal for the Study of Radicalism* 4, no. 1 (2010): 75–119.
Jameson, Fred. "But Their Cause Is Just: Capitalism, Not Zionism, Is the Problem's Real Cause." *Seven Days*, September 28, 1979, 19–21.
Jensehaugen, Jorgen. *Arab-Israel Diplomacy Under Carter: The US, Israel and the Palestinians*. London: I.B. Tauris, 2018.
Kahati, Yoram. "The Role of Education in the Development of Arab Nationalism in the Fertile Crescent During the 1920s." In *Political Thought and Political History: Studies in Memory of Elie Kedourie*, edited by Moshe Gammer, 22–38. London: Frank Cass, 2003.
Kahn, E. J. "Talk of the Town." *New Yorker*, December 9, 1950, 3.
Karabell, Zachary. *Architects of Intervention: The United States, the Third World, and the Cold War, 1946–1962*. Baton Rouge: Louisiana State University Press, 1999.
Kelman, Herbert C. "Interactive Problem Solving in the Israeli-Palestinian Case." In *Paving the Way: Contributions of Interactive Conflict Resolution to Peacemaking*, edited by Ronald J. Fisher, 41–63. Lanham, MD: Lexington Books, 2005.
Kerr, Ann Zwicker. *Come with Me from Lebanon*. Syracuse: Syracuse University Press, 1994.
Kerr, Malcolm H., ed. *Islamic Studies: A Tradition and Its Problems*. Malibu: Undena Publications, 1980.
Khalil, Osamah F. *America's Dream Palace: Middle East Expertise and the Rise of the National Security State*. Cambridge: Harvard University Press, 2016.
el-Khazen, Jihad. "Read with Me." *al-Hayat*, September 10, 2013, www.alhayat.com/Ayoon +Wa+Azan+(+Read+With+Me+).-a0342440125.
Khoury, Claude. "Talk to Syria and the PLO!" *Monday Morning*, July 18–24, 1983, 26–31.
Kimche, David. *The Last Option*. New York: Charles Scribner's Sons, 1991.
Klingenstein, Susanne. *Enlarging America: The Cultural Work of Jewish Literary Scholars, 1930–1990*. Syracuse: Syracuse University Press, 1998.
Küng, Hans. *Disputed Truth: Memoirs II*. London: Continuum, 2007.
Lançon, Daniel. *Jabès L'Egyptien*. Paris: Jean-Michel Place, 1998.
Leavitt, Daniel B. *Cogwheeling with History*. Jaffrey, NH: Savron Graphics, 2000.
Lewis, Bernard. *Islam and the West*. New York: Oxford University Press, 1993.
Lindqvist, Line. *Religious Freedom and the Universal Declaration of Human Rights*. Cambridge: Cambridge University Press, 2017.
Lippman, Thomas W. *Arabian Knight: Colonel Bill Eddy USMC and the Rise of American Power in the Middle East*. Vista, CA: Selwa Press, 2008.
Makdisi, Jean Said. *Teta, Mother and Me: An Arab Woman's Memoir*. London: Saqi, 2005.
Makdisi, Nadim K. *The Syrian National Party: A Case Study of the First Inroads of National Socialism in the Arab World*. PhD diss., American University, 1960.
Malik, Charles H. "A Christian Reflection on Martin Heidegger." *Thomist* 41, no. 1 (1977): 1–61.
Malik, Charles H. "A Job for the Businessman." *Fortune*, November 1958, 120–1, 190.
Malik, Charles. "A Near Eastern Witness to Christian Missions." *Theology Today* 5, no. 4 (1949): 527–32.

Malik, Charles. "A New Dawn in the East." *Vital Speeches of the Day* 18, no. 1 (October 1, 1951): 29–32.
Malik, Charles. "An Appreciation of Professor Whitehead." *Journal of Philosophy* 45, no. 21 (1948): 577–82.
Malik, Charles. "Call to Action in the Near East." *Foreign Affairs* 34, no. 4 (1956): 637–54.
Malik, Charles. "Christian Morals in International Affairs." *Harvard Divinity School Bulletin* 24, no. 1 (1960): 1–16.
Malik, Charles. "Continuity of US Policy." *Journal of Palestine Studies* 4, no. 1 (Autumn 1974): 159–62.
Malik, Charles H. "Faith and Reason in the University." *Modern Age* 28, no. 4 (1986): 314–20.
Malik, Charles Habib. "Faith, Truth, Freedom." In *Addresses Delivered at the Centennial Day Convocation, Dec. 3, 1966*. Beirut: AUB, 1966.
Malik, Charles. "From a Friend of the West." *Life*, March 31, 1952, 53–64.
Malik, Charles, ed. *God and Man in Contemporary Christian Thought*. Beirut: American University of Beirut, 1970.
Malik, Charles, ed. *God and Man in Contemporary Islamic Thought*. Beirut: American University of Beirut, 1972.
Malik, Charles. "History-Making, History-Writing, History-Interpreting." *Center Journal* 1, no. 4 (Fall 1982): 11–42.
Malik, Charles. "How to Beat Communism in the Middle East." *U.S. News and World Report*, March 29, 1957, 88–90.
Malik, Charles H. "Ideals for Export." *Harvard Business Review* 40, no. 1 (January–February 1964): 51–9.
Malik, Charles. "Lebanon and the World." In *Lebanon and the World in the 1980s*, edited by Edward E. Azar and Robert F. Haddad, 1–22. College Park: Center for International Development, University of Maryland, 1983.
Malik, Charles. *Man in the Struggle for Peace*. New York: Harper and Row, 1963.
Malik, Charles. "Middle Eastern-American Relations." In *Proceedings of the First Annual Conference of the American Friends of the Middle East, Inc.*, 106–8. New York: AFME, 1953.
Malik, Charles. "Much Is Required." *Al-Fusul Al-Lubnaniya* 3 (Summer 1980): 24–34, http://www.maroniteacademy.com/uploads/courses/Charles%20Malek's%20letter%20to%20the%20Maronites.pdf
Malik, Charles H. "My Philosophy." In *Qualities of Life: Critical Choices for Americans*, vol. 7, 395–400. Lexington, MA: D. C. Heath, 1976.
Malik, Charles. "Reflections on the Great Society." *Saturday Review*, August 6, 1966, 12–15.
Malik, Charles. *The Challenge of Human Rights: Charles Malik and the Universal Declaration*. Edited by Habib C. Malik. Oxford: Charles Malik Foundation and Centre for Lebanese Studies, 2000.
Malik, Charles. "The Drafting of the Universal Declaration of Human Rights." *UN Bulletin of Human Rights* 86/1 (1986): 18–26.
Malik, Charles. "The Historic Moment." *Harvard Alumni Bulletin*, July 5, 1953, 760–1, 768–9.
Malek, Charles. "The Impossible and the Possible." *Monday Morning*, May 17, 1976, 16–18.
Malik, Charles Habib. "The Individual in Modern Society." In *The One and the Many: The Individual in the Modern World*, edited by John Brooks, 135–56. New York: Harper and Row, 1962.

Malik, Charles. "The Metaphysics of Freedom." In *Freedom and Man*, edited by John Courtney Murray, 183–200. New York: P. J. Kenedy and Sons, 1965.

Malik, Charles. "The Near East: The Search for Truth." *Foreign Affairs* 30, no. 2 (January 1952): 231–64.

Malik, Charles. "The Near East Between East and West." In *The Near East and the Great Powers*, edited by Richard N. Frye, 11–23. Port Washington, NY: Kennikat Press, 1969.

Malik, Charles H. "The Peace of God and the Peace of Man." *Princeton Seminary Bulletin* 49, no. 2 (October 1955): 6–12.

Malik, Charles. "The Price of Peace." *UN Bulletin* 10, no. 9 (May 1, 1958): 434, 459–60.

Malik, Charles. "The Problem of the West." *Vital Speeches* 45, no. 15 (May 15, 1979): 458–63.

Malik, Charles. "The Spirit Matters First." In *White House Sermons*, edited by Ben Hibbs, 85–92. New York: Harper and Row, 1972.

Malik, Charles. "The Struggle for Peace." *BYU Studies* 8, no. 4 (1968): 396–406.

Malik, Charles H. "The Two Tasks." *Journal of the Evangelical Theological Society* 23, no. 4 (December 1980): 289–96.

Malik, Charles H. "The United Nations as an Ideological Battleground." In *The United Nations in Perspective*, edited by E. Berkeley Tompkins, 14–28. Stanford: Hoover Institution Press, 1972.

Malik, Charles. "The West Misses Its Calling in Lebanon." *Wall Street Journal*, March 28, 1984, 32.

Malik, Charles H. "The World Looks at the American Program." *Annals of the American Academy of Political and Social Science* 335, no. 1 (1961): 132–40.

Malik, Charles H. "The World Promise of America." *Vital Speeches of the Day* 47, no. 17 (June 15, 1981): 538–42.

Malik, Charles. "Ultimate Questions of the Middle East." *New York Times*, February 17, 1979, 21.

Malik, Charles. Untitled Statement. In *World Neighbors: Working Together for Peace and Plenty*, 20–27. Washington, 1952.

Malik, Charles. *War and Peace*. New York: National Committee for A Free Europe.

Malik, Charles H. "What One Learns." *Middle East Forum* 31 (February 1956): 14–15.

Malik, Charles. *Will the Future Redeem the Past?*. Richmond: Virginia Commission on Constitutional Government, 1960.

Malik, Habib C. "Kierkegaard's Reception in the Arab World." In *Kierkegaard's International Reception, Tome III: The Near East, Asia, Australia, and the Americas*, edited by Jon Stewart, 39–95. Farnham: Ashgate, 2009.

Mallios, Peter Lancelot. "What Is Contrapuntalism? An Interview with Edward Said on Joseph Conrad." *Culture.pl*, December 1, 2017, https://culture.pl/en/article/what-is-contrapuntalism-an-interview-with-edward-said-on-joseph-conrad.

Marmura, Michael E. "George Fadlo Hourani." *Journal of the American Oriental Society* 105, no. 1 (1985): 3–6.

Marshall, Jonathan V. *The Lebanese Connection: Corruption, Civil War, and the International Drug Traffic*. Stanford: Stanford University Press, 2012.

McManus, John. "Feastday Speech for Brother Francis." *Mancipia: The Report of the Crusade of Saint Benedict Center*, November/December 2009.

Melham, Edmond. *Antun Saadeh: National Philosopher*. Beirut: Dar Fikr, 2010.

Ménargues, Alan. *Les Secrets De La Guerre Du Liban*. Paris: Albin Michel, 2004.

Mikhail, Hanna. *Politics and Revelation: Mawardi and After*. Edinburgh: Edinburgh University Press, 1995.

Mitchell, Timothy. "The Middle East and the Past and Future of Social Science." In *The Politics of Knowledge: Area Studies and the Disciplines*, edited by David L. Szanton, 74–112. Berkeley: University of California Press, 2004.

Mitoma, Glenn. "Charles H. Malik and Human Rights: Notes on a Biography." *Biography* 33, no. 1 (Winter 2010): 222–41.

Moore, Peter C., ed. *Youth in Crisis*. New York: Seabury Press, 1966.

Mowshowitz, Israel. *A Rabbi's Rovings*. Hoboken: Ktav Publishing House, 1985.

Moyn, Samuel. *Christian Human Rights*. Philadelphia: University of Pennsylvania Press, 2015.

Munro, John M. *A Mutual Concern*. Delmar, NY: Caravan Books, 1977.

Mujais, Salim. *Antoun Saadeh: A Biography*. Beirut: Kutub, 2009.

Naff, Thomas, ed. *Paths to the Middle East: Ten Scholars Look Back*. Albany: SUNY Press, 1993.

Naftali, Timothy. *Blind Spot: The Secret History of American Counterterrorism*. New York: Basic Books, 2005.

Newman, Barbara, with Barbara Rogan. *The Covenant: Love and Death in Beirut*. London: Bloomsbury, 1991.

Nisan, Mordecai. *The Conscience of Lebanon: A Political Biography of Etienne Sakr (Abu-Arz)*. London: Frank Cass, 2003.

Norling, Torgeir. "A View from the East: Sadik al-Azm." *Global Knowledge*, August 11. 2006, http://www.siu.no/nor/Front-Page/Global-knowledge/Issues/No-1-2006/A-View-from-the-East-Sadik-al-Azm.

Nusseibeh, Hazem Zaki. *Jerusalemites: A Living Memory*. Nicosia: Rimal Publications, 2009.

O'Connell, Jack. *King's Counsel: A Memoir of War, Espionage, and Diplomacy in the Middle East*. New York: W. W. Norton, 2011.

Othman, Enaya Hammad. *Negotiating Palestine: Encounters between Palestinian Women and American Missionaries, 1880s-1940s*. Lanham: Lexington Books, 2016.

Pakradouni, Karim. *Le Paix Manquée: Le Mandat D'Elias Sarkis, 1976–1982*. 2nd ed. Beirut: Éditions FMA, 1984.

Pakradouni, Karim. *Le Piège: De la malédiction libanaise à la Guerre du Golfe*. Paris: Bernard Grasset, 1991.

Pearson, Drew. *Diaries, 1949–1959*. Edited by Tyler Abell. New York: Holt Rinehart Winston, 1974.

Penkower, Monty Noam. *Decision on Palestine Deferred: America, Britain, and Wartime Diplomacy, 1939–1945*. Abingdon: Routledge, 2013.

Penrose, Stephen B. L., Jr. *That They May Have Life: The Story of the American University of Beirut, 1866–1941*. Princeton: Princeton University Press, 1941.

Perlmutter, Amos. "Glimpses of War." *Encounter*, November 1982, 85–92.

Phares, Walid. *Lebanese Christian Nationalism: The Rise and Fall of an Ethnic Resistance*. Boulder: Lynne Rienner, 1995.

Polmar, Norman, and Thomas B. Allen. *Spy Book: The Encyclopedia of Espionage*. New York: Random House, 1998.

Priester, Roman. "Notables Interviewed on Future, Relations with Israel." *Ha'aretz Weekend Supplement*, September 17, 1982, 7–9.

Quandt, William B. *Camp David: Peacemaking and Politics*. Washington: Brookings Institution, 1986.

Raafat, Samir. "Zionist Heyday on Zamalek's Al-Kamel Mohammed Street." *Egyptian Mail*, September 11, 1993, http://www.egy.com/judaica/93-09-11.php.

Rabah, Makram. *A Campus at War: Student Politics at the American University of Beirut, 1967–1975.* Beirut: Dar Nelson, 2009.

Rabinovich, Itamar. *The War for Lebanon, 1970–1985.* Revised Edition. Ithaca: Cornell University Press, 1985.

Randal, Jonathan C. *Going All the Way: Christian Warlords, Israeli Adventurers, and the War in Lebanon.* New York: Vintage, 1984.

Rathmell, Andrew. *Secret War in the Middle East: The Covert Struggle for Syria, 1949–1961.* London: I.B. Tauris, 1995.

Reich, Cary. *The Life of Nelson A. Rockefeller: Worlds to Conquer, 1908–1958.* New York: Doubleday, 1996.

Reid, Donald M. *The Odyssey of Farah Antun.* Minneapolis: Bibliotheca Islamica, 1975.

Rejwan, Nissim. "Dr. Charles Malik on Israel: A Recent Arab Reappraisal." *New Outlook* 16, no. 4 (May 1973): 19–22.

Roosevelt, Archie. *For Lust of Knowing: Memoirs of an Intelligence Officer.* Boston: Little, Brown, 1988.

Rouleau, Eric. "Cairo: A Memoir." *Cairo Review of Global Affairs*, Summer 2012, www.thecairoreview.com/essays/cairo-a-memoir.

Rubin, Andrew N. "Edward." *Alif* 25 (2005): 15–17.

Russell, A. J. *For Sinners Only.* London: Hodder and Stoughton, 1932.

Russo, John Paul. *The Future Without a Past: The Humanities in a Technological Society.* Columbia: University of Missouri Press, 2005.

Rustom, Mohammed. "In Memoriam: Michael E. Marmura, 1929–2009." *Arabic Sciences and Philosophy* 20, no. 1 (2010): 177–84.

Sack, Daniel. *Moral Re-armament: The Reinventions of an American Religious Movement.* New York: Palgrave Macmillan, 2009.

Said, Edward. "American Perception of Palestinians and Arabs." *New Outlook* 19, no. 1 (January 1976): 27–30.

Said, Edward W. "A Palestinian Perspective." In *The Arab World: From Nationalism to Revolution*, edited by Abdeen Jabara, 192–200. Wilmette, IL: Medina University Press International, 1971.

Said, Edward W. "A Palestinian Voice." *Columbia University Forum*, Winter 1969, 24–31.

Said, Edward W. "Arab and Jews." *Journal of Palestine Studies* 3, no. 2 (1974): 6–9.

Said, Edward. "A Road Map to Where?" *London Review of Books*, June 19, 2003, 3–5.

Said, Edward W. "Begin's Zionism Grinds On." *New York Times*, June 11, 1982, 31.

Said, Edward W. "Bonding Across Cultural Boundaries." *New York Times*, February 27, 2000, AR43.

Said, Edward W. Commencement Speech, American University of Beirut, June 28, 2000, http://www.aub.edu.lb/activities/public/graduation/ed-said.html.

Said, Edward W. *Culture and Imperialism.* New York: Vintage, 1993.

Said, Edward. "Defamation, Zionist-Style." *al-Ahram Weekly*, 26 August–1 September 1999, http://weekly.ahram.org.eg/Archive/1999/444/op2.htm.

Said, Edward W. "Desert Flowers." *Middle East Forum* 35, no. 9 (1959): 32.

Said, Edward W. "Arab and Jews: 'Each Is the Other.'" *New York Times*, October 14, 1973, 217.

Said, Edward. "Edward Said Reflects on the Fall of Beirut." *London Review of Books*, July 4, 1985, 3–4.

Said, Edward. "Fire and Steel." *Observer*, March 19, 1989, 49.

Said, Edward W. *From Oslo to Iraq and the Road Map.* New York: Vintage Books, 2005.

Said, Edward. "Fueling the Arab Fire Next Time." *Guardian*, August 12, 1990, 12.

Said, Edward W. "Getting to the Roots." *American Report*, November 26, 1973, 1, 10–12.
Said, Edward. "Holy Land of My Fathers." *Observer*, November 1, 1992, 49–50.
Said, Edward W. "Ideas Massacred in Thuggish Tirade." *Independent*, September 4, 1990, 18.
Said, Edward W. "Intellectual Origins of Imperialism and Zionism." In *Zionism and Racism: Proceedings of an International Symposium*, 125–30. London: Billing and Sons, 1977.
Said, Edward. "*Intifada* and Independence." *Social Text* 22 (Spring 1989): 23–29.
Said, Edward. "Keynote Address." In *Jerusalem Today*, edited by Ghada Karmi, 1–21. Reading: Ithaca Press, 1996.
Said, Edward W. "Keynote Address." In *Holy Land, Hollow Jubilee: God, Justice and the Palestinians*, edited by Naim Ateek and Michael Prior, 17–32. London: Melisende, 1999.
Said, Edward. "Living in Arabic." *Al-Ahram Weekly*, February 12–18, 2004, http://weekly.ahram.org.eg/prit/2004/677/cu15.htm.
Said, Edward W. "Memory, Inequality, and Power: Palestine and the Universality of Human Rights," *Alif* 24 (2004): 15–33.
Said, Edward. "Meeting with the Old Man." *Andy Warhol's Interview*, December 1988, 112–15, 194.
Said, Edward. "My Encounter with Sartre." *London Review of Books*, June 1, 2000, 42–43.
Said, Edward. "My Guru." *London Review of Books*, December 13, 2001, http://www.lrb.co.ok/v23/n24/edward-said/my-guru.
Said, Edward. "Naguib Mahfouz and the Cruelty of Memory." *Counterpunch*, December 15, 2001, http://www.counterpunch.org/2001/12/15/naguib-mahfouz-and-the-cruelty-of-memory/.
Said, Edward W. "Nasser and His Canal." *Daily Princetonian*, October 11, 1956, 2.
Said, Edward W. "Nationalism, Human Rights, and Interpretation." In *Freedom and Interpretation: The Oxford Amnesty Lectures 1992*, edited by Barbara Johnson, 175–205. New York: Basic Books, 1993.
Said, Edward W. "On Genet's Late Works." *Grand Street* 36 (November 1990): 26–42.
Said, Edward W. *On Late Style*. New York: Random House, 2006.
Said, Edward W. *Out of Place*. New York: Alfred A. Knopf, 1999.
Said, Edward W. "Paradise Lost." In *Best American Travel Writing 2001*, edited by Paul Theroux, 276–85. Boston: Houghton Mifflin, 2001.
Said, Edward W. *Peace and Its Discontents: Essays on Palestine in the Middle East Peace Process*. New York: Vintage Books, 1996.
Said, Edward W. *Power, Politics, and Culture: Interviews with Edward W. Said*. Edited by Gauri Viswanathan. New York: Vintage, 2001.
Said, Edward W. "'Purifying,' Israelis Called It." *New York Times*, September 29, 1982, 27.
Said, Edward W. *Reflections on Exile and Other Essays*. Cambridge: Harvard University Press, 2000.
Said, Edward W. *Representations of the Intellectual*. New York: Pantheon, 1994.
Said, Edward W. "Shattered Myths." In *Middle East Crucible*, edited by Naseer H. Aruri, 410–27. Wilmette, IL: Medina University Press International, 1975.
Said, Edward W. "Some Satisfactions for the Palestinians." *New York Times*, January 8, 1988, 31.
Said, Edward. "The Arab Portrayed." *Arab World* 14, no. 10–11 (October–November 1967): 5–7.
Said, Edward W. "The Burdens of Interpretation and the Question of Palestine." *Journal of Palestine Studies* 16, no. 1 (Autumn 1986): 29–37.

Said, Edward W. *The Edward Said Reader*. Edited by Moustafa Bayoumi and Andrew Rubin. New York: Vintage, 2000.
Said, Edward W. *The End of the Peace Process: Oslo and After*. New York: Vintage, 2001.
Said, Edward W. "The Formation of American Public Opinion on the Question of Palestine." In *The Second United Nations Seminar on the Question of Palestine*, August 25–29, 1980, http://unispal.un.org/UNISPAL.NSF/0/7057B228AE31A9E9852574C9004EE90D.
Said, Edward W. "The Franco-American Dialogue: A Late Twentieth-Century Assessment." In *Traveling Theory: France and the United States*, edited by Ieme van der Poel and Sophie Bertho, 134–56. Cranbury, NJ: Associated University Presses, 1999.
Said, Edward. "The Lost Liberation." *Guardian*, September, 9, 1993, 20.
Said, Edward. *The Moral Vision: André Gide and Graham Greene*. BA thesis, Princeton University, 1957.
Said, Edward. "The One-State Solution." *New York Times Sunday Magazine*, January 10, 1999, 36–39.
Said, Edward W. *The Palestine Question and the American Context*. Beirut: Institute for Palestine Studies, 1979.
Said, Edward W. *The Pen and the Sword: Conversations with David Barsamian*. Monroe, ME: Common Courage Press, 1994.
Said, Edward W. "The Phony Islamic Threat." *New York Times Sunday Magazine*, November 21, 1993, 62–65.
Said, Edward W. *The Politics of Dispossession: The Struggle for Palestinian Self-Determination, 1969–1994*. New York: Vintage Books, 1994.
Said, Edward W. *The Question of Palestine*. New York: Times Books, 1979.
Said, Edward W. *The Shadow of the West*. Directed by Geoff Dunlop. Falls Church, VA: Landmark Films, 1985. VHS.
Said, Edward W. *The World, the Text, and the Critic*. Cambridge: Harvard University Press, 1983.
Said, Edward. "Tragically, a Closed Book to the West." *Independent on Sunday*, August 12, 1990, SR28.
Said, Edward W. "Visions of National Identity in Palestine and Lebanon." In *Small States in the Modern World*, revised ed., edited by Peter Worsley and Paschalis Kitromilides, 25–42. Nicosia: New Cyprus Association, 1979.
Said, Edward, and Charles Glass. *Edward Said: The Last Interview*. Directed by Mike Dibb. London: Institute of Contemporary Arts, 2005. DVD.
es-Said, Mona. "The Dangerous President of the United States." *Monday Morning*, December 7–13, 1981, 50–7.
Said, Najla. *Looking for Palestine: Growing Up Confused in an Arab-American Family*. New York: Riverhead Books, 2013.
Said, Wadie E. *Crimes of Terror: The Legal and Political Implications of Federal Terrorism Prosecutions*. New York: Oxford University Press, 2015.
Salameh, Franck. *Language, Memory, and Identity in the Middle East: The Case for Lebanon*. Lanham, MD: Lexington Books, 2010.
Salem, Elie A. *My American Bride*. London: Quartet Books, 2008.
Salem, Elie A. *Violence and Diplomacy in Lebanon: The Troubled Years, 1982–1988*. London: I.B. Tauris, 1995.
Salibi, Kamal S. "Recollections of Lebanon in the 1940s and 1950s." *Bulletin of the Royal Institute for Inter-Faith Studies* 5, no. 2 (Autumn/Winter 2003): 126–30.
Saunders, Bonnie F. *The United States and Arab Nationalism: The Syrian Case, 1953–1960*. Westport, CT: Praeger, 1996.

Sayigh, Rosemary, ed. *Yusif Sayigh: Arab Economist, Palestinian Patriot*. Cairo: American University of Cairo Press, 2015.

Scates, Shelby. *War and Politics by Other Means: A Journalist's Memoir*. Seattle: University of Washington Press, 2000.

Schaar, Stuart. *Eqbal Ahmad: Critical Outsider in a Turbulent Age*. New York: Columbia University Press, 2015.

Schiff, Zeev, and Ehud Yaari. *Israel's Lebanon War*. Translated by Ina Friedman. New York: Simon and Schuster, 1984.

Schlesinger, Stephen C. *Act of Creation: The Founding of the United Nations*. Boulder: Westview Press, 2003.

Schomer, Howard. "From 'Just War' to 'Just Peace': CPS and War Resistance Among Congregationalists." *Mennonite Quarterly Review* 66, no. 4 (October 1992): 598–614.

Seelye, Laurens Hickok. "An Experiment in Religious Association." *Journal of Religion* 2, no. 3 (May 1922): 303–9.

Segev, Tom, and Haim Watzman. *A State at Any Cost: The Life of David Ben-Gurion*. New York: Farrar Straus Giroux, 2019.

Sharabi, Hisham. *Embers and Ashes: Memoirs of an Arab Intellectual*. Translated by Issa J. Boullata. Northampton, MA: Olive Branch Press, 2008.

Sharabi, Hisham. *Governments and Politics in the Middle East in the Twentieth Century*. Princeton: Van Nostrand, 1962.

Sharabi, Hisham. *The Peaceful Solution: Illusions and Realities*. Beirut: Fifth of June Society, 1971.

Sharabi, Hisham. "The Transformation of Ideology in the Arab World." In *A Middle East Reader*, edited by Irene L. Gendzier, 71–88. New York: Pegasus, 1969.

Sharkey, Heather J. *American Evangelicals in Egypt: Missionary Encounters in an Age of Empire*. Princeton: Princeton University Press, 2008.

Sharlet, Jeff. *The Family: The Secret Fundamentalism at the Heart of American Power*. New York: HarperCollins, 2008.

Shlaim, Avi. "Husni Zaim and the Plan to Resettle Palestinian Refugees in Syria." *Journal of Palestine Studies* 15, no. 4 (1986): 68–80.

Shlaim, Avi. *Lion of Jordan: The Life of King Hussein in War and Peace*. New York: Alfred A. Knopf, 2008.

Singh, Amritjit, and Bruce G. Johnson, eds. *Interviews with Edward W. Said*. Jackson: University of Mississippi Press, 2004.

Sleiman, André. "'Zionising' the Middle East: Rumours of the 'Kissinger Plan' in Lebanon, 1973-1982." In *Conspiracy Theories in the United States and the Middle East*, edited by Michael Butter and Maurus Reinkowski, 76–99. Berlin: De Gruyter, 2014.

Smith, Dinitia. "Arafat's Man in New York: The Divided Life of Columbia Professor Edward Said." *New York*, January 23, 1989, 40–6.

Sofer, Sasson. *Zionism and the Foundations of Israeli Diplomacy*. Cambridge: Cambridge University Press, 1998.

Souki, Samyr. *Middle Eastern Tales*. New York: Vantage Press, 1994.

Spears, Edward. *Fulfilment of a Mission*. London: Archon Books, 1977.

Stocker, James R. *Spheres of Intervention: US Foreign Policy and the Collapse of Lebanon, 1967-1976*. Ithaca: Cornell University Press, 2016.

"Symposium: US Foreign Policy in the Middle East." *Journal of Palestine Studies* 10, no. 4 (Autumn 1980): 3–34.

Syrkin, Marie. "The Arabs' Modest Proposal." *Jewish Frontier* 38, no. 1 (January 1971): 14–18.

Taky Deen, Said. *Bridge Under the Water*. Beirut, 1957.
Tannous, Afif I. *Village Roots and Beyond*. Beirut: Dar Nelson, 2004.
Telmissany, May, and Stephanie Tara Schwartz, eds. *Counterpoints: Edward Said's Legacy*. Newcastle: Cambridge Scholars Publishing, 2010.
Thompson, Todd. "Albert Hourani, Arab Christian Minorities and the Spiritual Dimension of Britain's Problem in Palestine, 1938–1947." In *Christians in the Middle East Conflict*, edited by Paul S. Rowe, John H. A. Dyck, and Jens Zimmermann, 66–83. London: Routledge, 2014.
Toward Peace in the Middle East. Washington: Brookings Institution, 1975.
Tyler, Patrick. *A World of Trouble: The White House and the Middle East from the Cold War to the War on Terror*. New York: Farrar Strauss Giroux, 2009.
Vaisse, Justin. *Zbigniew Brzezinski: America's Grand Strategist*. Cambridge: Harvard University Press, 2018.
VanDeMark, Brian. *American Sheikhs: Two Families, Four Generations, and the Story of America's Influence in the Middle East*. Amherst and New York: Prometheus Books, 2012.
van de Ven, Susan. *One Family's Response to Terrorism: A Daughter's Memoir*. Syracuse: Syracuse University Press, 2008.
Veeser, H. Aram. *Edward Said: The Charisma of Criticism*. New York: Routledge, 2010.
Wallach, John and Janet Wallach. *The New Palestinians*. Rocklin, CA: Prima Publishing, 1992.
Walzer, Michael, and Martin Peretz. "Israel Is Not Vietnam." *Ramparts*, July 1967, 11–14.
Weiner, Justus Reid. "'My Beautiful Old House' and Other Fabrications." *Commentary*, September 1999, 23–31.
Weir, Ben and Carol Weir. *Hostage Bound, Hostage Free*. Philadelphia: Westminster Press, 1987.
West, Cornel. "The Legacy of Edward Said," October 1, 2015, https://www.thejerusalemfund.org/5327/the-2015-edward-said-memorial-lecture-with-dr-cornel-west.
"What Future for the Palestine Arabs?" *War/Peace Report*, June–July 1970, 3–11.
White, Edmund. *Genet: A Biography*. New York: Alfred A. Knopf, 1993.
Wild, Stefan. "Gott und Mensch im Libanon." *Der Islam* 48, no. 2 (1972): 206–53.
Wilford, Hugh. *America's Great Game: The CIA's Secret Arabists and the Shaping of the Modern Middle East*. New York: Basic Books, 2013.
Woodward, Bob. *Veil: The Secret Wars of the CIA, 1981–1987*. New York: Simon and Schuster, 1987.
Wylie, Philip. *The Innocent Ambassadors*. New York: Rinehart, 1957.
Yamak, Labib Zuwiyya. *The Syrian Social Nationalist Party: An Ideological Analysis*. Cambridge: Center for Middle Eastern Studies, 1966.
Zamir, Meir. "The Lebanese Presidential Elections of 1970." *Middle Eastern Studies* 16, no. 1 (January 1980): 49–70.
Zamir, Meir. *The Secret Anglo-French War in the Middle East: Intelligence and Decolonization, 1940–1948*. Abingdon: Routledge, 2015.
Zisser, Eyal. *Lebanon: The Challenge of Independence*. London: I.B. Tauris, 2000.

Index

Abbas, Mahmoud (Abu Mazen)   167
Abd Rabbo, Yasir   194, 204
Abu-Lughod, Ibrahim
   and Association of Arab-American
      University Graduates   120–1, 201
   at Birzeit University   201
   and Edward Said   100–1, 114, 120–1,
      161–3, 173, 181, 189–92, 201, 210
   and Palestine National Council   119,
      166–7, 192, 198
   and Yasir Arafat   119, 168, 178
Acheson, Dean   9, 39, 49
Adwan, Kamal   127–8
Ahmad, Eqbal
   and Daniel Berrigan   129, 178
   and Edward Said   121, 163–4, 171–3,
      181, 200, 205, 210
   and Noam Chomsky   121, 163–4,
      219
   and Kissinger kidnapping case   121,
      129, 171, 219
   and PLO   163–4, 171–3
Ajami, Fouad   167, 181–3, 196, 211
Akl, Said   29, 70, 135, 147
Alsop, Joseph   59–60
Alter, Robert   108, 112, 227
American Friends of the Middle East   31,
   48–51, 55–6, 71, 77, 79, 100
American Israel Public Affairs
   Committee   79, 144, 177
American Lebanese League   142, 144,
   149
American University of Beirut
   and Arab nationalism   6, 21, 27, 32
   assassinations and kidnappings   152,
      155–6, 159
   centennial   77–80
   founding   5–6
   student unrest   7–8, 81, 86–90
   US funding   33, 46, 55, 73, 78, 134,
      142, 163

Arabian-American Oil Company   7,
   41–2, 45, 49, 52, 55
Arab League   38, 41, 44–5, 53, 96, 114,
   139
Arafat, Yasir
   and Black September   119, 124
   and Charles Malik   91–2
   and Edward Said   10, 119, 130–1,
      168–72, 176–84, 189–92, 198–9,
      203–6, 225–6
   and Hanna Mikhail   119, 164, 222
   and Israeli invasion of Lebanon   153,
      176
   and Oslo Accord   201–3
   and Palestine National Council   119,
      180
   and PLO-Lebanese Forces
      alliance   159, 191–2
   and Saddam Hussein   194–6
   and Sadik al-Azm   124, 127
   and Shafiq al-Hout   169–70
   and Stephen P. Cohen   175, 183–4
   UN speech   130–1
   and US-PLO dialogue   11, 192–4, 218
Arazi, Tuvia   37, 45
Arendt, Hannah   44, 111
Arens, Moshe   154–5
Ashrawi, Hanan Mikhail   126, 165–6,
   192, 198, 201–4
Assad, Hafez   136, 165, 180–1, 226
Association of Arab-American University
   Graduates   120–1, 124, 127–9,
   162, 166–8, 172, 200–1, 219
Athenagoras I, Patriarch   73–4, 80
Auster, Paul   117, 128
Al-Azm, Fawz   72, 113
Al-Azm, Sadik
   at American University of Beirut   72,
      78–81
   arrested   83
   and Charles Malik   72, 78–81

and Edward Said   113, 124, 127,
    173–4
on "God and Man" symposium   78–
    81, 83
and Palestinian movement   113, 119,
    123–4, 127–8

Badeau, John   9, 94–9, 108, 120
Badr, Rev. Habib   157, 167
Badr, Rev. Youssef   3, 52, 93, 97, 157
Badre, Albert   27, 67, 127
Badre, Lily   27, 67, 93
Bahnan, Rev. Fuad   103, 107, 211
al-Banna, Sami   123–4, 127, 195
Barakat, Halim   127, 130
Barenboim, Daniel   201, 211
Bar-On, Mordechai   184, 193
Baroody, Jr., William J.   74, 91
Bechtel Corporation   7, 55
Begin, Menachem   140–1, 145, 152–4,
    186, 193
Beidas, Yusef   73, 96
Ben-Eliezer, Benyamin   135–6
Ben-Gurion, David   7, 9, 43–4
Berri, Nabih   157, 181
Berrigan, Daniel   121, 129, 178, 228
Birzeit University   165, 169, 175, 199, 201
Blackmur, R. P.   100, 177
Bliss, Rev. Daniel   5, 19
Bliss, Rev. Daniel (grandson)   43, 77
Bliss, Rev. Howard   5–6, 19–20
Bolling, Landrum   179, 218
Bourguiba, Habib   64, 111
Brewer, Sam Pope   56, 59–63
Brower, Reuben   105, 177
Brzezinski, Zbigniew   108, 137–8, 166,
    216–21
Buber, Martin   42–4, 227
Buchman, Rev. Frank   22–3, 53
Bunche, Ralph   45–7
Bundy, McGeorge   64, 67, 76
Bush, George H. W.   196, 200
Bush, George W.   209, 224
Bustani, Fuad   70, 137, 158–9

Camp David Accords   1, 144–6, 149, 186
Carter, Jimmy   8–10, 137–46, 149, 165–9,
    179–80, 200–2, 214, 217–18
Case, John   55, 69, 73

Casey, William   8, 82
Cassin, René   41–2
Cavafy's "Waiting for the Barbarians"   86,
    211
Central Intelligence Agency
    and American Friends of the Middle
        East   48–9, 71, 79
    and Columbia   220
    and Egypt   9, 99
    and Harvard   182–3
    and Iran   7, 41
    and Jordan   10, 58, 64, 118
    and Lebanon   8, 56, 59–62, 72, 83,
        139, 154, 182
    and PLO   131
    and Princeton   104
    and Syria   45, 54, 58
Chalabi, Ahmad   83, 195, 211
Chamoun, Camille
    and Chehab regime   64, 69, 84
    and independence movement   34
    and Lebanese Front   135–9, 142, 148,
        151–9, 166, 227
    as president of Lebanon   7–8, 50,
        53–5, 58–63, 70–2
Chamoun, Dany   136, 147, 159
Chamoun, Dory   144, 149
Chehab, Fuad   7, 62–3, 69–70, 73, 84,
    214
Chiha, Michel   35–6, 44
Chomsky, Noam
    and Association of Arab-American
        University Graduates   120
    and Edward Said   13, 120, 163, 211,
        219–20
    and Eqbal Ahmad   219
    and 1967 Arab-Israeli war   112
    and PLO   163–4
    on responsibility of intellectuals
        218–19
Clayton, Iltyd   33–8
Cleland, W. Wendell   72, 94
Clinton, Bill   200–3
Close, Arthur   52–3, 58
Close, Dora Eddy   33, 52
Close, Harold   33, 40, 52
Close, Raymond   52, 59, 62
Coe, Doug   78, 141–2
Coffin, Jr., Rev. William Sloane   75

Cohen, Stephen P.   115, 175, 183–4
Columbia University
    and Charles Malik   76, 108
    Edward Said Chair   36
    School of International Affairs   76, 108, 193, 217, 220
    student unrest   108–9, 114–17, 120, 125, 217
Conrad, Joseph   69, 107, 124–5, 177
Copeland, Miles   52, 98–9
Cordier, Andrew   76, 108, 114
Cortas, Emile   20, 126–7, 171, 179, 199
Cortas, Michel   20, 86, 118, 127
Cortas, Mona Malik   86, 118, 127
Cortas, Wadad Makdisi
    and Charles Malik   21
    and Edward Said   118, 171
    and Eva Malik   67
    and Institute for Palestine Studies   122
Council on Foreign Relations   44, 55, 59
Crawford, Archie   27, 33

Dakkak, Ibrahim   169, 192
Darwish, Mahmoud   130–1, 186, 192, 198, 201
Dean, John Gunther   149, 172
de Beauvoir, Simone   169
de Botton, Gilbert   97
Dedijer, Vladimir   45, 125
de Gaulle, Charles   6, 31, 64, 74
Dellinger, David   171–2
de Man, Paul   105, 109, 113
Derrida, Jacques   109, 113–14, 128, 229
Dodge, David   33, 52, 152–4
Dodge, Rev. Bayard   5–6, 19–21, 27–8, 33, 42, 98–9, 167
Dulles, Allen
    and Charles Malik   26, 52–4
    and CIA fronts   48, 50
    as Director of Central Intelligence   7, 51, 56
    and Edward Said   104
    as foreign service officer   6, 31
    and Kim Roosevelt   54, 98
    and Near East College Association   26, 33, 38, 44
    and Stephen Penrose   33
    and Syria   6, 52–4
    and Van Engert   31, 48
Dulles, John Foster
    and Bandung   54
    and Charles Malik   47–9, 52–5, 57–9, 61–2, 67, 149
    and Communism   7, 67, 149
    and Lebanon   58–63
    and Nasser   57–8
    and Presbyterian Church   51, 56
    and Syria   61
    at UN organizing conference   37
    and William Ernest Hocking   37
Dulles, Rev. Avery   39

Eban, Abba
    as ambassador   46, 60
    as British officer   33, 36, 94
    and Charles Malik   60, 152, 227
    as foreign minister   9, 130
Eddé, Raymond   84, 134–7
Eddy, Jr., Rev. William   99, 102
Eddy, Sr., William
    and American Friends of the Middle East   49
    and Aramco   42, 52
    and Charles Malik   56
    and CIA   42, 52
    and Close family   52
    and Harold Hoskins   27
    and Lebanon   62–3
    as State Department official   38, 41
Egypt
    Free Officers' coup   9, 51, 98–9
    Muslim Brotherhood   8, 59, 98–100
    Suez War   9–12, 57–8, 70, 102, 214
    Victoria College   8–9, 29, 97, 102, 118, 162, 207
Eisenhower, Dwight
    and Charles Malik   64
    Eisenhower Doctrine   7, 59–61, 103
    and Lebanon   7, 11, 60–3, 156, 214
    and Henry Luce   58
    and Nelson Rockefeller   55
    and prayer breakfast   53
    and Rev. Edward Elson   51
    and Suez War   9, 12, 57–8, 214
Elliott, William Yandell   47, 64, 67, 216, 221

Elson, Rev. Edward   50–1
Engel, Monroe   107, 126
Engert, Cornelius Van Hemert   31, 48, 51, 55, 77
Epstein (Elath), Eliahu   38
Eveland, Wilbur Crane   54–9, 64, 118, 133

Falk, Richard   114, 167, 172–3, 219
Farhang, Mansour   223–4
Farouk, King   8, 48, 98
El-Fattal, Randa Khalidi   131
Fawaz, Leila   185
Fistere, John   56–8, 63, 69
Forbes, Rev. James   198, 211
Ford, Gerald   74, 90–1, 137, 179, 214, 217
Ford Foundation   53–5, 71
Foucault, Michel   1, 3, 126, 169
Frangieh, Suleiman   8, 84, 89, 134–9, 155, 166, 217
Frangieh, Tony   136, 142, 166
Frayha, Anis   28, 124

Geagea, Samir   142, 157–60
Gemayel, Amin   135, 154–9, 180, 191, 225
Gemayel, Bashir
  and Charles Malik   91, 141, 147–8, 152–3, 156, 225
  as commander of Lebanese Forces   5, 137, 140–2, 147–51, 167
  and Elie Salem   225
  and Israelis   135–6, 141, 148–53
  kidnapped by PLO   91
  as president of Lebanon   8, 151–3
  and United States   148–9
Gemayel, Pierre
  as Cabinet member   157
  and Chehab regime   84
  and Lebanese Front   135–9, 148, 155, 166, 229
  and Phalange   8, 28, 55, 70, 133, 154, 226
Genet, Jean   117, 126–8, 222
Ghaleb, Abdulhamid   55–7
Gibb, H. A. R.   30, 40, 49, 64, 71, 105, 170, 221
Gildersleeve, Virginia   38, 43

Gilpatric, Chadbourne   26, 46
Glass, Charles   126–7, 210
Glendon, Mary Ann   14, 228–30
Godley, G. McMurtrie   134
Graham, Rev. Billy   53, 147
Graham-Brown, Rev. G. F.   23, 32, 107
Gramsci, Antonio   3, 83, 171

Habib, Philip   137–8, 152–4, 168, 217
Haig, Alexander   8, 149–51, 175
Harkabi, Yehoshafat   121, 161–2, 169–70
Harvard University
  Center for Middle Eastern Studies   64, 71, 105, 130, 182–3, 221
  Summer School   47–8, 68–9, 216–17
Hatfield, Mark   78, 142
Heath, Donald   55–61
Heidegger, Martin   2, 24–5, 29, 65, 75, 91, 107
Helms, Jesse   134, 146
Hertzberg, Rabbi Arthur   115, 129, 183
Hitchens, Christopher   164, 185, 197, 202, 211, 228
Hitti, Philip   19–20, 27, 30, 36–7, 40, 49, 71, 98
Hobeika, Elie   157–8
Hocking, William Ernest   24, 37–40, 45, 49
Hoover, J. Edgar   51, 121
Horan, Hume   64, 222
Hoskins, Harold
  and Allen Dulles   26
  as American University of Beirut trustee   27, 32–3, 40–2, 53–5
  and Charles Malik   32–3, 40, 55
  and John Foster Dulles   55
  and Near East College Association   26
  and William Eddy   27
Hourani, Albert   185
  on Arab nationalism   33
  as British officer in Cairo   33–6
  and Charles Issawi   29
  and Charles Malik   27–36, 49, 53, 71
  and Edward Said   170–1
  and H. A. R. Gibb   30, 170
  as Oxford don   70–1, 77, 185
Hourani, Cecil
  On Ahmad Shukairy   112

at American University of Beirut 30
at Arab Office in Washington 39, 43
as British officer in Cairo 33–5
and Charles Malik 30, 34, 64, 148
and Eqbal Ahmad 121
and Habib Bourguiba 64, 112, 121
on Israel 112
and Kim Roosevelt 43
and Saad Haddad 148
Hourani, George 30, 99
al-Hout, Shafiq
    and Edward Said 130, 163, 166, 169–70, 175
    on one-state solution 166
    and Palestine National Council 166, 180–1
    as PLO official 91, 126, 163–4, 169, 194, 201
    at United Nations 130, 163–4, 169
Hovsepian, Nubar 173, 192, 198
Humphrey, Hubert 81, 217
Humphrey, John 41, 89
Huntington, Samuel 56, 165
Hurewitz, J. C. 72, 115
Hussein, King 62
    and Black September 85, 118–20, 123, 221
    and CIA 58, 64, 118
    and Palestine National Council 180
    and PLO 10, 180, 183–5, 191
Hussein, Saddam 194–5, 199, 229
Husseini, Faisal 193, 198–9, 201

Ibn Saud, King 7, 39, 56
Institute for Palestine Studies 122–3, 171–3
International Christian Leadership 53, 78–81, 138, 141
Israel
    alliance with Lebanese Forces 2, 8, 135–44, 148, 172
    ban on talking to PLO 11, 178–9, 193
    as "colonial-settler state" 85, 114–15, 120–1
    Munich Olympics attack 87–8, 124–6, 162
    1967 Arab-Israeli war 12, 80, 111–12
    1982 invasion of Lebanon 8, 151–6, 175–8

Oslo negotiations 11, 183–4, 201–2
Palestinian terrorist attacks 116, 221
targeting of PLO officials 88, 116, 126–8, 162, 174–5, 182, 191, 222
Issawi, Charles
    at American University of Beirut 30, 40
    and Charles Malik 29–30, 47, 64, 71
    at Columbia 64, 67, 76, 108, 112
    at Princeton 167

Jabès, Edmond 93, 128
Jackson, Jesse 13, 180
Jamali, Fadhel 21, 38, 54, 62
James, C. L. R. 186, 216
Jameson, Fredric 107–8, 172, 221–3
Jennings, Peter 202, 211
Jewish Defense League 120, 182, 185, 194
al-Jisr, Sheikh Nadim 78, 83
Johnson, Lyndon 9–10, 74–5, 81, 86, 108, 111, 196, 214
Jumblatt, Kamal 63, 91, 135
Jumblatt, Walid 155–7, 218
Jurdak, Angela 27, 37
Jurji, Rev. Edward 20, 40, 98

Kaddoumi, Farouk 119, 166, 192
Karame, Rashid 61–5, 155–7
Kassis, Father Charbel 8, 135–8
Kelada, Naguib 22, 94
Kelman, Herbert 115, 184
Kennedy, Edward 149
Kennedy, Jacqueline 73, 191
Kennedy, John F. 9, 67–70, 73, 85, 106
Kennedy, Robert 68, 73
Kerr, Elsa 31, 71, 162
Kerr, Malcolm
    at American University of Beirut 154–7, 177
    assassination 155–7, 179
    and Charles Malik 71–2, 154, 157
    and Dennis Ross 200
    and Edward Said 162, 170–1, 179
    and Rashid Khalidi 177
Khalaf, Salah (Abu Iyad) 119, 181, 192
Khalidi, Ahmad S. 30, 70
Khalidi, Rashid 36, 177, 192, 198, 206

Khalidi, Walid
  at American University of Beirut 70, 122, 173
  and Edward Said 166, 177, 218
  and Institute for Palestine Studies 122–3
  and John Gunther Dean 172
  and PLO 131, 172
  and Robert Oakley 189
  and Saeb Salam 70
Khashoggi, Adnan 97, 162
Khomeini, Ayatollah 145–6, 169, 195, 223–4
Khoury, Bishara 34–5, 50
al-Khoury, Faris 6, 44, 54
Kierkegaard, Soren 3, 32, 75
Kimche, David 140–1, 150
Kirkpatrick, Jeane 156, 175
Kirkwood, Samuel 8, 77, 81, 85–7, 202
Kissinger, Henry
  and Charles Malik 84, 87–9, 92, 133–4, 137–8, 217
  and Edward Said 190
  and Hanna Mikhail 221–3
  at Harvard 10, 74, 216–17, 221
  kidnapping plot 121, 129, 219
  and Lebanon 134–8, 159, 217
  and Philip Habib 137, 154
  and PLO 169, 178, 189, 218
Küng, Hans 77–80

LaRouche, Lyndon 125–6
Leary, Lewis 21, 33, 108, 114
Lebanon
  Amal militia 156–9, 181
  American hostages 152, 156–9, 163, 182, 210
  Constitution 30, 34–5, 59, 71–2, 152
  Druzes 133, 142, 149, 155–6
  Hezbollah 8, 203, 208
  independence movement 34
  "Islamic Jihad" 155, 159, 182
  Israeli invasion 151
  Lebanese Forces 5, 8, 137, 147–9, 154–60, 226
  Lebanese Front 5, 8, 135–42, 148–51, 158–60, 172, 187, 217, 229
  Maronites 5, 8, 134–7, 147, 154, 224
  massacres of Palestinians 135–6, 178

  1958 Civil War 62, 71–2, 156
  1975 Civil War 5, 8, 133
  Parti Populaire Syrien 28, 31–4, 40, 46, 52–4, 58, 62, 67–70, 94
  Phalange 28, 55, 133–7, 147, 151, 159
  and US Marines 7–8, 153–6, 179–80
  War of the Camps 181
Levin, Harry 105–8, 227
Lewis, Bernard 71, 101, 113, 167, 176, 183–5, 211
Lodge, Jr., Henry Cabot 64, 85
Luce, Henry 50–1, 56–8
Lukacs, Georg 107, 227
Lyotard, Jean-Francois 181

Maalouf, Fakhri 27–8, 31, 39, 95
McClintock, Robert 61–2
McGhee, George 47
McGovern, George 87, 134, 146, 180
Mahayri, Issam 55, 70
Makdisi, Anis 21, 28, 77, 94
Makdisi, Jean Said
  in Beirut 127, 160–3, 171, 174, 179
  childhood 98, 102
  in Dhour el Shweir 205
  in Jerusalem 109
  and Maire Jaanus 106
  marriage 106–7
  in Washington 113, 122
Makdisi, Nadim 67, 94, 163
Makdisi, Samir 67, 100, 106–7, 113, 163, 171
Makiya, Kanan 123, 195–6, 211
Malik, Baheej 32–4, 64, 73
Malik, Charles Habib
  on Abrahamic faiths 101, 117, 141, 144–6
  and Albert Hourani 27–36, 49, 53, 71
  and Allen Dulles 26, 52–4
  as ambassador 6–7, 36–55
  and American Jewish Committee 144
  on American University of Beirut 35, 77–8
  as American University of Beirut professor 27–36, 55–8, 70–92
  as American University of Beirut student 19–21
  on Arabs 41, 88

and Arab nationalism 3, 6, 70, 79, 228
and Athenagoras-Pope Paul VI meetings 73, 80
at Bandung Conference 54
and Bashir Gemayel 91, 141, 147–8, 152–3, 156, 225
on Camp David Accords 144–6
on campus radicals 86, 150–1
at Catholic University of America 148–50, 176
and Cecil Hourani 30, 34, 64, 148
as Chamber of Deputies member 59–64
on classics of Western thought 29–31, 39–41, 44–7
on Communism 42, 46–7, 50–2, 57, 67–8, 70–1, 79–82, 145, 149, 215–16
Congressional testimony 79, 142–3
and Cyrus Vance 137–41, 217
and David Rockefeller 69, 73, 86, 108, 137
on developing nations 48–50, 68–9, 73
and Edward Said 2–5, 99–103, 106–7, 111–13, 116–17, 122, 166–7
and Eleanor Roosevelt 1, 40–4, 48, 98
encounters with Israelis 37–8, 44–5, 65, 152, 155
as foreign minister 58–63, 186
on freedom 34–5, 50–2, 75–7, 157, 215
and George Said 4, 27, 31–5
"God and Man" symposium 77–81
as Greek Orthodox Christian 3, 19, 74
and Hanna Mikhail 166, 221
as Harvard student 23–7
and Heidegger 2, 24–5, 29, 65, 75, 91, 107
and Henry Kissinger 84, 87–9, 92, 133–4, 137–8, 217
and Hisham Sharabi 37, 69–71, 76–7, 85
and Iltyd Clayton 33–6
on intellectuals 59, 214–16
on Islam 22, 34, 59, 101, 147, 168, 172

on Islamic Revolution in Iran 145–6
on Israel 45–7, 153, 172, 227
and John Fistere 56–8, 63, 69
and John Foster Dulles 53–4, 58, 61–2
and Lebanese Front 135–8, 148, 151, 159
and Kim Roosevelt 45, 54, 59
on Lebanon as bridge between East and West 33–4, 150, 156–7
and Malcolm Kerr 71–2, 154, 157
on Maronites 147, 154, 224
and Nasser 5, 54, 57–9, 73, 101
on Nazi Germany 25, 30
and Nelson Rockefeller 50, 55, 90, 92, 133–4, 137
and 1958 US Marine landing in Lebanon 62–3, 139, 156
on Orientalism 41, 49, 157
on Palestinian question 87–92, 133, 152
on Palestinians in Lebanon 89, 136–40, 143, 148, 152, 230
on PLO 91–2, 133
at prayer breakfasts in Washington 53, 80–1, 134, 141, 144
and Richard Nixon 63, 68, 74, 81–4, 87, 217, 226
and Robert Kennedy 68, 73
and Roman Catholic Church 27–8, 74, 147
and Sadik al-Azm 72, 78–81
on spiritual crisis in America 75, 82–3, 86, 90
and Syria 54–5, 58–9, 143
as UN General Assembly president 63–5
on United Nations 54–6, 85–6, 138, 158
on United States as Christian nation 12, 47, 214
and Universal Declaration of Human Rights 40–5, 54, 82, 89–90, 158–9, 228–30
at UN organizing conference 6, 36–8
on UN partition plan for Palestine 41–4, 96
and Wadie Said 22, 33–5, 94–5

on Western civilization 34, 68, 73, 157
and Wilbur Crane Eveland 54, 59, 64, 118, 133
Malik, Dr. Habib 19
Malik, Eva Badr
    in Charles Malik's philosophy circle 27-9
    and Edward Said 94, 97-101, 106, 113
    and Elsa Kerr 31, 154
    and Hilda Said 1, 3, 27, 109
    and League of Lebanese Women 34
    and Malcolm Kerr 154
    and 1958 Lebanese civil war 60
    and Wadad Cortas 67, 118
Malik, Habib Charles 100, 153, 167, 228
Malik, Rev. Gabriel 31, 39
Malik, Rev. Ramzi 32, 39
Malik, Zarifa 3, 19, 34
Marmura, Michael 96, 99, 205
Marmura, Rev. Elias 93, 96, 205
Marshall, George 41-3
Meir, Golda 121, 130, 162
Meouchi, Paul Cardinal 70, 83
Mikhail, Hanna (Abu Omar)
    and Alan Dershowitz 221
    and Charles Malik 221
    disappearance 164-6, 223
    and Edward Said 64, 105, 119, 126, 203, 206, 220-3
    and H. A. R. Gibb 105, 221
    and Henry Kissinger 221-3
    and Hume Horan 64, 222
    and Jean Genet 126, 222
    and Jihan Helou 126
    and Quakerism 126, 220, 223
Morgenbesser, Sidney 111, 227
Mossadegh, Mohammed 7, 41, 48
Moughrabi, Fouad 192-4
Moynihan, Daniel Patrick 144-6
Mroueh, Kamel 76, 79, 202
Mubarak, Hosni 154, 186, 203
Murphy, Richard W. 157, 183, 223
Murphy, Robert 7, 62-3
Musa, Munira Badr 93
Musa, Rev. Shukri 93, 199

Nader, Ralph 106, 165
Naguib, Mohammed 51-2, 98, 101

Naipaul, V. S. 130
Nasir, Hanna 174, 201
Nasir, Kamal
    assassinated 88, 128, 162
    and Charles Malik 32
    and Edward Said 10, 94, 115-16, 128
    and PLO 88, 115-16, 128, 162
Nasrallah, Sheikh Hassan 208-9
Nasser, Gamal Adbel 214
    and Bandung 54
    and Charles Malik 5, 54, 57-9, 101
    and Communists 100, 105
    and John Badeau 9
    and Kim Roosevelt 98, 101
    and Lebanon 60-1
    and Muslim Brotherhood 100
    and PLO 10, 119
    and Suez War 57-8, 102, 214
Near East College Association 26, 33, 38, 44
Near East School of Theology 30, 103, 122, 157
Netanyahu, Benjamin 146, 182, 190-1
Nixon, Richard
    and Charles Malik 63, 68, 74, 81-4, 87, 217, 226
    and Israel 129
    and prayer breakfast 53
    and William Yandell Elliott 68

Oakley, Robert 134, 200
Obama, Barack 177, 206
O'Brien, Conor Cruise 114, 186
O'Connell, Jack 10, 64, 118

Pakradouni, Karim 134, 138-9, 157, 159
Palestine Liberation Organization
    and Ahmad Shukairy 10, 112
    Black September 85-8, 119, 123-6
    Democratic Front for the Liberation of Palestine 83, 118-19, 124, 185
    Fatah 10, 123-4, 127, 164, 179-80, 221-2
    Lebanese Forces alliance 159, 191-2
    Oslo Accord 11, 201-3, 209
    Planning Center 85, 123, 222
    Popular Front for the Liberation of Palestine 10, 119, 124, 178, 185
    Research Center 123, 126-7, 179, 222

Palestine National Council 1, 10–11, 119, 166–7, 180, 185–6, 192, 198
Palestinian Authority 201, 204–6, 220, 230
Parker, Richard 139–41
Paul VI, Pope 73–4, 80
Peled, Matti 179–81
Penrose, Jr., Stephen 21–3, 33, 40–2, 46, 51–8, 155
  and Allen Dulles 33
  and American Friends of the Middle East 51
  at American University of Beirut 21, 42–3, 46
  and Chadbourne Gilpatric 46
  and Charles Malik 21–3, 40, 51–5
  and Lewis Leary 21, 33
  and Near East College Association 21, 33
  as OSS officer in Cairo 21, 33
Peretz, Martin 114–15, 121, 130, 182, 185
Perlmutter, Amos 152, 182
Philby, St. John 56
Princeton University
  and CIA 104
  Near Eastern Studies 30, 40–1, 98–101, 167
Pusey, Nathan 51, 63

Quandt, William 89, 139, 163, 166
Quay, Rev. James 22, 43, 94, 98

Rabin, Yitzhak 11, 121, 135, 138, 167, 199, 202
Rabinovich, Itamar 162, 206
Reagan, Ronald 8, 11, 148–9, 154, 175, 179, 190, 214
al-Rifai, Zaid 10, 97, 118
Robertson, A. Willis 53, 138
Robertson, Pat 138
Rockefeller, David 69, 73, 78, 86, 108, 137
Rockefeller, Nelson 50, 55, 90–2, 133–4, 137, 217
Rockefeller Foundation 22, 26, 41, 46, 55, 137
Rogers, William 89, 119
Roosevelt, Eleanor 1, 40–4, 48, 98
Roosevelt, Franklin 32, 37–9
Roosevelt, Jr., Archie 43–5
Roosevelt, Jr., Kermit "Kim"
  and American Friends of the Middle East 71
  and Cecil Hourani 43
  and Charles Malik 45, 54, 59
  and Egypt 9, 52, 98–101
  and Iran 7, 41, 48
  and Lebanon 59
  as OSS officer in Cairo 58
  and Sam Souki 162
  and Syria 54
Ross, Dennis 200–2
Rostow, Walt 67, 76, 89
Rushdie, Salman 185–6, 199–201, 205, 228
Russell, Bertrand 23, 124, 213

Saadeh, Antun
  and Charles Malik 29
  execution 46, 52
  and Fakhri Maalouf 28, 31
  and Fayez Sayegh 32, 95
  and Hisham Sharabi 40, 46, 95
  and Nadim Makdisi 94
  and Sadik al-Azm 72
  and Yusif Sayigh 28–9
Sadat, Anwar 119, 141, 144–6, 168, 175, 218
Sadr, Imam Musa 78, 83, 136
Safran, Nadav 72, 182–3, 221
Said, Albert Boulos 95, 128
Said, Boulos 32, 93, 109, 198
Said, Edward W.
  and American Arab Anti-Discrimination Committee 176–7, 180
  and American Council for Palestine Affairs 192–4
  on American perceptions of Palestinians 114–16, 163, 173, 180
  on American University of Beirut 127, 130
  in Amman 115–17, 174–5, 199
  and Arabic 28, 95, 124–6, 131, 192, 205
  on Arabs and Jews 111, 116, 129, 181

and Association of Arab-American
   University Graduates   162, 166–8,
   200–1
and Barack Obama   177, 206
Beginnings   1, 109, 124
in Beirut   10, 106–7, 115, 123–30,
   161, 167, 170–5, 199, 205, 208
in Birzeit   199–201, 204
and Charles Malik   2–5, 99–103,
   106–7, 111–13, 116–17, 122, 166–7,
   181–2
childhood   8–9, 93–7, 207–8
and Christopher Hitchens   164, 185,
   202
Covering Islam   174, 182
and Cyrus Vance   168–72
in Dhour el Shweir   35, 94–5, 98, 100,
   106, 118, 205
encounters with Israelis   115, 121,
   161–2, 169–70, 178–81, 184, 190–3,
   206
and Eqbal Ahmad   121, 163–4, 173,
   200, 205, 210
and Fouad Ajami   167, 181, 211
as go-between for US and PLO   166–
   72, 176, 189–90
on Gulf War   196–7, 224
and Hanan Ashrawi   165–6, 192, 198,
   204
and Hanna Mikhail   64, 105, 119, 126,
   203, 206, 220–3
as Harvard student   9, 104–8
on human rights   130, 161, 229
and Ibrahim Abu-Lughod   100–1,
   114, 120–1, 163, 175, 201, 210
and Institute for Palestine
   Studies   122–3, 171–3
on intellectuals   203, 213–14, 220,
   226–8
and *Intifada*   189–91
on Iraq War   210–11, 229
on Islamic Revolution in Iran   169,
   172, 223–4
on Israeli invasion of Lebanon   176–8
and Jacques Derrida   109, 113–14,
   128
in Jerusalem   95–6, 109, 198–9,
   204
and John Badeau   95–7, 120

and Joseph Conrad   69, 107, 124, 130,
   177
as lapsed Anglican   3, 96, 205
and Maire Jaanus   106–7, 110, 114
and Marxism   83, 109, 171, 174, 223
on Middle East "experts"   185, 196, 211
as Mount Hermon student   9, 97–9
on Nasser   12, 101–2
on nationalism   165, 197, 229
on 9/11 attacks   209–10
on 1967 Arab-Israeli war   4–5, 12,
   111–12, 116
and Noam Chomsky   120, 163–4,
   211, 218–20
on one-state solution   115, 118, 121,
   207
Orientalism   1, 161, 165, 170–6, 186,
   211
on Oslo Accord   11, 201–3, 209
Out of Place   174, 205–8, 223
and Palestine National Council   10–
   11, 119, 166–7, 180–1, 185–6, 192
and Palestinian resistance
   movement   1, 10, 123
on PLO misconceptions of United
   States   171–2, 193–4
on political Islam   199–203, 206–7,
   224
as Princeton student   4, 9, 99–104
The Question of Palestine   1, 201
and Rashid Khalidi   177, 206
on religion   3, 13, 103–4, 116–17, 165,
   208–9, 214, 228–30
at religious conferences   176, 183,
   189, 205–6
on Saddam Hussein   194–5, 199
and Sadik al-Azm   124, 173–4
and Salman Rushdie   185–6, 199–201,
   205, 228
and Shafiq al-Hout   130, 163, 169, 175
South Africa trip   197
stone-throwing incident   208–9
and Students for a Democratic
   Society   115–16
on "terrorism"   169, 178, 185, 193, 210
on two-state solution   130, 183, 219
and Weiner controversy   96, 207–8
and Yasir Arafat   119, 130–1, 170,
   175, 178, 182, 191–2, 199

on Yasir Arafat 168–9, 179, 203, 206, 225–6
and Zbigniew Brzezinski 166, 216–18
on Zionism 121, 164, 186, 207
Said, George Boulos 4, 27, 31–5
Said, Grace 103, 113, 171, 174
Said, Hilda Musa
  in Beirut 113, 176, 179
  and Elsa Kerr 31, 154, 162
  and Eva Malik 1, 93, 109
  and Maire Jaanus 107
  and Rev. Fuad Bahnan 103, 211
Said, Huda Farradj 73, 83
Said, Joyce 102, 109–10, 113, 185
Said, Mariam Cortas
  in Lebanon 123–7, 179
  marriage 21, 110, 118, 122
Said, Nabiha 93, 96, 105, 128
Said, Najla 161, 171, 179, 198–9, 208, 211
Said, Robert Boulos 95, 109
Said, Wadie Edward 204, 208–11
Said, Wadie Ibrahim
  in Beirut 107, 113, 122
  and Charles Malik 22, 33–5, 94–5
  in Jerusalem 95–6, 109
  and John Badeau 9, 94, 97
  and Sam Souki 56, 162
  and Standard Stationery Company 93, 98, 104, 107
Said, Yousif Boulos 96, 198
Sakr, Etienne (Abu Arz) 152–4, 159
Salam, Saeb 50, 58, 61–3, 70, 84, 128, 153
Salem, Elie 156, 163, 225
Sarkis, Elias 8, 84, 134–42, 147–9, 152
Sarton, George 23–4, 40
Sartre, Jean-Paul 75, 107, 125–6, 169–70
Saunders, Harold 76, 89
Sayegh, Anis 123, 126–7
Sayegh, Fayez
  and Antun Saadeh 28, 95
  and Charles Malik 27, 95
  and Eisenhower Doctrine 103
  and George Said 27, 32
  and Parti Populaire Syrien 28, 40, 95
  and "Zionism is racism" resolution 164
Sayigh, Yusif 27–32, 180

Schoenman, Ralph 102, 124, 227
Schomer, Rev. Howard 26–9, 42, 159
Seelye, Rev. Laurens 19–20, 23–6, 100
Seelye, Talcott 20, 136, 223
Shaath, Nabil 123, 131, 178, 192–3, 198
Shafi, Haidar Adbel 199, 204
Shahak, Israel 129, 172
Shah of Iran 48, 144–5, 169, 223–4
Shamir, Yitzhak 149, 189, 193
Sharabi, Hisham
  at American University of Beirut 37, 40, 46, 85
  and Charles Malik 37, 69–71, 76–7, 85
  and Edward Said 124, 177
  at Georgetown University 69, 169
  and Palestinian resistance movement 85, 122, 126, 177–8
  and Parti Populaire Syrien 31, 40, 46, 52, 55, 70, 95
Sharon, Ariel 8, 151–2, 175–8
Shukairy, Ahmad 10, 21, 54, 112
Shultz, George 10–11, 157–8, 189–92
Solh, Riad 34, 46
Solh, Sami 50, 58, 64
Sontag, Susan 108, 211
Souki, Sam 56, 73, 162
Spears, Edward 34–6
Stephanopoulos, George 202
Syrkin, Marie 121
Szathmary, Arthur 26, 46, 100, 227

Takieddine, Said 52, 60–1
Thompson, Dorothy 48, 51
Toynbee, Arnold 30, 49, 112, 214
Trilling, Diana 108, 169
Trilling, Lionel 108, 111, 227
Truman, Harry 6–7, 37–43, 47–8, 214
Tsimang, Mendi 197–8
Tueni, Ghassan
  and Charles Malik 52
  and Edward Said 229
  as Harvard student 95
  and Parti Populaire Syrien 52
  and Sam Souki 73
  and Suleiman Frangieh 84
Tuqan, Ahmad 72, 119

United Nations
  admission of Israel 45–6

Conference on International
    Organization   6, 36–8
and 1958 Lebanon crisis   62–3
Palestine partition plan   7, 41–4, 96
and Palestinian question   11, 130–1,
    163–6, 173, 178–9, 192
Security Council Resolution 242   169,
    180, 190–2, 218
UNESCO translation project   30,
    39–40
Universal Declaration of Human
    Rights   40–5, 54, 82, 89–90, 158–9,
    228–9
United States
and American University of
    Beirut   7–8, 33, 55, 73, 78, 142
and Egyptian Free Officers' coup   9,
    98–9
and 1957 Lebanese elections   59–61,
    71–2
1958 Marine landing in Lebanon   7,
    62–3, 156
1982 Marine landing in Lebanon   8,
    155–6, 179–80
Office of Strategic Services   21, 32–3,
    41, 58, 72
and PLO   10–11, 169–70, 175,
    192–4
Protestant missionaries in Near
    East   3–5, 19, 22–3, 27, 52, 104,
    157

Vance, Cyrus
    and Charles Malik   137–41, 217
    and Edward Said   10, 168–9, 172
Veeser, Harold   115, 198
Vereide, Rev. Abraham   53, 78

Walzer, Michael   114–16, 121, 130, 196,
    219
Wazzan, Shafik   152, 155–6
Weir, Carol   157, 183
Weir, Rev. Benjamin   157, 182–3
West, Cornel   198–200, 228
Whitehead, Alfred North   2, 23, 29, 65
Wild, John   23–4, 65, 79

Yariv, Aharon   162

Zahlan, Anthony   124
Zahlan, Rosemarie Said   67, 101, 104, 113
Zionism   24, 47, 88, 121, 164–7, 186,
    206–7
Zurayk, Constantine
    at American University of Beirut   6,
        27, 32–3, 42, 53, 56
    and Charles Malik   20, 27, 30–5, 42,
        53
    and Edward Said   20, 127, 130
    at Syrian embassy in Washington
        39–40
Zurayk, Najla Cortas   20–1, 27, 30–2,
    122, 127